D1481494

GERMAN WOMEN IN THE EIGHTEENTH AND NINETEENTH CENTURIES

GERMAN WOMEN IN THE EIGHTEENTH AND NINETEENTH CENTURIES

A Social and Literary
History

EDITED BY
RUTH-ELLEN B. JOERES
AND
MARY JO MAYNES

INDIANA UNIVERSITY PRESS • BLOOMINGTON

Publication of this volume has been made possible by grants from the following: the Fritz Thyssen Foundation, the National Endowment for the Humanities, the Council for European Studies, and the University of Minnesota.

Manufactured in the United States of America

Library of Congress Cataloging in Publication Data
Main entry under title:

German women in the eighteenth and nineteenth centuries.

Essays from an Apr. 1983 meeting held at the University of Minnesota and sponsored by its departments of German, History, and Women's Studies.
1. Women—Germany—Social conditions—Congresses.
2. Women—Germany—History—Congresses. 3. Women—Employment—Germany—History—Congresses. 4. German literature—History and criticism—Congresses. 5. Women in literature—Congresses. 6. German literature—Women authors—History and criticism—Congresses. I. Joeres, Ruth-Ellen B., 1939–   . II. Maynes, Mary Jo.
III. University of Minnesota. Department of German.
IV. University of Minnesota. Department of History.
V. University of Minnesota. Department of Women's Studies.
HQ1623.G47   1986   305.4'0943   84-48542
ISBN 0-253-32578-1

1 2 3 4 5   89 88 87 86

CONTENTS

INTRODUCTION. RUTH-ELLEN B. JOERES AND MARY JO MAYNES   ix

Work and Ideas about Work for Women

Teamwork in Saxon Homeweaving Families in the Nineteenth
Century
    A Preliminary Investigation into the Issue of Gender Work
    Roles
    Jean Quataert   3

Labor Force Participation, Life Cycle, and Expenditure
Patterns
    The Case of Unmarried Female Factory Workers in Berlin
    (1902)
    Rosemary Orthmann   24

The Viennese Enquête of 1896 on Working Women
    John C. Fout   42

Women's Work as Portrayed in Women's Literature
    Renate Möhrmann   61

Women and the Literary Enterprise in Nineteenth-Century
Germany
    Patricia Herminghouse   78

Women and the Professions in Imperial Germany
    James Albisetti   94

Motherhood and Work
   The Concept of the Misuse of Women's Energy,
      1895–1905
   Kay Goodman   110

Feminisms

"That girl is an entirely different character!" Yes, but is she a
   feminist?
   Observations on Sophie von la Roche's *Geschichte des
      Fräuleins von Sternheim*
   Ruth-Ellen B. Joeres   137

"And this shield is called—self-reliance"
   Emerging Feminist Consciousness in the Late Eighteenth
      Century
   Ruth Dawson   157

Discipline and Daydreaming in the Works of a
   Nineteenth-Century Woman Author: Fanny Lewald
   Regula Venske   175

On a Feminist Controversy
   Louise Otto vs. Louise Aston
   Hans Adler   193

The Nineteenth-Century Deaconessate in Germany
   The Efficacy of a Family Model
   Catherine M. Prelinger   215

Gender and Class in Working-Class Women's Autobiographies
   Mary Jo Maynes   230

The Concept of Feminism
   Notes for Practicing Historians
   Richard J. Evans   247

Women's Words and Women's Self-Definition

Inside Assimilation
    Rebecca Friedländer's Rahel Varnhagen
    Deborah Hertz   271

On Travel Literature by Women in the Nineteenth Century
    Malwida von Meysenbug
    Wulf Wülfing   289

". . . nothing more than a German woman."
    Remarks on the Biographical and Autobiographical
        Tradition of the Women of One Family
    Gudrun Wedel   305

The Struggle for an Identity
    Working-Class Autobiographies by Women in
        Nineteenth-Century Germany
    Juliane Jacobi-Dittrich   321

CONTRIBUTORS   347

INDEX   351

INTRODUCTION

Recent efforts to incorporate the study of women into the research agendas of several of the humanistic disciplines have had profound consequences. Scholars have found that the attempt to describe and understand the female experience has forced them not only to seek out new sources and methods of analysis, but even to rethink basic analytic categories. Frequently, the challenge has been so demanding that it has been necessary and fruitful to construct new theories and research methods through interdisciplinary borrowing, a process that has helped overcome the incapacity of any one disciplinary tradition simply to include women on its own terms.

In the United States, the fields of history and literature have been especially affected by feminist revisions. Women's historians at American universities have been pioneers in the study of women and have led the whole field of American history in new directions. Gerda Lerner's *The Majority Finds Its Past* and William Chafe's *Women and Equality,* to name only two among myriad studies, are popular and influential interpretations of American women's experiences.[1] American scholars have also been involved in helping to write the history of European women: Louise Tilly's and Joan Scott's *Women, Work, and Family,* based on research about France and England, has become a model for the study of the female experience in the past. American literary scholars such as Elaine Showalter *(A Literature of Their Own)* and Sandra Gilbert and Susan Gubar *(The Madwoman in the Attic)* have led the way in establishing feminist criticism as a respected method of analyzing both American and European literature.[2] Journals such as the University of Chicago Press's *Signs* have contributed an interdisciplinary focus by involving not only literature and history, but also anthropology, linguistics, and sociology in the effort to indicate the broad and appropriate application of feminist theory.

Until very recently, however, Americans have done almost no work on the particular subject of German women's history and literature, nor was this study highly developed in Europe. To an extent far greater than elsewhere, it seems, the feminist investigation of German women has primarily involved researchers marginal to the academy and peripheral to the major academic disciplines. Indeed, German historiographic and literary-critical work has begun to recognize the need to include the study of women only within the last twenty years. As a result of this situation, scholars on both sides of the ocean have often felt frustrated and isolated in their search for sources about German women and their attempts to establish contacts with others sharing their interests. Nevertheless, several recent or forthcoming volumes attest to a new vitality in the interdisciplinary study of German women in the past. An anthology that reports the results of a recent meeting at the University of Bielefeld, site of a new center for research on women, is one example; another anthology of essays on the social history of German women in the nineteenth century and edited by the American historian John Fout, is a further one. Both volumes suggest that the time is ripe for an examination of German women's history, and that interdisciplinary efforts are certain to play a large role in such an investigation.[3]

As scholars of the social and literary history of German women, we have been keenly aware of the isolation of and the growing interest in our fields. With these considerations in mind, we decided to undertake the step of calling together for the first time in the United States a sizable group of social historians and literary scholars from both sides of the Atlantic whose shared interest is the investigation of the social conditions and ideas that shaped the world of women in pre-World-War-One Germany and were, in turn, reshaped by those women. The following essays are the result of that April 1983 meeting.

The interdisciplinary conference that produced these papers brought together scholars from the United States, England, and the Federal Republic of Germany. All of them have previously published in the area of scholarship on German women; indeed, all are still very actively involved in such pursuits. They are acutely conscious of the need for interdisciplinary awareness and they are all in search of methods that will accommodate or facilitate their research on German women in the past. By coming together to discuss their current work, they hoped not only to share research results, but more importantly to discuss those results with scholars familiar with the basic problems of German women's social and cultural history who are approaching those problems from a variety of perspectives. The conference program was thus designed to facilitate broad participation and exchange between scholars from different disciplinary backgrounds. Social historians spoke of their work with women's autobiographies. Literary scholars discussed the history of the women's movement in Germany. Opportunities arose throughout the meeting, not only to have questions answered, but to formulate new questions, to illuminate areas that have been neglected, and to point out ways in which the constraints of a single disciplinary tradition have perhaps distorted or limited our perceptions of German women in the past.

The conference papers centered on a few common themes likely to encourage interdisciplinary dialogue. The first of these—work and the meaning of work for women—is hardly a surprising choice for anyone familiar with feminist scholarship in any context. Work is an essential part of life, but it has always been viewed somewhat ambivalently in the spectrum of women's experience. Tied as it is to gender role and gender distinction, it has often served to delineate and to control, to define and to limit the spheres available to women. As a paradigm of the female dilemma, it can serve admirably to indicate gains and losses over the course of history. As a theme, work brings together a great variety of approaches to the study of women and can be shown to be a determining element shaping the literature and the historical condition of women. The fact that women have always worked and that their progress in general has often been tabulated according to the kind and locus of the work they do suggests the salience of the theme for broad interpretations of women's history.

The essays in the section on women and work present a series of contributions to our understanding of the subject even when they are read individually. Their juxtaposition with one another, however, enriches them. While each one contributes an analysis of patterns of work or explores evidence about norms concerning work for women, the collection as a whole suggests some characteristic differences in the ways in which women in different social classes and occupational milieux worked and regarded work.

Jean Quataert leads off with an essay that is both a detailed case study and the beginning of a broader analysis of the historical evolution of the gender division of labor. She is particularly concerned with gender roles among homeweaving families in the Oberlausitz district of Saxony, but her discoveries there have led her to formulate a new chronology and perhaps a new dynamic to account for the connections between economic change and women's work roles. Of all the essays in this section, Quataert's presents the most sanguine portrait of working women. Their lives may not have been rosy, but at least they were not unduly oppressed by exclusion from the possibility of earning the means to support themselves or by the constraints of an ideology of spheres. The other essay on the work of women in the popular classes, that by Rosemary Orthmann on the working women of Berlin, reflects the same equanimity on the issue of women participating in the work force. To be sure, their work as paid laborers was distinctly connected with the female life cycle. Moreover, the well-being of a woman worker was inseparable from her situation at home. Orth-mann's analysis suggests, in fact, that the kind of residential situation in which a single woman worker lived was a good indicator of her ability to make ends meet on her wages. Still, the prevalence of work among Berlin working-class women, especially prior to marriage, meant that the issue of work remained in the realm of necessity, and going to work was not in itself a moral dilemma. John Fout's contribution, based on a turn-of-the-century survey of working women in Vienna, addresses the interplay of work and homelife for women there, and brings to light an interesting new source for looking at the working women of Central Europe. His findings suggest that women in Vienna held a greater variety of jobs over a longer period of their lives than has been assumed on the basis of studies conducted in other regions of Europe.

When we enter the world of middle-class women, the emphasis on the simple development of strategies for working and living from one's wages is displaced by the evidence of ambivalence about working for money, of resorting to disguises and subterfuges covering up female enterprise, and of complex efforts to justify women working at all. Patricia Herminghouse discusses the social world of the numerous professional women writers who lived in Germany in the nineteenth century. She points out how common it was for those women to hide behind initials and pseudonyms, to meet with discouragement on the part of their husbands or fathers, to be overlooked by literary critics and historians. In part, she suggests, these subterfuges are understand-able reactions to the prevailing prejudices against female writers, but they also exacerbated the problem by rendering invisible that very substantial number of women who were earning their livelihood from the pen. Renate Möhrmann takes this problem a step further. She examines the contents of some of the writings of these women to see how they portray the working woman. Her discovery that the portraits of working women in fiction were rarely positive—despite the fact that in their nonfictional, polemic writings many of these women were advocates of feminine emancipation—indicates that the tenets of the ideology of spheres were perhaps more pervasive than we have thought. James Albisetti's analysis of those middle-class women who did begin to enter the professions at the end of the nineteenth century presents a less stark picture. He notes a certain degree of success for women in some professions, most notably medicine and primary and secondary school teaching. But the success of women even in these professions was limited: they were by and large restricted to the han-dling of female clients, and most professional women obeyed the unwritten law that career and family were impossible to combine.

In short, the examination of attitudes and behavior of middle-class women suggests an ambivalence toward women's work that was widespread and deep. Kay Goodman's essay on the reception in Germany of the ideas of the Swedish writer Ellen Key at the turn of the century only reinforces this impression: Key's popularity can be viewed as an index of the timidity or confusion within the ranks of advocates of women's rights in Germany. Key offered an alternative to the demand for female equality. Her emphasis on the differences between men and women, on the special virtues of women, allowed women to argue that certain work roles were acceptable for some women, but not work in general for all women. Goodman's thought that Key was influential not only among some sectors of the middle-class women's movement but even among some working-class women who advocated women's rights brings us full circle to the question of whether social class barriers indeed were barriers with respect to attitudes about women's work. Perhaps working-class women felt the same kind of ambivalence, which persisted for them alongside the statistical normality of paid work.

The second unifying theme of the volume we have called "feminisms." Any discussion of women's history must involve the effort to provide an appropriately concise definition of feminism while at the same time acknowledging the need for flexibility and imagination: thus "feminisms." A historical use of the term, however, encounters immediate difficulties as soon as it refers to a point before the present century. Nevertheless, we need to discuss the history of feminism, to make comparisons between different places and different times. The slow and reluctant character of the turn-of-the-century German women's movement, for example, is especially evident when it is compared to its more fiery and radical counterparts in England and the United States at the same time. But even to make a statement such as that requires a firm concept of female progress against which to measure these movements. The series of papers that constitutes this section attacks the problem of clarification and definition on several levels. Through the use of a variety of source materials, the essays attempt to determine what might be labelled feminist at various points in German history when the term itself was not even in use. Their intentional chronological arrangement permits a look at the process of an evolving definition.

Ruth-Ellen B. Joeres discusses an eighteenth-century novel that she sees as an effort by its author, Sophie von La Roche, to move beyond the limits within which women were normally contained. At the same time, the clear hesitation that was to be the hallmark of many German women who were moving slowly toward self-awareness can also be found in the La Roche text, and the resulting portrait becomes a study in ambivalence. Ruth Dawson, while emphasizing the positive contribution of eighteenth-century progressive thinkers in their discussion of German women, also takes up the controversial question of why those who were concerned early on with the issue of female emancipation were nonetheless singularly reticent when it came to establishing the role that work was to play in that emancipation. The mixed message presented by such openly progressive polemic texts is duplicated in fictional writings as well; an impression of the often uncertain nature of liberalizing tendencies is thus reconfirmed. Regula Venske's essay on the nineteenth-century writer Fanny Lewald provides another example of ambivalence, here as it is directed toward work and self-discipline. At the same time, Venske expands her discussion to include the less obvious, yet equally significant subjective world of Lewald's thoughts and dreams, where uncertainty about a woman's role expectations is also in evidence. In his discussion of the differing perspectives of two prominent middle-class activist women in nineteenth-century Germany, Hans Adler reveals the important role that religion played in the formation of early German feminist thought. His approach as a literary critic is in many ways complemented by that of the historian Catherine Prelinger, who explores the connections between religious thought and women's changing self-definition in her use of the model of the early deaconess movement. The contradictory place of religious women as well as of religion itself is brought to the fore, and the significance of the forms and practices of religion for early German feminist thinking is established in both essays. Turning her attention to the question of what, if any, indication of feminist thought can be found in the autobiographical writings of German working-class women at the turn of the century, M. J. Maynes provides an essential note of caution in the matter of textual interpretation. The Procrustean method that might like to find positive evidence of feminism among all progressive women is held in check by her more precise look at the personal writings of such women, who often displayed the uncertainty and ambivalence found in the writings of their middle-class sisters. Richard Evans rounds out this section of the volume with a provocative demand for rigor in conceptualization and labelling in the discussion of feminist ideas in the past. Particularly in the case of German women, whose awareness of their place in society was so often marked by ambiguity, and whose actions did not always tally with their words, such a call is worthy of attention.

The last area of focus centers on sources about women in the past and how they expand our understanding of women's self-definition. In all the volume's essays the question of sources keeps recurring, but these last contributions bring it to the fore. Although each has a substantive point to make, each also pays a great deal of attention to the process of uncovering and using certain kinds of sources, in particular sources that record the direct testimony of women of the past. It is also interesting that in this section disciplinary boundaries begin most obviously to break down. There are doubtless different ways of reading and interpreting texts, but the very act of seeking out clues to past meaning and past condition through an interpretation of words unites the social and literary historian.

Each selection deals with a different kind of text, and techniques for analysis vary accordingly. Deborah Hertz examines a series of fascinating letters by the Berlin salonière Rahel Varnhagen. Although Hertz uses the letters primarily to make an argument about Varnhagen's ethnic and sexual self-awareness, she also comes to grips with what such a set of documents means to the social historians of women. Wulf Wülfing's contribution takes a different approach. He searches for women removed from their usual context—through travel—to see what their accounts of travel suggest about the condition and assumptions of these women on the margin. Gudrun Wedel, whose work to date has entailed the collection and annotation of a huge number of women's autobiographies and biographies, reflects in her essay on the nature of such writings, and looks at the process whereby German women came to write about their lives. The analysis of female autobiography is also the focus of the essay by Juliane Jacobi-Dittrich, who is concerned with reading these sources in order to uncover the process of feminine personality formation in working-class and middle-class milieux.

These essays, like those in the other two sections of the volume, show the start of an interdisciplinary process of discovering sources and applying them creatively, of recapturing for German women their place in the past, of cooperation in feminist scholarship across national as well as disciplinary boundaries. They should be viewed as a beginning, for the purpose of our meeting was not to produce a closed circle, but rather to open channels. Where might we go from here? The conference indicated the value and importance of discovering and developing clusters of areas of interest to all of us and the value of the use of theoretical tools from both our disciplines to investigate those clusters. Among possible areas for exploration are autobiographies and biographies by women, which need to be viewed not only as sources of information about the contours of women's lives, but also as sources of more subjective insights. In addition, there is a clear need for more work on the role of religion as a shaping force in the lives of German women in the past, not only as a form of suppression and control, but also as a source of liberating ideas and experiences. Certainly many of the essays suggest that our understanding of the overpowering importance of gender roles and expectations can benefit from further social- and literary-historical analysis, as can our understanding of feminism as a many-sided and often contradictory concept.

This interdisciplinary venture has also reinforced our belief that any attempt to recapture and understand the past must incorporate the methods and sources of both our disciplines. This is all the more true of the study of women from a feminist perspective. The lack of data, the disappearance or destruction of archival materials, the overt and the more subtle methods of censorship and control, the bias and self-censorship, the frustrating subjectivity of many of the early chroniclers of women: we have all seen and experienced the barriers that can arise in the work on our subject. But we have also realized that our joint efforts can help us immensely in our effort to revise and augment the history of German women. The goal of a feminist history is not only to determine what women have done and thought and experienced in the past—it is also to investigate the context in which those women lived and how that context shaped their development—and, by extension, the present in which we live. We hope and plan to pursue that goal through further cooperative efforts.

The conference that produced the essays which comprise this volume was supported both financially and in less tangible but equally important ways by many organizations and individuals whom we would like to thank. We are very grateful to the following for their generous funding: the Fritz Thyssen Foundation, the National Endowment for the Humanities, and the Council for European Studies, as well as the Office of International Programs, the College of Liberal Arts, the Graduate School, and the Center for Western European Studies, all of the University of Minnesota. The strong encouragement provided by the three sponsoring departments of German, History, and Women's Studies at the University of Minnesota was a great help to us. The organization of Women Historians of the Midwest was also supportive; we thank them for their assistance. The Minnesota Historical Society deserves mention, especially for the exhibit of contemporary documents that it assembled for the benefit of conference participants. The St. Paul History Theater's eloquent reading of scenes from its production of *Lady Knight* brought home to us the realization that women's history—American or German—is rich and full and wonderfully colorful. We also wish to express our gratitude to Linda Pickle and Regina Schulte for their contributions, and to Edith Waldstein, Ilse Brehmer, Elke Frederiksen, and Richard Evans, whose willingness to serve as moderators and discussants at the conference sessions was very much appreciated.

We would also like to express our appreciation to the following sources for their kind permission to reproduce some of the illustrations included in this volume: Ingeborg Weber-Kellerman and the Beck Verlag of Munich, the Deutsche Verlags-Anstalt of Stuttgart, the Fackelträger-Verlag of Goseriede, and Foto Marburg.

Without the calm and knowledgeable assistance of Leslie Denny, of the University of Minnesota Department of Conferences, we wonder if the meeting could have been held at all. We thank her not only for her competence, but also for her wit and imagination in helping us through many chaotic stages. The ever-present support and encouragement of Erhard and Ron, as well as the patience of Melissa, Timothy, and Daniel at moments ranging from distraction to crisis are gratefully noted.

Minneapolis
Summer 1983

NOTES

1. Gerda Lerner, *The Majority Finds Its Past: Placing Women in History* (New York: Oxford University Press, 1979); William Chafe, *Women and Equality: Changing Patterns in American Culture* (New York: Oxford University Press, 1977).

2. Louise Tilly and Joan Scott, *Women, Work and Family* (New York: Holt, Rinehart and Winston, 1978); Elaine Showalter, *A Literature of Their Own. British Women Novelists from Brontë to Lessing* (Princeton: Princeton University Press, 1977): Sandra M. Gilbert and Susan Gubar, *The Madwoman in the Attic. The Woman Writer and the Nineteenth-Century Literary Imagination* (New Haven, London: Yale University Press, 1979).

3. Our inclusion of names and titles is not meant to be comprehensive, particularly since new materials are appearing with ever-greater frequency. The Bielefeld anthology mentioned here, for example, that emerged from a meeting held in December, 1982, was published in the fall of 1983 by Schwann-Bagel Verlag in Düsseldorf under the editorship of Ilse Brehmer, Juliane Jacobi-Dittrich, Elke Kleinau, and Annette Kuhn as volume IV in the series *Frauen in der Geschichte* (its title: *"Wissen heisst leben. . . ." Beiträge zur Bildungsgeschichte von Frauen im 18. und 19. Jahrhundert*).

John Fout's collection will be published by Holmes & Meier; its title is *German Women in the Nineteenth Century: A Social History*. Among the German publications that have appeared recently, mention should be made not only of the entire series of *Frauen in der Geschichte*, edited by the historian Annette Kuhn and a variety of coeditors from a number of disciplines, but also of a new anthology edited by Karin Hausen, *Frauen suchen ihre Geschichte* (Munich: Beck, 1983). An earlier interdisciplinary collection in which literature, history, biology, and aesthetic theory are represented is Gabriele Dietze, ed., *Die Überwindung der Sprachlosigkeit. Texte aus der neuen Frauenbewegung* (Darmstadt, Neuwied: Luchterhand, 1979, 1981²).

*Work and Ideas about Work
for Women*

TEAMWORK IN SAXON HOMEWEAVING FAMILIES IN THE NINETEENTH CENTURY
A PRELIMINARY INVESTIGATION INTO THE ISSUE OF GENDER WORK ROLES

Jean H. Quataert

Human societies have exhibited great diversity in constructing the cultural roles of men and women. In recent decades, investigations by archaeologists and anthropologists have uncovered an amazing variety of gender relations that challenge long-held assumptions of universal male dominance and sexual divisions of labor. These patterns include noble women in African tribes functioning as "fathers" and passing on wealth, status, and power, and great ladies in Western feudal society actively managing the family estates. So, too, the symbolic and structural equality of the Balinese made sex distinctions practically irrelevant in everyday life, and, among the pygmy Mbuti in Africa, men and women both hunted and gathered. Cross-cultural studies show in general that foraging, fishing, and semi-intensive agricultural societies are characterized by sex integration, relative female autonomy, and enhanced ritual roles for women. But even in communities that hunt big game or rest on advanced agriculture, male dominance may be counterbalanced by actual, if informal, female power.[1]

In the Western world, the history of gender differentiation and the reasons for changes in sex role assignments are poorly understood and documented. Ironically, even recent research on family life and work patterns has contributed to perpetuating assumptions about the pervasiveness of sexual divisions of labor. For example, considerable literature now exists on the preindustrial Western peasant household based on private property. In some analyses, such as the feminist study of *Household and Kin* by Swerdlow and Bridenthal, these household structures are presented as the typical family and work unit of the past for the majority of people; the book is surprisingly silent on contemporaneous alternative living and working patterns for the lower classes. The studies demonstrate clearly that peasants assigned jobs by gender and age. The preindustrial, subsistence peasant world relied on considerable sex role divisions. Men's work and women's work existed separately: men plowed and sowed the fields, and in the fall, women were found threshing. Women also did the housework, cooked, cared for children, and tended the livestock and garden. The larger the farm, the greater the division of tasks.[2] Yet each individual in the household provided indispensable services to the survival of the whole: the death of one member put extraordinary strains on the household unit. Men and women were crucial productive members of this peasant family economy; however, they did different kinds of work.

Industrial society perpetuated sexual divisions of labor, for it, too, rests on sex segregation in the labor market, as the latest research has described so well.[3] Industrialization gave rise to "women's work" in the so-called light, consumer industries such as textiles, apparel, tobacco, or low-skilled office jobs in the tertiary sector. Nearly simultaneously, it created employment essentially for men, among the blue-collar work force in heavy industry, in the mines, and in construction. Such divisions, of course, confounded the historic feminist slogan of "equal pay for equal work"—only recently, and at present only in the professions, have men and women been doing the same jobs. Industrial ideology anchored role divisions even more securely in society by positing something new in the nineteenth century: notions of "proper" roles corresponding to presumed sex characteristics. The public realm came to be defined as men's proper sphere of activity, and women, seen first and foremost as nurturing and caring creatures, were held responsible for the smooth functioning of the private family. In Germany, these new norms developed out of the bourgeois social order in the late eighteenth century.[4] They reflected material changes in family life (the separation of production and consumption) as well as growing professionalization of bureaucratic and university careers. In these educated families, the wife's role was supportive at home; the husband's was productive outside. This description, however, became prescriptive and normative and, through a variety of mechanisms, increasingly institutionalized in the emerging industrial world.[5]

At first glance, it might appear quite inevitable that modern, industrial society would rest on clearly defined gender work roles. After all, preindustrial peasant life assigned work by gender and age and by the late eighteenth century, the educated *Bürgertum* in Germany was developing an elaborate ideology to justify its own version of such divisions. But the capitalist industrial world hardly evolved "naturally." It was a product of concrete choices and resolutions, and, in some geographic areas of Germany, the onset of the factory age disrupted a pattern of work and family living that was remarkable for the *absence* of clear sex divisions of labor. Contemporaneous with the preindustrial peasant work unit were the households of weavers, spinners, nail- and scyth-makers, and potters, to mention but a few work tasks that were performed in the home. This labor was neither urban nor organized along guild lines. Rather, beginning in the mid-seventeenth century, economic development and the evolving world market stimulated *rural* production outside the guilds. These home-industry households, producing for a distant market, shared with peasants a rural setting but, in marked contrast to peasant labor, work patterns broke the bonds of gender role divisions.[6] The couple shared productive functions, and it appears that housekeeping tasks were exchanged as well.

This essay investigates household living and working among rural homeweavers in the Oberlausitz, a textile district in historic Saxony. It offers a case study and rests on detailed and systematic archival research. The prime motive behind the choice of the case-study method originally reflected a desire to test, through archival work on the local and provincial levels, many of the exciting hypotheses and assumptions that feminist historians have put forth. Women's history by now has generated enough broad questions to inform this data gathering. But some other benefits of archival work quickly became apparent. Above all, it was archival materials that showed a pattern of shared work activities among men and women in the Oberlausitz hand textile industry. Yet these work relationships are not discussed in the *published* studies of hand textile production that began to appear in the late nineteenth century Germany. At that time, middle-class critics of industrial capitalism—associated, for example with the "Socialists-of-the-Chair," the *Verein für Sozialpolitik* (Social Policy Association) and a variety of bourgeois feminist groups—began to study aspects of the "social question." Their investigations add up to a whole corpus of literature in which homeweaving figures prominently. But archival evidence demonstrates that these studies seriously misrepresent the role of women in rural homeweaving. How could this have happened?

The historic record (the written works on history that have been passed down through the ages) is not synonymous with history (the actual experiences of men and women in the past). Rather, the former reflects the choices and assumptions (often implicit) of the historian. Furthermore, issues not deemed significant are not recorded. For a variety of reasons, work relations in home industry production have been slighted as a topic of investigation. Historians were not interested in women's work and, until recently too, a woman-centered perspective was absent from the inquiries.

At the turn of the century, the German historical economists saw rural manufacturing as a unique type of business enterprise, separate and distinct from the production of both artisan and factory. Labor interested them only to the extent that such production pitted two "classes" against one another: the dependent "weavers" and the socially more powerful "distributors." They failed to ask who produced the goods at home. By contrast, other authors were concerned with labor specifically; here a line of analysis has stamped the literature until today. This "school" of late nineteenth-century thought distinguished between two types of domestic industry: the old and the new—and gender of the workers became the central dividing characteristic. The "new" was a child of industrial capitalism, a product of increasing division of tasks and the massive influx of lower-class people into urban areas. In the cities, women and girls worked at home to augment the family fund while family men took on factory employment or other work outside their place of residence. In short, the "new" home industries were dominated by female, usually married, labor; the prime example was the ready-made garment industry that blossomed in Germany's larger cities. By contrast, the "old" embraced traditional domestic industry—rural handweaving, for example—fighting, by the late nineteenth century, a pathetic and, in the long run, unsuccessful battle for survival. Its workforce, so the literature argues, was male, and the job represented a life's profession for the worker. These family men, however, were helped by their family members. In this picture, men were the weavers and women and children did the preparatory tasks of winding the bobbins and the yarn. One dynamic note, however, informed this interpretation: with the inexorable decline in handweaving, men were leaving the profession so it was becoming increasingly feminized as well as aged—a trend universally lamented—but the authors leave no doubt that previously handweaving had been a "male monopoly."[7] Yet, strikingly, no evidence for such family work patterns actually is offered. It becomes quickly apparent that these and later authors are describing an ideal notion of the family that was spreading in the new industrial world: a residential unit comprised of a husband—head and chief breadwinner—and his dependents, whose labor, particularly in the lower classes, was needed to help ends meet. Both portraits of old and new home industry conform to this ideal.

Archival evidence, however, imposes a different conclusion for older, rural manufacturing. Such production downplayed gender work roles in favor of a family "teamwork," although these families lived and worked in a patriarchal legal setting that enhanced men's position. The husband represented the family unit to the outside world: the small businesses typically appeared in his name in municipal registers, as did account books, and the joint family wage usually was paid directly to him. To the public world, then, the "team" had a head. But among these rural weavers in the Oberlausitz, roles were interchangeable and fluid, as will be demonstrated shortly. The private family setting accommodated an alternative work life to the division of labor by gender. This leaves undetermined—and the subject for another essay—the extent to which women's broad economic roles translated into public activity like, for example, involvement in machine wrecking in the 1830s and 1840s, demonstrations, and later unionization. Furthermore, role sharing should not be equated with familial harmony. These families were subjected to the stresses and strains of increasing economic hardship in the nineteenth century. Yet one careful student of cross-cultural patterns offers an interesting hypothesis. She writes that "men and women must be physically as well as conceptually separated in order for men to dominate women."[8] In other words, sex segregation—which was greatly minimized in these rural home-industry households—is a necessary, but not solely sufficient, ingredient for male dominance as well as aggression and violence.

This essay begins with a brief history of the emergence and spread of handweaving in the South Oberlausitz. It then assesses the centrality of weaving in women's lives and reconstructs a pattern of shared productive and home tasks. The arguments, by necessity, are preliminary and designed to stimulate discussion of the economic, demographic, technological, and even political reasons that may account for the extent of gender role assignments in a given society.

The Oberlausitz is little known in the historic literature. Yet for historians of work and family life, it offers an instructive case of rural textile manufacturing extending over centuries. Despite shifting political fortunes, its ties to weaving have been long and continuous. Weaving for the market originally was monopolized by urban woolen and linen guilds. The oldest guild in the area was the clothmakers of Zittau, chartered in 1312.[9] In the fifteenth century, South German, and particularly Nuremberg, capital turned to organizing a lucrative linen trade, and the Oberlausitz began its gradual incorporation into the larger market economy. Growing prosperity in Europe and changing fashion among the upper classes increased demand for linen. Nuremberg houses excelled in dyeing and finishing woven linen cloth; they already had contact with woolen Oberlausitz clothmakers and their representatives soon began to control production and marketing of linen itself.[10] Cities in the Oberlausitz grew prosperous and powerful by this trade and gradually bought up many surrounding villages that once had belonged to feudal lords.

Rural homeweaving emerged during the Thirty Years' War when the urban guilds lost their monopoly over textile production. The devastation and disruption of the war had weakened the guilds; they no longer could meet steady demand. In 1638, bowing to the inevitable, the Zittau city council permitted its villages to weave for the market; it controlled, however, the trading of linen goods and, until 1810, the cloth could only be sold in urban centers. Other councils and overlords followed suit. In return, each village weaver had to pay a loom tax—a feudal levy that continued until 1848.

A century of changes in agriculture had paved the way for this development. As is well known, agrarian prices began to rise in the sixteenth century, which in Germany spurred lords to extend their feudal estates. East of the Elbe generally, this process consolidated large Junker *Rittergüter* (estates of the nobility), establishing noble economic, social, and political dominance over the countryside. This did not occur in the South Oberlausitz. In part, urban power frustrated the nobility's intentions; in part, peasants in the province occupied land under favorable conditions; and the original settlement pattern in row villages had left considerable meadow and common lands unoccupied. During the century from about 1550 to 1650, these lands came to be occupied by gardeners, cottagers, and small-scale lessees. In short, social differentiation—not hardening serfdom—appeared in the Oberlausitz countryside.[11] Seeking profits, feudal lords had attracted cottagers, hoping to obtain a stable supply of cheap labor for their estates. They encouraged weaving and spinning and other manufacturing as supplemental income for the long winter months. Likewise, peasants had an incentive to parcel out their lands in hereditary tenancy; the amount paid often exceeded what they could obtain from the sale of agricultural products. Sons of peasants settled on their fathers' lands or on the commons and worked as day laborers for

Table 1

Landowners and the Land-poor in
Select Oberlausitz Villages,
1565 and 1586

Village	Landowners, A	Land-poor, B	Percentage B of Total
Seifhennersdorf, 1565	553	310	36.0
Eibau, 1565	432	310	41.7
Gross-Schönau and Bertsdorf, 1586	710	670	48.5

Source: Arno Kunze, "Vom Bauerndorf zum Weberdorf: Zur sozialen und wirtschaftlichen Struktur der Waldhfendörfer der südlichen Oberlausitz im 16., 17., und 18. Jahrhundert," *Oberlausitzer Forschungen: Beiträge zur Landesgeschichte* (Leipzig, 1961), p. 170.

brothers or others. As cottagers, they could marry and form their own families and escape the fate of remaining single manservants *(Hausleute)* on their fathers' land. And weaving cloth and spinning yarn improved their economic position in this hilly and only moderately fertile province.

The villages of the South Oberlausitz experienced marked growth in the numbers of land-poor settlers who could not live from agriculture alone. Table 1 divides the population of several villages into two categories: landowners and their family members, including girl and boy servants, who all lived from agriculture (A) and the land-poor—cottagers, other small lessees, and landless tenants (B).

In each case, the number of land-poor, who had detached themselves from the feudal sector, was considerable. In Gross-Schönau, with Bertsdorf, such groups represented nearly half the population in 1586. The settlement of cottages can be traced with some precision in the village of Gross-Schönau. In 1586 there were 33, in 1620, 48 were recorded; in 1700, there were 214, and together they housed 782 looms; in 1777, the number of cottages had climbed to 400.

The data could be multiplied for each village but the pattern remains the same: cottagers were the fastest growing social class in the South Oberlausitz in the early modern period. They owned very small plots of land (on average, one-quarter of a Saxon *Scheffel* or .17 acre) and supplemented their income by weaving. Once the villagers obtained the right to weave for the market, the number of cottagers making weaving their *main* livelihood spread rapidly. Weaving received added stimulus as a result of the settlement in the Oberlausitz of numerous

Bohemian Protestant refugees who fled the Counter-Reformation. Saxony remained Protestant and these settlers brought with them their long experience in weaving and high skill levels. Numerous new weaving villages were founded in the second half of the seventeenth century—Neu-Eibau, Neu-Schönau—by the Bohemian refugees.[12] At the end of the century, one account estimated that two-thirds of the population in the South Oberlausitz was engaged in homeweaving for the market; the area had one of the densest populations in all of central Europe.[13] Its inhabitants were not really bound by either feudal or guild restrictions, and they fashioned a new material culture that included an appropriate "sex-role plan."[14]

In the latter part of the seventeenth century, the British began to search for new sources of linen cloth. Expulsion of the Huguenots in 1685 had disrupted their profitable French connection; in its place came the Oberlausitz village, the producing end of a chain that included cloth manufacturing firms in Hamburg, Leipzig, and Dresden. British capital introduced a different product to the area—bleached linen cloth—and brought in new technology to improve quality. While the actual weaving process continued to be decentralized and dispersed in the cottages of weavers, commercial capital now controlled more tightly the other stages of production. Distributors provided the raw materials (the bleached yarn which they obtained primarily from Silesia) and they arranged the finishing and dyeing of the cloth. They took over sales, too. The finishing stage typically was done in centralized workshops. Ongoing investment in the course of the eighteenth century transformed these distributors into the area's first industrialists.[15]

With the incorporation of the district into the world economy, its weavers became increasingly dependent on foreign demand and prey to foreign competition. Wars, tariffs, even mechanization in distant lands affected deeply the quality of life in the remote Saxon province. In 1770, for example, the British shifted linen production to Ireland. They hoped to displace Irish clothmakers and secure for themselves alone the lucrative wood trade. The Napoleonic Continental System (1806–1811), by halting foreign trade, further disrupted linen production in the Oberlausitz; the industry never fully recovered, in part because of the revolution in cotton manufacturing that was occurring in England. Demand for linen began to fall sharply at the end of the eighteenth century. Henceforth, cheaper cotton goods increasingly dominated the market.

During the Continental System, hand cotton manufacturing had been introduced into the South Oberlausitz. Unemployed linen weavers could use their own looms for cotton manufacturing. Production continued to be organized by distributors, now responsible for dispensing cotton yarn. While the Napoleonic policy artificially stimulated the new industry by keeping out British goods, cotton weaving weathered the dislocations of the post-Napoleonic era and became increasingly important to the area, as an 1831 survey of distribution of looms by type of product demonstrates. In the province that year there were around 10,579 hand looms for cotton, 4,114 for linen cloth, and 937 for intricate picture weaving (Damask).[16] No mechanical looms were counted; the Oberlausitz weaver still worked with hand technology and ingenuously shifted from product to product that had not yet undergone mechanization: linen cloths, damask, and increasingly, colored yarn *(Buntweberei)*. Thus, Oberlausitz weavers remained marginally competitive, although the price was growing impoverishment throughout the nineteenth century. But as late as 1885, handweaving still was a very important source of family livelihood. A major survey of work in the administrative district of Zittau shows that handweaving that year represented the occupation of 12 percent of a total population of 73,750.[17] This percentage does not include family members supported by the occupation nor those engaged in textile-related handicraft. In some villages, the numbers far surpassed the average; in Middle and Lower Oderwitz, for example, 28 percent and 35 percent, respectively, of each total population worked in handweaving.

As seen, it was in the course of the eighteenth century that the Oberlausitz was drawn ever more fully into the world economy. Henceforth, a majority of its populace was engaged in weaving for a distant market. Until the mid-nineteenth century, when railroad construction and urban building opened up seasonal jobs for men, *all* family members worked together in weaving. There was surprisingly little job differentiation in weaving households. Traveler accounts and municipal surveys are unambiguous on that score. While each village, to be sure, had its local artisans—the shoemaker, tavernkeeper, fruit or vegetable grower and, of course, the peasant—most of the people lived by weaving. One commentator described life in the village in the early nineteenth century: "In the so-called weaver-villages, men and women, sons and daughters weave. The oldest and the children sit near the looms and wind the bobbins and prepare the spools. All are interdependent and rely on one another. . . ."[18] Is this description accurate? How were work tasks assigned in the home in the nineteenth century? To what extent was gender or age important in dividing up work?

Rural homeweaving was work activity outside guild control. This independence offered distinct advantages to women: guilds restricted female labor, and it appears that organized, official training in general discriminates against women. For example, not until the 1880s did the Saxon government become involved in supervising job training in weaving. By then concerned over the precipitous decline of hand-weaving, officials introduced the newest handloom technology and sought to retool weaving skills; several weaving schools (Webschulen) also were opened. Women explicitly were excluded from these pro-grams.[19] But in the interim two and a half centuries, labor relations went essentially unregulated. The periodic efforts by the rulers in the eighteenth century to restrict women's work in weaving in order to promote domestic feudal service were disregarded completely. In es-sence, rural manufacturing represents a period of relative laissez-faire in labor regulation: a long hiatus between guild control on the one hand and state intervention that characterizes industrial capitalism on the other. The major exception proves the theme that official organiza-tion discriminates against women: Damask weaving was introduced in Gross-Schönau in the second half of the seventeenth century. It was highly skilled, minutely regulated, and secretive; it was also the exclu-sive domain of men. But in raw and bleached linen weaving and, after 1800, in the cotton cloth goods industry that began to encroach on indigenous linen production, any "lad" or "girl" could learn the trade. The verb erlernen (training through practice) was applied equally to men and women. A girl would take a short apprenticeship with a weaver and then return home to "work as" (agieren) a "master." Equally important, the new weaver, in turn, would teach others, in-cluding family members. In the main, these work skills were survival tools, passed on in the home from generation to generation.[20]

Probate records offer added proof of women's significant participa-tion in weaving. The Bautzen archives for the Oberlausitz preserved one in ten of the documents in the nineteenth century and sought representativeness: there are weavers' last wills (Nachlässe) divided by sex, by owners or renters of homes, and by economic position as wage earner or self-employed. The estate's records contain a variety of evidence. First, they indicate the extent to which girls inherited looms. The practice of females inheriting work tools was widespread and affirms the family's recognition of the centrality of weaving in women's lives. For example, Auguste Eichler inherited the family loom in 1872; her brother received the small home. The young Christiane Luise, niece of the deceased weaver Johanne Schmidt, was given her aunt's work tools in 1872 over the claim of her four brothers.[21] Typically, these family units in the South Oberlausitz had two or more looms. The girls brought their inheritance into their marriages as young brides.

This is the second type of evidence. By custom, the wife's property remained her own *(eheweibliches Einbringen)* and it showed up as a debt on the deceased husband's ledger. Here can be seen the women's economic contribution at the outset of marriage. Women brought in looms, to be sure, and other work tools, but also cash. Johanna Keil, the wife of Karl Gottlieb, cottager and weaver in Upper Sohland who died in 1860, contributed 100 RT *(Reichstaler)* cash at marriage and contracted a 130 RT debt for their cottage. Her money, so it appears, helped the couple buy their home. The wife of a poorer weaver and renter, Karl Röthig, had helped out with 40 RT cash at marriage. Johanne Christiane was married to the weaver and cottager Gottlieb Tietsch, who died in 1883. Her marriage had begun with some financial security. She offered 285 RT cash, 45 RT for buying flax, and 40 Ellen (1 Elle = 56.8 cm) of woven bleached linen which she apparently made before her wedding. Marie Elisabeth Zöllner's claim on her husband's estate in 1873 nearly exceeded his total assets. It added up to a sizeable amount of 3,038 Taler. At marriage, she gave 700 NT *(Neutaler)* cash, flax worth 30 Taler, a dairy cow, a goat, and potatoes: she also gave 1000 NT worth of bleached yarn, a loom (which her husband had sold) and later added an inheritance from her brother. The heirs were forced to sell his estate to pay off the debt to his wife.[22]

The wife's contribution of cash and tools offered real economic advantages to the young couple. At a time when looms and related work tools were quite inexpensive (looms cost about 5 RT during the nineteenth century, although the sum varied slightly depending on the quality of the wood), even 40 RT cash permitted the couple to begin marriage with some financial advantage. They did not have to save to buy the necessary work tools. Furthermore, the custom of separating out the wife's contribution created, in fact, a second economy in the household. The estates' records refer to the *ehemännliche Wirtschaft* (the joint economy—i.e., what the husband and wife contributed in the course of marriage over which the husband had control) and the *eheweibliche Wirtschaft*. For Marie Zöllner, her wealth represented real security for her later years and generally such monies supported women in widowhood. They obtained after the death of a husband what they had put into the marriage as a young bride. Evidence also exists that the wife's inheritance was passed on to daughters and remained in the female line. The last will and testament of Johann Gottlieb Hänsch in Lower Berthelsdorf, who died in 1856, stipulated that his daughter Johanne Rahele receive the following items that belonged to her mother: "1 blanket, 6 pillow cases, a loom with a spinning wheel and reel, a middle-sized wardrobe, a larger wardrobe, a cupboard, and an easy chair."[23] This reality of distinct economic units was so powerful that a husband perceived himself as a user rather than co-owner of his wife's property when she had inherited a home. He "was using the property," as Karl Gottlieb Korfelt described it in a petition to the Saxon government in 1847. His own words are very revealing: "In 1845 I married Marie Schubert from Turchau, and now I am a family weaver [*Familien Weber*]! Since my wife inherited the house from her father, I am using it profitably and am very industrious in my work."[24]

Probate records offer additional evidence for the paramount role of weaving in the life of the South Oberlausitz women. These are the sales contracts. Such contracts were a form of premodern old age insurance among property owners and, as seen, most homeweavers in the Oberlausitz were cottagers, although the number of renters was rising in the nineteenth century. The sales contracts guaranteed the parent or other survivor *(Ausgedinge)* and the unmarried children minimal maintenance. They show unmistakably the effort made to insure that women would be able to continue to weave after the death of one of the breadwinners. As Johann Weber in 1872 so nicely stated, he wanted his wife to continue "her much-loved occupation"— weaving.[25] In the sale of his cottage in 1861, Johann Gottlieb Hensel stipulated that the buyer provide his widow with free lodging in the home or build her a home large enough to house a loom "comfortably." In addition, she was assigned a shed for her goat. Other contracts were much more detailed. The testament of a linen manufacturer Karl Reichel in Oberoderwitz secured for his wife Anna Dorothea a room of her own large enough to set up a loom, spinning rod, and small table easily and gave her the option of employing a weaving-girl *(Weber Magd)*. It required the purchaser of his estate (in this case his son Karl Gustav) to provide fuel and lighting. Anna Dorothea was given unlimited use of one of 6 rooms of her choosing in which her weaving assistant was permitted to set up a bed. Further, she was to receive yearly 6 bushels of potatoes, 3 of corn, and a pound of butter and a jug of good milk each week. So, too, Martha Elisabeth was given a room in the Neuberthelsdorf residence and the right to set up a loom, spinning rod, and reel.[26]

Other types of archival documents help establish actual work patterns in the home. In 1810, the Oberlausitz homeweavers received special rights to hawk their wares; this was a milestone in the development of rural weaving in the province because previously goods manufactured in the countryside had to be sold in cities. Hawking assumed increasing importance as local handweavers faced serious machine competition—first by England, then the Rhineland and Southern Germany, and finally by the early mechanized textile mills for Orleans cloth in the city of Zittau itself. Offering supplemental income, hawking, among other activities, helped these increasingly impoverished handweavers survive the disastrous famine decade of the 1840s. Yet the Saxon government, bowing to pressure from its other constituents who continuously complained of unfair advantage, began to curtail the Oberlausitz peddler. In December 1844, weavers had to prove need; then an official pass was issued to the family member allowed to hawk only goods personally made. This control lasted until freedom of trade was proclaimed in the Oberlausitz in January 1862. In turn, weaver families petitioned for permission and described their living and work relations in justifying the request.

For nearly twenty years, from 1844 to 1862, hundreds of petitions were sent off to the Saxon government that give a glimpse into the weavers' homes. Further, local officials commented on the request and corraborated the story. These unique documents show a pattern of shared "teamwork." Husbands were given passes; so were wives and daughters. For example, at the sudden death of her father Jacob Hättig in Bertsdorf in 1858, his married daughter Christiane Rössler petitioned for permission to hawk his goods and settle his business for two years. She had accumulated enough experience as daughter and later as wife working in her own home. The request was granted. The rather amusing case of Johanna Christiane Gacht, who talked her way out of a fine for illegal hawking of wares, shows that women peddled goods without official permission. But when the husband was away, the wife ran the family work unit, continuing to weave and meet work contracts and stocking goods for subsequent sale. Conversely, when the wife was out hawking, the husband took care of the home, looking after children and tending the small garden. Roles were exchangeable and not defined by gender. The documents, in fact, affirm the crucial importance of such role sharing, ironically in part by reverse example. A few cases exist (although they are by no means typical) in which a survivor petitioned the Saxon government to assume the peddling rights of a wife who had died unexpectedly. Johann Scholze from Hainewalde was such an individual. In his petition of 1850 he described sex division of labor in his home: he "finished the goods and [his] wife alone undertook the selling and hawking."[27] While the municipal officials supported Scholze's request, they predicted the family's imminent downfall. Due to rigid sex role divisions, Scholze was ill-informed about customers along the hawking circuit and was unable to maintain the household. Role sharing, then, was a matter of practical necessity in this era of high mortality and economic deprivation.

The pattern of shared work roles continued throughout the century since it was rooted partially in technology. Initially, the distributor controlled the preparation stages of production only in the cotton industry. He bought up the spun yarn, had it bleached and dyed and then carefully prepared for weaving. But with the spread of the warping frame in the Oberlausitz, much of the so-called preparatory work was done outside the weaver's home, in other households geared to the textile industry or in the homes of agents and distributors which more and more came to resemble centralized workshops.[28] Weavers typically picked up the warp spools already wound and chained off, and even the bobbins. Thus, role divisions by age and sex were less likely to materialize among weavers. To be sure, if young children lived in a family they earned their keep by winding the bobbins. A charming and informative reminiscence of a 79-year-old weaver, August Flügel, who had been born in 1877, describes typical children's work:

> In my parent's home, father and mother sat at the looms. Beginning at
> 6 years of age, we six children had to help out. We had to warp the
> yarn and wind the bobbins. But soon I was also winding bobbins as
> wage labor. In 4 or 5 days, I had to prepare for weaving a good 5
> pounds worth of yarn. . . . We were paid just pittance and often had to
> wait in long lines to deliver the bobbins. . . .[29]

This was the only work children could do but it was not exclusively children's work. Furthermore, children grow up and leave the family and the once young parents become an aged couple. Each family has its own family cycle, and work patterns vary over time. The dominant description in the historic literature of distinct gender and age work patterns does injustice to a reality that was much more complex, although it might capture a family at a moment in time. But even if these preparatory tasks were done at home, the jobs were not exclusively gender-specific. Municipal officials in the late nineteenth century, confounded by what they saw in the home, painstakingly sought to piece together the fluidity of jobs in homeweaving households. At times, adult male weavers wound the bobbin (the so-called children's work); at other times, they commissioned an adult neighbor. True, wives might prepare the warp; so would husbands, and often husband and wife wove on one piece alternately. Furthermore, insurance records late in the century document an amazing relationship that appeared in the later stages of a family cycle. This picture turns stereotypes totally upside down. Among the elderly, men who tended to age earlier prepared the warp and wound the bobbins (to save money) for their more healthy wives who continued to weave.[30]

The evidence presented so far has established the importance of weaving as a life's profession for the women. It compels recognition that males and females shared productive work roles including, for half of the century, the hawking of goods. One final issue remains to be considered in this joint family venture. Were "reproductive" tasks exchanged as well? Simply put, did men do housework? This question—which is of considerable contemporary interest—nonetheless represents a modern analytic perspective that rests on different spheres of production and reproduction. Such division was not characteristic of the preindustrial world. After all, it was industrial development that physically separated work from the home, divided life up, and by and large assigned different activities to the sexes. These polarities, then, informed the very theoretical constructs that social scientists have devised to analyze life in industrial societies. This is not to say that such concepts are inapplicable to an earlier age. But, rather, such clear division of spheres was foreign to the thinking of people who, for example, worked in rural manufacturing. Housework was fully integrated into family life that included labor for pay (weaving), cooking and cleaning, gardening, and raising children and goats (unpaid household tasks). In researching such family production in protoindustrial societies, Hans Medick persuasively shows that men and women exchanged the so-called reproductive activities as well as productive roles. The notion of teamwork embraces household tasks, too. For example, he cites a traveler in the Rhineland in 1816 who remarked that men "cooked," "milked" and "swept" when the wife was busy meeting work orders. Medick also argues for an equality of consumption: women were seen drinking in taverns and smoking, a testimony to their important economic position because these two forms of relaxation usually were reserved for the male breadwinner.[31]

My own evidence on the issue of household tasks is sketchy but suggests a compatible conclusion. A detailed survey taken in 1895 in the South Oberlausitz sheds light not only on the activities in weaver households at the time but, by extrapolation, on earlier patterns. This survey was undertaken in the area after the *Bundesrat* (Germany's Federal Council) extended old age and disability insurance to the self-employed in homeweaving. The pollsters visited each home and interviewed the members, asking about work, family relationships, home tasks, employers, wages, hours, etc.[32] The survey demonstrates that men at home did housekeeping, although invariably the pollsters added "for the wife," showing *they* knew that housework was woman's work. For example, the husband of Auguste Heinze, full-time homeweaver in Mitteloderwitz, was a construction worker. The poll probably was taken in the winter and at the time he was caring for the home. Wilhelm Wendler's case was similar. He admitted candidly that his wife went into the factory and he ran the home. The husband of Julianne Neumann offers a different example. In a letter to the insurance officials, he stated that since his marriage in 1874 his wife had borne twelve children (not all survived). The decline in handweaving incomes pushed him into the factory; now, he was the sole breadwinner (he complained) and *no longer* could help his wife care for the home and raise the small children.[33] He leaves no doubt, however, that previously he had done so and that he was expected to help.

For Karl Neumann and many others like him, the transition to factory employment was a deterioration in the quality of life since they no longer could meet expectations and participate in the education of their children. In the course of time this division of labor—women in the home and men working outside—would come to be seen as "natural." But for the transition generation between domestic and factory employment it was not. Inspectors' reports reinforce the picture obtained from archival materials. As income from handweaving continued to plummet, family members sought other jobs. There were more jobs available for men and, as seen, in the last third of the nineteenth century former male handweavers took on seasonal employment, particularly in construction or agriculture. Their wives would work in the mills in the winter months and husbands would care for children, shop, cook, and clean. In the spring, however, wives would return home and husbands would leave to work for wages. In one large mill, this was true of 51 of 279 married women workers, or 18 percent. In a textile factory in Eibau, 20 families arranged their lives in a similar fashion.[34] Thus, part of the large turnover in the factory workforce reflected a modification of the "teamwork." Couples continued to exchange unpaid domestic tasks but now in ways appropriate to the early industrial era.

The material in this essay captures a lost past. Rural manufacturing prior to industrialization was a crucial stage of economic growth and capital accumulation. Recognized today as a major transition phase of feudal, agrarian society, such development loosened feudal ties and promoted market activity. It represents a fascinating example of economic practices that include the sharing of work by men and women in a family setting. Yet such gender relations are not discussed in the historic literature on traditional home industry; and it requires extensive archival research in both judicial and administrative collections to recover their reality.

It appears that these work patterns owe their origin to several basic causes. The first was the economic deprivation and poverty that characterizes preindustrial society generally. This meant—and it was true for peasant households as well—that all family members, male and female, had to contribute to family maintenance. What set home industry off from peasant agriculture were two additional factors: the work could be done indoors and it was not as inexorably seasonal as farming. In addition, the home industry families were integrated into national and even international markets and from the start worked for wages. Cash income was increased when both partners wove; inheritance patterns have shown that wives of cottagers typically brought their own looms into the marriage. To the extent that these families were part of a market economy, their members thought of time as money. We can speculate that to save time they readily helped one another out by sharing the nonpaid labor tasks as well. Furthermore, agriculture involves many jobs—plowing, sowing, harvesting, growing crops and vegetables, tending animals, possibly even marketing, to name a few. Such complexity was met by division of labor, and gender became one of the bases for assigning work. There were fewer steps in home weaving; one person could be responsible for various operations and even the whole process of production. This did not mean that age and sex played no role in dividing work tasks. As seen, children did certain kinds of jobs as did old people who were losing their strength. What mitigated such clear divisions in the case of Oberlausitz weaving households was technology. The preparatory stages— winding the bobbins and warping the yarn—increasingly came to be performed in the homes of distributors or other households that specialized in such work. In the nineteenth century, in both the linen and cotton industries, weavers picked up the warp and bobbins fully wound; they needed merely to dress the loom and this was done by a specialist *(Andreherin)* at night so the weavers—male and female— would not lose time. Finally, the absence of guild control as well as state regulation of labor was a critical variable in the ability of women to assume such broad productive roles. In the public organization of work—whether it is specifying steps in apprenticeship training, organizing secondary and university education, or, as in the Renaissance artist ateliers, offering nude models[35]—women have been disadvantaged, unable to compete, and assigned secondary, supplemental function. But these rural households were independent of the guilds and essentially unaffected by state regulation, which in the nineteenth century generally was minimal. They broke out of the feudal, agrarian context and constructed their own gender work patterns. Changes in gender relations, however, are embedded in the historic process. The onset of the industrial age would once again transform women's work and reintroduce greater sex differentiation as a basis of cultural work.

NOTES

The basis of this chapter was a paper presented to An International Conference on German Women in the 18th and 19th Centuries: Condition and Consciousness, April 15–17, 1983, University of Minnesota. Research in the archives of the German Democratic Republic and the libraries of the German Federal Republic was made possible by a Research Fellowship of the National Endowment for the Humanities (1980–1981), a Grant-in-Aid of the American Council of Learned Societies, and a Study Visit from the German Academic Exchange Service (Summer, 1982). I wish to thank all three foundations for their support.

1. Peggy Reeves Sanday, *Female Power and Male Dominance: On the Origins of Sexual Inequality* (Cambridge, 1981), pp. 15–19, and 21–24. See, as well, Amy Swerdlow, Renate Bridenthal, et al., *Household and Kin: Families in Flux* (Old Westbury, New York, 1981), p. 3, and Ann Oakley, *Woman's Work: The Housewife, Past and Present* (New York, 1974), p. 11.

2. A detailed description of women's work in peasant communities is found in Renate Schulte, "Bauernmägde in Bayern am Ende des 19. Jahrhunderts," pp. 10–11, paper discussed at the conference "Condition and Consciousness," April 15–17, 1983, University of Minnesota. Also, Louise Tilly and Joan Scott, *Women, Work and Family* (New York, 1978).

3. Robyn Dasey, "Women's Work and the Family: Women Garment Workers in Berlin and Hamburg before the First World War," in Richard J. Evans and W. R. Lee, eds., *The German Family* (London, 1981), pp. 221–55; Barbara Franzoi, "Women Home Workers, 1870–1914," paper presented at the 1982 American Historical Association meeting, Washington, D.C. Also, Wolfram Fischer, *Wirtschaft und Gesellschaft im Zeitalter der Industrialisierung* (Göttingen, 1972), pp. 250–51.

4. Karin Hausen, "Family and Role Divisions: The Polarisation of Sexual Stereotypes of Work and Family Life," trans. Cathleen Catt, in Evans, *German Family*, pp. 51–83; Birgit Panke, "Bürgerliches Frauenbild und Geschlechtsrollenzuweisungen in der literarischen und brieflichen Produktion des 18. Jahrhunderts," *Frauengeschichte. Beiträge 5. zur feministischen Theorie und Praxis* (Munich, 1981), pp. 6–11.

5. I am presently working on a book that traces the precise mechanism whereby middle class notions of proper roles were spread to working-class people and the extent to which working-class women actually internalized such norms.

6. Hans Medick, "Haushalt- und Familienstruktur als Momente des Produktions- und Reproduktionsprozess," in Heidi Rosenbaum, *Seminar: Familie und Gesellschaftsstruktur* (Frankfurt/M., 1978), pp. 295–96. Recently, historians have shown considerable interest in preindustrial *rural* production of goods for the interna-

tional market. In today's literature, it is called "protoindustrialism." Historians see it as a major transition phase of feudal society and they have analyzed it in terms of population growth and density, fertility strategies, household formation, and family labor. See, for example, Peter Kriedte, Hans Medick, Jürgen Schlumbohm, *Industrialisierung vor der Industrialisierung. Gewerbliches Warenproduktion auf dem Lande in der Formationsperiode des Kapitalismus* (Göttingen, 1977).

7. See the series *Hausindustrie und Heimarbeit in Deutschland und Österreich,* Vols. 1–4, Schriften des Vereins für Sozialpolitik (Leipzig, 1899); also, *Heimarbeit und Hausindustrie in Deutschland,* herausgegeben im Zusammenhange mit der Deutschen Heimarbeit-Ausstellung 1906 in Berlin vom Bureau für Sozialpolitik (Berlin, 1906); and the two works by Robert Wilbrandt, *Die Weber in der Gegenwart* (Jena, 1906) and *Die Frauenarbeit: Ein Problem das Kapitalismus* (Leipzig, 1906). Also documents in the Zentrales Staatsarchiv, Potsdam, RMdI, Nr. 6729–33; Die Verhältnisse der Hausindustrie und der Heimarbeit, 1882–1911; Nr. 6736: Die Beschränkung der Heimarbeit, 1901–1905; and Reichlandsbund. Pressarchiv. Nr. 8458: Heimarbeiter und Hausindustrie. International. 1906–1911.

8. Sanday, *Female Power,* pp. 7 and 75.

9. Chronologie. Stadtmuseum Zittau.

10. Arno Kunze, *Die nordböhmisch-sächsische Leinwand und der Nürnberger Grosshandel* (Reichenberg, 1926), pp. 14–17, 48–53; "Die Baumwollweberei des sächsischen Oberlausitz," *Der Textil-Arbeiter,* Vol. 24, Nr. 6 (9 February 1912).

11. Arno Kunze, "Der Weg zur kapitalistischen Produktionsweise in der Oberlausitzer Leineweberei im ausgehenden 17. und zu Beginn des 18. Jahrhunderts," in E. Winter, ed., *E. W. von Tschirnhaus und die Frühaufklärung in Mittel- und Osteuropa* (Berlin, 1960), p. 20; Edmund Gröllich, *Die Baumwollweberei der sächsischen Oberlausitz und ihre Entwicklung zum Grossbetrieb* (Leipzig, 1911), pp. 9–11. Fritz Hauptmann, *Woher wir Kommen,* Vol. 2, *Das Zittauer Land* (Privatdruck Marburg, 1976), pp. 121 and 167.

12. "Die Exulanten in der Oberlausitz," *Oberlausitzer Rundschau* (hereafter *OR*) Vol. 8, Nr. 9 (5 May 1961); also, Theodor Schütze, *Um Bautzen und Schirgiswalde: Ergebnisse der heimatkundlichen Bestandsaufnahme im Gebiet von Bautzen und Schirgiswalde* (Berlin, 1967).

13. Gröllich, *Die Baumwollweberei,* pp. 1–2; G. Korschelt, "Beiträge zur Geschichte der Webindustrie in der sächsischen Oberlausitz," *OR,* Vol. 11, Nr. 19 (5 October 1964), p. 293 (reprint of an 1867 article). Helmut Sieber, *Oberlausitz* (Frankfurt/M. 1968), p. 69.

14. For example, weaving determined the layout of the numerous long, narrow villages that emerged along both sides of the many small streams; it accounted as well for the unique structure of weaver cottages, the *Umgebinde* house—literally, a four-sided structure within a wooden house. The former had its own foundation so the shaking of the loom would not spread throughout the dwelling. These homes dominate the landscape even today. Sanday (*Female Power,* p. 3) discusses how cultures select a sex-role plan.

15. A. Kunze, *Zittaus Weg in die Welt* (Zittau, 1956), pp. 26–28.

16. "Die Baumwollweberei" (9 February 1912).

17. Richard von Schlieben, "Untersuchungen über das Einkommen und die Lebenshaltung des Handwebers im Bezirke der Amtshauptmannschaft Zittau, *Zeitschrift des K. Sächsischen Statistischen Bureaus,* Vol. 31 (Dresden, 1885), pp. 156–190.

18. Christian Pescheck, "Geschichte der Industrie und des Handels in der Oberlausitz," *Neues Lausitzisches Magazin,* Vol. 29, 1852, p. 8; for municipal accounts see

Staatsarchiv Dresden (hereafter StAD), Nr. 6257, Bl. 274–277: detailed report of work among Oberlausitz weavers, 1848. Also, Konrad Sturmhoefel, *Illustrierte Geschichte der Sächsischen Lande und ihrer Herrscher* (Leipzig, n.d.), p. 639.

19. For examination of the position of the guilds towards women's work see, particularly, Wilbrandt, *Frauenarbeit,* pp. 3–7; for the Saxon government's effort, Staatsarchiv Dresden, Aussenstelle Bautzen (hereafter B), Kreishauptmannschaft Bautzen (hereafter KB), Nr. 13820: Chamber of Commerce reports, 1881 and 1884; B, Amtshauptmannschaft Zittau (hereafter AZ), Nr. 1492: weaving school in Weigsdorf, 1881–1882 and Nr. 1481–1482: the weaving and commercial school in Seifhennersdorf, 1881–1914.

20. *Praktische Darstellung der Oberlausitzer Leinwand-Fabrikation nebst ihren Mängeln, zum Beweis dass, verschiedene Abhülfe und Verbesserungen dabei höchst nöthig sind, sowie wo dieselben anzuwenden,* von einem Fabrikanten, Herrnhut, 1837. Archival documents on hawking use the verb *erlernen* in describing both male and female weavers. For example, StAD, Nr. 6257: the hawking trade among Oberlausitz, Sebnitz, and Zwönitzer weavers, 1840.

21. B, Gerichtsamt Herrnhut, Nr. 226: Nachlass der Inwohner u. Weberin Johanne Schmidt, 1872; Nr. 231: Nachlass des Lohnwebers Johann Gottlieb Eichler, 1872.

22. B, Amtsgericht Schirgiswalde, Nr. 2116: Nachlass des Häuslers und Webers Karl Gottlieb Keil, 1860; Amtsgericht Löbau, Nr. 1783: Nachlass des Inwohners und Webers Karl Gottlieb Röthig in Waldorf, 1854; Amtsgericht Schirgiswalde, Nr. 2471: Nachlass des Häuslers und Webers Carl Gottlieb Tietsch in Weisa, 1883; Gerichtsamt Herrnhut, Nr. 240: Nachlass des Häuslers und Webers Johann Christoph Zöllner aus Oberoderwitz, 1873.

23. Amtsgericht Herrnhut, Nr. 128: Nachlass Johann Gottlieb Hänsch, Freihäusler und Weber zu Nieder Berthelsdorf, 1856.

24. B, KB, Nr. 11237, Bl. 38–39: petition to receive a hawking pass, Turchau, 10 October 1847.

25. Amtsgericht Herrnhut, Nr. 229: Nachlass des Hausbesitzers und Webers Johann Carl Weber aus Ober-Ruppersdorf, 1872.

26. Amtsgericht Schirgiswalde, Nr. 1912: Nachlass des Freiangesessenen und Webers Johann Gottlieb Hensel in Weisa, 1861; Amtsgericht Herrnhut, Nr. 247: Nachlass des Gartenbesitzers und Leinwandfabrikanten Karl Gottlieb Reichel in Oberoderwitz, 1873 and Nr. 128: Nachlass Johann Hänsch, 1856.

27. StAD, Nr. 6259, Bl. 56–58: 26 March 1858, petition by Rössler; B, KB, Nr. 11237, Bl. 44–46: 4 April 1851 for the case of Gacht; and ibid., Bl. 171–175: for Scholze.

28. Gröllich, *Die Baumwollweberei,* pp. 19 and 76.

29. "Die Erinnerungen alter Weber," Schöne, *Bautzener Land: Weberort Wehrsdorf* (Bautzen, 1956), p. 26.

30. B, AZ, Nr. 8082, Bl. 70–76: report on work life among handweavers, 21 April 1902; also Nr. 8225: insurance documents on extending disability and old age insurance to homeweavers, Niederoderwitz.

31. Medick in Werner Conze, ed., *Sozialgeschichte der Familie in der Neuzeit Europas* (Stuttgart, 1976), pp. 280–281.

32. The archival source for 31 of the area's municipalities contains not only the detailed survey taken in 1895 but, for the next several decades, letters, petitions, and court cases by family members protesting a variety of decisions. It is a unique and exciting set of documents, made doubly interesting because the Oberlausitz had been so isolated; the homeweavers were relatively unaffected by growing state regulation of

work or the new ideologies on gender roles and family life. Their responses thus partially reflected the values and assumptions of an earlier age. Two worlds are revealed in the survey: the world of traditional home industry and that of the modern, industrial state equipped with new notions of proper roles for the sexes.

33. For the remarks on Heinze, see B, AZ, Nr. 8223: Mittelweigsdorf #97 on the survey; for Wendler in Bertsdorf, Nr. 8210, Bl. 26: (no date—around July 1896); and Nr. 8238, Bl. 106–107: 14 July 1896 on Neumann's complaints, Spitzkunnersdorf.

34. *Amtliche Mitteilungen aus den Jahres-Berichten der Gewerbe-Aufsichtsbeamten,* Berlin, 1899, II, p. 1075. The case of the Eibau families is mentioned in Wilbrandt, *Die Weber,* p. 126.

35. Linda Nochlin, "Why have there been no Great Women Artists?" in Thomas B. Hess and Elizabeth C. Baker (eds.), *Art and Sexual Politics* (New York, 1971), pp. 1–39. Nochlin demonstrates that the requirements for "great" art were more than talent and creativity and required a course of study which was not available to women.

LABOR FORCE PARTICIPATION, LIFE CYCLE, AND EXPENDITURE PATTERNS

THE CASE OF UNMARRIED FEMALE FACTORY WORKERS IN BERLIN (1902)

Rosemary Orthmann

One of the major concerns of both critics and supporters of female participation in the nineteenth- and early twentieth-century labor force, particularly in industry, was the detrimental effect of such activity on the worker, her family life, and society. Supporters emphasized the need for social legislation to protect working women against the physical and moral hazards of factory life and to provide them with better training. Critics, on the other hand, concentrated on the perceived pernicious effects of female labor force participation, including increased promiscuity, disintegration of the family unit, and endangerment of future generations. Recent research, however, has shifted the emphasis away from the negative elements of female labor force participation and focused attention instead on the positive economic contributions working women made to their families, both in terms of ensuring their survival and improving their living standards.[1]

This shift reflects a conscious effort by scholars to place women's work within the context of their families and, in so doing, to bridge the gap in the literature between women's and family history. Most of the studies concentrate primarily on the woman's role as producer within the working-class family; they evaluate the types of jobs she performed, the conditions under which she worked, and the determinants of that paid or unpaid labor.[2] Her role as a consumer and the distribution of the fruits of her labor receive only secondary attention in the literature, due largely to the scarcity of appropriate source materials.[3] Common to all studies, however, is the underlying assumption that the family in the late nineteenth and early twentieth centuries was the basic unit for making decisions and that each member of the family filled a particular economic role toward achieving and maintaining a certain level of subsistence. That role at any given time depended to a large extent on demographic profiles of the individuals and families involved.

According to these studies, a working-class woman was most likely to work for wages outside the home before she married, that is, before her primary responsibilities centered around child care and household management. If she lived at home she was expected to contribute to the family economy. Her contribution took the form of paid or unpaid labor, depending on the labor supply within the family (the father's income and the age/sex distribution of its members) and the market demand for her labor.[4] As a young married woman she might work outside the home to augment her husband's earnings. Once she bore a child, however, her time at home, nurturing her offspring and performing domestic tasks, became more valuable. In times of crisis, such as unemployment, illness, or death of her spouse, she might reenter the labor force. Or she might take in lodgers, washing, or piecework to augment the family's income and still attend to her domestic responsibilities. As long as her children lived at home and worked, however, her monetary contribution to the family was small relative to that of the children.[5] The wife and mother, accordingly, was valued more highly for her unpaid labor within the family, and the daughter, for her earnings as well as her assistance in the household. Female labor force participation would thus appear to be largely a life-cycle phenomenon, varying with the age, marital status, and child-related responsibilities of women over the course of their lifetime.

Although these studies offer valuable insights into the family decision-making process and the woman's role within the family economy, they do not evaluate the actual distribution of the women's earnings within the family or the specific uses to which the women and their families put this money. Different expenditure patterns could well reflect different individual and familial considerations. Those families, for example, in which the daughter handed over all or almost all of her earnings, probably exercised greater control over their offspring than those in which the daughter kept some of her earnings for herself. On the other hand, those daughters who contributed all or almost all of their earnings for necessary items, such as food and housing, had less opportunity than others to directly purchase other consumer items that might improve the quality of their lives or the lives of their families.

By using family budgets or census data that concern households, scholars also tend to neglect the economic role of those individuals who fall between stages of the family life cycle. Studies typically define the stages in such a way that individuals enter into a new family of marriage directly upon leaving the old family of birth.[6] Such categorizations unfortunately ignore the range of options available to young, working-age adults in the leaving-home stage of the life cycle. They can, for example, continue to live at home while working and postpone marriage, or they can leave home to go to work and live with kin or set themselves up in lodgings well before getting married. Of particular interest in this study are those women who had already left home but had not yet formed their own families. Technically, they still belonged to their families of birth; but, as a result of living on their own or with others, they were no longer under the direct control of those families. One might expect their expenditure patterns to differ from those of the workers who still lived under that control.

A unique source of data, which tabulates information on age, occupation, income, housing, and expenditures for a large group of individual workers, allows the historian to address these issues directly. After a brief description of these data, this paper will evaluate the population they represent in terms of the woman's life cycle and then turn to the differential expenditure patterns of unmarried female factory workers in greater Berlin.

Data

In the fall of 1902, on the occasion of an imperial inquiry into the length of the factory workday for women, the factory inspectorate responsible for greater Berlin[7] carried out an independent investigation into the style and cost of living of unmarried female factory workers. According to directives, the three female assistants conducted personal interviews with workers employed full time in various branches of industry, chosen in numbers approximately proportional to the total number of women employed in each branch.[8] The assistants completed a questionnaire on a wide variety of issues for each worker while still in the factory and referred in many cases to the company records to ascertain or verify wage information.[9] At the completion of their interviews, the assistants then tabulated the results of the investigation for each worker. It is these individual-level tabulations, and not the questionnaires, that have survived for the historian's perusal.

The sample does not comprise a random distribution of workers, but it does constitute a considerable number of cases chosen to approximate the larger factory population in its occupational distribution. The number of women actually interviewed, 939, represents 1.3 percent of the total female workers, age fourteen and over, under the jurisdiction of the factory inspectorate.[10] A closer examination of the distributions of these two groups of women according to industrial branch, as in table 1,[11] reveals that the assistants succeeded quite well in interviewing women in relative proportion to the total factory population. Of the nine branches under consideration, only Forestry Byproducts was grossly overrepresented. This inclusion of a greater proportion of soap factory workers tends to bias the sample slightly in favor of the younger workers and those who lived at home and earned a wage below the median value.

It is more difficult to substantiate how well the sample group represented all female factory workers in terms of housing patterns and age

Table 1

Female Labor Force Participation in Factories and
Workshops by Industrial Branch, Greater Berlin, 1902

Branch of Industry	Unmarried Women 14 and older, Special Inquiry		All Women 14 and older, All Factories and Workshops		Special Inquiry as Percent of Whole Population
	Absolute No.	(%)	Absolute No.	(%)	
Metalworking	68	(7.2)	3902	(5.5)	1.7
Machine Manufacturing	77	(8.2)	8662	(12.3)	0.9
Chemicals	8	(0.9)	576	(0.8)	1.4
Forestry Byproducts, Soaps	33	(3.5)	599	(0.9)	5.5
Textiles	45	(4.8)	4568	(6.5)	1.0
Paper	165	(17.6)	9339	(13.3)	1.8
Food, Drink, Tobacco	58	(6.2)	3389	(4.8)	1.7
Clothing, Cleaning	422	(44.9)	32013	(45.4)	1.3
Printing	52	(5.5)	4460	(6.3)	1.2
Other	11	(1.2)	2928	(4.2)	0.4
Total	939	(100.0)	70436	(100.0)	1.3

Table 2

Age Structure of the Female Work Force in
Factories and Workshops, Greater Berlin, 1902

Age Category	Unmarried Women 14 and older Special Inquiry		All Women 14 and older, All Factories and Workshops		Special Inquiry as Percent of Whole Population
	Absolute No.	(%)	Absolute No.	(%)	
14–15	40	(4.3)	5194	(7.4)	0.8
16–21	429	(45.7)	24703	(35.0)	1.7
over 21	469	(50.0)	40539	(57.6)	1.2
Total	938	(100.0)	70436	(100.0)	1.3

structure. No statistics exist for the entire factory work force, for example, that detail systematically the living situations of working women. Working daughters and wives might appear in the households of working-class males who kept records of their budgets, but those women who were not living at home would surface only in terms of the rent and/or board they paid to those households as lodgers. When compared to women who participated in the domestic or home industry, however, factory and workshop workers were probably less fettered by the demands of child care and household management, since their working conditions required them to work outside of the home, under someone else's close supervision, and for longer periods without interruption or distraction. Factory workers accordingly could be expected to be at that point in their life cycles when domestic demands were smallest: young, unmarried, and living at home or else renting before forming their own families. Just what percentage of the female factory work force consisted of married women, unfortunately, is not clear. It is unlikely, however, that the proportion would be quite as large as that for the entire female labor force of independent wage earners (in the industrial branches under investigation) or 8.4 percent in 1900.[12]

Some information does exist on the age structure of the total factory and workshop population. The factory inspectors unfortunately did not tabulate their statistics on the number of workers by marital status, but they did record crude age categories for women: 14–15, 16–21, and over 21. A closer examination of the distributions of the sample and larger population by age category, as in table 2, indicates that the special investigation has a larger proportion of women twenty-one or younger, concentrating in the age category sixteen through twenty-one. This bias may be explained in part by the deliberate inclusion of only unmarried women in the special investigation. Married women would tend to raise the proportion of workers over age twenty-one.

Factory Labor Force Participation and the Life Cycle

Although the age structure of the work force in the special investigation may favor the younger women slightly, table 2 indicates nonetheless that factory and workshop positions tended to attract very young women. Forty-two percent of the female workers in all factories and workshops and one-half of those in the special investigation were twenty-one or younger. When the age structure of the workers in the special investigation is contrasted with that of all female workers in industry, including those who worked in small, unmechanized shops or out of their homes, the relative youth of unmarried female factory workers becomes clear. Nearly 69 percent of the women interviewed were under the age of twenty-five. By contrast, fewer than one-half (46.4 percent) of all the female workers employed in industry in greater Berlin in 1907 fit that category,[13] although the pool of potential workers was proportionally larger.[14] Clearly, factories and workshops drew from a younger female population than industry in general.

If factory labor force participation were primarily a life-cycle phenomenon, limited largely to young, unmarried women, one would expect to find the majority of workers below the average age at which women married. In the special investigation this was certainly the case. More than three-quarters of the workers (78.7 percent) were younger than 26.1, the mean age at marriage for women in the city of Berlin.[15] Of the remaining workers, only 6 percent of the total were thirty-five or older. It seems likely, then, that some factory workers, especially in the age group 27–34, delayed marriage while working, but almost all of them could expect factory labor force participation to be but a passing phase of their young, unmarried lives.

An unusual piece of information on each worker in the special investigation supplies further evidence as to the worker's life-cycle stage. The interviewers asked every worker with whom she was living. Fifty-eight and one-half percent of the workers replied that they lived with their mother, father, or parents. In other words, a young, unmarried woman in the factory labor force was slightly more likely to live at home than elsewhere. Another 7.2 percent had already left the family nest but wandered only as far as their siblings or other relatives. In all, nearly two-thirds of the unmarried female factory workers lived with relatives.

The remaining one-third of the factory work force had left home and relatives to find shelter with strangers or people not related to them. They chose basically between two options. They either rented a bed, or part of a bed, as a night lodger in someone else's household; or they rented a room as a lodger (or, in a few cases, an apartment), the more expensive but private alternative. More women (20.4 percent of the cases) chose the cheaper option, which entitled them only to a place to sleep during the night. Only 13.8 percent of the workers afforded their own room or apartment.

In moving away from home and relatives, these workers did not necessarily forsake a family-type living situation. Studies on both the United States[16] and Germany[17] argue that lodging and night lodging, respectively, offered young, urban migrants an important means of socialization into city life. A "malleable" or "half-open" family structure developed in response to the demand for low-cost housing, itself a product of migration, high intracity mobility, low wages (both for the household head and lodger), and a serious housing shortage.[18]

It is, unfortunately, impossible to determine to what extent the workers who rented from people other than relatives did so because they had no relatives living in greater Berlin. The interviewers did not record any information on the migration histories of either the worker or her family. Some of the women could have migrated from outside greater Berlin, with no contacts in the city other than their landlords and coworkers. Others could simply have changed lodgings within the city, leaving behind relatives or previous housing accommodations for different ones. Both options seem plausible in view of the attractiveness of the urban area to migrants and Berlin's characteristically high intracity migration.[19]

Although evidence about their migration histories is not available, the historian may nonetheless gain a better understanding of the workers and their housing situations by examining simultaneously their age structure. The distribution of age groups by housing category, as in table 3, reveals a pattern one would expect to find: the proportion of workers who lived with their parents decreased with age, and the proportion of those who rented rooms increased. In specific terms, workers in the youngest age group (and even the next older) were most likely to live at home, while those in the most mature age group tended to rent their own rooms or apartments. Living with other relatives or nonrelatives provided a middle ground between these two extremes: in both categories women in their early twenties (the largest single age group) predominated, but more women chose to live with people other than relatives. As a result, next to living at home, a worker in her twenties was most likely to rent a bed in someone else's household.

Table 3

Age Structure by Housing Category
Unmarried Female Workers in Factories and Workshops,
Greater Berlin, 1902

Age Group	Percent in Each Housing Category:				Absolute Frequency
	With Parents	With Other Relatives	With Non-Relatives	Own Room/Apt.	
14–19	80.4	4.7	13.0	1.9	316
20–24	56.1	8.2	27.0	8.8	330
25–29	41.1	10.1	26.2	22.6	168
30–54	32.3	7.3	14.5	46.0	124
All Ages	58.4	7.2	20.5	13.9	938

Of particular interest is the relatively large proportion of workers in the most mature age group who were still living at home: nearly one-third of the unmarried female factory workers, age thirty or older, were living as members of their parents' households. This finding suggests that these workers experienced a particularly long period of parental authority during which they were subject to the considerations of the family economy. Their working-class sisters who no longer lived with parents or relatives, on the other hand, presumably were freer to dispose of their earnings as they saw fit.

Living with relatives other than parents was the housing situation that factory workers experienced with least frequency. Those who did, however, comprised similar proportions of the four age groups under consideration. Unlike the other three housing categories, which exhibited clear age-related patterns, living with relatives apparently appealed to factory workers for reasons that went beyond age. Perhaps the absence of parents (through death or separation) and the desire to maintain a familial setting compelled these workers to live with their relatives. In any event, factories and workshops seem to have recruited workers primarily from parental households and secondarily from those in which the worker rented from nonrelatives.

The distinction between workers who lived at home and those who had already left home gains further clarification by examining some of the occupations in which these women engaged. A cross-tabulation of occupation by age, controlling for housing, reveals that those occupations with the youngest workers had especially high concentrations of women who lived at home: all of the workers, age 14–19, in the soap factories and most of those, age 14–24, in the confectionery factories (69 percent). In addition to the nature of the work involved—light, manual labor, particularly suited to girls just out of school with no industrial training—the employment policy of one of the soap factories offers an explanation of this phenomenon. According to the factory inspectorate assistant, the employer of two-thirds of these soap factory workers hired only young female workers, paid them low wages, and then let them go when the work ran out.[20] Young women who lived at home would be in a better position to survive, economically, under these conditions than workers who lacked that financial support system.

In contrast to these particularly young workers, the ironers in the clothing and cleaning trades presented the most mature work force. Three-quarters of the oldest ironers, thirty or over, and 40 percent of those in their later twenties rented their own rooms or apartments; another 40 percent of this latter group rented beds from people not related to them. These workers were clearly at a different point in their life cycles than those who still lived at home but worked for meager wages at light, manual tasks. Ironing required training and a good deal of physical strength. For their labors, however, the women were rewarded with relatively high wages. They tended to be former domestic servants, which, in the case of Berlin,[21] suggests strongly that they had migrated from outside the area and left home some years earlier.

In those occupations that seemed to appeal to both younger and older women—unskilled work in the machine, chemical, and textile branches and the operation of sewing machines in factories and workshops—the proportion of workers who lived at home was approximately equal to the proportion of women who had moved out. As an illustration, 57 percent of the unskilled workers in the machine and chemical industries who were in the age group 20–24 lived at home, while 31 percent rented beds, and 9 percent rented rooms. In the next older age group, 24–29, the proportions reversed: two-fifths of the workers lived at home, one-third rented beds, and one-fifth rented rooms from nonrelatives.

The women who operated sewing machines in factories were slightly younger than their counterparts in workshops (and better paid). It is also interesting that there seemed to be a distinct difference in the housing situations that both groups of workers experienced. Although in both groups a similar proportion of women lived with parents or other relatives (slightly less than 60 percent), factory workers tended to rent beds more frequently than rooms. Women who operated sewing machines in workshops, on the other hand, lived with equal frequency in both categories. Of even greater interest, however, is the contrast in the housing situations of the most mature sewing machine operators. While nearly three-quarters of the factory workers in the age group thirty and over lived at home, the same proportion of workshop laborers rented their own rooms. The workshop positions clearly appealed to women who were more independent of others in their housing situations.

Several further distinctions are worth noting. The majority of workers in skilled positions lived at home: more than three-quarters of those in the textile and clothing branches, over one-half of the skilled metal workers, and more than two-thirds of the bookbinders and printers. For nearly all of the skilled seamstresses and textile workers in the most mature age group, this meant a particularly long period under the direct control of their parents. This finding also suggests that these workers were the daughters of relatively prosperous factory workers, artisans, or shopkeepers, who could afford both to pay the apprenticeship fees and to wait to bring home pay until they had obtained a relatively high-paying position. Employment in the low-paying, ready-made clothing industry, on the other hand, which required little training, would more likely appeal to a woman who needed to make money quickly, such as one dependent on her own earnings for survival. One group likely to fit this description is the numerically largest category of unskilled seamstresses and assorted workers in the clothing and cleaning branches. Twenty-one percent of them lived with people not related to them.

Expenditures and the Life Cycle

Although unmarried women did not specify why they entered the factory labor force, it is possible nonetheless to draw conclusions about their motivations from their activities as consumers. If their income went exclusively or mostly toward necessary items such as food, rent, and utilities, their basic concern in going to work was probably economic survival. If they were able to purchase items that were not necessities, however, they probably were concerned also with improving their own or their family's quality of living. The presence of several categories of women in different phases of the leaving-home stage of the life cycle provides the opportunity to compare and contrast the expenditure patterns of these factory workers.

Let us look first at the worker's necessary expenditures, those for food, rent, and utilities. When expressed as a percentage of her earnings (including her factory wage and other weekly earnings), they reveal how much the worker actually pays in terms of how much she

Table 4

Necessary Expenses as Percent of Earnings, by Housing Category,
Unmarried Female Workers in Factories and Workshops, Greater Berlin,
1902

Percent of Weekly Earnings Spent on Necessary Items	Percent of Each Housing Category:				Percent of All Housing Categories (N = 897)
	With Parents (N = 541)	With Other Relatives (N = 68)	With Non-relatives (N = 175)	Own Room/Apt. (N = 113)	
Less than 50	17.9	2.9	4.6	2.7	12.3
50–60	19.6	23.5	9.7	5.3	16.2
60–70	15.2	22.1	26.3	15.9	17.9
70–80	14.4	25.0	25.1	22.1	18.3
80–90	9.1	8.8	20.6	25.7	13.4
90–100	22.6	17.6	8.0	14.2	18.3
More than 100	1.3	0.0	5.7	14.2	3.7
	100.1	99.9	100.0	100.1	100.1

takes home, without outside subsidies. The median value of the computed variable, 72.2 percent, suggests that economic need was indeed a powerful motivation but not the only contributing factor to female labor force participation. A closer look at the percentage breakdown in each housing category, as in table 4, reveals some distinct patterns.

Of the workers who lived at home, the largest single category spent all or nearly all (greater than 90 percent) of its earnings for necessary items. In 22.6 percent of the cases, unmarried women worked essentially to defray the cost of their families' food, rent, and utility bills. Not far behind in relative frequency, however, was another group of workers who paid less than 60 percent but more than one-half of their earnings for food, rent, and utilities. This category accounted for 19.6 percent of all the workers who lived at home.

In spite of these two relatively large categories, women who lived at home seemed to be fairly evenly distributed along a continuum from 40 through 60, 60 through 80, and 80 through 100 percent contribution of their earnings to the family income. It would appear, then, that no single family strategy regarding the dispensation of the daughter's earnings prevailed, except that the daughter was expected to contribute *something* to the family income.[22] Only six women reported free room and board from their parents and thus had their entire earnings at their own disposal.

Among the workers who lived with other relatives, including siblings, there was a greater tendency to expend more than one-half of their earnings for food, rent, and utilities. They were, however, less likely than the workers who lived at home to spend all or nearly all of their earnings on these items. Nearly three-quarters of these workers concentrated their necessary expenditures in the range from 50 through 80 percent of their earnings. Financial demands from relatives other than parents were, apparently, confined more to the middle range of values than in the nuclear family household.

The workers who did not live with parents or relatives were more likely than those who did to exceed their earnings in paying for necessary items. While only 1 percent of those who lived with relatives (parents, in this case) reported spending more than their earnings allowed, 9 percent of those who lived apart from relatives went over their limits on food, rent, and utilities. For workers renting the considerably more expensive rooms or apartments, making ends meet was particularly a problem. Over 14 percent of them overextended themselves, and an additional 14.2 percent spent all or nearly all of their earnings on necessary items. The combined figure of 28.4 percent suggests strongly that these women worked just to pay their necessary bills, although their bills were considerably higher than in any other housing category.

The women who lived with nonrelatives tended to spend 10 percent more, overall, on food, rent, and utilities, than the workers who lived with other relatives. While the latter group concentrated its expenses in the range from 50 through 80 percent of its earnings, those who lived with strangers tended to allocate from 60 through 90 percent of their available monies for necessary expenditures. This group, the most frugal of all, had the lowest percentage of workers who spent more than 90 percent of its earnings on food, rent, and utilities. This was the group in which numerous women admitted to cutting back on food when finances became tight or when the rent had to be paid. The main meal for them sometimes consisted only of a roll.

There were obviously different considerations at work in the woman's allocation of her earnings for necessary items, depending on her phase in the leaving-home stage of the life cycle. Those who still lived at home or with other relatives tended to contribute prearranged lump sums for their room and board to the head of the household. In return, the workers received not only full pension but also certain extras, such as free laundry, outings, and even pocket money. The workers who rented from strangers or acquaintances, on the other hand, generally did not benefit from such in-house subsidies but had to pay for every service rendered. In the case of those who rented only a bed, whose earnings were least likely to fall into the highest quartile, this often meant cutting back on one necessary item to buy another. The workers who rented their own rooms or apartments, by contrast, may have spent more on necessary items, but they also had more money to spend and perhaps higher expectations out of life. Nearly one-half of this group fell into the highest earnings quartile. They undoubtedly enjoyed the least crowded housing of any group and in this sense enjoyed greater privacy than those workers who slept with two or more relatives in one room or those who slept on cots set up in the busy kitchens of strangers.

A closer examination of the single most important budgetary expenditure, food, reveals that the worker who lived at home had a clear advantage over her working-class sisters. She was most likely to spend the least amount of money on food; that is, with food expenditures divided into four categories of an equal number of cases, the largest proportion of women who lived at home (34.5 percent) fell into the lowest quartile. The workers who lived with other relatives, on the other hand, were most likely to spend an amount in the next higher quartile, just below the median. Of the workers who rented from people not related to them, those who rented beds were most likely to spend an amount in the next-to-highest quartile, just above the median. The workers who rented rooms, however, were most likely to spend the most of any group on food. Forty-six percent of these workers fell into the highest quartile of food expenditures. Of particular interest here is the fact that even when taking into account who cooked the main meal, just over one-half of these women spent the most on food *and* cooked their own meals. They presented a clear contrast to those workers who rented beds, spent less on food, but tended to eat out (in a restaurant or canteen) more frequently. With control over their diets, women who rented their own rooms clearly were willing to spend more on food than those who had others cook for them.

In order to put this discussion of necessary expenses into perspective, I now turn to the total of the worker's fixed weekly expenditures and its relationship to her total weekly income (factory wage, other earnings, and a few cases of cash subsidies). Included in the fixed weekly expenditures are not only necessities but also regular child or family support payments, taxes, savings deposits, debt repayment, insurance premiums, club dues, pocket money, and allowances for entertainment, newspapers, and transportation. Not included in the regular weekly expenditures are such occasional expenses as clothing or extraordinary outlays for family support or entertainment.

What appeared earlier as the modal or most common category for workers living at home is now even clearer in table 5: one-quarter of these women were expected by their families to cover their own expenses. In contrast to these workers, however, was the slightly larger group of women who spent or handed over less than 60 percent of their total weekly income and all the others who were distributed fairly evenly along the range from 60 through 90 percent. The degree of familial control over the daughter's income thus varied widely among these unmarried workers.

In comparing this category of workers, who lived at home, with the other three, it becomes abundantly clear that other fixed expenses played a larger role in a worker's budget when she did not live at home. The relative distribution of workers by housing in tables 4 and 5 indicates that the addition of other regular expenses to the budget of a worker living at home met with an increase in the proportion who paid out more than 70 percent of their available monies and a decrease among those who spent 70 percent or less. In the other three housing categories, however, the dividing line was higher (80 percent). Working daughters, apparently, could benefit financially from living at home not only in terms of in-house subsidies for necessary items but also for additional expenses, such as pocket money or outings. They were, at the same time, however, subject to parental control. The more financially independent women, those in the other three categories, could not necessarily benefit from such in-house subsidies. They had

Table 5

Total Fixed Expenses as Percent of Income, by Housing Category
Unmarried Female Workers in Factories and Workshops,
Greater Berlin, 1902

| Percent of Weekly Income Spent on All Fixed Items | Percent of Each Housing Category: | | | | Percent of All Housing Categories (N = 765) |
	With Parents (N = 448)	With Other Relatives (N = 61)	With Non-relatives (N = 163)	Own Room/Apt. (N = 93)	
Less than 50	11.6	1.6	3.1	1.1	7.7
50–60	15.6	14.8	5.5	2.2	11.8
60–70	12.5	19.7	21.5	9.7	14.6
70–80	15.4	21.3	20.2	16.1	17.0
80–90	12.1	14.8	26.4	29.0	17.4
90–100	24.6	16.4	11.7	19.4	20.5
More than 100	8.3	11.5	11.7	22.6	11.0
	100.1	100.1	100.1	100.1	100.1

to pay for the additional expenditures themselves, or in a few cases, with outside funding.

Among those workers who lived with other relatives, the most common category remained those who spent from 70 through 80 percent of their income. At the same time, however, those who paid more than 80 percent of their available funds increased. This rise took place largely in the proportion of women whose income did not cover their expenses. With other expenses included, 11.5 percent of these workers could no longer make ends meet.

The addition of other expenses proved even more burdensome for the workers who did not live with parents or relatives. Of those who rented a bed for the evening, the modal category switched from the lowest in the 60 through 90 percent range to the highest. Again, more of the workers were pushed beyond the limits of their available funds. A slightly higher percentage of women than in table 4 spent all or nearly all of their income in a week, and the proportion that exceeded its limits doubled.

The group of workers most overburdened with fixed weekly expenditures again turned out to be the women who rented their own rooms or apartments. Although, as in table 4, they were most likely to fall in the category that expended from 80 through 90 percent of its income every week, that proportion increased in table 5, as it did in the category of workers that barely covered its expenses. The most dramatic increase, however, occurred in the proportion of women whose expenses exceeded their incomes: over 22 percent of the women fell into this group, the category with the second highest frequency among these workers.

Economic necessity clearly played an important role in the lives of these unmarried female factory workers. Eighteen percent just barely managed to cover the cost of their food, rent, and utilities, and another 4 percent exceeded their earnings limits when they paid for these items. These percentages rose to 20.5 and 11, respectively, when all regular expenditures were taken into consideration. And yet there were evidently workers for whom economic need was not the primary, or only, consideration. Women who lived at home were equally likely to fall into the quartile of workers with the largest and smallest balance of expenditures over income, depending on the household's strategy regarding the disposition of the daughter's income. Workers who lived with other relatives, on the other hand, were fairly evenly distributed among the three quartiles with a positive balance.

Those workers who did not live with parents or relatives were most likely to have a small but positive balance of expenses over income once they made all the regular weekly payments. Those in night lodging were also, like the workers who lived with other relatives, least likely to run a deficit and perhaps most frugal in their tastes. The women who rented rooms or apartments were, like the workers who lived a home, very likely to run a deficit but least likely to run a large surplus (unlike those at home).

Living with relatives was apparently a financially secure arrangement for the worker. Although she was expected to contribute some, if not all, of her earnings to the household income, she was likely to receive other services, gratis, in return. Once she left the family fold, however, she was most likely to have little money left after the regular bills were paid; and, in order to support a lifestyle that included her own room or apartment, she could also expect to exceed the limits of her income.

NOTES

Research for this paper was supported by a grant from the International Research and Exchanges Board (IREX).

1. See the suggestive article by Peter N. Stearns, "Adaptation to Industrialization: German Workers as a Test Case," *Central European History* 3, 4 (December 1970), p. 327; his follow-up study, *Lives of Labor: Work in a Maturing Industrial Society* (New York: Holmes and Meier, 1975), pp. 276–77; Neil McKendrick, "Home Demand and Economic Growth: A New View of the Role of Women and Children in the Industrial Revolution," in *Historical Perspectives: Studies in English Thought and Society,* ed. Neil McKendrick (London: Europa Publications, 1974), pp. 152–210.

2. See the seminal study by Louise A. Tilly and Joan W. Scott, *Women, Work, and Family* (New York: Holt, Rinehart and Winston, 1978); Robyn Dasey, "Women's Work and the Family: Women Garment Workers in Berlin and Hamburg Before the First World War," in *The German Family: Essays on the Social History of the Family in Nineteenth- and Twentieth-Century Germany,* eds. Richard J. Evans and W. R. Lee (London: Croom Helm or Barnes and Noble Books, Totowa, N. J., 1981), pp. 221–55; Martha Haley Fraundorf, "The Labor Force Participation of Turn-of-the-Century Married Women," *Journal of Economic History* 39 (June 1979), pp. 401–18; Claudia Goldin, "Household and Market Production of Families in a Late Nineteenth Century American City," *Explorations in Economic History* 16 (1979), pp. 111–31; Carol Groneman, "'She Earns as a Child; She Pays as a Man': Women Workers in a Mid-Nineteenth-Century New York City Community," in *Class, Sex, and the Woman Worker,* eds. Milton Cantor and Bruce Laurie (Westport, Conn.: Greenwood Press, 1977), pp. 83–100; Elyce J. Rotella, "Women's Labor Force Participation and the Decline of the Family Economy in the United States," *Explorations in Economic History* 17 (1980), pp. 95–117.

3. A notable exception is Michael R. Haines, "Industrial Work and the Family Life

Cycle, 1889–1890," in *Research in Economic History,* ed. Paul Uselding (New York: Academic Press, 1979), pp. 289–356; see also McKendrick.

4. Haines, p. 309.

5. Goldin, p. 112; Haines, p. 302.

6. Evelyn Millis Duvall, *Marriage and Family Development,* 5th ed. (Philadelphia: J. B. Lippincott Company, 1977), p. 144; John Modell, "Patterns of Consumption, Acculturation, and Family Income Strategies in Late Nineteenth-Century America," in *Family and Population in Nineteenth-Century America,* eds. Tamara K. Hareven and Maris A. Vinovskis (Princeton: Princeton University Press, 1978), p. 233; Haines, p. 298.

7. The factory inspectorate of greater Berlin had jurisdiction in 1902 over the cities of Berlin, Charlottenburg, Schöneberg, and Rixdorf (later Neukölln).

8. Draft of an Edict, 9 September 1902, State Archive, Potsdam (subsequently abbreviated SAP), Pr. Br. Rep. 30 Berlin C. Police Presidium, Tit. 44–47, Nr. 2018, Bl. 1.

9. "Bericht für Berlin C betr. die Lebenshaltung der unverheirateten Arbeiterinnen," 26 January 1903, SAP, Pr. Br. Rep. 30 Berlin C, Police Presidium, Tit. 44–47, Nr. 2018, Bl. 4; "Bericht für Berlin O betr. die Lebenshaltung unverheirateter Arbeiterinnen," 23 January 1903, SAP, Pr. Br. Rep. 30 Berlin C, Police Presidium, Tit. 44–47, Nr. 2018, Bl. 85.

10. The factory inspectorate was responsible in general only for those industrial concerns that employed at least ten workers and used mechanical power.

11. Figures for the population of women workers in all factories and workshops in tables 1 and 2 were gleaned from the "Annual Report" of the Factory Inspectorate for greater Berlin, 1902, SAP, Pr. Br. Rep. 30 Berlin C, Police Presidium, Tit. 47, Nr. 1946, Bll. 115–17. The data for the special investigation in this and all subsequent tables were gleaned from the appendixes to the reports of the three divisions of the Berlin factory inspectorate involved in the inquiry: SAP, Pr. Br. Rep. 30 Berlin C, Police Presidium, Tit. 44–47, Nr. 2018, Bll. 22–43, 60–81, 101–13.

12. This figure was computed from the pertinent statistics in Statistisches Amt der Stadt Berlin, ed., *Die Grundstücks-Aufnahme Ende Oktober 1900 sowie die Wohnungs- und die Bevölkerungs-Aufnahme von 1. Dezember 1900 in Berlin und dreiundzwanzig Nachbargemeinden . . . ,* sect. 2 (Berlin: Kommissionsverlag von Leonhard Simion, 1903), pp. 38–40.

13. This figure was computed from the pertinent occupational statistics in Statistisches Reichsamt, ed., *Statistik des Deutschen Reichs* 207,1 (1910), pp. 377, 382, 387, 392.

14. The figures 19.2 percent (1900) and 22 percent (1905) were computed from the appropriate statistics in Statistisches Amt der Stadt Berlin, pp. 6, 8; Statistisches Amt der Stadt Berlin, ed., *Die Grundstücks-Aufnahme von Ende Oktober 1905 sowie die Wohnungs- und die Bevölkerungs-Aufnahme vom 1. Dezember 1905 in der Stadt Berlin und 29 benachbarten Gemeinden,* sect. 2 (Berlin: Verlag Puttkammer & Mühlbrecht, 1911), pp. 105–06, 108–09.

15. The pertinent data for Charlottenburg, Schöneberg, and Rixdorf were not available. This figure should, nonetheless, represent the situation well since the overwhelming preponderance of women, working or not, came from Berlin. Statistisches Amt der Stadt Berlin, *Veröffentlichungen des Statistischen Amts der Stadt Berlin* (1900), suppl. 1: *Tabellen über die Bewegung der Bevölkerung der Stadt Berlin im Jahre 1900,* p. 47.

16. John Modell and Tamara K. Hareven, "Urbanization and the Malleable House-

hold: An Examination of Boarding and Lodging in American Families," *Journal of Marriage and the Family* 35, 3 (August, 1973), p. 470.

17. Lutz Niethammer, with Franz Brüggemeier, "Wie wohnten die Arbeiter im Kaiserreich?" *Archiv für Sozialgeschichte* 16 (1976), p. 125; Franz Brüggemeier, and Lutz Niethammer, "Schlafgänger, Schnapskasinos und schwerindustrielle Kolonie: Aspekte der Arbeiterwohnungsfrage im Ruhrgebiet vor dem Ersten Weltkrieg," in *Fabrik—Familie—Feierabend: Beiträge zur Sozialgeschichte des Alltags im Industriezeitalter*, eds. Jürgen Reulecke and Wolfhard Weber (Wuppertal: Peter Hammer Verlag, 1978), p. 156.

18. Modell and Hareven, p. 470; Brüggemeier and Niethammer, p. 156.

19. Clemens Wischermann, "Wohnungsnot und Städtewachstum: Standards und soziale Indikatoren städtischer Wohnungsversorgung im späten 19. Jahrhundert," in *Arbeiter im Industrialisierungsprozess: Herkunft, Lage und Verhalten*, eds. Werner Conze and Ulrich Engelhardt, Industrielle Welt, vol. 28 (Stuttgart: Klett-Cotta Verlag, 1979), p. 223.

20. SAP, Pr. Br. Rep. 30 Berlin C, Police Presidium, Tit. 44–47, Nr. 2018, Bl. 65.

21. N. Brücker, "Die Entwicklung der grossstädtischen Bevölkerung im Gebiete des Deutschen Reiches," *Allgemeines Statistisches Archiv* 1 (1890), p. 646.

22. Tilly and Scott, p. 177.

THE VIENNESE ENQUÊTE OF 1896 ON WORKING WOMEN

John C. Fout

The focus of my current research is working-class life in the decade of the 1890s in Germany and Austria and my hope is to write a social history of the working-class in that era. I seek to reconstruct both the work experiences of male and female workers and their personal lives. At this stage of my research I have been working with worker auto-biographies, primarily those of working-class women,[1] and it is for that reason that I turned to the Viennese Enquête of 1896. This essay is a preliminary report on that document, the most remarkable collection of women's autobiographical material I have yet discovered. After a brief commentary on the Enquête itself, this essay will report on some observations of working-class life that I have extrapolated from this work.[2]

Inquiries into working conditions in industry, such as this one, were common in the nineteenth century, although most were conducted under the auspices of the state, or by labor unions. The Viennese Enquête was almost unique as it came about through the efforts of a private organization, *the Ethische Gesellschaft;* that society was a branch of an international movement that had begun with the founding of the New York Society for Ethical Culture in 1872. The first German branch was formed in 1892 and the first Austrian group shortly thereafter. The German journal, *Ethische Kultur,* was published in Berlin beginning in 1893 and the First International Congress was held in Zürich in 1896. These societies believed in social reforms based on sound ethical principles and they advocated active involvement in the social problems of their day. Two clauses of the manifesto issued at the Zürich Congress are worth quoting here:

We demand for woman the possibility of the fullest development of her mental and moral personality, and we would strive to bring about in all departments of life an uncurtailed expression of the equal worth of her personality with that of man.

Especially we regard the fate of working women in industry (whether in the factory or at home), and also in domestic service, as one of the most grievous evils of our time, and would strive to restore, throughout the whole people, the conditions of a healthy family life.[3]

The Austrian society organized the Enquête and was responsible for most of the financial support necessary to conduct it. The commission that actually sat and heard the testimony consisted of prominent Viennese leaders, politicians, and *Reichsrat* deputies representing the Liberal, Democratic, Christian-Socialist, and Social Democratic parties, businessmen, trade unionists, local and national government officials, academics, and women—both middle-class feminists (Marie Baroness von Vogelsang, Thérèse Schlesinger, and Auguste Fickert) and socialist women (Anna Bozek, Marie Krasa, and Adelheid Popp).[4]

The commission sat for 35 sessions for a total of 118 hours and heard testimony from 260 people, 59 males and 181 working women: in addition, though far fewer than they had hoped for, 20 factory owners. The male witnesses included workers, labor union officials, and representatives of local government, especially from the *Krankenkassen,* since women's health problems were severe in certain industries. Many factory owners who were invited to attend, refused to do so, and it was pointed out by witnesses and Commission members that the conditions in some of their factories were the most appalling. Women were reluctant to testify, particularly from branches of industry that were notoriously antiunion. During the hearings, two women who appeared were fired. It had been decided, after fierce debate within the commission, that all women who came before them would be designated by number rather than by name, and, though they would be asked to describe in detail working conditions in their present place of employment, the name of the firm would not be divulged publically. However, the Viennese press gave extensive coverage of the hearings, and frequently firms were identified by name in those reports and some of the most dreadful circumstances were described. It was the factory owners' reaction to those accounts that led to the dismissal of the two women.[5]

The women who did come forth represented over fifty industries, though there were fewer women from certain trades, and from others none. For example, the Commission was not able to convince any telephone or telegraph operators that it was safe to appear. Though union leaders played a crucial role in bringing women before the Commission, in the end there was quite a reasonable balance between nonunion women (the majority) and women who belonged to various types of unions. Adequate numbers of single and married women testified as well as women from large factories, small firms, and home industry.[6] Significantly, the testimony was taken down by stenographers and printed verbatim in this volume, totalling 666 pages. The data are in fact so massive that I am computerizing them for greater facility in analysis. Autobiographical statements by 181 women would be valuable to historians on any level but there was another advantage here, namely, a well-conceived and sophisticated questionnaire that was concerned with both the workplace and the home, was devised as the basis for the interrogation of each witness. Unfortunately, not all witnesses were asked all the questions; testimony from some ran one or two pages, others to four or five pages. Yet even that inconsistency cannot denigrate the overall value of this marvelous source. Given the constraints of space, this essay can only offer a limited perspective on the Enquête. I shall share what I think are my most important conclusions. In turn, to substantiate these remarks, some testimony from individual workers will be integrated into the text, primarily in the last third of the paper. I should add that this research is in an early stage. The next step will be archival research in Vienna, to acquire quantitative data from factory inspectors' reports, *Krankenkassen* officials, government statistics on population and numbers of women employed and in which industries, reports and statistics from labor unions, working-class newspapers, et cetera. It will also be important to question how representative Vienna was by comparison with other large central European (especially German-speaking) cities and other capitals, such as Paris and London.

Comments from such a large cross section of women workers have led me to question many of the assumptions that have emerged from the recent research on the paid and unpaid employment and personal lives of working-class women in the late nineteenth century.[7] It is not that these assumptions are necessarily invalid, rather they are too simplistic for a sophisticated understanding of the social history of everyday life. In searching for broad universals in the material, I realized that for *every* generalization there were always significant exceptions. Moreover, I believe that the decade of the 1890s was an important turning point in the history of women's employment patterns in Vienna. In almost every industry, wages were being depressed, and since women were on the lowest rung of the economic ladder, reduction in wages that were already low meant that the standard of living of women and working-class families was declining in Vienna in the 1890s. Equally significant was the fact that factory owners in some industries realized that it was possible to replace the higher-paid skilled manual labor of men with machines tended by considerably lower-paid women workers. These aggressive capitalists also sought to increase profits by stepping up production. They did this by increasingly resorting to piecework wages as a substitute for an hourly or weekly wage. That practice forced workers to compensate for wage reductions by working harder, and faster, in order to keep their incomes constant; a vicious situation that often drove women to work beyond their level of endurance.

These and other changes in the character and pattern of work in general meant that women's work specifically was undergoing a kind of minirevolution in Vienna and that phenomenon can be illustrated in a number of ways. One can single out a number of industries in which women were rapidly replacing men in certain occupations. In the bookbinding business, 50 percent of the employees were now women, while only a few years before, there had been almost no women employed in those firms. In 1895 alone, of the 930 women who were registered with one *Krankenkasse*, the sickness insurance fund, 299 were newly listed, and of those, 119 were women who were doing this work for the first time. In lithography, of 759 assistants, *Hilfsarbeiter(innen)*, two-thirds were women. In recent years most manual labor had been replaced by machine work and the ratio of men and women employed had been reversed; before it was two-thirds men and one-third women. These women workers were paid about 30 percent less than the men even though both were doing the same work.[8] In the sheet metal industry an ever larger share of the work was done by machines; and, whereas earlier, large and small firms had employed men entirely, now the large factories were employing women exclusively; small firms, it was reported, still relied on male workers. Men's wages ranged from 10 to 14 florin a week but women were paid 3 to 7 fl. for the same work.[9] In the hat industry, where formerly the heaviest physical labor had been accomplished by the manual labor of men, the work could now be done by machine— and naturally women tended those machines. Skilled male workers had earned 10 to 16 fl. a week, now the women received 3 to 6 fl.[10] In the brush industry, there had not been extensive mechanization, but over the preceding three decades wages had been depressed by 10 to 12 percent. As a result, an industry that had once used male workers only, now had a work force that was about 32 per cent female.

This changeover from men to women was taking place in clerical work as well. It should be emphasized that the overwhelming majority of the occupations surveyed in this inquiry were those of the working-class women, but in some instances, the testimony was concerned with women whose class background was middle- or lower-middle-class. Secretaries, clerk typists, and bookkeepers, working in banks, insurance firms, lawyers' offices, and in the clerical departments of factories, had, even in the most recent past, been positions held by men without exception. Now women were being hired to do the same work, but not surprisingly, the women—who more often than not were better qualified than males—were usually paid on a salary scale that was 20 to 50 percent lower. When a male stenographer was hired, his starting wage would be 40 to 50 fl. a month. Some very skilled women started at 25 or 30 fl., but many others were paid as little as 10 or 15 fl.[11] Some concrete examples can illustrate this situation. Witness number 149 was seventeen years old. She had graduated from a *Bürgerschule* and spent a year studying foreign languages and was fluent in five. She then studied two years in a *Handelsschule* where she won first prize as the fastest and most proficient stenographer in her class; she could do 120 words per minute. These schools placed women in jobs and she had been promised a position in a lawyer's office with a starting salary of 40 or 45 fl. When she reported for work, the lawyer told her "You understand that ladies are not so highly paid; one can get you cheap. I can only offer you 25 fl." She had the courage to turn down that offer, and he relented and said he would pay her 30 fl., which she accepted. Another woman was already working in that office for 25 fl., but shortly thereafter the first woman was let go. The seventeen year old was doing the work of two women.[12] Witness number 148 reported that she had worked six years as a secretary/bookkeeper in the business office of a company that manufactured women's lingerie. When she began she started at 35 fl. a month and eventually worked her way up to a salary of 70 fl., a very high salary for a woman. That same firm now hired equally qualified women at a starting salary of from 5 to 15 fl. a month.[13] Employers could take advantage of the fact that hundreds of women were graduating at this time from business schools. Witness number 154 worked as a clerk in a large insurance firm, where she did the same work as male clerks. Her monthly income was 30 fl. with no possibility of an increase. Men had a starting salary of 40 fl., and the workers were segregated—women in one room, men in another.[14]

Replacing men with women caused a number of problems. Most male witnesses, factory owners, and workers, and some women, described employment in gender-specific terms. That is, certain work was men's work because it was more strenuous, better suited to them, or because it required more education. Other work was women's work because indeed it was less arduous or because it supposedly conformed to women's physical capacities and dispositions. With the changeover, what new explanation could be ventured? The men blamed it on economic conditions and commented no further. The women had a more rational answer as they understood the situation very well. They pointed out that employers were simply taking advantage of the depression in prices by replacing higher-paid men with lower-paid women so that there would be minimal resistance to wage reductions. Employers knew that women were so desperate for work that they were forced to accept employment on any terms. Another facet of the problem was the friction between female and male workers that resulted from one sex replacing the other. The men resented being fired from jobs that they regarded as men's work, and the women complained bitterly that they were doing the same work as the men, and, according to them, generally doing it better. They were very proud of that. They believed that the bosses were exploiting them just because they were women. They also took exception to the fact that in almost all cases, the supervisor was a man.

In characterizing women's work in the late nineteenth and early twentieth centuries, Louise Tilly and Joan Scott in their seminal study of women workers in England and France, *Women, Work and Family,* argued that "most jobs for women in the twentieth century—the new and the old—required few skills and offered relatively low pay." Moreover, "in all the twentieth-century cities, women tended to be concentrated in a narrow range of occupations." They lumped women's work into the following categories: textiles, domestic service, business/professional, commerce and home manufacture, garment making, and a large category of unspecified work.[15] In so doing, I will argue, they have oversimplified a very complicated situation. The Viennese Enquête surveyed the following occupations and branches of industry:

arsenal workers	cigarette paper makers
bakeries	clerical workers
bookbinding	confectioners
bottle-cap makers	construction
brick makers	corset makers
brush makers	dress makers
cardboard box makers	dye works

embroidery
fan/comb makers
flower makers
furriers
galvanizers
glove makers
gold embroidery
gold/silver lace makers
hat makers
incandescent light fixtures
jute production
lamp makers
laundresses
leather industry
lingerie
lithography
metal cutters/polishers
metal industry
milliners

necktie seamstresses
newspaper carriers
paper products
rag sorters
ready made clothes
rubber products
screw factories
sheet metal work
slaters (roofers)
straw hat makers
telephone operators
terra cotta workers
textiles
theater
tobacco
umbrella makers
valance knitters
veterinary institute
whalebone industry[16]

Within each industry, there could be dozens of individual occupations, as factory work processes were intricate and complicated. Though these branches might indeed be organized "in a narrow range of occupations," to do so would not adequately explain what women's work was all about.

Tilly and Scott further explained that single women generally did different work than married women. If we summarize their argument; women's work was gender-specific, it was determined by whether one was married or single (for example, mostly single women worked in factories), and it was unskilled. I would argue that in order to reconstruct women's employment experiences we must, as has been the practice increasingly in the study of men's work, proceed occupation by occupation, or at least with related occupational categories. There are many advantages to such an approach. Working conditions and wages on each job were quantitatively different, and, in terms of the skill required, many occupations were certainly not all unskilled, even in terms of working-class jobs, the focus here. Taking a broader perspective is less patronizing toward women's work. Just as in men's work, there are really three categories of women workers: unskilled, semiskilled and skilled. Some jobs could be learned in a few hours or days, others took three to six months and required real manual dexterity, and other occupations took two or three years before they could be mastered. Working conditions in large factories, where mostly unskilled workers were employed, were shaped by rigid factory discipline and generally the most inhumane treatment and filthy surroundings. In contrast, work in small firms, employing perhaps ten to thirty workers, was often more appealing in terms of working conditions (although few workplaces could be described as pleasant) and many of these occupations used semiskilled or skilled workers. In turn, women working in home industry had yet another set of circumstances with which to deal. While some factory employment was surely regarded by employers as work for single women, other factory jobs were for the most part held by married women.

Employment was also age specific. Some occupations were dominated by young women and in others, older more experienced women were needed; naturally they would mostly be married. Some jobs were quite detrimental to women's health—if not outright dangerous—but workers would willingly take such risks if reasonably high salaries were offered. Some low paying work might provide steady employment year round, while other higher paying occupations were seasonal, and workers would only be employed for a few months of the year. For married women, one occupation might be chosen over another just because it was closer to home, making child care a less complicated problem. Single or married women might alternate within a given year between home and factory work when one or more occupations (sometimes in related industries) were seasonal. A young woman without a family—this was especially true for orphans and migrant workers—might take a job that provided room and board and perhaps even an apprenticeship. If room and board were provided, that might make the job attractive even though the work itself might not be particularly suitable. Apprenticeships were popular with young girls from large families who could not pay for additional schooling. Apprenticeships meant terribly low pay and all too often minimal training, but room and board was generally provided, and many young girls thought it would lead to a better paying job. Unfortunately they were frequently treated like domestic servants.

Many married women would take advantage of a skill they had learned as a single woman, in the garment industry mainly, and for family and financial reasons they would want to either work at home or start their own business. These female entrepreneurs would make arrangements with one or more factories to sew goods (ties, corsets, men's shirts) at home. They were paid by the piece. They could work alone, or if sufficiently skilled, they would oversee women whom they hired to work for them; these entrepreneurs were called *Zwischenmeisterinnen*. Large factories might make agreements with dozens of these women, who in turn as a group hired hundreds of seamstresses, many only semiskilled.

Though many women had family obligations that limited their opportunities and choices, perhaps the majority of women workers were able to adopt specific strategies in choosing their work; indeed they had to make many different decisions in what was a varied and confusing job market. Women were without a doubt exploited by their employers, but that does not mean that they were mindless victims of the system. They often had a clear understanding of the options open to them and decided accordingly, depending on what solution fit their own personal needs. When they found themselves in an intolerable job, for example, they might have to accept it for a time, but they eventually found ways to circumvent the situation. If the wages were too low or if the supervisor was too brutal, they would move on to another factory. Naturally those women with no skills were the most powerless, and, of those, the most pathetic group were older, unmarried or widowed women who had to take any work they could get, whether it was agreeable or not.

I would like to illustrate and substantiate many of the general observations made in the preceding pages. I shall compare and contrast working conditions in various industries (particularly those less commonly discussed) and the experiences of single and married women. I will try to demonstrate the interrelationship between work and family life, especially to demonstrate the many factors that have to be considered to reconstruct the daily lives of working-class women.

Using single women as a category of workers is very helpful, but generalizations about them as a group are dangerous. Let us look at quite a varied group of single women. Witness number 96 was eighteen years old and for the past year she had been working in a dead-end job in a candy factory where she operated a small machine that cut bonbons. Prior to that she had worked in a government arsenal for three years. Typically she had begun work at fourteen. She evidently left her first job because she was being sexually harassed by a lieutenant. Like most unskilled workers she then went door to door until she managed to find work in the candy factory. There were seventy people employed there, about half men and half women. All the women were single except for three. She was paid a pitiful weekly wage of 4 fl., which meant she could not possibly survive alone. Her father had died ten years before, and her mother had a very small pension and could not work because she was ill. She had a sister who also worked and the three of them paid 9 fl. a month for a small two-room apartment. In the candy factory there was a ten hour day, with an hour for lunch.

Most factories had recently adopted the ten hour day; it had been eleven, but factory owners were under pressure to accept the shorter schedule. Of course, there were no longer any morning or afternoon breaks; the workers had to accept that trade-off. Men in that factory earned up to 12 fl. for work that was similar to what the women did. Working conditions were decent, and the boss treated the women well (though he paid them poorly). There were no serious health hazards, but she frequently cut her fingers on the machine she used. This woman was not unionized but did belong to the *Krankenkasse,* which cost her 10 Kreuzer a week. She owed money to the local *Greissler,* a kind of small grocery store that allowed workers to buy on credit. She wanted to be able to go to the theater but could not possibly afford it on her salary. She belonged to a local *Volksbildungsverein,* which had a lending library; and on Sundays the *Verein* provided two hours of dancing lessons which she attended. Otherwise she had to help with the housework. Breakfast was generally coffee and a *Semmel,* and lunch at the factory, which she bought locally, was often milk and some vegetables—maybe a little wurst. Not infrequently she had no money for dinner, and on Sundays there was only a little meat. She had no future prospects, since her mother could not pay for training or an apprenticeship.[17]

Witness number 110 was single, perhaps seventeen years old, had a child, and lived with her parents. Six people lived in a two room apartment: her parents, her sister and her husband, and the witness and her child. They paid 13.50fl. a month for the apartment. Her mother was too old for wage work so she cared for the child. Her father was unskilled and earned 7 fl. a week. She worked in a factory that employed 100 people, more women than men, and she earned a little over 4 fl. a week sorting and cleaning whalebones which were used for stays in women's clothing and for fans. She was paid a daily wage, although some women were paid by piece work; they worked all year. The male supervisor was decent, but the women hated the factory owner as he addressed all the women, young and old alike, as *du.* The wages were very low, and though there was no sexual harassment, the boss often hit the women on the head with packages. He swore at the women regularly, and when a woman with a child asked for a raise, he replied, "What do I care about your child?" None of the women was unionized, but they belonged to the *Krankenkasse.* Our witness could not afford to go anywhere; her only amusement was taking her child for a walk.[18]

Witness number 98 was in her early thirties and single, supposedly. In actual fact, she had a common-law husband and two children, one twelve years old and one six months. She worked right up to the day of the birth of her second child as her "man" only earned 98 kr. a day at the railway warehouse. Babysitting and food for the children cost 40 kr. a day, and they paid 9.50 fl. a month for a two room apartment. They could not afford to get married, as they did not have the money for the necessary papers; she came from Saxony and did not meet required resident status. Her "husband's" wages barely paid the rent, and they owed the *Greissler* 15 fl. They were hungry quite often, she said. The woman who cared for their children was very poor, had three children herself and was a stranger to them; she was not sure how well her children were cared for in that family. For lunch at work, she and two other women split the cost of buying coffee, and a little milk and sugar. Generally she had a *Semmel* with the coffee. Eating in the *Volksküche*, the cheapest place for a worker (although they all said the food was terrible), was too expensive for her, as it was for many women, since their wages were lower than men's. She worked in a very small factory filing and polishing spoons (she was called an *Essbesteckfeilerin*) and was paid by the piece. She averaged 5 fl. a week in the good season doing sixty to seventy dozen spoons a day. Her job used to be men's work. She paid for the files herself; she spent about 50 kr. for twenty and they lasted her about six months. She worked from seven in the morning until six at night with an hour for lunch and no other breaks. There were fines and deductions taken from her salary as a rule. The heavy season was from March to August and the off-season was from September to February when she was laid off days at a time; her wages then sank to 3 or 4 fl. a week—hence they were always in debt. Her free time was spent doing the housework. She had worked in that firm for eight years, and she emphasized that jobs in the metal industry were hard to come by; she was evidently happy to have steady work. The industry was highly unionized but she did not belong to the union.[19]

Witness number 132 was also single and a skilled shoemaker. She learned cobbling at age seventeen and had been doing that work for twenty-one years. She obviously was in her late thirties and lived in a one-room apartment she shared with another woman. Together they paid 14 fl. a month. She paid 12 kr. a week to the *Krankenkasse,* and she did not belong to the union. She was the only woman in a small firm that employed eighteen workers. She sewed women's and men's shoes by hand and with a machine, and she earned 8.5 fl. a week. She worked year round, although the work was seasonal and some of the younger workers were let go for part of the year. She worked from seven in the morning until seven at night, with an hour for lunch and no breaks—but workers could eat on the job. She had few amusements, as she was often sick, but enjoyed reading the newspaper. The boss provided their lunch, otherwise she bought all her food from a local *Gasthaus.* She lived rather well by the standard of most single women workers.[20]

Witness number 118 was also single and in her early thirties. She was a skilled seamstress and sewed men's shirts, earning about 7 fl. a week. She, and two other women who were married, worked for a *Zwischenmeisterin* in the latter's apartment, where two of three rooms served as the workplace. The witness and the other workers ate their lunch there, and it was a pleasant place in which to work. Her own residence was a one room apartment (she lived alone) for which she paid 6 fl. a month. She made her own clothes. They worked from seven to seven and did a little overtime at home—but our witness did it only when she was in the mood (sewing button holes on shirts). She ate out (and well), and she liked to go on excursions and to the theater. (All workers were on the job six days a week, so whether they had the money to go out or not, their free time was severely limited.)[21]

The last single woman to be considered, witness number 121, was perhaps twenty-one years old and lived with her parents. She was a seamstress who sewed ties but was only semiskilled. She and three other women worked in the residence of a *Zwischenmeisterin* whom she noted was very humane. The work was seasonal, and in the summer she earned only 2 fl. a week. In the heavy winter season she earned up to 6 fl. (with overtime she might make up to 8 fl.). She liked to go to the *Volkstheater,* where she could purchase the 20 kr. seats. Yet she could not do that often because her family was in debt. She had three brothers—two of them were apprentices and earned only 2 or 3 fl. Her father was a construction worker, but his work was seasonal. He was well paid in the summer but earned little in the winter. Her mother and one younger brother did not work. Their two room apartment cost 11 fl. a month. The two older brothers slept in one bed in the kitchen, and there were two beds in the second room, one for her parents and one for her and her younger brother. She had to buy all her clothes on time and had to pay exorbitant *Raten* (interest). The family ate so little meat that she said, "one can hardly call it meat at all"—the men ate the meat, not the women. She belonged to the *Krankenkasse* and joined a socialist union, because, as she said, "my father is a Social Democrat."[22]

All the women cited above share the fact that they were single, yet their personal and family circumstances were certainly quite varied. One group of women, in fact, was not even included—single women living with a "lover," although witness number 132 could have had a lesbian relationship with the woman she lived with—who knows? What is important, I think, is to consider how quantitative data from official statistics, for example (which would have lumped all these women into the category of "single women"), would be very misleading. Moreover, taking a life-cycle approach has other problems. In each case, one must take into account whether a woman lived alone, with her family, or with someone else. In the latter two instances especially, what financial or family responsibilities were demanded of that woman, and did she have dependents? Furthermore, what was her salary, and what share of that money had to go for the family and what share went for her own upkeep? Given the character of her job, what were the problems or benefits of her employment, what were the working conditions, and what future prospects might she have? Was her job seasonal, or did she have work year around? Given all those considerations, how was she able to spend her free time? Without a doubt, the contemporary image of the young, single, high-living or frivolous "factory-girl" does not realistically describe these women.

Let us now look at some examples of married women workers. Witness number 100 was one of the two women mentioned in the introduction who was fired because of her testimony before the commission. Her case gives us some insight into the plight of older workers. Though she did not give her age, she was probably in her late forties or perhaps early fifties. Though married, she had no idea of the whereabouts of her husband, who had left her and Vienna eighteen years before. They had had three children; one died at seven months, a second died at three years of a brain concussion, and the third, a daughter, living and now twenty-one, was a cripple who could not work as she had heart trouble. Her mother was responsible for her support. They had a two-room apartment for which they paid 10.60 fl. a month, and they shared it with a woman lodger who paid 2 fl. a month. Our witness was a spoon maker and had worked for the same firm off and on for twenty-seven years. She worked piece work and averaged 6 fl. a week when work was full time; in the slow season she only worked three-quarters of the day. The firm employed almost three hundred workers—women and men worked in separate rooms. Some men did the same work as women for the same pay, but making forks was strictly men's work, and it paid more. She spent the day pouring liquid metal into molds. She made twenty-six or twenty-seven spoons a day working nonstop with 30 other women in the *Giesserei*. The male overseer treated the women well, she said. She belonged to the *Krankenkasse* but not to the metal workers' union as some women did. They worked a ten hour day with one hour for lunch and two fifteen-minute breaks. She was barely literate, so her only amusement was having her daughter read the newspaper out loud. Otherwise, she just did housework in her free time. She was fired because she reported to the commission that when it rained, water leaked into the *Giesserei*. She also told them that the workplace used to be a bowling alley. Her boss was furious, as her testimony was reported in the newspaper. When she returned to work she learned that she was to be fired, but not until the end of the week as she owed the foreman money. Knowing she was to be fired, she quit in midweek of her own accord because she had no money to pay back the man; she had only earned 2 fl. that week.[23]

Witness number 147 was in her late fifties and was a straw hat maker—but the season lasted from December to Pentecost, barely five months. It took two or three years to learn the work, so it was highly skilled. During the season she took home 10 to 12 fl.—some of the very talented and fast working women earned 15 to 16 fl. a week. Most of the women were married. Men and women worked in this small firm, though separately, and the men (there were very few of them) did the finishing. The women had to buy the needles and twine from the factory owner, who sold them to the workers for a profit, which infuriated the women. In season they worked eleven or twelve hours a day and took additional work home two or three nights a week. At the factory most of the work was done by machine, and it was very strenuous. Yet the women worked themselves very hard; they were paid by the piece and tried to earn as much as possible since the season was short. To some extent, how much one earned depended on the quality of the materials received from the foreman. The best went to the women who were willing to be "intimate" with him, and for that reason this witness earned less. Generally, she said, he had one of the women living with him.

In the off-season she was a home worker, making cigar tips. The whole family worked at it and they could make 1,000 a day, which she then sold in the evenings. In the off-season the family went 30 to 40 fl. in debt and had to mortgage their belongings. Her husband was sixty-three and a metal grinder but was out of work, as most companies only hired younger men; he helped her with the cigar tips. In any official statistic, he, not she, would be listed as the breadwinner. They paid 8.50 fl. for a two room apartment. They had seven children; one had died and three still lived at home: two sons aged thirteen and six and a twenty-six-year old daughter who was a cripple who suffered from hydrocephaly when she was eighteen months old. Despite that incredible life this witness belonged to a union and, though she had little to enjoy in life, did try to take the family on outings—and they always attended the union's annual *Gründungsfest.*[24]

Witness number 71 lived in abject poverty. She was a widower whose deceased husband had been a day laborer. They had six children, two who had died young, two whom she had placed in an orphanage, and two, a boy and a girl, who lived with her. She was a home worker, and in season she sewed aprons. Some years before she had purchased her sewing machine on time. She worked for a *Zwischenmeister* who could only give her a little work; after deductions for her supplies, she only earned about 2.40 fl. a week. She had to deliver and pick up supplies daily; her son and daughter helped her after they came home from school. To get extra money she was a dishwasher and picked up about 1 fl. a week that way. Her rent was 7 fl. a month, and she and her children lived on coffee, bread, and potato or rice soup—nothing else. The *Vincenzverein* gave her bread and potatoes each week, and another charity gave her clothes at Christmas and bought the children's school books. She could not get help from the welfare authorities as she was not a legal resident of Vienna. She was only semiskilled.[25]

A nineteenth-century English observer wrote about women workers: "whatever mill, yard, factory or workshop you enter, you will find the women in the lowest, the dirtiest, and the unhealthiest departments."[26] No comment could better describe the situation for women in the building, brickmaking, and roofing trades in Vienna, occupations in which the majority of the women were married. The men and women who worked in these trades were primarily migrant workers from Bohemia. Some traveled back home in the winter when there was no work; others eventually became permanent residents of the city. The impact on the health of the women who worked in these trades was cataclysmic—almost all their children died, mainly because the women did so much heavy physical labor. Their diets were also poor since wages were low.

Witness number 88 was fifty-two years old and a *Dachdecker* (a slater or a roofer); her husband did the same work. They had had seven children, but five of the seven had died. Two sons were now grown and on their own. She went to work about 5:45 A.M. and mixed mortar and then put it in a cart. She was harnassed like a horse and had to pull the cart to the construction site, where she carried two or three hundred containers of the mortar a day up and down the ladders for the men who did the construction work. At about 6:00 P.M. she had to reload the cart and pull it back to the warehouse. She earned 85 kr. a day for this work.[27]

Witness number 87 was evidently in her thirties. She bore three children, and they all died. Both her husband and her mother, who lived with them, were ill, so she supported all three. She earned 80 kr. a day, also as a slater. (This work used to be done by men, but mostly married women did it now.) Their diet was very poor, but when her husband worked she liked to drink beer and eat wurst on the job—she ate while she worked (but not by choice). The cart she pulled to the construction site was filled with the mortar, up to two hundred tiles and all the tools. Some of the men helped push the cart but not always. She went up and down the ladders all day but only got four or five hours of sleep as she got up at 5:00 A.M. and usually did not get to bed until midnight because she had the housework to do. On Sundays she did the mending and took care of her mother, who was bedridden.[28]

Witness number 94 worked in the building trade where she also mixed and carried mortar. She had two children, but they both died at birth. Her work was very similar to roofing, as she carried the mortar up and down ladders, after having, of course, mixed it and dragged the cart to the construction site. Her foreman was infamous for his ill-treatment of the women. He and some of the other men often beat the women, and he always addressed them as *du,* even the women in their fifties. The men called the women every filthy name possible and tried to look up their dresses when they climbed the ladders. Most women were pressured to have sex with the foreman. As a rule he had one of them living with him for periods of time, until she was discarded. The witness was thirty-two and her husband was a bricklayer who earned almost 2 fl. a day; she earned 75 or 80 kr. a day—and, with overtime, 4 or 5 fl. a week in season, which ran from March to October. In the off-season they went 30 to 40 fl. in debt. They mortgaged their furniture and had to sign for food at the *Greissler* to live in winter, as their only work was shoveling snow. They paid 23 fl. quarterly for their two room apartment and had a lodger. This witness belonged to the *Krankenkasse* but not in the winter, as they could not afford it. She was afraid to join a union. In her free time she did the housework—otherwise nothing. She could not read. She was born in Bohemia and went into domestic service, she then married and had been working in construction for twelve years.[29]

The constraints of space prohibit me from citing further examples of married women's work experiences, but clearly working-class women played a major role in the family economy. My contention is that indeed most working-class married women worked for pay, either inside or outside the home during most of their married lives.[30] We can also see that the responsibilities of the married women were extremely complex and terribly demanding. After working for wage work, there were both household and childrearing responsibilities to consider. These women had almost no free time, and they were constantly juggling their responsibilities depending on family needs, which often determined whether they were working for wages at home or in a factory or other workplace. Also, married women's work was more varied, I believe, than earlier studies have thought possible. We are still burdened with nineteenth-century notions, espoused by middle-class observers and social scientists, that married women did not work. Moreover, the type of paid employment available to married women was also quite broad.

This essay has attempted to offer some insights into the complex world of working-class Viennese women in 1896. It has tried to prove how a sophisticated analysis of their everyday life must be built on a detailed study of the wide range of occupations these women pursued. I have also argued that to understand their world one must have an integrated view of their work experiences and their personal lives. The circumstances for single and married women were both similiar and yet quite different, and their work was complex and varied. They indeed worked long hours at low pay, but not all were unskilled— some women were either semiskilled or highly skilled and trained for long periods to learn very intricate work. Their wages and working conditions, as well as their living arrangements, were widely divergent and depended to a great extent on their family situations. Many women were closely attached to families, while other single women were quite independent. It will take considerable additional research to explain how they lived, and many assumptions about their lives will have to be reevaluated. Autobiographical material should be used whenever possible and carefully integrated with statistical data, but those data must be evaluated cautiously.

NOTES

1. I must note here that because of the constraints of space, footnotes must be kept to a minimum. See my article, "The Woman's Role in the German Working-Class Family in the 1890s—from the Perspective of Women's Autobiographies," in John C.

Fout, ed., *German Women in the Nineteenth Century. A Social History* (New York: Holmes & Meier, 1984). Some of the most important autobiographical sources are: Ottilie Baader, *Ein steiniger Weg*. *Lebenserinnerungen* (Berlin: Vorwärts, 1921); Doris Viersbeck, *Erlebnisse eines Hamburger Dienstmädchens* (München: Ernst Reinhardt, 1910); *Im Kampf ums Dasein. Lebenserinnerungen eines Mädchens aus dem Volke als Fabrikarbeiterin, Dienstmädchen und Kellnerin* (Stuttgart: Karl Weber, 1908); *Aus der Gedankenwelt einer Arbeiterfrau, von ihr selbst erzählt* [Frau Hoffman], ed. by C. Moszeik, Pfarrer (Berlin: Edwin Runge, 1909); Phyllis Knight (with her son, Rolf Knight), *A Very Ordinary Life* (Vancouver, Canada: New Star Books, 1974). For Austria, see Adelheid Popp, *The Autobiography of a Working Woman*, trans. by E. C. Harvey (Chicago: F. G. Browne, 1913) and *Gedenkbuch 20 Jahre Österreichische Arbeiterinnenbewegung*, Im Auftrage des Frauenreichskomitees, ed. by Adelheid Popp (Wien: Vorwärts, 1912). Published collections have now made "pieces" of many of these works available (as they are obscure): Eleanor S. Riemer and John C. Fout, eds., *European Women. A Documentary History 1789–1945* (New York: Schocken, 1980); Wolfgang Emmerich, ed., *Proletarische Lebensläufe* 2 vols. (Reinbek bei Hamburg: Rowohlt, 1974/5); Friedrich G. Kürbisch and Richard Klucsarits, eds., *Arbeiterinnen kämpfen um ihr Recht* 2nd edition (Wuppertal: Peter Hamm Verlag, 1981).

2. *Die Arbeits- und Lebensverhältnisse der Wiener Lohnarbeiterinnen* Ergebnisse und Stenographisches Protokoll der Enquête über Frauenarbeit, abgehalten in Wien vom 1. Marz bis 21. April 1896 (Wien: Erste Wiener Volksbuchhandlung, 1897). Hereafter cited as *Enquête*.

3. Gustav Spiller, "Ethical Movements," in *Encyclopedia of Religion and Ethics* (New York, 1913/1922), vol. 5, p. 413.

4. *Enquête*, pp. iii–v, xv–xvi. For some comments on the Enquête by a participant (she was middle class but she later became a socialist) see Thérèse Schlesinger, "My Road to Social Democracy," in Riemer and Fout, pp. 95–99; that was quoted from the original in *Gedenkbuch* 107–9. See also Thérèse Schlesinger Eckstein, "Die Lage der Lohnarbeiterinnen in Wien," *Der sozialistische Akademiker* 3 (1897), pp. 227–33 (later that journal was called *Sozialistische Monatshefte*).

5. The two women who were fired were numbers 41 and 100; see pages 122–23 and 616–17 for number 41 and pp. 351–54 and 434–35 for number 100.

6. Josef Ehmer, in his absolutely first-rate article, "Frauenarbeit und Arbeiterfamilie in Wien: Vom Vormärz bis 1934," *Geschichte und Gesellschaft*, 7 (1981), p. 454, emphasized (and I do not really disagree) that the trade union role meant the survey was biased in favor of "industrielle Unternehmen."

7. See, for example, Louise A. Tilly and Joan W. Scott, *Women, Work, and Family* (New York: Holt, Rinehart and Winston, 1978); chapters 11 and 12 in *Becoming Visible*, eds. R. Bridenthal and C. Koonz, (Boston: Houghton Mifflin, 1977); or R. J. Evans and W. R. Lee, eds., *The German Family* (Totowa, NJ: Barnes & Noble, 1981).

8. *Enquête*, pp. 3–4, 18–19. For some help in figuring prices, see David F. Good, "The Cost of Living in Austria: 1874–1913," *Journal of European Economic History*, 5 (1976), pp. 391–400.

9. *Ibid.*, pp. 419–20.

10. *Ibid.*, pp. 104 and 381.

11. *Ibid.*, pp. 275 and 277.

12. *Ibid.*, pp. 580–83.

13. *Ibid.*, pp. 578–80.

14. *Ibid.*, pp. 589–90.

15. Tilly & Scott, pp. 162 and 166.

16. *Enquête,* p. 675. This list is in no way complete—other occupations were not considered at all, for example, domestic service and prostitution.

17. Ibid., pp. 335–39.

18. Ibid., pp. 388–90.

19. Ibid., pp. 341–46.

20. Ibid., pp. 494–96.

21. Ibid., pp. 439–40.

22. Ibid., pp. 446–51.

23. Ibid., pp. 351–54, 434–35.

24. Ibid., pp. 573–77.

25. Ibid., pp. 230–31.

26. "What are Women Doing," *English Woman's Journal,* March, 1861, p. 53 (also quoted in Riemer and Fout, p. 1).

27. *Enquête,* pp. 268–73.

28. Ibid., pp. 268–73.

29. Ibid., pp. 328–33.

30. Again, I would recommend the Ehmer essay for excellent material on married women workers. See also essays by Barbara Franzoi and Jean H. Quataert in my book—see note 1.

WOMEN'S WORK AS PORTRAYED IN WOMEN'S LITERATURE

Renate Möhrmann

> Mostly, however, the silence of the women themselves went unnoticed, drowned by the noise of the endless discussion about femininity.
>
> —Silvia Bovenschen

The ensuing reflections do not aim at a further compartmentalization of a feminist theme, so usual within the framework of increasing academic specialization. On the contrary, the question of the presentation of female work in the literature of those women who wrote themselves is raised in an effort to draw attention to the silence of women alluded to in the introductory quotation, to reveal the traces of their submerged effectiveness and to contribute to the reconstruction of female cultural work. Here literature is of special importance. For, unlike the usual exclusion of women in the course of historical, political, and scientific processes of development, literature cannot manage without its feminine element. The question of how the female writers themselves portrayed their heroines, however, which projections of femininity they preferred, and in which way the empirical woman was reflected in their works has, until now, been a matter attracting only slight interest.

It can thus be assumed that the relationship between the female writer and her female subject is not an unchangeable one, but rather takes on very different forms in the course of the historical-cultural process. In this respect, a systematic discussion of the proposed question is not possible. Categorical attempts at analysis without reference to history would oversimplify the matter. However, since I do not wish to reduce the subject to a subjective selection of individual examples or to allow it to be led into methodological randomness, my focus will be limited to a particular literary epoch in the nineteenth century and a selected group of female writers. If, in this context, the choice falls upon the German women writers of the *Vormärz* (the period preceding the Revolution of 1848), it is for the very reason that they do not constitute an arbitrary generation of female authors. Women like Fanny Lewald, Luise Mühlbach, Mathilde Franziska Anneke, Louise Otto-Peters, Ida Hahn-Hahn, Louise Aston, Therese von Bacheracht, or Louise Dittmar—just to mention the most committed and the most important few—represent the first generation of female writers in the history of German literature who no longer exercised their literary talent only occasionally and as an unrewarding hobby, but who actually wrote on a professional basis.

The female writers of the *Vormärz* were consequently rebellious and revolutionary women who were themselves very familiar with everyday working life and had firsthand experience of the twofold demands made on them by "work" and "love."

One misunderstanding should be cleared up at the outset. If the following analysis concentrates solely on the presentation of the professional, paid, and regularly practiced literary occupation of women, without considering the description of domestic work as practiced by the huge majority of women, it should certainly not be seen as a denial of the all too frequent hard work involved in a woman's domestic duties. The concern of the following analysis is not the creation of a hierarchical scale into which women's jobs should be fitted, but rather the relationship between female reality and female fiction, namely between the female writer and the picture of femininity she creates in her literature. In concrete terms, therefore, the question is whether and in which way the employment of women (which was becoming more and more self-evident in the course of the nineteenth century and was turning into an economic factor) found a literary equivalent in the works of female writers.

A false picture is, of course, created if women's literature is discussed separately and outside the accepted poetological norms. Also, it must not be overlooked that topics such as employment and everyday working life, which were on the whole long overdue, did not make an appearance in literature until the second half of the nineteenth century and since time immemorial had taken second place to the confusion of the heart and the adventures of the mind. It was exactly this dilemma, the lack of poetological simultaneity, that Fanny Lewald was referring to when she defended the new functions of the novel against the old ones. "What sort of great, poetic significance can the sufferings of a poor manual worker or a little seamstress have—those who have to struggle with harsh reality for their daily bread", asks her reactionary representative, who then concludes apodictically: "In the struggle for survival, there is no trace of beauty or poetry."[1] But such a dictum is not accepted without contradiction. The author leaves the last word in the matter of 'the novel' to the representative of the progressive movement, who is at the same time the representative of the younger generation: "As soon as the novel begins to concentrate on unsatisfied needs instead of directing its attention toward those needs that have already been satisfied, the typical form of the novel, that of a pleasant world, will no longer be possible, and the novel of harsh reality and sharp individualisation will become necessary."[2] Lewald had also formulated her aesthetic credo in no uncertain terms elsewhere: "A novel without exact relation to the time in which it was written is seldom a successful piece of work."[3] In this way, she approved the tendentious novel and granted poetic dignity to "the struggle for survival."

The same was true of the majority of female writers in the *Vormärz* period. Almost all wanted their stories to serve as contemporary documents as well as to influence the present. Apart from Fanny Lewald, it was Louise Otto-Peters and Louise Dittmar in particular who, in their theoretical writings, drew attention to the economic discrimination against women and who firmly called for their gradual integration into professional life. For female gainful employment was still regarded as a kind of family disgrace which detracted from the credit and reputation of the father, lessened the daughter's chances of marriage, and was, as far as possible, kept secret.

Before the fictitious picture of the working woman can be examined in detail, her real-life employment possibilities must be outlined briefly, such as they were between the beginning of the nineteenth century until the key year of 1869, the year of the general enforcement of freedom of trade and, along with it, the lifting of the guilds' exclusion of women within Germany. Here the respective classes enjoyed very different prospects. Female gainful employment is known to have been regarded as a family stigma only for women and girls of the upper classes. Women of the proletariat had had to learn very early on to support themselves and to contribute to the upkeep of the family just as the men did.[4] The term "the gentle sex" had never applied to them. For them, there were generally three areas of activity: agriculture, domestic service, and, with increasing industrialization, factory work connected with home industry.

Gainful employment was not envisaged for the daughters of the educated classes. They were reared solely for marriage despite the fact that the number of unmarried women rose continually throughout the nineteenth century and, around 1890, almost one-half of all women were affected (of 16.9 million adult women, only 8.8 million were married[5]). Nevertheless, middle-class girls wanting a career came up against barriers everywhere. "The areas of greatest importance to the state such as military service, administration, the administering of justice and legislation, [were] almost completely closed to women."[6] They were barred from any studies which could lead to academic professions. German trading regulations prevented commercial independence. Manual work was denied them through the exclusion rights of the corporations, and even the secret crocheting and sewing resorted to by a large number of impoverished middle-class women ran short as a result of the factory work taken over by women of the proletariat.

Thus, only two possibilities to work remained for the daughters of the upper classes, namely teaching and art. The former generally took the form of governess while the latter was attainable only in the dramatic arts, singing technique, or writing. The fact that the art academies had dictated a ban meant that the fine arts remained largely closed to them. If, with this background in mind, one considers the novels of such female writers who had themselves successfully opposed the program aimed at female domestication and who, often in the face of a family veto, had fought undeterredly to attain their own employment, the contradiction is clear. For these "women of letters"— who in their essays uttered highly subversive "thoughts about the education of girls,"[7] pleaded "for the commercial activity of women,"[8] and urgently demanded "the right of women to earn a living"[9]—were hardly guided in the writing of the novels by their own first-hand experiences. So the majority of their literary writings, in spite of their great commitment to the *Zeitgeist* and the trend on the reflective level, can more aptly be classified under the heading of the romantic novel and the novel of renunciation; most conflicts presented can be described as affairs of the heart, and the emancipatory energies of the heroines can very often only be recognised in the rejection of the demanded marriage of convenience and the insistence on "the Right Man."[10] The theme of female employment, however, is rarely seriously discussed, and the struggle for the survival of the seamstress described by Lewald in her polemic writing is nowhere to be found in the fiction. The few examples out of approximately three hundred novels by the female writers whom I have examined that deal with female working life were thus all the more informative for the complex of questions posed here.

It must be immediately pointed out that the pictures of female work sketched at this time stemmed either from the field of domestic service or from art, as was the case in reality. Such congruence between extrafictional and fictional reality cannot necessarily be regarded as the sine qua non of tendentious literature. After all, imagination reaching far beyond the bounds of reality could very well be utilized as a means of tendentious education: consider, for example, Esther Vilar's American female Pope. The fact that the women writers here remain guided by reality and do not stretch their imagination beyond reality with respect to female work can best be interpreted as a lack of imagination on their parts. This will become clear through a closer look at individual examples.

A further striking feature is that from the large variety of servants' jobs, one above all attracted quite special literary attention, namely that of the lady's maid. Not the cook, the nanny, the wet nurse, the governess, nor even the chambermaid or the seamstress—none was able to win a place like hers in the female literature of the *Vormärz*, even if it was only a marginal place. There are reasons for this. According to the German dictionary compiled by the Brothers Grimm, "the lady's maid is a maiden in the service of a princess or a noblewoman . . . distinct from the chambermaid, often also from the maids-in-waiting who are below her in rank, and distinct also from the housekeeper who runs the household."[11] The special feature of the position of lady's maid is the fact that "[she] *alone* [is responsible for] personal attendance upon the mistress of the house."[12] The result was an intimate and exclusive knowledge of the master and mistress, which generally led to a separate, superior position in the hierarchy of the servants. For the literary transposition of this character, this meant that with her every appearance, a small piece of the story surrounding the master and mistress could be delivered as well, and the joys and sufferings of the aristocratic female immediately became the object of the narrative.

But what do we actually find when we examine the evidence? The figure of the lady's maid is not present at all in the work of Therese von Bacheracht, Louise Aston, and Louise Otto-Peters. This is hardly surprising in the case of a writer like Bacheracht, whose work (with the exception of *Heinrich Burkart*) concentrates almost exclusively on the discreet charms of the aristocracy. This absence is, however, striking in the work of a writer like Aston who, in her novels *Aus dem Leben einer Frau* (From the Life of a Woman) and *Revolution und Contrerevolution* (Revolution and Counterrevolution) clearly showed literary sensitivity for the working classes, and equally in the work of Otto-Peters, who made the working life of men from the lower classes the subject of whole novels, for example, *Ludwig der Kellner* (Ludwig the Waiter) and *Schloß und Fabrik* (Castle and Factory).

On the other hand, occasional and more or less scattered portrayals of the lady's maid are to be found in the novels of Ida Hahn-Hahn, Fanny Lewald, and Luise Mühlbach. Ida Hahn-Hahn presents a quite realistic example in her novel *Zwei Frauen* (Two Women). It must be said, however, that this remains her sole contribution to the theme of the serving girl. Dorothee Brand, who serves the Countess Sambach as lady's maid, is, although not exactly a main character, certainly no episodic character either. She is introduced already in the first third of the novel and until the end is continually integrated into the plot. In the course of the plot, strong emotional bonds develop between her and the Countess. It is interesting that Hahn-Hahn shapes the character of Dorothee according to her social background and interprets it in a social context. The reader not only learns that Dorothee is a servant, but also the reason why. In her description, the author goes so far as to explain the circumstances of the parents and, clearly in the cause of female emancipation, shows the brother's life as a parallel in order to indicate the contrasting fates of brother and sister. The two are the children of a schoolteacher whose untimely death leaves them in a state of destitution, worsened by the ensuing illness of their mother, which puts a particular strain on the girl. Thus, the task falls to the thirteen-year-old Dorothee to do the necessary housework and to look after her elder brother by "cooking, sewing and washing for him."[13] She herself can only attend school for a few years; her brother goes to university to become a doctor. Dorothee supports herself by working as a seamstress until, owing to failing eyesight, she is forced to abandon this source of income and is obliged to go into domestic service.

The hardships of the servant's job—the fact that the individual is, to a large extent, deprived of his/her rights and must be permanently on call—are expressed in the novel. "You have no idea of the dependent status that awaits you, or of the moods to which you will be exposed,"[14] is the brother's comment on hearing of his sister's decision to work as a lady's maid. But Dorothee objects very realistically to her brother's suggestion that she should become a companion or a governess: "You are wrong about me: I could not do any of that, for I lack the necessary education, knowledge, and experience."[15]

Here, Hahn-Hahn describes the situation regarding job allocation as in no way predetermined by fate, but rather dictated by society. She does not regard the different incorporation of brother and sister into the social hierarchy as resulting from their internal disposition, but as the result of external factors. By contrasting the lives of Dorothee and Leonor Brand, she can effectively demonstrate that the mere fact of belonging to the female sex resulted in greater professional dependence and worse prospects of promotion than was generally the case for the male sex. But this is followed by an idealistic tour de force of the author, who again completely destroys the viewpoint of society by declaring the acceptance of social injustice to be the mark of a noble mind. For, contrary to the horrors of a position in domestic service as depicted by her brother, Dorothee finds in the Countess Sambach a loving and gentle mistress with whom she can increasingly identify, indeed to such an extent that the sufferings and joys of the Countess become her own, although she wishes for and wants nothing more at all for herself. In this respect, the author can, without great poetological effort, steer the perspective from the story of the lady's maid to that of the mistress's drama and make a smooth transition from the servant's report to the aristocratic love story. For Dorothee has, in the meantime, been promoted to the alter ego of the Countess and consequently no longer needs her own personal portrayal.

The portrait of the lady's maid differs in the novels of Luise Mühlbach. In her *Frauenschicksal* (Female Fates)—a tetralogy consisting of *Das Mädchen* (The Girl), *Die Gattin* (The Wife), *Die Künstlerin* (The Female Artist) and *Die Fürstin* (The Princess)—the figure of the lady's maid occupies a section of her own. She is the principal character in the novel *Das Mädchen* (The Girl), whose life is portrayed in seven exemplary stages. In contrast to Hahn-Hahn, Mühlbach describes the destruction of a female existence from the perspective of the person concerned. Christine goes under because, in contrast to Dorothee, she does not take to heart the rules of resignation which applied to her class and because she demands her own share of happiness in life. The author leaves us in no doubt of her partiality for the behaviour of the lady's maid. The story of high-ranking people is inserted merely as a signal for a tale of exploitation. "She [Christine] was a mere lady's maid, how could she be foolish enough to demand joy and pleasure from life, a privilege only of the rich and elegant."[16]

The very character of the tetralogy shows us that Mühlbach conceived her story as an exemplary one. Female fates were in those days generally contained within the four patterns of femininity adopted by her. In the case of the absence or even rejection of the marriage pattern, there remained for the female existence, apart from the exception of the noblewoman, mostly only the shelter of domestic service[17] or the departure into the realm of art. It is certainly no literary invention that domestic service often offered girls more dangers than security. This is also confirmed by other female writers. Fanny Lewald is outraged at the frequent and unscrupulous seduction of serving girls, at "how many there are who are unaccustomed to seeing anything more in the daughters of the poor than objects for the satisfaction of their lust."[18] And Gertrud Bäumer also points to the fact that female servants "have the most illegitimate children out of all groups of female earners."[19] In light of this fact, the picture of the lady's maid drawn by Mühlbach corresponds more accurately to empirical reality than that of Hahn-Hahn.

Although Fanny Lewald's interest lay largely in middle-class women and their life-style, she too examined in her theoretical and her literary writings the problem of the serving girl. In particular the essays *Andeutungen über die Lage der weiblichen Dienstboten* (Sketches on the Position of the Female Servant) and *Osterbriefe für die Frauen* (Easter Letters for Women) are sympathetic and emphatic pleas for the improvement of serving girls' working conditions.

> At the age of fourteen or fifteen, they [the children] are confirmed, and then the boy's apprenticeship begins. The girl, however, has no such apprenticeship. She is to go to strangers to become a servant. The girl "in service," however, is "in service" day and night. On workdays and holidays, at any hour, the master and mistress have a right to her services. Much work, great exertion, bad treatment, little time for recovery from illness and even less pay, these are for women the first fruits of life among strangers.[20]

The decided bias for the serving-girls contained within these comments cannot be overlooked. It is therefore all the more astonishing— and that leads right to the heart of the confounded problematic nature of the subject—that the same is not true of the fictional texts. They do occasionally contain a female servant, as in *Das Mädchen von Hela* (The Girl of Hela), *Eine traurige Geschichte* (A Sad Story), and *Die Kammerjungfer* (The Lady's Maid), and it is also true that Lewald's servants always appear as lady's maids. The bias of the theoretical texts is, however, not in evidence. This is particularly striking in the two-volume novel *Die Kammerjungfer* (The Lady's Maid), for which this figure is nonetheless selected as the titular heroine. But, in fact, the lady's maid Marie Redlich can only attract the undivided attention of the reader on the book cover. The novel itself is an eloquent example of how the real interest of Lewald lies in the mistress of her lady's maid and how she uses the title-figure above all as a medium for a story centered on the master and mistress. It is striking that Lewald introduces the girl almost listlessly and that she cannot direct her narrative attention back quickly enough to the "interesting" mistress or her "energetic" fiancé. The reports come constantly from other perspectives, from that of her up-and-coming fiancé Karl, who is continuing his studies, or from that of her mistress Lora. The conclusion is such that Karl, a pocket-size Wilhelm Meister who has meanwhile done everything (been able to do everything) to educate himself, breaks off the engagement with Marie and marries her mistress instead, while Marie, who is left over, is given the elderly manservant, Ludwig, as a husband. The moral of this story is not so much "cobbler, stick to your last!" but indicates rather that this should only be true of his female counterpart. Advancement as such is not condemned; however, it is not envisaged for women of the lower classes. This is an amazing conclusion for a female writer who, in her theoretical writings, committed herself so wholeheartedly to the cause of the female servant.

Of interest in this connection is the ideological disparity between documentary and fictional articulation, the ambivalence between theoretical progression and fictional status quo. This topic has scarcely been discussed, even in the field of feminist research. Even a critic like Gisela Brinker-Gabler, who so firmly supports feminist concerns, lumps everything in this connection together. Thus, one can read: "Fanny Lewald devoted particular attention to the situation of female servants. After an essay (Sketches on the Position of Female Servants) published as early as 1843, she treats this problem in her literary works as well."[21] The dilemma, however, lies exactly in the fact that she does not discuss it in her literature, but only in theory. This contradiction, as far as it is proved to be constitutive for the female literature of this time, should not be glossed over but investigated. For we can assume that it will shed more light on the cultural fate of woman and her literary silence (or concealment) than is at first sight apparent.

When the literary sketches of the *Lady's Maid* are compared with one another, one sees that Luise Mühlbach has given this character the greatest literary authenticity. However, she too undeniably concentrates first and foremost on the spectacular moments of such a fate. The everyday life of such an existence, the quite normal difficulties are not aesthetically recorded by her either. The fact that "the main difficulties of the servant's job lie in its cross between a patriarchal and an employee relationship"[22] is nowhere clearly stated.

Indeed, how are the professions open to middle-class women and girls, namely governess and artist, reflected in literature? How is the most frequently practised profession of them all, that of governess and teacher, embodied in the novels of the female writers of the *Vormärz?* The answer may prove surprising: it is not portrayed at all—or almost never.

With respect to the female artist, however, the picture is quite different. Female writers and stage artists are frequently protagonists of women's novels. The fact that it was the actress who attracted the mounting interest of the first generation of female writers can be accounted for by the exceptional position occupied by women in the theatre. "For the actress was the first, for a long time the only 'female profession' "[23] and, more important still, "the only profession in which woman has achieved total equality with man and where she can stand as man's equal at his side."[24] And so it can with some justification be claimed that "female emancipation . . . was first recognisable . . . in the theatre."[25] Fanny Lewald writes:

> For me, the meeting with female stage artists had another quite special significance, because it provided me with a picture of the kind of independence and personal meaning toward which my whole soul aspired. For hours, while sewing and knitting, I was able to imagine how blissfully happy I should be to be independent, to have a self-supporting profession like these women. When pretty Clara Stich's uncle Crelinger once teasingly upbraided her, she answered him laughing: "You can't speak to me like that, I am a court actress, I am a royal official!"[26]

The price for this increased independence was generally the loss of social respectability. The job of actress lay in the problematic area of the absence of rights and representation. Particularly the large hosts of actresses who did not stand on the uppermost rung of success were encouraged, by virtue of the economic situation within the theatre of the day, to increase their meagre earnings through the financial support of "interested" admirers. However, libertinage was the property of their professional class. Actresses had always enjoyed greater moral freedom, were not judged according to the usual code of morals, and found themselves, to a certain extent, occupying the still permissible marginal area of ruling morality.

These brief comments already make it clear that the professional picture of the actress was a highly differentiated one with little standardization. In the novels of the female writers of the *Vormärz* it must be said, however, that only one variant is given a hearing, namely the celebrated diva or prima donna, who stands at the top of the ladder of artistic success in the glory of unlimited admiration. The majority of the others, who every season renewed their struggle for employment and all too often fell victim to extreme material need, have no place in their literature. This is true of Mühlbach as well as of Lewald, who both portrayed female stage artists on occasion. In the case of Lewald, the relevant figures, apart from various peripheral characters, are the actress Sophie Harkourt in *Eine Lebensfrage* (A Question of Life), the singer Regine in *Wandlungen* (Changes), and the actress Hulda in *Die Erlöserin* (The Female Liberator).

In spite of differences of detail, a common basic structure can be seen in their biographies. They are all successful social climbers. Orphaned early on, they are forced to find a means to support themselves. Drama serves to earn them a livelihood. They all climb the ladder of success to the topmost rung and manage the ascent almost without difficulty. Having stepped beyond the oppressive confines of their origins, they succeed within a short period in taking up residence in "stately houses" and "elegantly furnished rooms." "Surrounded by magnificent luxury," they have succeeded in calling the "reception hall" and "liveried servants" their own. They are largely spared the hardships of the acting profession. All the protagonists become brilliant actresses, "the greatest artists in their field,"[27] and all without any particular hurdles to overcome; they achieve within the shortest possible time the breakthrough to fame. Contracts with national and international stages alike fall into their laps, so to speak. They are assured of public favour, for they know how "to fanaticize" the public continually. The reader is given the impression that the ascent to the heights of dramatic art—where young, beautiful and enthusiastic women are concerned—is no particularly difficult undertaking.

A likewise common feature of all the female stage artists portrayed is the fact that, though they occupy the ultimate position in their art, this does not represent for them *the ultimate*. For, over and above the glory of the female artist, the loving woman in them reigns supreme. And this part of them is not so eager to gain the favour of the public as to preserve the love of the loved one. When faced with the choice between her art and the man she loves, she would without hesitation choose the latter. The orientation point of the "one and only" remains for her the determining element in life. "To overcome death," Sophie Harkourt announces to her interlocutor, "that is easy, but how should I live without Julian's love and what am I but an ordinary woman without Julian's transfiguring love? What am I without Julian? What is left for me if I lose him?"[28] And on hearing the obvious answer advanced by her interlocutor: "Art"—Sophie replies with apodictic severity: "I shall never again set foot on the stage."[29] Similar evaluations from Lewald with respect to the hierarchy of heart and art are to be found elsewhere as well. The latter—Lewald speaks in a way contrary to her own experience—can satisfy a woman for a while. However, it cannot fulfill her. Only love can do that.[30] And so all her actress figures are, first and foremost, great lovers with great noble hearts. They are capable of succumbing to passions, but they never have affairs. Furthermore, they are for the most part "lovers for the first time." The disorderly side of this profession, untouched by the glamour, remains unmentioned.

Thus the fates of actresses are rendered harmless and are described according to the pattern of the novels of renunciation. The scintillating contradictory versatility of the actor's life serves solely as a foil, in order to convey the well-known stories of the female heart in new drapings. The independence of the actress and the freedom her profession allowed her, so emphatically praised by Lewald in her autobiography, are not exploited in fiction.

Most of what has been observed in Lewald's work is likewise true of the actresses in the novels of Mühlbach. They too embody the highest achievements of their art, have scarcely experienced any difficulties during their ascent, and enjoy lasting public favour. They are young, beautiful, and nobleminded. But in some respects Mühlbach goes beyond the biographical portrayals given by Lewald. In any case, the unglamorous reverse side of the acting profession is not totally avoided. Not all biographies are success stories or stories of renunciation. Mühlbach's intense preoccupation with the portrayal of the female stage artist is clearly shown by the fact that the author devotes a whole novel to her within the tetralogy *Woman's Fate*. She is not, as in the works of Lewald, one of the protagonists, but the main protagonist, which means that, from the purely economic aspect of the novel, a larger circle of characters connected with her can be integrated into the plot, and much more space is made available for the theme of the "actress." Thus, from the very beginning, alongside the celebrated Emilie Minden is the uncelebrated Ernestine who, used by men as fair game and not able to cope with the hardships of her fate, takes her own life. "Need and her isolation in the world had caused Ernestine to go into the theatre, but her plain face hindered her in everything; maybe she had talent, but it was not tested, for 'lovers must be beautiful,' said the director."[31] When, in a kind of parallel montage, the author closely associates the high-flying heroine with the fate of a minor character, the possible decline of the celebrated actress is, for the reader, at least a potential danger.

But in yet another, more significant point, Mühlbach shifts the emphasis slightly in her portrayal of the actress. Thus, Catharina, the prima donna in *Der Zögling der Natur* (The Pupil of Nature), questions the basic principle that love represents the ultimate fulfillment of woman. Although she expresses the most passionate feelings for Antonio, she has more than this "one thought" and never forgets her own position as a professional woman. When Antonio presents her with a choice between withdrawal "with him into the peace of nature" to the exclusion of all but their love, and the continuation of the lifestyle she is used to but without him, she decides in favour of the latter. "Love alone does not bring happiness," she avows without reservation, "to be happy, you require all life's trimmings. . . ; in the midst of this noisy, tempestuous world I feel at ease, and though I often long for a quiet, secret hour of conversation with you—if this hour stretched into eternity, I could die of boredom!"[32] The novelty of this novel lies in the fact that Mühlbach interpreted such a figure neither as a cold-blooded career woman nor as a wanton femme fatale.

It is also of particular interest to find out how the figure of the female writer—that is, the authors' own profession—is treated in their fiction. In the process, one must bear in mind that their position was a difficult one by virtue of the fact that they, unlike the actresses, received scarcely any ideological support from their male colleagues. As long as men like Gervinus slandered the literary activities of women as "literary tea parties," or Scherr denounced their public debut as "tastelessness and shamelessness," and Gutzkow, referring to the same, even questioned the value of their sex, the female writers of the *Vormärz* were exposed to a double set of obstacles, namely that of the reigning set of family norms and that of a cartel of male critics. The fact that in their hard fight for freedom in their profession they met with prejudices similar to those in the restricted sphere of the family, when they discovered that even their literary colleagues expected them to represent a traditional picture of the woman as a female bearer of male wishes: all this could not help but exert an influence on their literary production.

Thus it is characteristic that in both of the novels in which she treated her own biography, *Aus der Gesellschaft* (From Society) and *Gräfin Faustine* (Countess Faustine), Ida Hahn-Hahn should indeed present her main character as a writer, though not in the modern sense of the professional woman as she herself actually was. Thus Countess

Schönhold and Countess Faustine do indeed write novels in their hours of leisure which are "incomparable in their grace of imagination and depth of feeling";[33] however, this activity scarcely arouses the interest of the author. Her heroines' writing assumes far more the status of a fine accessory, a further bonus in order to increase their interest. Here, pruned writing is shown. The thorns, very familiar to the author herself, are carefully swept out of the path of her heroine.

Fanny Lewald provides a very different picture indeed. While Hahn-Hahn aestheticises the literary activity of her female protagonist, Lewald tends to ridicule it. This is particularly true of her novel dealing with female novelists, *Adele* (Adele). The heroine, described as an old-maidish type, seizes on the writing profession not out of literary interest, but in order to help herself get over the loss of her unfaithful lover. Thus Adele's first novel *On the Genius of the Poet,* in which she reveals her love to the public, is a conglomeration of sentimental, embarrassing details which makes her the laughing-stock of those around her. This negative portrait of Lewald's has already been criticized by Marieluise Steinhauer,[34] and Regula Venske concludes that there can "be no question . . . of a genuine interest in the problem of a female writer."[35]

It is with some amazement that we realize that the author of this novel adopts the very picture men had of bluestockings pushing their way into the limelight and of hysterical old maids disappointed in love being the only ones making up the contingent of female writers: a writer who in her own "life story" had propounded the view "that unemployment . . . had degraded the female character."[36]

Literary work is treated seriously in the novels of Luise Mühlbach and particularly in her three-volume novel *Aphra Behn* (1849), where it is certainly to her advantage that the work revolves around an authentic female writer, who is introduced as the first professional female writer in the history of literature.[37] In spite of such examples, however, the astounding result remains: the woman described in fiction limps far behind her female creator. The artistic character preserves the socially approved pictures of femininity intact and does not adopt the reality of the female artist. Had the novels examined been works of the conservative phalanx, of such writers as Ottilie Wildermuth, Elise Polko, or Julie Burow, who never undermined the female status quo, the result could not have been more astonishing. Different behaviour could have been expected from female writers who publicly advocated "the right of women to employment."

But even more striking is the contradiction between emancipatory demands on the one hand, and regressive female portrayal within the works themselves on the other. For it is not true that the professional woman in her social existence does not figure at all in the writings of the female writers of the *Vormärz*. She just does not appear in the novel. In the documentary writings, however, she is clearly present. Worthy of consideration, therefore, is the discrepancy between documentary discernment and fictional shortsightedness, and the reason why that which had been recognized in the essays could not be transformed into fiction. This leads to the following concrete question: why does the woman writer not express in her art that which she is well aware of in reality? In turn, the complicated and thus far rarely discussed question is raised of the relationship between female writers and literary transformation, and the utilization of the supply of images available, towards the production of which women themselves had scarcely contributed.[38] One of the first to air her view on this subject was Virginia Woolf:

> It was strange to think that all the great women of fiction were, until Jane Austen's day, not only seen by the other sex, but seen only in relation to the other sex. And, how small a part of a woman's life is that; . . . Hence, perhaps, the peculiar nature of women in fiction; the astonishing extremes of her beauty and horror; her alternations between heavenly goodness and hellish depravity—for a lover would see her as his love rose or sank, was prosperous or unhappy.[39]

But there are weighty reasons for these "curiosities." For, even though the novel is the most recent and least fixed genre in the normative sense, it was, at the time when women were turning to literature, already stamped with a repertoire of images derived from the male imagination. There were no models for the professional woman. Not even a *Bildungsroman* had been devoted to her.

Literature was based on the polarization of the sexual characters, which resulted in the representation of the powers of reason falling to man, while woman was seen as the ruler of affairs of the heart. The decisive point was that the access and attachment of women writers to the medium of literature had developed via the images of femininity favored by men. No one could escape the authority of such images. For it was not the authority of the paterfamilias of which they were so suspicious, but rather the authority of the lover, above all an authority that appeared in the guise of freedom, for it represented the cause of art. Its atavistic reverse side was not as easily recognizable.

Thus, female literary perception underwent training according to the male patterns of perception. In order to master the novel genre, the female novice writer was obliged to accept the truth of that which the man had already perceived. This distorted her picture of herself. "For the true nature of woman, her sexuality, her everyday behaviour, the scattered signs of her autonomy"[40] were not presented in male works of art. Here the leading writers of the genre imposed on them a direction which led them away from their own experiences. The same was not true of the documentary presentation of reality. The low position of the documentary genre within the hierarchy of literary activities had warded off normative demands. It was, to a certain extent, still unformulated. Here, the female writers did not have to bow to any foreign norms. So it is that they sketch quite different pictures of women in their essays and reports from those they were able to sketch in their novels. To overlook such contradictions is to make insufficient allowance for the social pressure under which the first generation of female writers lived. For the following observation of Virginia Woolf was to retain its alarming validity for a long time to come:

> The indifference of the world which Keats and Flaubert and other men of genius have found so hard to bear was in her [woman's] case not indifference but hostility. The world did not say to her as it said to them, Write if you please; it makes no difference to me. The world said with a guffaw, Write? What's the good of your writing?[41]

translated by Sarah Wilson.

NOTES

1. Fanny Lewald, *Wandlungen* (Berlin: Otto Janke, 1864), vol. 1, pp. 84–85.

2. Ibid., pp. 86–87.

3. Lewald, *Eine Lebensfrage* (Leipzig: F. A. Brockhaus, 1845), vol. 1, p. 198.

4. Louise Otto, *Das Recht der Frauen auf Erwerb* (Hamburg: Hoffmann & Campe, 1866), p. 14.

5. *Handbuch der Frauenbewegung,* ed. Helen Lange and Gertrud Bäumer (Berlin: W. Moeser, 1902), vol. 4, p. 24.

6. Ibid., p. 62.

7. See Lewald, "Einige Gedanken über Mädchenerziehung," *Archiv für vaterländische Interessen oder Preußische Provinzial Blätter,* ed. O. W. L. Richter (Königsberg: 1843).

8. See Lewald, "Für die Gewerbstätigkeit der Frauen," *Westermanns Monatshefte* 1869, 26.

9. See Otto, *Das Recht der Frauen auf Erwerb.*

10. See Ida Hahn-Hahn, *Der Rechte* (Berlin: Alexander Dunker, 1845).

11. Jacob and Wilhelm Grimm, *Deutsches Wörterbuch* (Leipzig: Hirzel 1873), p. 122.

12. Lily Braun, "Die weiblichen Dienstboten", *Frauenarbeit und Beruf,* ed. Gisela Brinker-Gabler (Frankfurt a.M.: Fischer, 1979), 41. Italics mine.

13. Hahn-Hahn, *Zwei Frauen* (Berlin: Alexander Duncker, 1846), vol. 1, p. 143.

14. Ibid., p. 151.

15. Ibid., p. 141.

16. Luise Mühlbach, *Frauenschicksal* (Altona: J. F. Hammerich, 1839), vol. 1, p. 26.

17. See Wilhelm Kähler, *Gesindewesen und Gesinderecht in Deutschland* (Jena: 1896), pp. 7–37.

18. Lewald, *Osterbriefe für die Frauen* (Berlin: Otto Janke, 1863), pp. 137–38.

19. Bäumer, *Die Frau in Volkswirtschaft und Staatsleben der Gegenwart* (Stuttgart/ Berlin: Deutsche Verlags-Anstalt, 1914), p. 182.

20. Lewald, *Osterbriefe für die Frauen,* pp. 26–32.

21. Lewald, *Meine Lebensgeschichte,* ed. Gisela Brinker-Gabler (Frankfurt a.M.: Fischer, 1980), p. 25.

22. Bäumer, *Die Frau in Volkswirtschaft und Staatsleben der Gegenwart,* p. 181.

23. Julius Bab, *Die Frau als Schauspielerin* (Berlin: Oesterheld & Co., 1915), p. 53.

24. Heinrich Stümcke, *Die Frau als Schauspielerin* (Leipzig: Friedrich Rothbarth, 1905), p. 113.

25. Rudolf K. Goldschmidt, *Die Schauspielerin* (Stuttgart: Walter Hädecke, 1922), p. 9.

26. Lewald, *Leidensjahre* (Berlin: Otto Janke, 1862), vol. 2, p. 67.

27. Lewald, *Lebensfrage,* vol. 1, p. 156.

28. Ibid., pp. 185–86.

29. Ibid., p. 186.

30. See Lewald, *Wandlungen,* vol. 4, p. 41.

31. Mühlbach, *Frauenschicksal,* vol. 2, p. 24.

32. Mühlbach, *Der Zögling der Natur* (Altona: J. F. Hammerich, 1842), p. 223.

33. Hahn-Hahn, *Aus der Gesellschaft* (Berlin: Duncker und Humblot, 1838), p. 51.

34. See Marieluise Steinhauer, *Fanny Lewald, die deutsche George Sand* (Berlin: Diss. 1937).

35. Venske, Regula, *Alltag und Emanzipation. Eine Untersuchung über die Romanautorin Fanny Lewald* (Hamburg: MA thesis, 1981), p. 74.

36. Lewald, *Leidensjahre,* vol. 1, p. 269.

37. Mühlbach, *Aphra Behn* (Berlin: M. Simion, 1849), vol. 2, p. 283.

38. See Silvia Bovenschen, *Die imaginierte Weiblichkeit. Exemplarische Untersuchungen zu kulturgeschichtlichen und literarischen Präsentationsformen des Weiblichen* (Frankfurt a.M.: Suhrkamp, 1979), p. 12.

39. Virginia Woolf, *A Room of One's Own* (New York, Burlingame: Harcourt, Brace & World, Inc., 1957), p. 86.

40. Gisela von Wysocki, "Frauen—Bilder im Aufbruch. Hinweise auf ihren Gebrauch", *Kursbuch* 47 (1977), pp. 95–96.

41. Woolf, *A Room of One's Own,* p. 54.

WOMEN AND THE LITERARY ENTERPRISE IN NINETEENTH-CENTURY GERMANY

Patricia Herminghouse

In examining women writers' relationship to the literary enterprise, the concern of this paper is not primarily aesthetic. Rather the focus is on what one might call their "working conditions": the conditions which governed women's relationship to the institutions of literature and literary life in that period. Implicit in the discussion, of course, is the assumption that there *were* women who wrote in the first place, even if—because of accidental neglect or deliberate exclusion—they have disappeared from contemporary literary history. The token respect accorded to a few writers, such as Annette von Droste-Hülshoff or Marie von Ebner-Eschenbach, may even serve to reinforce a kind of literary Darwinism which leads us to regard seriously only the few who have survived the scrutiny of the guardians of the canon of nineteenth-century literature.

But there were thousands of women writers, as one can quickly ascertain from older reference works, such as Sophie Pataky's two-volume *Lexikon deutscher Frauen der Feder* (Encyclopedia of German Ladies of the Pen)[1], a bio-bibliography containing nearly 5000 entries from Marie Aabel's *Bayerische Knödelküche* (Bavarian Dumpling Cookery) to Baroness von Zwierlein's *Rheinische Lieder und Sagen* (Rhineland Songs and Stories). In addition to Pataky, Marianne Nigg's *Biographien der österreichischen Dichterinnen und Schriftstel-*

lerinnen (Biographies of Austrian Women Writers and Poets)[2], Heinrich Gross's three volumes of *Deutschlands Dichterinnen und Schriftstellerinnen in Wort und Bild* (Texts and Portraits of Germany's Women Writers and Poets)[3] and Ernst Brausewetter's three volumes of *Meisternovellen deutscher Frauen* (Master-Novellas of German Women)[4] give ample evidence of the extent of women's literary productivity. But both Brausewetter's assertion that his anthology was meant to provide witness to the artistic creativity of women in the area of literatur[5] and Pataky's reference to the imperfections of existing aids for finding out about women writers and their achievements[6] confirm that, even in their own time, there were definite deficits in knowledge about these women. More recently, Elisabeth Friedrichs compiled a lexicon of over 4000 women writers, based on her search of more than 400 sources, in an attempt "to focus scholarly attention once again on the many women writers of the eighteenth and nineteenth century who have been unjustly forgotten and to thereby make a contribution to the history of women's independence."[7] In thirty journals alone, she found 1552 novels and novellas, 3235 shorter prose works, 4756 poems, and 3656 reviews—a total of 13,200 works, many of which have never appeared between the covers of a book. Without focusing specifically on women writers, Franz Brümmer's *Lexikon der deutschen Dichter des 19. Jahrhunderts* (Encyclopedia of German Writers of the Nineteenth Century)[8] also alerts us to names and titles not included by his female colleagues—enough to justify my estimate that women comprised from one-fourth to one-third of the total number of literary authors in this period: a far cry from the minuscule proportion of them who have survived in more contemporary reference works. The purpose in introducing this flood of statistics is to document that, despite their virtual invisibility today, women did participate very actively in literary life in the nineteenth century, from writing popular drama to political poetry, from editing family papers to literary journals, and to suggest that it may be instructive to consider the professional rather than the strictly aesthetic aspects of their literary activities. Although the focus here is on the belletristic work of women, the fact that women were also producing immense numbers of practical, nonfiction publications—household handbooks, cookbooks, travel literature, and the like—only serves to indicate the importance of attempting to examine social aspects of their activity in the world of publishing.

Like so many other features of economic, cultural, and social life in the late eighteenth and early nineteenth century, literary life also underwent transformations, some of which can only be sketched in the

broadest outlines here. The marked increase in literacy and the corresponding qualitative and quantitative changes in the reading public
since the Enlightenment were reflected in a dramatic expansion of the
literary marketplace. As the growth of readers' clubs and lending libraries in the last decades of the eighteenth century demonstrated very
clearly, there were not only more readers but also more demand for
new works to read. Literary production increased and, for the first
time, it became possible for men such as Gotthold Ephraim Lessing
and Christoph Martin Wieland to derive their primary financial support
from writing, to make a profession rather than an avocation of their
literary activities. The commercialization of literary enterprise began;
literature, especially the novel, became a market commodity subject to
the material laws of production, distribution, and consumption.
Through the early decades of the nineteenth century, the publishing
industry itself was transformed by the Industrial Revolution, with major
improvements in the technology of printing and the mechanisms for
distributing printed materials. Newspapers and journals proliferated,
adding journalism to the list of lucrative new professions open to the
middle class. Yet, the same social forces which united to define the
nature, role, and destiny of woman in the domestic sphere and to keep
her out of the public sphere worked against her ambitions in the
literary market place as well as in other forms of productive work.

In the rapidly changing social order of the late eighteenth and early
nineteenth century an intense effort was made to prescribe and en-
force woman's "proper" role in the reproductive sphere of home and
family, to separate private from professional life. The development of
new work patterns and the establishment of a "productive" sector
outside the domestic sphere were bolstered by the propagation of
theories which attributed the division of labor by sex to psychological,
rather than physiological traits which limit woman's participation in the
world of "real work." But not only did such theories support woman's
exclusion from the productive sector of the economy; by attaching
sentimental instead of economic merit to her work, they also trivialized
the labor she continued to do in the domestic sphere and ultimately
awakened her desire for liberation from the cult of house and family.[9]
Already in 1815, the Brockhaus encyclopedia (Conversations-
Lexikon) offered a neat division of the roles of the sexes: "Man ob-
tains, woman sustains. . . . man resists fate itself and defies force, even
in defeat. Woman, however, submits willingly and finds comfort and
succor, even in her tears."[10] Even towards the end of the century, when
"women's literature" had indeed become big business, an editor's
proud defense of the fact that he had been publishing women in his

journal for years reveals his underlying reservations about their actual suitability for a serious career as writers:

> These days women are working with their hands and their heads in order to earn money. We have come to accept this. But it ought not give us reason to think less of women. Their industriousness in this area must also be considered a virtue. Personally, I do feel that women are capable of certain forms of artistic rendering in painting and writing.[11]

There is no point in repeating here the entire tradition of nineteenth-century theories of women's inferiority or even dragging out the all-too-familiar remarks of Arthur Schopenhauer, Friedrich Nietzsche, or Otto Weininger. Their blatant misogyny is more transparent to analysis and critique than are the more subtle ideologies which, throughout the century, simultaneously proclaimed woman's domestic role as the mediatrix of civilized traditions while supporting her exclusion from the cultural sphere. With an astonishing universality that dates at least as far back as Kant's postulation of the male principle as the sublime *(das Erhabene),* and the female as "beauty," socially conditioned differences between the sexes have been conceptually justified as "natural." In the relations of the sexes, Kant's notion that "one side must be subordinate to the other"[12] provided the foundation of a cultural myth about the "nature of woman" and her "natural vocation" which was internalized by women as well as men. This reduction of women to a male perception of their biology was immensely effective in binding them economically, intellectually, legally, and socially into dependency on men at a time when social and economic changes were actually altering the function and composition of the family. In fact, these very changes—which produced, among other things, an increase in leisure time—actually seemed to foster a renewed emphasis on "women's natural destiny." "The state *(der Staat)* is masculine gender, and the social groups [the peasantry *(das Bauerntum),* the bourgeosie *(das Bürgertum)*] are *generis neutrius:* what about women? They should remain in the 'family', which, after all, reflects its predominantly feminine character already in the gender of the noun."[13] The author of this astonishing linguistic analysis, Wilhelm Heinrich Riehl, is typical of any number of nineteenth-century writers and thinkers who were determined that transformations in ways of working and living were not to be accompanied by transformations in women's expectations or lessened acquiescence to their domestic role. His immensely popular sociology of the family *(Die Familie),* first published in 1854, cleverly indicates that the social inequality of men and women corresponds to the laws of nature and that, in fact, physical and intellectual differences between man and woman grow greater with increasing civilization; hence any attempt by women to reduce these differences amounts to a regressive step back down the road to barbarism. This line of argumentation illustrates the kind of double bind which can be created by postulating women's limitations and then criticizing those who try to transcend them as unwomanly. Riehl does concede the value of some education—within bounds—for women, provided that it serves the needs of others:

> Woman's education should not be an end in itself. . . . Husband, family, friends, the entire environment of a woman benefit directly from the bountiful fruits of noble, educated womanhood. Let woman rule through serving others, let her free man from his limitations by limiting herself, exert influence by appearing to be influenced.[14]

Despite the fact that by the end of the nineteenth century women comprised almost one-third of the wage earners in Germany, the stereotypes of woman's nature and role persisted tenaciously in a mutually reinforcing relationship with the kinds and amount of formal education available to women in this period. As the general statistics introduced at the beginning of this paper as well as a more specific examination of the number of women among the regular writers for the most popular family journal in nineteenth-century Germany indicate, women were similarly productive in the literary enterprise, despite the oblivion to which their contributions have been consigned. Not counting a few women who may be unrecognizable behind initials or male pseudonyms, 27 of the 99 authors who published at least two stories in the *Gartenlaube* between 1853 and 1900 were women.[15] The significant change is not that women began to write in ever-increasing numbers, but that they began to write for money, even though few of them wrote as their main occupation and even fewer belonged to professional groups, such as the General Association of German Writers *(Allgemeiner deutscher Schriftstellerverein)*, which by 1880 numbered only four women among its membership of 150.[16] This reflects the fact that, for most women, writing was a sort of cottage industry which they could carry on in whatever moments could be spared from their "proper" role in the domestic sphere. With the exception of the most popular women, such as E. Marlitt and W. Heimburg, whose royalties from the journals to which they brought so many readers equaled or exceeded those of their male counterparts, most women could not subsist on their income from writing. But because they did not need to, they also posed a threat to male writers, who feared economic competition from their willingness to accept lower honoraria. Once a woman got something published in even a minor local paper, sans royalty, she would seek better opportunities, a disgruntled colleague noted:

> Next she gets a small honorarium, she tries another journal. This time she succeeds in placing one or more stories and now she is convinced that she is an incipient genius and that writing is her profession. Her little stories or sketches are then collected into a volume; a publisher is easily found because the royalty she expects is so modest—more modest than that of most writers—and that tempts many a book dealer, so her book is sent out into the world. Now the little weekly, provincial or daily journal is no longer good enough for her. She sets herself a greater task: a novel, etc.[17]

Since specifics are often more instructive than generalities, I shall use the example of one particular writer, Fanny Lewald, to illustrate the way in which a woman became involved in the literary enterprise. I have chosen Lewald because, apart from the early romantic women writers who have been the object of so much attention recently, she is a pioneer among the generations of bourgeois women writers in the nineteenth century. Furthermore she has left us memoirs and letters which reflect with striking clarity the conflicts faced by a woman with literary ambitions. The mixed feelings with which, despite her successes, she regarded her participation in the literary enterprise emerge very clearly, for example, in a letter she wrote to Karl Gutzkow in 1848:

> If I were rich, I would write anyhow, because I have developed a need to clarify my own thinking in this way; but I doubt that I would let anything more be published. I've lost my love of the public and I don't feel like existing just to amuse them. It hurts me to think that I now have to publish the novel that I finished months ago. I know that you surely understand this, since you see that we women are only taken half seriously in Germany. But I hate half-measures.[18]

Lewald also is a particularly good example because she was, particularly in the first three and a half decades of her life (1811–1845) covered in the memoirs, a self-conscious professional. Even after her marriage to Adolf Stahr in 1855, when her attitudes about women's roles became somewhat more conventional, she continued to publish prolifically and to receive handsome honoraria for her enduringly popular work. Marieluise Steinhauer reports that the advance publication of one of her novels in a Viennese newspaper in 1871 created such heavy demand for the paper that it resorted to printing separate copies of the serialization. In the last years of her life, Lewald was paid up to thirty Marks per manuscript page, so that in 1886, for example, the advance publication alone of her novel *Familie Darner* (The Darner Family) earned her 18,000 Marks.[19] Thus, although the dilettants who wrote as a pastime may have received only a pittance for their work, the successful professional women writers seem to have earned at least as much as most of their male peers—and appreciably more than most of the men we tend to regard as significant today.

What, we might ask ourselves as a first consideration, would produce the virtual invisibility of so many women in the literary enterprise of the nineteenth century? First of all, as one can infer from a work such as Otto Berdrow's *Frauenbilder aus der neueren deutschen Literaturgeschichte* (Portraits of Women from Recent German Literary History), they were hidden in the shadows of men. Asserting that one cannot begin to understand an important writer without understanding his relationship to important women in his life, Berdrow explains that he intends to give a true and unadorned account of these women as mothers, sisters, girlfriends, brides, and wives of famous literary personalities. "One cannot ignore the fact that only a few of these women possess any literary significance of their own, that most of them would hardly be known in broader circles, had not the light of a great (male) artist illuminated their path through life."[20] Secondly, at least for their contemporaries, women writers were hiding behind pseudonyms, as Pataky illustrates with some 1500 examples from the eighteenth and nineteenth century. It may be objected that men, too, have used pen names—one need only mention Jeremias Gotthelf, Nikolaus Lenau, and Charles Sealsfield—but even where considerations of political reprisal or social standing dictated the choice of a pen name, its use was far more prevalent among women than men. And, to my knowledge, there is no male author who felt compelled to conceal his sexual identity behind a pseudonym such as Louise Otto's "Otto Stern"—or at least an initial, which was supposed to hide the writer's gender, such as W. Heimburg or E. Marlitt. While the very assumption of a pseudonym may signal a realistic assessment of the possibilities open to women who wanted to attempt the leap from the private sphere of the female to the public sphere of the male, it also served to perpetuate cultural biases which denied women's creative potential. Johannes Scherr was certainly not alone in his opinion that "the contingent of females, who force themselves on the public without being asked, consists either of ugly old maids . . . or of slovenly housewives and undutiful mothers."[21]

The fact that women had to hide their sexual identity by writing anonymously or pseudonymously reflects a form of repression and self-consciousness not shared by their male colleagues, a recognition that they ought not have had ambitions which extended beyond the domestic sphere and that women who wrote could not expect serious treatment by publishers or critics. Thus it is not surprising that Heinrich Gross introduced his three-volume anthology of women writers with the comment that the reading public tended to mistrust writing by women

> so that the women writers were forced by the editorship of the daily papers and journals to engage in the pious fraud of denying their gender and wrapping themselves in male pseudonyms, so that the impartial reader would surely not find out that the author of the much-admired lead article, the intelligent feature, etc. is—a female![22]

For some years, Fanny Lewald was one of these hundreds of hidden women writers, and her memoirs provide illuminating details about why she had to veil her literary identity. Raised in a bourgeois, assimilated Jewish milieu in Königsberg—the home, too, of Kant, whose remarks on the character of the sexes she reports having read with great interest at the age of sixteen[23]—Lewald reports how eagerly she devoured the educational opportunities which her father made available to all of his children—with differences between sons and daughters, of course. She did have the privilege of attending school until she was thirteen or fourteen, at which time girls were forced to discontinue their formal education and devote all their time to preparing themselves for their role as bourgeois housewives and mothers. But even in school, Lewald became aware that boys were being educated for making a living, girls for making a marriage. Lewald's account of her prolonged dependency as a potentially marriagable daughter—lasting until after the death of her mother in 1843, by which time she was over thirty years old—is rich in details about the lengths to which the bourgeoisie would go to prevent its women from disgracing the family with earned income. For her father, even her modest ambition to work as a governess was an unthinkable blemish on the family reputation. For Lewald, on the other hand, her confinement to the pointlessly repetitive domestic tasks that her mother insisted were woman's lot in life, was demoralizing and demeaning—at least until she invented a system to classify it for herself as productive work:

> One day I had the idea of keeping a little book, in which I meticulously entered how many handkerchiefs I had hemmed, how many pairs of stockings I had darned, whatever I had done for the family that day by

way of sewing, dressmaking, giving music lessons. At the end of the
month I calculated the financial value of all of this. As petty as the sums
were, they gave me a certain satisfaction.[24]

In circumstances such as these, how then did a woman ever come to
publish? In the case of Fanny Lewald, whose father resisted her ambitions—but nonetheless encouraged her intellectual development—
and who did not have a husband, it was her cousin August Lewald,
editor of the liberal journal *Europa,* who published some excerpts of
her letters describing local events in 1840 and then invited her to send
him further contributions. Her cousin's gesture rekindled her interest in
her private "scribbling" as well, and at the suggestion of her father and
a brother, who gave her more criticism than encouragement, she sent
August some of her short prose for comment. Not only did he react
positively; he sent her an honorarium for its immediate publication. "I
read the letter again and again," Lewald recalls, "and I felt as if I were
perceptibly growing and gaining in stature."[25] Faced with his daughter's resolve to pursue a career even less respectable than that of
teaching and the burdens of supporting eight children, Lewald accepted the inevitable with good grace, attaching only one condition to
his consent—that her authorship remain anonymous:

> You're thirty years old and unmarried and I cannot say, "Here's a
> fortune which will keep you independent for the rest of your life." . . .
> So do what seems right to you and God grant that it be to your good.
> But I must make one express condition: No one is to know anything
> about your writing.[26]

To preserve her anonymity, honoraria for her work in the form of
checks payable "to bearer" were cashed for her by her father. Rather
than chafe under this enforced anonymity, Lewald acknowledges the
support her father, and later her husband, gave her literary activities.
Yet the modern reader of these memoirs is taken aback by the childlike
quality with which a daughter in her thirties or a wife in her fifties
espresses her appreciation for the freedom she was granted to develop
her artistic personality:

> I had my greatest reward when my father showed his pleasure with me
> and my work. Because, no matter how much I was set on indepen-
> dence and living in the world, I was still so attached to my father and
> his house that everything which I achieved seemed to acquire real
> value only through the thought of the impression it would make on my
> father.[27]

When, as a successful writer in her thirties, she finally secured her father's permission to live with an aunt who ran a boarding house in Berlin, she could hardly be said to have gained "a room of her own." Her room, little more than a passageway between the music room of her aunt and that of another boarder, was subject to a steady stream of traffic by visitors to the house, domestic servants, cooks, and cleaning equipment.[28] When, despite the rules of propriety for a single woman of the middle class, she was finally able to get a modest apartment of her own, she marveled at the sense of freedom she felt at being able to leave a manuscript lying on her desk without everyone who happened by leafing through it![29] "I was very happy that I could use my time as I saw fit, that I could do or not do as I pleased, be as neat or messy, strict or relaxed as I chose."[30]

Clues as to how women writers perceived themselves and dealt with their literary ambitions can sometimes be read out of the biographical information which they submitted to the compilers of the older reference works cited above. If we look past the amount of space devoted to the careers of their fathers and spouses, it becomes clear that very few of them had the time and space necessary for substantial creative work. Perhaps this explains why there are proportionately more successful writers among childless women and women of the nobility and upper classes. But even the unmarried aristocrat Annette von Droste-Hülshoff had long periods of silence, euphemistically referred to as "creative pauses" *(Schaffenspausen),* during the years when she had to care for an ailing mother and sister. Whether women remained unmarried or childless in order to devote themselves to their art or whether they became writers because of the lack of husband or child, they tended to depreciate the depth of their own commitment to literature. This emerges poignantly when they try to explain their motives for writing. Most claim not to write for self-satisfaction but to meet real or perceived needs of others: "destitution," "father's death," "wish of my spouse" are typical of the reasons they give to justify entering the literary marketplace, to reassure others that there is integrity and harmony between their personal and their professional lives.[31] Among married women, with the exception of a few who were able to maintain careers established before their marriage, literary productivity usually begins or is resumed around their fortieth birthday; what went on during the intervening decades is buried without a trace in a statement such as, "She dedicated herself completely to the happiness of her family."

The tendency to treat women as "other" emerges in the awkwardness with which they are "integrated" into literary histories where, in a

curious parallel to recent American history, woman's place is at the
back of the book, the end of the chapter, or in separate, but hardly
equal, chapters and books, such as Heinrich Spiero's *Geschichte der
deutschen Frauendichtung seit 1800* (History of German Women's
Writing since 1800).[32] Even the liberal Rudolf Gottschall in his
Deutsche Nationalliteratur des 19. Jahrhunderts (German National Literature of the Nineteenth Century) buries them all in a chapter entitled
"Der Frauenroman" (Women's Novels).[33] Gottschall, like most critics,
has perceptible inhibitions about using the term "Dichterin" (woman
writer): circumlocutions such as "the social novel in the hands of
woman" or "ladies of the pen" are abundant, and Lewald herself
reports about the merriment which was caused among her classmates
by a teacher's reference to her as "Verfasserin" (authoress) of an
essay, which he praised generally despite his concern that the fantasy
of the author posed a potential threat to reason and morality.[34] Helena
Szepe has already sketched the bizarre history of the term "women's
writing" *(Frauendichtung)* as an attempt to put women writers "in their
place"—an attempt which reaches all the way to the present day.[35] But
even if we reject the notion of "women's writing" as a sort of genre
unto itself, it is interesting to speculate on whether there are any other
valid connections between gender and genre. Women seem to have
preferred writing novels to drama, although the bio-bibliographies of
the "lost" women writers indicate that far more of them at least tried
their hand at drama than we ever imagined. Perhaps someone will
someday devise a method for studying their relative success as poets;
for now one can only speculate on the significance of whatever might
have languished unpublished in desk drawers. But primarily, women's
writing is identified with women's novels, beginning with the epistolary
novels of the eighteenth century, which facilitated the transition from
reader to writer for women of that era. But we need to be cautious
about the put-down implicit in many theories about women's affinity
for the novel which, like Otto Heller's,[36] are based on the assumption
that women lack the discipline for anything more serious than narrative, that the novel is less demanding intellectually or more suitable as
a pastime or an outlet for female sensibilities. What might be more
worthy of emphasis are the inhibitions surrounding the classic genres
of drama and poetry which persisted as long as women were denied
access to formal education in the classics—or, for that matter, in any
subject which did not appear to have a direct bearing on their destiny
as wife and mother. In this sense, the novel as a relatively young
genre, unburdened by theoretical mystifications, probably did seem to
offer women greater freedom of expression.

If whole spheres of "real life," such as education, government, military office, and business were closed to women, is it at all surprising that domestic contents and traces of their private autobiography would rush in to fill the "vacuum of experience"?[37] Obviously the horizons of experience were more constricted for middle-class women than for women in the working class movements and those wealthier women who had opportunities for travel and social contacts. The connection between the material, historical, and psychological reality of women's lives and the authors' sense of their place in time and society, their consciousness of the contradictions between their personal interests and societal expectations of them, is bound to be reflected in what women do—or do not—write about. Perhaps it even explains why there are so few "great" women characters in their works. It is interesting to speculate on why the most acclaimed short stories by women in the nineteenth century, Droste-Hülshoff's "Die Judenbuche" (The Jew's Beech Tree) and Ebner-Eschenbach's "Krambambuli" and "Die Freiherren von Gemperlein" (The Barons of Gemperlein), are works in which the authors have almost totally suppressed their own femaleness.

Although we cannot be concerned here with the struggle for education—one of the few aspects of women's history which has been documented—the failure of women to gain access to higher education is reflected in their consequent exclusion from the roles of literary historian and literary critic. The implications of this for the reception of women's writing in the nineteenth century have already been outlined by Gisela Brinker-Gabler, who shows how effective clichés of male-female polarity have been in legitimating male cultural dominance and denying female artistic abilities.[38] Women, having been excluded from education and artistic training, were then blamed for their educational inadequacies. Given the assumption that artistic activity is against the nature of woman, critics' use of the term "truly feminine" to describe the literary production of a woman is ambiguous at best. Brinker-Gabler demonstrates this neatly with expressions such as "ignorance of the natural limitations of woman" to characterize Bettina von Arnim; "lacking in descriptive power, but exuding soulful feeling, rich in devoted, sentient femininity" for Betty Paoli's poetry; "masculine forcefulness" and "pithiness" for Droste-Hülshoff. Sex-linked criticism is the norm, not the exception, even in the case of a female critic who feels compelled to tie her admiration for a woman's literary achievement to "her impressiveness as model wife, mother, and housewife, her inexhaustible kindness towards the suffering and the poor, her untiring obligingness."[39]

It is disappointing that the sociologists of literature have thus far shed so little new light on the question of women writers. True, they have documented qualitative as well as quantitative changes in the reading public and drawn our attention to the connection between rising industrialization and the mass marketing of literature, which made "women's literature" into yet another industry by mid-century. But so much of the information and insights provided thus far by the sociologists seems of questionable applicability in the case of women writers. What about the nexus between a publishing industry controlled almost exclusively by men, the sociocultural opportunities open to women who might be inclined to write, and the real or perceived needs of the reading audience for their works—a reading audience which was generally assumed to be female, too? What happens when a woman sets out to make money by writing for women? Who determined what women wanted to read or should read or could read? Discussions of the literary market for women's writings seem predicated on the assumption that female readers were generally aesthetically incompetent. How much did women writers concern themselves with the critical reception of their works? Lewald's account of a story she was commissioned to write for the journal *Urania* is instructive in this regard: the story she wrote met with objections of the censor, who retracted his prohibitions on the publication of the issue when he found out that the author was a woman.

> This news, which was relayed to me from Berlin with great satisfaction, annoyed me beyond measure. . . . It seems wrong to me if one uses any standard for judging a work of art besides that which is based on the work itself, or if one lets other considerations influence the evaluation as those which relate strictly to the merit of the work and its effect on others. With an artistic product, it seems to me, it should be a question of the creation and not of the creator.[40]

The seeming absence of any social structures to support women's art—be it cafes, clubs, university circles, or academies—would seem to indicate that women worked in apparent isolation from one another. Although women did form some literary clubs of their own, such as the merry Berlin "Kaffeter" of the Biedermeier period,[41] there was, to my knowledge, no important group such as the "Tunnel over the Spree" for females. Yet we are aware in some cases how much personal contact with or even the mere reading of other women's texts meant to some women writers. Here again, Lewald provides us with valuable evidence, relating how the letters of Rahel Varnhagen became a source of hope and comfort to her. She drew comfort from seeing that

Rahel, in even less auspicious times, had overcome countless obstacles and finally enjoyed the success which attended achieving according to her own needs: "Vexations, heartbreak, love troubles, the urge for free development—she knew all of this, experienced and overcame all of it through sticking to her principles and to the truth. . . . There was something masculine, solid, and audacious in her spirit which I liked very much."[42] Lewald also emphasizes how much the opportunity to actually know other women writers, such as Therese von Bacharacht and Luise Mühlbach (Klara Mundt) meant to her.

As we begin to understand that traditional literary methodologies have provided us with insufficient information and erroneous assumptions about women's relationship to the literary enterprise, we recognize the need for asking new questions, attempting a re-vision of literary history that can make that which has become invisible visible once again. At present we do not have total vision, but at least we can begin to see that women's particular situation in the social and cultural structure of the nineteenth century is a matter of history and not of nature. Our efforts to understand how this historical situation affects the perceptions and portrayals of women writers, even their work habits, are part of this process of revision. New editions of texts and authors are beginning to provide the contours of the consciousness which informed their work while improved access to historical documentation is finally shedding light on the reality of their situation in the nineteenth century. In time we shall recognize more clearly the interplay between condition and consciousness in women as writers, workers in the creative arts.

NOTES

1. Sophie Pataky, *Lexikon deutscher Frauen der Feder* (Berlin: Carl Pataky, 1898; repr. Bern: Herbert Lang, 1971).

2. Marianne Nigg, *Biographien der österreichischen Dichterinnen und Schriftstellerinnen* (Korneuburg: J. Kühlkopfs Buchhandlung, 1893).

3. Heinrich Gross, *Deutschlands Dichterinnen und Schriftstellerinnen in Wort und Bild,* 3 vols. (Berlin: Fr. Thiel, 1885).

4. Ernst Brausewetter, *Meisternovellen deutscher Frauen mit Charakteristiken der Verfasserinnen und ihren Porträts,* 2 vols. (Berlin: Schuster und Loeffler, 1897–1898).

5. Brausewetter, xi–xii.

6. Pataky, p. vi.

7. Elisabeth Friedrichs, *Die deutschsprachigen Schriftstellerinnen des 18. und 19. Jahrhunderts* (Stuttgart: J. B. Metzlersche Verlagsbuchhandlung, 1981), p. vii.

8. Franz Brümmer, *Lexikon der deutschen Dichter des 19. Jahrhunderts* (Leipzig: Reclam, 1885).

9. Cf. Barbara Duden, "Das schöne Eigentum," *Kursbuch* 47 (1977), p. 132f.

10. *Conversations-Lexikon oder Handwörterbuch für die gebildeten Stände,* (Leipzig: ⁴1815), Vol. 4, p. 211. Quoted by Karin Hausen, "Die Polarisierung der 'Geschlechtscharaktere'—eine Spiegelung der Dissoziation von Erwerbs- und Familienleben," *Sozialgeschichte der Familie in der Neuzeit Europas,* ed. Werner Conze (Stuttgart: Ernst Klett, 1976), p. 366.

11. G. Spiethoff, *Die Großmacht Presse und das deutsche Schriftstellerelend* (Düsseldorf, 1883), quoted in Gross, p. iv.

12. Immanuel Kant, *Schriften zur Anthropologie* (Frankfurt a.M.: 1977), Vol. II, p. 648.

13. Wilhelm Heinrich Riehl, *Die Naturgeschichte des Volkes als Grundlage einer deutschen Sozialpolitik,* Vol. 3: *Die Familie* (Stuttgart and Berlin: Cotta, ¹²1904), p. 9.

14. Ibid., p. 90f.

15. Dieter Barth, "Das Familienblatt—ein Phänomen der Unterhaltungspresse des 19. Jahrhunderts. Beispiele zur Gründungs- und Verlagsgeschichte," *Archiv für die Geschichte des Buchwesens* XV (1975), cols. 212–14.

16. Reinhard Wittmann, "Das literarische Leben 1848 bis 1880," *Realismus und Gründerzeit,* ed. Max Bucher et al. (Stuttgart: J. B. Metzlersche Verlagsbuchhandlung, 1976), p. 203f. Wittmann also cites official statistics for Germany in 1882, according to which only 350 of the 19,380 persons who listed writing as their main profession were women (p. 204).

17. Article "Frauenliteratur" in *Blätter für literarische Unterhaltung* I (1863), Nr. 16, p. 291, quoted by Wittmann, p. 204.

18. Fanny Lewald to Karl Gutzkow, May 15, 1848, quoted in *Frauen im Aufbruch. Frauenbriefe aus dem Vormärz und der Revolution von 1848,* ed. Fritz Böttger (Berlin: Verlag der Nation, 1977), p. 379f.

19. Marielouise Steinhauer, *Fanny Lewald, die deutsche George Sand. Ein Kapitel aus der Geschichte des Frauenromans im 19. Jahrhundert.* Diss. phil. (Berlin, 1937), p. 128f., quoted by Regula Venske, *Alltag und Emanzipation. Eine Untersuchung über die Romanautorin Fanny Lewald,* Staatsexamen (Hamburg, 1981).

20. Otto Berdrow, *Frauenbilder aus der neueren deutschen Literaturgeschichte* (Stuttgart: Greiner und Pfeiffer, ²1900), p. vii.

21. Johannes Scherr, *1848. Ein weltgeschichtliches Drama* (Leipzig, ²1875), Vol. 2, p. 175f., quoted in Renate Möhrmann, *Die andere Frau* (Stuttgart: J. B. Metzlersche Verlagsbuchhandlung, 1977), p. 6.

22. Gross, p. iv.

23. Fanny Lewald, *Meine Lebensgeschichte* (Berlin: Verlag von Otto Jahnke, 1871), Vol. I, p. 276f.

24. Lewald, Vol. II, p. 6.

25. Lewald, Vol. II, p. 396.

26. Lewald, Vol. II, p. 399.

27. Lewald, Vol. III, p. 106.

28. Lewald, Vol. III, p. 159.

29. Lewald, Vol. III, p. 332.

30. Lewald, Vol. III, p. 329.

31. Elaine Showalter, *A Literature of their Own: British Women Novelists from Brontë to Lessing* (Princeton, N.J.: Princeton University Press, 1977) p. 61.

32. Heinrich Spiero, *Geschichte der deutschen Frauendichtung seit 1800* (Leipzig: B. G. Teubner, 1913).

33. Rudolf Gottschall, *Deutsche Nationalliteratur des 19. Jahrhunderts,* 4 vols. (Breslau: E. Trewendt, ¹²1901–1902).

34. Lewald I, p. 191.

35. Helena Szepe, "The Term 'Frauendichtung'," *Die Unterrichtspraxis* IX, 1 (Spring, 1976), pp. 11–15.

36. Otto Heller, *Studies in Modern German Literature* (Boston: Ginn, 1905), pp. 231–95.

37. Showalter, p. 79.

38. Gisela Brinker-Gabler, "Die Schriftstellerin in der deutschen Literaturwissenschaft: Aspekte ihrer Rezeption von 1835 bis 1910," *Die Unterrichtspraxis* IX, 1 (Spring, 1976), pp. 15–29.

39. Lina Morgenstern, (speaking about Ottilie Wildermuth) in *Die Frauen des 19. Jahrhunderts. Biographische und culturhistorische Zeit- und Charaktergemälde* (Berlin: Verlag der deutschen Hausfrauenzeitung, 1899), Vol. II, p. 355.

40. Lewald III, p. 232.

41. Cf. Ingeborg Drewitz, *Berliner Salons Gesellschaft und Literatur zwischen Aufklärung und Industriezeitalter* (Berlin, 1965).

42. Lewald II, 216ff.

WOMEN AND THE PROFESSIONS IN IMPERIAL GERMANY

James C. Albisetti

From the foundation of the German Women's Association and the Lette Association in the mid-1860s until 1914, a major focus of the organized women's movement in Germany was the improvement of the condition of the unmarried daughters of the middle classes by obtaining employment opportunities for them. In contrast to the failure of German women in this period to win the vote, full equality before the law, or an end to officially sanctioned prostitution, the fight for increased employment opportunities achieved some noteworthy successes. Lobbying efforts, newly created technical courses, and the needs of the German economy combined by the turn of the century to bring increasing numbers of women into sales and clerical positions, social work, and the postal and railway administrations.[1]

German women also strove in this era to gain access to traditional male careers with more formal educational and certification requirements: the professions of law, medicine, and teaching. In the context of Imperial German society, the demand to open these professions to women was more than just a call for expanded job opportunities; it was an assertion that women could handle and should have access to the elite courses of education that prepared for these careers. The push for women lawyers, physicians, and teachers was thus one of the most radical claims for equality advanced by the German women's movement before 1914. As such, it aroused significant opposition, even though opening the professions to women did not involve any threat of diluting the elite with recruits from the lower classes.[2]

This paper will examine the successes and failures of German women in their struggles to gain access to these professions. I will then look more briefly at the types and limits of solidarity among professional women, the problems of combining career and marriage, and the support that young women interested in professional careers received from their families.

German women had the least success up to 1914 in their fight to open the legal profession, but this was also the struggle into which they put by far the least effort. That this would prove to be the case had not been obvious in the early years of the women's movement. In 1867, Franz von Holtzendorff, a leader in the Lette Association, had spoken of law in the same breath as medicine when discussing desirable new careers for women. Five years later, the German Women's Association discussed the views of a Dr. Wendt on the need to train female lawyers who could handle divorce cases for women and perhaps defend female criminals.[3] Even in 1888, the recently founded Women's Reform Association included the legal faculties in its petitions to the state governments calling for admission of women to the universities.[4]

By the late 1880s and early 1890s, however, other women's organizations and most of the pamphlet literature had come to concentrate primarily on improving the position of women teachers and opening medicine to women.[5] What accounts for this neglect of law? Although one can speculate that the perceived need for women lawyers was less acute than that for physicians or teachers, the most important factor appears to have been the infinitesimal likelihood of achieving success. In a society where most lawyers were civil servants and most upper-level civil servants were lawyers, even strong supporters of increased employment opportunities for women had great difficulty imagining them in legal careers. Hedwig Kettler, a leader of the Women's Reform Association, admitted in 1889 that she was not proposing that women become mayors or judges.[6] Opponents treated the prospect of female attornies as a crude joke.[7] The probability of women gaining access to legal careers was so small that male physicians, when they feared that the government was about to allow women into their ranks, tried to prevent this by insisting that all professions be treated the same, knowing full well that law would remain closed.[8]

A few German women did study law at the University of Zurich in the late nineteenth century. The first to earn a degree was Emilie Kempin, married and the mother of three, who graduated in 1887 and after several years of struggle became a *Privatdozent* in 1891. Although a Swiss citizen, Kempin was active in the debate over the new Civil Law Code in Germany.[9] Anita Augspurg also studied law in Zurich and spent one semester in Berlin after the rules regarding female auditors at Prussian universities were eased in 1896. She never intended to be a practicing attorney or judge, and ended up employing her legal knowledge in the radical wing of the feminist movement. Frieda Duensing followed the same path of study in Zurich and Berlin, returning to social work after obtaining her degree in 1903. Other pioneers worked in advisory capacities for various organizations and information bureaus, including a counseling office established by the League of German Women's Associations in 1897.[10]

The number of women studying law remained extremely small, however, even after women gained the right to matriculate at Prussian universities in 1908. For the first three years, more women enrolled in the theological than in the legal faculties; and in the winter semester of 1913–14, just fifty women were enrolled in law in all of the German universities. Bavaria was the only state to open the first or *Referendar,* examination to women before World War I; but even there the second, *Assessor,* examination remained closed.[11] The history of women in the legal profession in Imperial Germany is thus almost no history at all.

Medicine proved to be a different story, although it also had its beginnings at the University of Zurich.[12] The first two German women to become physicians, Emilie Lehmus and Franziska Tiburtius, graduated from there in 1875. In the 1880s they were followed by Agnes Bluhm, Elizabeth Winterhalter, and Anna Kuhnow; in the 1890s, by many others. Because the commerical code of the Second Reich allowed anyone to practice the "healing arts," these women could practice inside Germany. Efforts to advertise themselves as certified physicians on the basis of Swiss examinations, however, led to several conflicts with the police. Despite such harassment, Tiburtius recalled that she and Lehmus, operating a clinic in Berlin, already by the mid-1880s "stood rather firmly on conquered ground."[13]

That the practice of medicine by German women advanced beyond these small numbers and restricted rights occurred largely because of a pamphlet and petition campaign that began in the late 1880s. The work that touched off this agitation, Mathilde Weber's *Ärztinnen für Frauenkrankheiten* (Female Physicians for Women's Diseases), reveals in its title the main argument used to justify admission of women to the medical profession. The largest of the many petitions of these years, which attracted about 55,000 signatures, called explicitly for "female physicians for women's diseases."[14] As I have argued in detail elsewhere, this argument had the greatest effect on the officials in Prussia and the Reich who initiated the action by the Bundesrat that opened medical certification to women in 1899.

In the years immediately following this action, medicine attracted a disproportionate number of the early *Abiturientinnen* in Germany.

Fifty-three of the 111 women who graduated from Helene Lange's preparatory course in Berlin between 1896 and 1906 chose medicine as their field of study. At the University of Freiburg in Baden, where full matriculation was opened to women with the *Abitur* in 1900, the medical faculty enrolled more than half of the female students until 1909. By the winter semester of 1913–14, 859 women were studying medicine at German universities. Of the 125 female physicians who responded to a survey published in 1912, the predominant number had specialized in gynecology or pediatrics, so that the perceived need for women to treat women was at least to some extent being met.[15]

Female physicians in Imperial Germany employed their skills in a wide variety of situations. Tiburtius and Lehmus ran their own clinic for women in Berlin, where, by 1892, 17,000 patients had received treatment. Among the other women trained in Switzerland, Agnes Bluhm and Jenny Springer worked part-time for health insurance organizations for female employees; Sieglinde Stier had a position on the staff of a mental hospital; and Agnes Hacker became, in 1900, the first female physician hired by the Berlin police force. As of 1905, at least three cities employed women as school physicians.[16]

That teaching was the profession that attracted the most women in Imperial Germany is hardly surprising. Yet it is easy to forget how late the rise of the woman teacher in Germany was. Two studies of the professionalization of elementary schoolteaching in Prussia, one covering the period through 1850 and the other that from 1850 to 1880, include not a word about the role of women—a neglect justifiable in the first case but not totally so in the second, because by 1878 there were approximately 1,500 women teachers in the Prussian elementary schools.[17] According to Marie Calm, prospects and pay for women were so poor around 1870 that half of those qualified to teach sought their livelihood abroad. Many others, including Helene Lange, began their careers as governesses; as late as 1899, twenty-six percent of women teachers in Germany were employed by private families.[18]

In Catholic areas, the tradition of teaching nuns made for a somewhat greater openness to women in the schools. In Bavaria, a ministerial decree of 1836 even suggested that girls should be taught primarily by women. The lack of adequate training facilities and sufficient candidates prevented the achievement of this goal, but Munich alone had 118 women teachers by 1869.[19] In Germany as a whole, Catholic women outnumbered Protestants among elementary teachers until at least the 1890s.[20]

The number of women teachers in both the elementary and the higher girls' schools did grow substantially during the Second Reich.

By 1900, 22,000 women taught in German elementary schools, along-side of 122,000 men; in Prussia alone, there were 13,700 female and 74,500 male elementary teachers in 1901.[21] In large part, this increase occurred because the low pay and status of these positions failed to attract enough men to fill them, a situation especially acute during the 1870s and again around the turn of the century.[22] Both the male elementary teachers who were struggling to be recognized as *Gebilde-ten* and the university-trained men in the girls' schools who were striving for equal pay and rank with Gymnasium teachers tended to view the increasing number of women in their ranks as a major obsta-cle to their ambitions.[23] No common external threat helped to over-come this hostility between men and women teachers in Germany as the fight against clerical influence did in France; in fact, the overrep-resentation of Catholic women among the elementary teachers caused many men to fear a return of clerical influence in the schools.[24]

The two- or three-year "seminars," or normal schools, that trained women teachers recruited their students almost exclusively from the higher girls' schools attended by the daughters of the upper middle class. Those seminar graduates who took positions in the elementary schools were thus generally from a higher social class than their male colleagues, which often proved to be another source of conflict.[25] In the early years of the twentieth century, men teachers frequently tried to demonstrate that women teachers were no less expensive in the long run than men, arguing that they took more sick days and more often suffered mental breakdowns than did their male colleagues. Hostility between men and women came to a head at the annual German Teachers' Convention in 1906, where extremely critical re-marks by one speaker caused women to walk out. This protest eventu-ally led to adoption of a conciliatory resolution stressing the equal value of male and female teachers.[26]

For women teaching in the higher girls' schools, the main problem was not gaining acceptance, but escaping from a burdensome second-class citizenship that stemmed in part from prejudice, in part from their limited training. In the mid-1890s, women comprised 75 percent of the teachers in the private girls' schools, but just 33 percent in the public schools, those run by the city or state governments. At this time, just one out of 125 public girls' schools in Prussia had a woman as director; for the Reich as a whole, over 90 percent of public schools were headed by men.[27] Women in the public schools usually taught only in the lower grades, instructing the older girls only in subjects such as needlework, singing, gymnastics, and occasionally foreign lan-guages. Even in the private schools, close to 90 percent of which were run by women, women teachers in the upper grades were severely hampered by their seminar training, which ended at age eighteen or nineteen and often included no study of science.[28]

The fight against this second-class citizenship necessarily became a fight for more advanced training for women teachers. Helene Lange's famous "Yellow Brochure" of 1887 centered on the need for such training, as well as on the desirability of having women play a greater role in the education of German girls.[29] Within the next few years, two other prominent women educators, Auguste Sprengel, the director of a public girls' school in Mecklenburg, and Anna Vorwerk, the head of a private school and seminar in Brunswick, echoed this call for more advanced education for women teachers. All three agreed at this time that women teachers should not attend the existing universities with their strong emphasis on scholarship. They called instead for *Frauenhochschulen* that would combine the pedagogical training of the seminars with more advanced work in specific disciplines.[30]

Prussia proved to be the state most responsive to these demands, supporting new courses and creating new examinations that enabled women to become *Oberlehrerinnen,* or upper-level teachers, a possibility not open to men trained at seminars. The first of these courses began in 1888 as an adjunct to the Victoria Lyceum in Berlin.[31] The second, founded by Anna Vorwerk and Auguste Sprengel, opened five years later in Göttingen, and was soon followed by others in Königsberg, Bonn, and Breslau. A special advanced course for Catholic women teachers was established in Münster in 1899.[32] Although all these courses were located in university towns and employed well-known professors, at the start they all operated independently of the universities.

By 1906, 408 women had taken the *Oberlehrerin* examination, which required two fields of preparation. Only 6 women chose to be tested in physics and chemistry, 19 in biology, and 47 in mathematics. In contrast, 239 took the examination in German, 154 in history, 131 in English, and 124 in French.[33] They thus gravitated overwhelmingly toward the literary fields for which the higher girls' schools and the seminars had predisposed them. It appears that those German women interested in science were pursuing careers in medicine rather than teaching.

Passing the *Oberlehrerin* examination did not mean instant promotion. Only 60 of 207 public girls' schools in Prussia in 1906 had two or more *Oberlehrerinnen* positions, 76 had one, and 71 did not have any. In the upper three grades of the public schools and the seminars, men still outnumbered women 1,160 to 221. Increasingly aggravating to the women with advanced training was the fact that they did not always receive higher pay than women who had attended only the seminars, and often earned less than men with seminar training. They could not claim equality with men who possessed university degrees, but in January 1906 they petitioned the Ministry of Education to set their salaries at 75 to 80 percent of those for academically trained men.[34]

By this time, however, these *Oberlehrerinnen* were about to be rendered obsolete by women with an *Abitur* and a university education. Shortly after the opening of medical certification to women in 1899, the board of directors of Helene Lange's Gymnasium course had petitioned the Prussian government also to allow women to take the examination *pro facultate docendi*. In the first years of the century, Saxony and Bavaria took this step before Prussia did, although in neither state was any woman ready to attempt the examination. Action in Prussia came in response to the application of Thekla Freytag, a graduate of Lange's course who had been studying mathematics. Her father, a high-level official in Berlin, wrote a letter to Minister of Education Konrad von Studt in March 1904 that resulted in her being admitted to the examination. Several other individual cases followed before a decree opened the examination to all qualified women in December 1905.[35] Applicants were informed that although the examination was the same given to men, they would not obtain the qualification to teach in the boys' schools that it normally gave.

After Prussia established regular courses for girls that led to the *Abitur* and opened matriculation to women in 1908, it also decided to phase out the special courses and examinations for *Oberlehrerinnen*. Women who had graduated from the seminars and taught for several years, however, now won the right to matriculate in the philosophical faculties and to take the examination *pro facultate docendi* without having to earn an *Abitur*. This "fourth way" to the universities, in addition to the traditional Gymnasium, Realgymnasium, and Ober-realschule, was not welcomed by many of the feminist leaders. Helene Lange wondered if it was not designed to discredit study by women, and was convinced that the government hoped through this measure to preserve more of the seminars and discourage the founding of Gymnasien for girls. Despite this hostility, however, in 1912 there were 787 women enrolled in the philosophical faculties who had chosen this route, compared to 772 women with an *Abitur*.[36]

No women reached the highest pinnacle of the educational structure in Imperial Germany, a university chair.[37] In Prussia, only two cases received serious attention as possible precedent setters, both at the

University of Bonn. In 1900, Adeline Rittershaus-Bjarnason, a scholar in old Scandinavian literature, applied to the university curator at Bonn about becoming a *Privatdozent.* After being directed to the ministry in Berlin and from there back to the university, Rittershaus did succeed in having the question of a woman *Privatdozent* brought before the philosophical faculty. It rejected the idea by a vote of sixteen to fourteen, without going into the specifics of her qualifications. Rittershaus later became an instructor at the University of Zurich.[38]

By 1906 the faculty at Bonn had changed its mind, and supported the *Habilitation* of Countess Marie von Linden, a zoologist who was already employed in a laboratory there. On this occasion, the Ministry of Education consulted all the university faculties about the general question of female professors, receiving a wide variety of responses. It decided in the end to reject the proposal; but Linden received a raise, the title of professor, and directorship of a parasitology laboratory.[39]

There are a variety of intriguing instances of solidarity among professional women in the Second Reich. Some received financial support for their education in the form of fellowships granted by the German Women's Association. Among them were Marie von Linden, who had help in getting her fellowship from Mathilde Weber, and Hildegard Ziegler, who studied in Zurich before becoming, in 1895, the first woman to pass the Gymnasium *Abitur.*[40] The most ambitious project to give financial aid to women students, however, never came to fruition. After the Prussian decree of 1908—opening matriculation to women—had allowed professors to exclude women from their courses in "exceptional circumstances," Ottilie von Hansemann offered a 200,000 Mark scholarship fund to the University of Berlin on the condition that this clause be rescinded. The Ministry of Education could not be bribed, however, and after several years she withdrew the offer.[41]

Female physicians in Germany did not form their own organization until after World War I, but they clearly had an informal network before then. An important link in this network was Marie Heim-Voegtlin, the first female physician in Switzerland, who for many years steered women who graduated from the medical faculty in Zurich to the only German physician willing to give them further training, Franz Winckel, who worked first in Dresden and later in Munich.[42] Women in private medical practice apparently received much of their business from other single women with careers. Rahel Straus described her clientele in Munich as being "primarily working women from the more educated classes: teachers, secretaries, upper-level office workers."[43]

Women teachers in the Second Reich did establish a number of self-help organizations. As early as 1875 the German Pension Institute for Women Teachers and Educators was founded under the protection of Crown Princess Victoria; by 1895, it had accumulated retirement funds of 4,500,000 Marks and was paying pensions to 377 women. Bavarian teachers created a similar organization in 1890. As of the mid-1890s, retirement homes for women teachers existed in at least seven locations; and Anna Vorwerk would soon found one for graduates of her seminar in Wolfenbüttel. All these groups combined in 1895 to establish the "General German League of Charitable Institutions for Academically and Technically Trained Women Teachers."[44]

The sense of common endeavor and purpose among women teachers received a strong boost from the journals and organizations founded in the 1880s and 1890s. When Marie Loeper-Housselle began to publish *Die Lehrerin in Schule und Haus (The Woman Teacher in School and House)*, she admitted that women teachers did not yet constitute a conscious community; but for Gertrud Bäumer and countless other women this journal began to forge such a consciousness. In 1885 as well, Pauline Herber founded the Association of Catholic Women Teachers, which began publishing its own journal three years later. Of the greatest importance was the creation in 1890 by Helene Lange and others of the German Women Teachers' Association, which grew to almost 30,000 members by 1910.[45] In contrast to the organizations of men teachers, these women's groups embraced teachers at both elementary and secondary schools.

This solidarity did begin to break down somewhat as the level of education among women teachers became more varied. The first *Oberlehrerinnen* fought to raise their pay above that of their less well-trained colleagues; and, as might be expected, women who passed the examination *pro facultate docendi* demanded a similar advantage over the older *Oberlehrerinnen*. In their petitions for full matriculation rights, women with the *Abitur* often argued that less qualified women auditors should be excluded from the universities. This elitist stance also manifested itself in the hostility to the "fourth way" that allowed seminar graduates to study in the philosophical faculties after 1909: the German Women's Association refused to give its fellowships to women who took this path to the universities.[46] After the turn of the century, an increasing sentiment developed in favor of separating the seminars for teachers in the elementary schools from those preparing women for the higher girls' schools, a change carried through in Prussia after 1908.[47]

Several disagreements arose between the women whose interests centered on their own studies and careers and more radical elements in the feminist movement. Helene Lange reports that around 1907 Minna Cauer and Anita Augspurg complained about "ungrateful women students" who were not getting involved with feminism. Lange dismissed this charge as unfair, but Rahel Straus's explicit refusal as a student to join the Association for Women's Education and University Studies suggests the problem was a real one.[48]

The issue of coeducation in secondary schools rather seriously divided the more radical feminists and the women teachers. In the early years of the twentieth century, Baden, Württemberg, Hesse, and Saxony began allowing girls into some boys' secondary schools, largely to save the expense of separate schools for a small number of girls. In 1903, the Association for Women's Education and University Studies declared itself in favor of universal coeducation. For women teachers who had been struggling to win greater control over girls' education, however, coeducation seemed to promise the reversal of all their gains, because it was extremely unlikely that women would be able to teach in coeducational secondary schools. In 1908 the Association of Catholic Women Teachers spoke out in opposition to any coeducation. Not until 1913 did the Women Teachers' Association make a declaration, following Lange's lead in accepting coeducation as a supplement to single-sex schools only in areas where girls did not have their own secondary schools.[49]

A similar disagreement arose over the issue of married women continuing to teach, something that was banned in almost all the German states. Feminists began fighting against this form of discrimination in the first years of the century, but found little support among the teachers themselves. That Catholic women did not frequently challenge the Church's emphasis on celibacy for lay as well as religious teachers is understandable, but most Protestant teachers also rejected the possibility of combining their "calling" with marriage. Practical considerations also played a role in this defense of the discriminatory status quo: single teachers feared that married women would create more competition for jobs and might, by treating their work as of less importance than their families, lower the image and status of all women teachers. Helene Lange took a middle position on this issue, condemning what she saw as an unjustified restriction on teachers' personal lives but arguing that women generally could not and should not combine a teaching career and marriage.[50]

Female physicians could marry; and of the 125 who answered the survey in 1912, 78 were single, 42 were married, and 5 had been widowed. Only 4 had abandoned their careers upon marriage. A study of 1,078 women who matriculated in Prussian universities between 1908 and 1912, published in 1917, found 346 to be married, but only 121 of these still active in their careers. Of the other 225 married women, 181 had dropped out of the university at the time of marriage, and thus were not teachers giving up their jobs, a practice that was suspended during World War I in any event. Of the 732 single women in the survey, 528 had completed their studies and were still active in their professions.[51]

If most professional women in Imperial Germany did not have husbands and children to support them in their jobs, this does not mean that they did not have familial support when they decided to pursue careers. One can certainly find cases of a Helene Lange orphaned at sixteen, a Ricarda Huch able to study in Zurich only because her father was in Brazil and could not prevent it, or a Marie von Linden who pursued her degree at Tübingen against her father's will.[52] Yet more striking is the number of professional women who had parents or relatives who were both socially prominent and sympathetic to their career aspirations. Linden herself had an uncle who, as a minister of state in Württemberg, helped open the doors of Tübingen to her. Franziska Tiburtius, who at first taught German at girls' schools in England, had a brother who was a physician and who stimulated and supported her decision to study medicine. Rahel Straus, whose father had died while she was a girl, had an uncle who paid for her studies. Anna Vorwerk, still living at home in her late twenties, received significant financial and moral support from her father in the founding and running of her school.[53]

Thekla Freytag was not the only professional woman to receive important help from her father in dealing with the Prussian bureaucracy. Something similar happened to Else von der Leyen, one of the first graduates of Lange's Gymnasium course and then one of the first two female physicians to be trained entirely in Germany. In 1898 her father, a *Wirklicher Geheim-Oberregierungsrat* in the Ministry of Public Works, successfully put pressure on Minister of Education Robert Bosse to admit her to the preliminary examinations in medicine on the basis of audited courses before the Bundesrat allowed certification of female physicians on this basis. Among other early graduates of Lange's course who entered medicine, Frida Busch's father was a professor of surgery at Bonn, Margarete Breymann's and Hermine Edenhuizen's fathers were practicing physicians, and Clara Bender's father was, as mayor of Breslau, instrumental in the founding of a girls' Gymnasium in that city.[54] Käthe Windscheid, the first German woman granted a doctorate at Heidelberg, was the daughter of a law professor. Hildegard Ziegler's grandfathers were both Gymnasium directors, her mother and one grandmother had their teaching certificates, and her aunt taught at the Königin-Luise-Stiftung. The first thirteen women to pass the examination *pro facultate docendi* in Prussia included not only Thekla Freytag, but also Carola Barth, the daughter of the liberal politician Theodor Barth, and three noblewomen—Christine von Wedel, Elise von Keudell, and Countess Gabriele von Wartensleben.[55] When the interests of their own daughters were at stake, many members of the German elite clearly proved to be very favorably inclined toward increased educational and employment opportunities for women.

The record of women in the professions in Imperial Germany is thus an ambiguous one. The desired expansion of educational and employment opportunities was achieved, something worth noting for those who overemphasize the resistance to change in this era. Yet the continued exclusion of women from university teaching and the legal profession indicates that educated women were far from achieving full equality. The rapidly growing number of women teachers and the emergence of female physicians at least partially satisfied the perceived need to have girls and women taught and treated by members of their own sex, a need expressed more often and more urgently around 1890 than it had been before. Even these female physicians and teachers, however, were restricted to the handling of their own sex in a way that their male colleagues were not.

This last fact points to perhaps the greatest paradox about professional women in Imperial Germany. Their successful efforts to obtain and protect a sphere in which to work led them to adopt strategies and accept compromises that left them in positions of inferiority within their own professions. To feminists interested in a broader pursuit of equality, actions such as the rejection of coeducational secondary schools and of marriage by most women teachers represented an unwarranted sacrifice of long-term goals to short-term gains. For the active professionals, however, self-interest and sisterhood did not always coincide.

NOTES

1. See Louise Otto-Peters, *Das erste Vierteljahrhundert des Allgemeinen Deutschen Frauenvereins* (Leipzig, 1890); Lilly Hauff, *Der Letteverein in der Geschichte der Frauenbewegung* (Berlin, 1928); and Lily Braun, *Die Frauenfrage* (Leipzig, 1901), esp. pp. 99–171.

2. Konrad Jarausch has recently demonstrated that the first generation of women students came "from more elitist backgrounds, and from more college-educated families," than their male colleagues: *Students, Society, and Politics in Imperial Germany* (Princeton, 1982), p. 109.

3. Franz von Holtzendorff, *Die Verbesserungen in der gesellschaftlichen und wirtschaftlichen Stellung der Frau* (Berlin, 1867), p. 23; Otto-Peters,p. 25.

4. Gustav Cohn, "Die deutsche Frauenbewegung," *Deutsche Rundschau* 86 (Jan.–Mar. 1896), p. 411.

5. See James C. Albisetti, "Could Separate Be Equal? Helene Lange and Women's Education in Imperial Germany," *History of Education Quarterly* 22, 3 (Fall, 1982), pp. 301–17; idem, "The Fight for Female Physicians in Imperial Germany," *Central European History* 15, 2 (June 1982), pp. 99–123.

6. Views of Felix Dahn and Wilhelm Lexis in Arthur Kirchoff, ed., *Die akademische Frau* (Berlin, 1897), pp. 20, 206; Hermann Grimm, "Zur Frauenfrage," *Deutsche Rundschau* 74 (Jan.–Mar. 1893), p. 311; Hedwig Kettler, *Was wird aus unseren Töchtern?* (Weimar, 1889), p. 32.

7. See the famous caricature of Jeanne Chauvin, the first woman admitted to the bar in France, putting forward her "last and best evidence"—her breasts. This was recently reproduced in Eda Sagarra, *An Introduction to Nineteenth-Century Germany* (Harlow, 1980), p. 249.

8. *Deutsche Medizinische Wochenschrift* 24 (1898), pp. 435–36.

9. Elise Oelsner, *Die Leistungen der deutschen Frau in den letzten vierhundert Jahren auf wissenschaftlichem Gebiete* (Guhrau, 1894), pp. 113–14; Schweizerischer Verband der Akademikerinnen, *Das Frauenstudium an den Schweizer Hochschulen* (Zurich, 1928), pp. 34–39.

10. Lida Gustava Heymann, with Anita Augspurg, *Erlebtes—Erschautes: Deutsche Frauen kämpfen für Freiheit, Recht, und Frieden, 1850–1940,* ed. Margrit Twellmann (Meisenheim am Glan, 1972), pp. 17–19; Ricarda Huch, et al., *Frieda Duensing: Ein Buch der Erinnerungen* (Berlin, 1922), p. 231; Helene Lange and Gertrud Bäumer, eds., *Handbuch der Frauenbewegung,* Vol. V: *Die deutsche Frau im Beruf* (Leipzig, 1906), pp. 251–52.

11. Zentrales Staatsarchiv, Historische Abteilung II, Merseburg, Kultusministerium, Rep. 76 Va, Sekt. 1, Tit. VIII, No. 8, Vol. XIII; Gerda Caspary, *Die Entwicklungsgrundlagen für die soziale und psychische Verselbständigung der bürgerlichen deutschen Frau um die Jahrhundertwende* (Heidelberg, 1933), p. 76; Laetitia Boehm, "Von den Anfängen des akademischen Frauenstudiums in Deutschland," *Historisches Jahrbuch* 77 (1958), p. 319.

12. See Albisetti, "Female Physicians," for a more detailed treatment of the fight to open the medical profession.

13. Ilse Szagunn, "Agnes Bluhm—Ärztin und Forscherin," *Die Ärztin* 16 (1940), p. 5; Marie Elisabeth Lüders, *Fürchte dich nicht* (Cologne, 1963), p. 45; Franziska Tiburtius, *Erinnerungen einer Achtzigjährigen* (2nd, enl. ed.; Berlin, 1925), p. 196.

14. Mathilde Weber, *Ärztinnen für Frauenkrankheiten: Eine ethische und eine sanitäre Notwendigkeit* (Tübigen, 1888); Reichstag, *Anlagen,* 8th legislature, 2nd session, p. 778.

15. Gertrud Bäumer, *Geschichte der Gymnasialkurse für Frauen zu Berlin* (Berlin, 1906), unpaginated appendix; Ernst Theodor Nauck, *Das Frauenstudium an der Universität Freiburg im Breisgau* (Freiburg im Breisgau, 1953), p. 28; Caspary, p. 75; Helenefrederike Stelzner, "Der weibliche Arzt: Nach gemeinsam mit Dr. Margarete

Breymann gepflogenen statistischen Erhebungen," *Deutsche Medizinische Wochenschrift* 38 (1912), p. 1,290.

16. Oelsner, p. 29; Szagunn, p. 5; Annemarie Blumenthal, "Diskussionen um das medizinische Frauenstudium in Berlin," (Diss., Free University of Berlin, 1965), pp. 27, 22; Hauff, p. 376; Stelzner, p. 1,243.

17. Anthony LaVopa, *Prussian Schoolteachers: Profession and Office, 1763–1848* (Chapel Hill, 1980); Helmut Meyer, "Das Selbstverständnis des Volksschullehrers in der zweiten Hälfte des 19. Jahrhunderts (1850–1880)," (Diss., University of Münster, 1965); Margrit Twellmann, *Die deutsche Frauenbewegung: Ihre Anfänge und erste Entwicklung, 1843–1889* (2 vols.; Meisenheim am Glan, 1972), 1:104.

18. Marie Calm, *Die Stellung der deutschen Lehrerin* (Berlin, 1870), p. 10; Helene Lange, *Lebenserinnerungen* (Berlin, 1930), pp. 94–95; Ilse Gahlings and Ella Moering, *Die Volksschullehrerin: Sozialgeschichte und Gegenwartslage* (Heidelberg, 1961), p. 29.

19. Helmut Beilner, *Die Emanzipation der bayerischen Lehrerin* (Munich, 1971), pp. 26–31, 36–38; Joseph Heigenmooser, *Überblick der geschichtlichen Entwicklung des höheren Mädchenschulwesens in Bayern bis zur Gegenwart* (Berlin, 1905), p. 68. Joanne Schneider indicates that there was a similar instruction in 1804: "An Historical Examination of Women's Education in Bavaria," (Diss., Brown University, 1977), p. 33.

20. Pauline Herber, *Das Lehrerinnenwesen in Deutschland* (Kempten and Munich, 1906), p. 40.

21. Wilhelm Karl Bach, *Die Lehrerinnenfrage* (Elberfeld, 1905), p. 9; Erich Dauzenroth, *Kleine Geschichte der Mädchenbildung* (Ratingen bei Düsseldorf, 1971), p. 153.

22. Beilner, p. 41; Gahlings and Moering, pp. 24, 58; Eduard Cauer, *Die höhere Mädchenschule und die Lehrerinnenfrage* (Berlin, 1878), p. 18; Elisabeth Stoffels, *Die Lehrerinnenfrage* (Paderborn, 1906), p. 11; Christine von Wedel, "Der Oberlehrermangel an Mädchengymnasien," *Preussische Jahrbücher* 138 (1909), p. 88.

23. Gahlings and Moering, p. 55; Beilner, p. 42; Otto Sommer, "Die Entwicklung des höheren Mädchenschulwesens in Deutschland," in Joseph Wychgram, ed., *Handbuch des höheren Mädchenschulwesens* (Leipzig, 1897), p. 31.

24. Gahlings and Moering, p. 56. For comparisons, see Peter V. Meyers, "From Conflict to Cooperation: Men and Women Teachers in the Belle Epoque," *Historical Reflections* 7 (1980), pp. 493–505; and Barry H. Bergen, "Only a Schoolmaster: Gender, Class, and the Effort to Professionalize Elementary Teaching in England, 1870–1910," *History of Education Quarterly* 22, 1 (Spring 1982), pp. 1–21.

25. Beilner, p. 43; Gahlings and Moering, pp. 45–47.

26. Stoffels, pp. 3–4; Bach, p. 20; Ralf Wichmann, *Geistige Leistungsfähigkeit und Nervosität bei Lehrern und Lehrerinnen* (Halle, 1905), passim; Gahlings and Moering, pp. 51–54, 60–61.

27. Jürgen Zinnecker, *Sozialgeschichte der Mädchenbildung* (Weinheim and Basel, 1973), p. 48; Emmy Beckmann, *Die Entwicklung der höheren Mädchenbildung in Deutschland von 1870–1914* (Berlin, 1936), p. 64; Helene Lange, *Entwicklung und Stand des höheren Mädchenschulwesens in Deutschland* (Berlin, 1893), p. 13.

28. Lange, *Entwicklung*, p. 13; Schneider, p. 33; Elisabeth Meyn-von Westenholz, *Der Allgemeine Deutsche Lehrerinnenverein in der Geschichte der deutschen Mädchenbildung* (Berlin, 1936), p. 70.

29. See Albisetti, "Could Separate Be Equal?"

30. Beckmann, p. 41; Martha Genzmer, *Anna Vorwerk: Ein Lebensbild* (Wolfenbüttel, 1910), p. 280. See also Auguste Sprengel, *Erinnerungen aus meinem Leben* (Berlin, 1932).

31. Material on the course at the Victoria Lyceum in ZStA-II, KM, Rep. 76 VI, Sekt. 14, Gen. ee, No. 17, Vols. I and II.

32. Genzmer, pp. 246–97; Maria Kley, *Die Studien- und Anstellungsverhältnisse der Oberlehrerinnen* (Bonn, 1907), p. 1; Hildegard Bogerts, *Bildung und berufliches Selbstverständnis lehrenden Frauen in der Zeit von 1885–1920* (Frankfurt and Berne, 1977), p. 129. For one woman's experience in such courses, see Marie Martin, "Meine Studienzeit in Göttingen," *Zeitschrift für weibliche Bildung* 26 (1898), pp. 422–29.

33. Kley, pp. 1, 5.

34. Data in ZStA, KM, Rep. 76 VI, Sekt. 1, Gen. ee, No. 5, Vol. IV; petitions of the Verband akademisch gebildeter und studierender Lehrerinnen and of the Verein katholisch deutscher Lehrerinnen, ibid., No. 5B, Vol. I.

35. Petition of 6 Dec. 1899 in ZStA-II, KM, Rep. 76 Va, Sekt. 1, Tit. VIII, No. 8, Vol. VII; reports from Saxony and Bavaria (Feb. and Mar. 1904), Thekla Freytag to Studt (26 Jan. 1904), *Senatspräsident* Freytag to Studt (7 Mar. 1904), memorandum by Studt (9 Mar. 1904), and Studt to Thekla Freytag (19 Mar. 1904), in Rep. 76 VI, Sekt. 1, Gen. z, No. 134, adhib. A, Vol. I.

36. Helene Lange, *Kampfzeiten: Aufsätze und Reden aus vier Jahrzehnten* (2 vols.; Berlin, 1928), 1:342–49; Judith Herrmann, *Die deutsche Frau in akademischen Berufen* (Leipzig, 1915), p. 32.

37. Dr. Elisabeth Altmann-Gottheiner habilitated in 1908 at the Handelshochschule in Mannheim, but this was not a true university: Caspary, p. 76.

38. Adeline Rittershaus-Bjarnason, "Kann eine Frau in Deutschland Privatdozentin werden?" *Frauen-Korrespondenz*, 11 and 14 Feb. 1902, copies of which are in ZStZ-II, KM, Rep. 76 Va, Sekt. 1, Tit. VIII, No. 8, adhib. II.

39. All materials, including rejection letter of 28 May 1908, ibid., adhib. III. See also Johanna Kretschmer, "Marie von Linden—die erste Studentin der Universität Tübingen," *Attempto* 33/34 (L969), pp. 78–88; and Elke Rupp, *Der Beginn des Frauenstudiums an der Universität Tübingen* (Tübingen, 1978), pp. 32–43.

40. Otto-Peters, pp. vii–viii, 50, 63, 71; Rupp, p. 38; Hildegard Wegscheider-Ziegler, *Weite Welt im engen Spiegel* (Berlin, 1953), p. 23.

41. Hermann, p. 31; Gerda Stücklen, *Untersuchung über die soziale und wirtschaftliche Lage der Studentinnen* (Göttingen, 1916), p. 65. See also the letter from Minister of Education von Trott zu Solz to Hansemann, 20 Nov. 1913, in ZStA-II, KM, Rep. 76 Va, Sekt. 1, Tit. VIII, No. 8, Vol. XIII.

42. Statement by Winckel in Kirchhoff, p, 124. See also Johanna Siebel, *Das Leben von Frau Dr. Marie Heim-Vögtlin* (Zurich, 1919).

43. Rahel Straus, *Wir lebten in Deutschland: Erinnerungen einer deutschen Jüdin, 1880–1933* (Stuttgart, 1961), p. 139.

44. Gotthold Kreyenburg, "Ein Kapitel aus der deutschen Frauenfrage," *Preussische Jahrbücher* 84 (1896), pp. 158–65; Beilner, p. 47; Genzmer, pp. 106–8, 219–32.

45. Bogerts, pp. 42–49; Gertrud Bäumer, *Im Licht der Erinnerung* (Tübingen, 1953), p. 126; Meyn, p. 170 and passim; Beilner, pp. 46–47, 78.

46. Various petitions dating from 1900 through 1902 in ZStA-II, KM, Rep. 76 Va, Sekt. 1, Tit. VIII, No. 8, Vols. VII–IX; clipping about the fellowships, from 1909, in Vol. XII.

47. Pauline Herber, "Vorschläge zu einem System der Vor- und Fortbildung der

Lehrerin für Volksschulen, mittlere und höhere Mädchenschulen," *Frauenbildung* 4 (1905), pp. 495–511; Gahlings and Moering, pp. 47, 57, 30.

48. Lange, *Kampfzeiten*, 1:324–25; Straus, p. 95.

49. Beckmann, pp. 172–75; Lange, *Die Frauenbewegung in ihren modernen Problemen* (2nd ed.; Leipzig, 1914), pp. 60–63.

50. Bogerts, p. 64; Beilner, pp. 160–63; Gahlings and Moering, pp. 62, 76–87.

51. Stelzner, p. 1,243; Ernst Bumm, *Über das Frauenstudium* (Berlin, 1917), pp. 13–14.

52. Lange, *Lebenserinnerungen*, p. 68; Ricarda Huch, *Autobiographische Schriften* (n. p., n. d.), p. 160; Rupp, p. 38.

53. Rupp, pp. 32–37; Tiburtius, pp. 108–10; Straus, p. 87; Genzmer, p. 39.

54. Note by Bosse in ZStA-II, KM, Rep. 76 Va, Sekt. 1, Tit. VIII, No. 8, Vol. VII; curricula vitae of women applying for the *Abitur* examination in Rep. 76 VI, Sekt. 1, Gen. z, No. 134, Vols. I and II.

55. Caspary, p. 74; Wegscheider-Ziegler, pp. 10, 18; list of applicants in ZstA-II, KM, Rep. 76 VI, Sekt. 1, Gen. z, No. 134, adhib A, Vol. I.

MOTHERHOOD AND WORK
THE CONCEPT OF THE MISUSE OF WOMEN'S ENERGY, 1895–1905

Kay Goodman

The most recent phase of the women's movement in the United States began with women rejecting the oppression they experienced in the home. Their roles as housewives and mothers were felt to confine and enslave, and they left them to fight for jobs, for education, for equal pay, and for equal rights. Work in the private sphere was seen to imprison; work in the public sphere to emancipate. Not always, but often the values of the marketplace supplanted those of the home as women struggled to prove their personal worth in a culture which had devalued the work performed in the home as well as the skills and talents which were appropriate to it. Now the realm of the family is claimed by the New Right. The space women fled when they demanded their right to personal growth is occupied by those who claim motherhood and love for human life as their own unique preserve.

As this important lacuna in feminist theory becomes all too apparent, feminists themselves are voicing their concern with these traditional areas of women's activity. Betty Friedan has announced a "Second Stage." Others like Mary O'Brien and Jill Lewis are evolving theories to "renegotiate the politics of the reproductive sphere," redefining motherhood to include public relationships, and contemplating the implications of genetic engineering for innovative forms of family life.[1] Simultaneously French feminists like Julia Kristeva, Hélène Cixous, and Luce Irigaray who proclaim the "future of difference" are becoming increasingly popular in the United States. This combined theoretical shift is of major significance, for with it comes a new emphasis on difference and the positive evaluation of female or motherly qualities rather than androgyny and equality.

We want to address the challenge of this debate boldly, with all the energy, imagination, and compassion called for by such a topic, but because of our history, we must also be exceedingly careful to set our terms clearly. We want to bear in mind the history of our mothers, grandmothers, and great-grandmothers; as mothers and as feminists; both in this country and elsewhere. What follows is a preliminary survey of an earlier German movement to bring feminists back to a discussion of motherhood and to assert a cultural mission for women.

When Katharine Anthony set about in 1915 to mediate the achievements and goals of the women's movement in Germany and Scandinavia for the American movement, she highlighted the differences between them.[2] She characterized the Anglo-Saxon movement by the slogan, "Votes for Women," and the Germanic one by "Mutterschutz" (protection for mothers). Each direction, she found, had defined itself at roughly the same time: the suffrage movement with Emmeline Pankhurst's demands of 1905 and "Mutterschutz" with Ruth Bré's founding of the *Bund für Mutterschutz* (League for the Protection of Mothers) in 1904, after she had read the writings of the Swedish feminist, Ellen Key. Although she juxtaposed English and American agitation for the franchise with continental efforts to revolutionize education and morality, Anthony observed at base a more fundamental agreement on feminist goals and viewed the sister movements as the two eyes of one face: each possessing its own particular perspective while the combined gaze yielded a vision of unique depth.[3]

Anthony was as correct in pointing to differing perspectives as she was in pointing to the role of Ellen Key, although Key's impact was far more widespread than her identification with the radical "Mutterschutz" would lead us to believe.[4] Indeed her influence had been gathering momentum for nearly ten years before the founding of the *Bund für Mutterschutz* and around a different, though not totally unrelated, slogan "Missbrauchte Frauenkraft" or "Women's Misused Energy".[5] That concept was first articulated in 1895 in a speech at a women's conference in Copenhagen. There Key explicitly directed comments against the movement and what Anthony had labelled "Anglo-Saxon" tendencies to encourage women to become the legal, social, political, and domestic equals of men. The immediate reaction among the German admirers of John Stuart Mill and the English feminist movement is exemplified by Hedwig Dohm's designation of Key as an "antifeminist."[6] Despite that initial reaction one soon finds Ellen Key's name and the concept of "women's misused energy" in the writings of virtually every branch of the German women's movement. Then, as now, continental feminists asserting the positive aspects of gender difference frequently opposed the struggle for equality of rights with such a vehemence that one might wonder whether or not the two lines of vision were in fact focused on the same object, or whether the combined women's movement was not a little cross-eyed.

The essay "Missbrauchte Frauenkraft" was published in Germany in 1898.[7] Key objected strenuously to what she correctly saw as the main thrust of the women's movement: the unqualified struggle for more educational and vocational opportunities for women and the encouragement of women to apply themselves in the same fields in which men had been active for centuries. Among those women who entered these fields she had detected a particular tedium. By competing with men, she maintained, women misused their energies, leaving their most natural talents uncultivated. The demands placed by work on men are so great that, were women to fulfill them, they would not be able to produce children. Science had shown that the development of muscles in an athlete drew strength away from the brain (8) and women also had to learn that their energies were limited; they could not both achieve and mother. If women continued educating themselves and working like men, they would become psychically modified in five or six generations and the human race would be endangered. She therefore advocated continuing the basic division of labor which had existed to that point in time (15).

Key was not merely a prophet of cultural doom, she also proposed that women would never be able to achieve the intellectual levels of men and questioned whether society had ever benefited that much from the work of women (33). An inborn inequality would never be overcome by mutual approximation of the sexes. No believer in the complexities of socialization, she maintained that working-class men had been at least as restricted in education as upper-class women, but had nevertheless produced more of significance. Even in religion or the domestic sphere women had not been as inventive as men. Only in two areas had women's work matched that of men: philanthropy and the interpretive arts such as acting and singing. Women, she believed, would never be as original as men; their genius was receptive rather than creative; and their role was to glorify the thoughts and actions of others, to create hero cults (62).

With considerable boldness, then, Key announced her hatred of the women's movement (64) as a struggle in the name of human rights. And yet, if she had taken the one-sidedly antifeminist stance for which Hedwig Dohm so roundly denounced her, she could not have inspired the imaginations of so many feminists. Despite their lack of general creativity and inability to take the initiative, women, Key maintained, would lead the "revolt against everything evil in society" (42). She came to this conclusion by asserting the positive aspects and talents of women in their role as mothers, the one role in which they excelled. However, Key did not propose that women should remain at home, in fact she advocated the economic independence of women, not wanting to force them into the most menial labor of all: domestic labor in a marriage of necessity. According to her the mistake of the women's movement had been to focus blindly on opening all positions for women, without considering their natural talents. She demanded work for women that would develop their particular personalities the same way men's work developed theirs (22).

If women continued to force themselves to do men's work "the sum of happiness and culture would only add to male values and not to an organic whole created by the harmonious union of two differently endowed creatures" (10). And here lies the crux of the matter: her fear that society as a whole would lose those values attributed to women. In motherhood, she claimed, lay the origins of altruism. Mothers alone taught faithfulness, modesty, love of the home and family (12). "The humanization of life . . . has been the unprecedented cultural task of women." (12) If women work they should avoid labor designed for men. That included not only those continents of knowledge and creativity charted by men, but factory work as well. Women's energies were most advantageously used in education, social welfare, and the peace movement. And, although Key attacked the goal of equality for women, she believed they needed the right to vote in order to assert "the power of motherliness" (42). Thus while Key supported the franchise and the expansion of new work areas her argumentation was quite different from those who supported them with reference to human rights.

"Missbrauchte Frauenkraft" is a problematic text for a feminist. On the one hand Key disparaged women's capabilities; on the other she elevated their traditional role in society and wanted to expand it to redeem the human race. Her own numerous contradictions, which Hedwig Dohm ruthlessly exposed, do not help in evaluating the text. The very existence of the treatise would seem to contradict her estimation of women's inability to contribute to intellectual discourse. But Key foresaw this objection and revealed, as proof of her position, that she had merely compiled her arguments from male sources, which she did not name. It is instructive to speculate on these, however, for they not only give us a sense of the climate in which she wrote, they also clarify some of her assumptions. Her emphasis on gender difference undoubtedly derived from what was then popularly accepted as the most advanced scientific research in anthropology, female physiology, and the brain.[8] Much of the argumentation about women's work then rested on often unspoken assumptions about women's physiological and biological nature. A discussion of women's work was impossible without addressing her role in the home as a function of her biology.

One of the most specious and influential of these "researchers" was Cesare Lombroso, a "criminal anthropologist" according to whom women demonstrated fewer brain anomalies than men and were therefore less likely to become either criminals or geniuses.[9] Since the number of anomalies supposedly advanced with civilization, women represented an atavistic form of human life (107). Lombroso also asserted that there was an inverse correlation between fertility and intelligence, so that to the degree that women could acquire intelligence, the culture as a whole would suffer. By his reasoning, furthermore, pent-up maternal feelings produced female criminals.

The German translation of *La Donna Delinquente* appeared in 1894, the same year as the German version of Havelock Ellis' *Man and Woman*. If Key did not read Lombroso she almost certainly read Ellis, and there she would have encountered a number of Lombroso's theories. In general, however, Ellis evaluated the investigations of Lombroso (and others like him) more evenhandedly. For instance he interpreted gender difference as a natural balance wherein women's childlike character counteracted men's depravities and extremes of behavior. He further claimed that gender difference was modifiable by human hands, although probably never possible to remove. In his conclusion Ellis even proposed that the future lay with women and the feminization of the human race. Although atavistic in his opinion as well, women were described as closer to the telos of human evolution. Thus, despite the highly dubious and extremely chauvinist research on the basis of which it was written, *Man and Woman* was popular among some feminists.

Two popular treatises by doctors appeared just about the time Ellen Key delivered her Copenhagen speech: the infamous pamphlet, "Über den physiologischen Schwachsinn des Weibes," by Paul Julius Möbius would go into many editions, and "Das Weib in seiner geschlechtlichen Eigenart" by Max Runge gained considerable credence because he asserted his authority as a gynecologist.[10] Both protested, on the basis of scientific research, the "unnatural goals of feminists." Significantly for our discussion, however, later editions of both works also cited Ellen Key as a reasonable woman of some talent.[11]

From this perspective Ellen Key is clearly in the company of anti-feminists, adding validity to their invectives.[12] While the more positive cultural mission that Key defined for women may have been suggested by Ellis, the most likely candidate is Theodor Gottlieb von Hippel, whose treatise, "Über die bürgerliche Verbesserung der Weiber" (On the Improvement of Women), appeared in 1792. Known as the first feminist treatise in Germany, that work advocated admitting women to all branches of educational, social, and political work since they would inevitably humanize, regenerate, and purify those spheres. This work was generally known among women at the end of the nineteenth century.[13]

The bourgeois women's movement in Germany had arisen in large part around the call for expansion of work opportunities for women. Many of the early feminists like Louise Otto-Peters and Fanny Lewald urged the right of women to earn their own living, that is, their right to economic independence so they would not have to prostitute themselves in undesirable arranged marriages. Additionally, some argued that women had the right to develop their personalities in work just as men. The most compelling argument of the early feminists in late nineteenth-century Germany, however, was that of sheer economic need. It was the argument least likely to meet controversy since it was an unavoidable social fact. Women significantly outnumbered men then and means simply had to be found to support them. They could no longer be assured of finding a financial haven in a man's home, and even if they did, conditions frequently necessitated their working. With the argument of economic need, therefore, bourgeois feminists could override any moral objections to opening new educational and employment possibilities for women. As a result, however, the movement as a whole seemed to address the plight of unmarried women more than married ones. Thus, like more recent American feminists, German bourgeois feminists had failed to address the issues of motherhood and the conflicts of marriage and work. Those issues only emerged after the movement had had some success in expanding educational and job opportunities for women.

The proletarian women's movement, of course, had arisen around issues related to the workplace and the exploitation of female labor. Under Klara Zetkin's strong guiding hand, that movement also emphasized moving women into the workplace and improving their working conditions. They, too, neglected issues related to motherhood and the home. Both wings of the women's movement in Germany focused on increasing the numbers of women working in the public sphere, and only a few referred to the principles of classical liberalism in their efforts to advance women's occupational rights.[14] Those feminists who argued from the position of classical liberalism did so without a large base either within the movement or in German politics as a whole.

With this difficulty and in the face of weighty attacks from the intellectual establishment, Key's solution to the rift in cultural politics must have seemed a palatable corrective. Before Key, Laura Marholm had tried to span the differences and redirect the tide of feminism in *Das Buch der Frauen* (1895). There she asserted that men were women's destiny and women were a mysteriously erotic principle. While the women's movement largely rejected Marholm, she did find considerable following among men. But Marholm's emphasis on female sexuality could not answer critics of the movement, male or female, with the same force as Ellen Key's redefinition of the goals of the women's movement in terms of motherhood. Indeed, the majority of German feminists did not even respond favorably to others of Key's writings on sexual emancipation. As early as 1903 Hedwig Dohm, a feminist of classical liberal standards, felt compelled to publish a book, *Die Mütter* (The Mothers), affirming her belief in motherhood but denouncing its cult, which she felt the majority rabidly and thoughtlessly articulated. She questioned, for instance, the value of motherhood when one occupied oneself with useless work in its name or when it meant hating someone else's child for the sake of one's own. But she could not stem the flood. Marie Diers apologized, in the introduction to her book, *Die Mutter des Menschen* (The Mother of Human Beings, 1905), for the energy with which she defended motherhood. Such energy, she explained, had seemed necessary two or three years previously, when she had written the book. To the extent that one can date massive shifts in a movement, it would seem that by 1905 motherhood had diverted much of the energy of feminist debate. One wonders, of course, if this was the feminist version of Eduard Bernstein's 1896 revision of Socialist theory: a reformulation of that theory in less confrontational terms and an accession, in some measure, to the status quo. Or was Key's position closer to a feminist re-vision of history (and the future) to acknowledge the significance and importance of women's role and talents? Only a closer look at the wide-ranging reception of Key's concept will provide a response.

One of the most reknown leaders of the movement for educational reform, Helene Lange, worked untiringly for equal opportunity for women in the schools. Yet even this advocate of equal treatment of the sexes complained, as early as 1895, of the one-sidedness of contemporary culture: "Women should bring their unique talent to bear on the cultural evolution of humanity, which until now has one-sidedly borne the stamp of men."[15] Writing too early to have been influenced by Key, her sources appear to be the same. Criticizing Lombroso, but drawing on Havelock Ellis, she believed women's natures possessed a more childlike purity and could therefore provide a necessary corrective to social life. The egoism apparent to so many in contemporary German society, and associated by Lange with men, could be combated by women engaged in social work. They were needed in prisons, hospitals, and schools.[16]

Only two years later she repeated the essence of that article, but altered significantly the posture of her remarks.[17] In 1897, she argued somewhat defensively against viewing women *only* as different. Lange stated positions Key would publish the following year. The origins of altruism, sympathy, and love lay in motherhood. These provided a balance to the abstract, speculative, systematic, and impersonal attitudes of men. While accepting difference she urged that that point of view not cause the similarities between men and women to be obscured. On the basis of her defensive stance and the number of sources she seems obliged to rally, it would appear that a debate about women's proper work sphere was already gathering momentum. Lange dismissed Laura Marholm's positive characterization of women as a "hysterical sexual being" as perverse. She cited instead Hippel and Olive Schreiner.

Despite her desire to see the complementarity of the sexes expanded from the domestic to the public sphere, 1898 would find Lange arguing that women's logic was no different than men's and that there was no reason they should not be admitted to the universities.[18] For women as for men, she wrote at the moment Key's pamphlet appeared, math remained math. Thus despite her belief in intellectual difference, she continued the struggle to have all the "mechanistic" restraints on women's options removed so that the "natural" ones might emerge.[19] *Die Frau,* the newspaper she edited, continued carrying numerous reports on the English feminist movement and included a column which discussed such jobs for women as embroiderer, stenographer, masseuse, artist, dairy maid, post office clerk and telegraph operator, sales clerk, sports teacher, fruit and vegetable gardener, bookbinder, nurse, midwife, railroader, etc. Many of these jobs were new for women at the turn of the century. Lange never expressed the cultural pessimism of Key or even of one of her closest associates, Gertrud Bäumer.

Surely it is not insignificant that the stormy debate on women's proper work raged around the more polemical figure of Ellen Key rather than the more coolly reasoning Helene Lange, who continued to fight for women's admission to universities. To be sure, the choice of Key as the rallying point may have had much to do with her more flamboyant style and her coinage of the slogan which carried the concept. It seems unlikely, however, that Key's more deprecatory comments on the women's movement did not also fulfill some of the needs of such a shift in direction. And, just as surely, that attitude also influenced the shape of the debate.

In 1904 Gertrud Bäumer, a life-long friend of Helene Lange's, acknowledged Key's role in the debate:

> Out of a more finely atuned sense of female individuality Ellen Key replaced the ideal of the mechanical work of a telephone operator and a factory worker with the many-sided accomplishments of motherhood and gave the women's movement, which had seen progress in these forms of work, the alternative concept of women's misused energy.[20]

Factory work might be necessary for some, but Bäumer argued against placing women in higher positions in industry and trade. Like Key, Bäumer was more inclined to see danger in engaging women's energy in "male" spheres of work. The egoism necessary in those spheres was irreconcilable with women's tradition of devotion, and women's "cultural mission" lay in preserving female sensitivity. If necessity demanded it, women should work in fields where their motherliness would be helpful and not a hindrance. The sciences demand too much intellectual concentration, but women could humanize other academic disciplines by directing research into areas of the home and other, more personal components of history. Throughout her writings Bäumer maintained that women could not fulfill their cultural mission if they remained in the home. Although she never campaigned for suffrage, she believed that women must possess political rights and access to public forums if they were to have an impact.

Bäumer's later works would modify slightly or expand various points, but more than anything her diction and the tone of her writing changed. By 1909 she saw a social crisis caused by the "overcivilization" of German life.[21] In a later work she defined the product of such a society, a "civilization person," as someone "living on the basis of reason, disciplined, goal-oriented, awake and dopey at the same time, banal and transparent, a microcosm of the powerful macrocosm: the machine age."[22] Men had created technology and capitalism; they had forced the separation of culture and work, learned to manipulate people for their own ends.[23] Only women could reinsert the soul into social life, but to do that they needed to recognize their mission, step out of the home and restore "the personal," "energies of the soul," and "wholeness" to society, to create a culture that was of the "Volk," "volksthümlich."[24]

Looking back on the women's movement in the 1920s, Bäumer believed the first phase of the movement had aligned itself with the forces of civilization, rather than culture; had mistakenly grounded its arguments for social reform in the concept which deemed the sexes to be equal: Key's disdained "human rights."[25] The second generation, however, posed additional difficulties for Bäumer. As she watched young women rejecting work as unfulfilling and noticed their increasing concern with free love and sexuality, she began to chastise them for refusing to accept the opportunity to change the nature of their work.[26] Although she had admired Key's emphasis on a social definition of motherhood, Bäumer could not accept the "New Morality" which followed from some of Key's later writing. Instead of being diverted by Key's notion of free sexuality, women were needed to take up their mission. They were "generically" the protectors of life (31).

Although Lange and Bäumer are usually associated with conservatism in the movement, it is difficult to apply that label in a strict sense to feminists who desired suffrage (albeit less actively than their British sisters) and motivated women to take up a national mission. They did not push women to return to the home, rather they sought to extend the family structure into the public sphere. Indeed, somewhat problematically, the notion of a cultural mission depended for them on the complementarity of the traditional family model. Literally and figuratively women would become the mothers of the nation.

In its struggle to open new opportunities for women, the first phase of the German movement had not excluded the notion of difference so much as it had ignored it. The phase which began after Key's "Missbrauchte Frauenkraft" emphasized it. While Lange worked to leave all possibilities open and to allow natural processes to sort things out, in general these feminists built their notion of a cultural mission for women on the premise, supported by highly questionable "scientific" research, that women were unable to perform equally well in the same categories with men. Their tactics focused the attention of women on new professions, like social work, and steered them away from ones in which they would run into competition with men.

The notion of complementarity thus cleverly avoided confrontation. It also meant that these feminists did not aim, in their social criticism, to subvert the social order so much as to provide a balance to the activities of men. For them the challenge of a cultural mission did not mean confrontation with established structures or necessarily even established ethics. "[Women] should expand family culture and, where necessary, help complement an essentially formula-oriented bureaucracy with a freer humanity, with understanding for what is personal."[27] To complement, not to replace. Women might work with prisoners, for instance, but the system of justice and the conditions which created criminals were not challenged. Similarly Key and Bäumer alluded to factory work and conditions as too foreign for women's natures without either proposing changes or challenging the appropriateness of factory work and/or conditions for men.

"The woman who, as a fully developed person, is at home outside the home will achieve the highest. She will bring her children a powerfully developed humanity and progressive strength. The goal of the women's movement is not the manly woman *(Mannweib)*."[28] Shortly before this statement, the author of these sentiments had found it natural for early feminists, reacting against their diminished productive role in the home, to strike out by emphasizing the "only human" *(nur Mensch)* in them, but she criticized the type of "new woman" glorified in feminist publications as grotesque and sexless, an abstraction walking around on two legs. As portrayed in the American and English movements the "new Eve" represented the most horrible assassination of every artistic sentiment (9). Fortunately, so the author continues, women themselves have been the ones to react with an alternative which does not return to the "only woman" *(nur Weib)* image of the protectors of the old order. Laura Marholm's image of the sensual, erotic woman is too one-sided for this author, but the writings of Ellen Key are described as particularly "sensitive."

We may expect Gertrud Bäumer to be a semiadmirer of Ellen Key, but we may be surprised to learn that the author of this tribute to the Swedish feminist was none other than Klara Zetkin, the powerful leader of the women's faction of the Social Democracy. Throughout her life Zetkin championed the end of women's isolation in the home. In her 1889 pamphlet, "Arbeiterinnen und Frauenfrage der Gegenwart" (Women Workers and the Woman Question of Today), she emphasized the economic changes which had led to the contemporary women's movement. Through these changes the illusion that eternal laws governed women's role in the home had been undermined. Since the loss of productive work in the home and the necessity for working-class women to engage in factory work, the housewife had become an "economic anachronism" (6). Zetkin considered the resulting economic independence of women and their inclusion in the public sphere to be advantageous. With women's entrance into the work force, she believed, would come the end of women's myopic, conservative perspective.

Nothing in the pamphlet of 1899 contradicted anything in that position, but it adds a perspective to Zetkin's image of women one does not usually associate with her. Despite advocating women's work, she did not foresee a future in which men and women would perform all tasks equally well. It would not, according to Zetkin, be appropriate to measure women's work, talent, and accomplishment with genius. Against a norm of average talent and accomplishment, however, women's work could prove itself, "even if its grade would not be equally good in all areas of intellectual endeavor." (16) Still, she preferred to wait until women had had sufficient opportunity to develop their potential, before passing judgments on its limits.

Two aspects of Zetkin's reception of Key's ideas moderate its actual effect on her position. One is her astute criticism of the "international brotherhood of scholars" and the other is the rejection of a specific "cultural mission" for women. Zetkin accused scholars and doctors of protecting their professional turf against competitors (12ff.). A few years later she concurred with Oda Olberg that it was mere head-in-the-sand politics *(Vogelstrausspolitik)* on the part of women to avoid discussion of the allegedly scientific work on the relationship of culture and fertility.[29] She felt nothing was gained by hasty retreats behind cries of "human rights" or paroxisms of fear at the thought of any debate on the effect of women's increased intellectual abilities on children. In her review of Olberg's book, *Das Weib und der Intellektualismus,* therefore, she lauded Olberg's careful revelation of the inconsistencies of various theories and the controversial nature of Möbius' sources (87). As for women's intellectual potential, Zetkin agreed with her response to Key: "Use for everybody, Misuse for nobody" *(Gebrauch für alle, Missbrauch für keinen).* (88)

Zetkin saw the issue of women's work neither in terms of solving the economic needs of middle-class women, nor in terms of a particular cultural mission; rather she aimed to make work for all people more meaningful. She disagreed that women had a particular cultural mission "to preserve life." Under capitalism neither men nor women shaped their work, their work shaped them. She envisioned a future, moreover, in which men would be freed to enrich their lives by domestic work, including the raising of children.[30]

Lily Braun often sat between the bourgeois and proletarian camps of the women's movement, offering some of its most innovative proposals. One might therefore expect her to do the same on this issue. And to some extent she does. Without actually mentioning Ellen Key in her book, *Die Frauenfrage* (1901), certain of Braun's arguments bear signs of similarities if not influence from that direction. She took seriously the conflict between women's "true" profession, motherhood, and employment in the public sphere, scorning as myths rumors from America that women could work full time and raise a dozen healthy children simultaneously. But she also found solutions to the domestic side of the dilemma in some of the American experiments in communal kitchens, living establishments, gymnasiums, and childcare.[31]

Despite her clarity in that domestic area Braun's conception of the potential role of women in the public sphere appears a little contradictory. On the one hand, she counters Key's analysis by offering historical and social explanations for the current status of women. On the other hand, certain comments suggest distinct agreement with Ellis and Key with regard to their doubts about the potential of women in men's fields. She echoes them when she comments that women have produced no geniuses and seem most capable in the interpretive arts, rather than the creative ones. Even in the fields where one would most likely expect to find innovations by women (cooking, washing, sewing), they are not forthcoming. Fields preferred by women—education, social work, medicine, office work, sales—corresponded, Braun found, in some ways to women's innate motherliness. Indeed, women's personalities reached their most perfect expression in social work, a field they had developed almost exclusively. And, she asked, "does not genius consist in the expression of one's personality?"(207) In general women decried despotism, slavery, and war where it existed. Like Key, Braun found women's appropriate work in those areas where her motherliness would come into play and where she would not duplicate the work of men. Only by complementing male skills with female ones would the first true cooperation of the sexes come about: "If the abilities of mind and heart were equal, the entrance of women into public life would be totally without value and would only lead to even more brutal competition."(207) It surprises that, as a feminist, Braun does not seem to consider the benefit of work for women and, as a socialist, she does not seem to envision humanizing all work.

Unfortunately, the imagination Braun had shown in finding new forms of domestic work was also not matched by her conceptions of new relationships among men and/or women. Even before the appearance of "Missbrauchte Frauenkraft" she had questioned the direction of the movement in "the classical land of the women's movement," England.[32] With all of Key's distaste for this phenomenon she, too, rejected the mannish intellectuals and the clever beauties who flaunted their sexual emancipation. To her, both were caricatures. She regarded "Ladies' Clubs" as helping the separation of the sexes "rather than the healthy tendency of the women's movement to bring the sexes closer together."[33] Her expression of rather traditional homophobia is accompanied here by her expression of regret at the loss of charm and goodness on the part of women *and* the loss of power and beauty *(Kraft und Schönheit)* on the part of men.[34] She presents her ideal: "The free woman will walk beside her man as a true comrade, not above and not below him. And from the womb of this new woman will grow the leaders of the *volk,* the bearers of the future: the new human race."[35] As early as 1895 the new woman, for Braun, was a womb for the propagation of a new race.

Lily Braun's essay of 1895 had appeared in the weekly periodical of the Social Democrats, *Neue Zeit.* When Ellen Key's *"Missbrauchte Frauenkraft"* appeared in 1898 the same journal published two reviews of it within a fairly short time. Considered together, they suggest both the ambivalence of the leftists toward her concept and the eventual speed with which it was accepted. Anna Schapire reviewed the text unfavorably, labeling it "the old philistine morality with a new coat of paint."[36] The second review was submitted before the first had even been printed, and the editors simply decided to publish both. For Ria Claassen, Ellen Key's essay was evidence of the viability of the women's movement.[37] The significance of the pamphlet lay "in its strong emphasis on the particular nature of women and its importance for culture."(598) Ellen Kay had finally broken out of the narrow, flattening perspectives on woman to understand her "in her profundity and originality." (599)

Adherents of the proletarian women's movement thus seem torn between attraction and ambivalence. Perhaps the general popularity of Key's suggestions, as well as the problems with them, surface best in a one-act play published by the *Arbeiterbühne: Missbrauchte Frauenkraft* by Ida Strauss (1905?).[38] The son of workers dies in the course of the play and the blame for his death is laid on the poor health of working-class mothers in general. If they work such long shifts and at home as well, they cannot properly attend to their health, which is so vital for raising strong children (and workers). The heroine of the play suggests to the baroness (wife of the factory owner) that male workers should be paid enough to support their families. For her insolence she nearly loses her position.

The clear assumption underlying this action is that women belong at home with their children. In this more accessible form—the plays in the series were available to theater groups at minimal costs—Key was understood to suggest returning women to the home, at least women who worked in factories. An opinion more in contrast to that of Klara Zetkin is hard to imagine. Additionally, and significantly, the heroine's recommendation, though her own belief, did not originate with her. She heard it first from a young doctor. Thus the historical origins and reception of the idea are manifest in the play as well. Obviously the conservative implications of Key's treatise had found their way into the working-class movement.

The range of Key's reception in the proletarian movement was as great as in the bourgeois movement: from Zetkin's fundamental sympathy, but rejection of the idea of a "cultural mission," to Braun's essential acceptance of one and Strauss' desire to return women to the home. Despite its impact, however, Key's slogan could mean very little for the platforms of this movement. Working-class women truly did not possess the luxury to consider more motherly forms of work, and so the debate within this flank of the whole movement took on more hypothetical forms. Nevertheless, both Zetkin and Braun accepted the affirmative emphasis on difference. After all, Zetkin modeled her ideal of a fulfilled human being on the pattern of women's lives: a combination of domestic and public work.

Key's formulation of the concept *Missbrauchte Frauenkraft* was favorably received by the majority of the combined bourgeois and proletarian women's movement in Germany. Only classical liberals resisted it. Its effect on the bourgeois movement was to dissipate efforts to expand educational and vocational opportunities for women. Exclusively biological explanations for difference made this inevitable. And while this eased social tensions considerably, it meant, to return to Katharine Anthony's metaphor of stereoscopic vision, that the women's movement essentially closed one eye and lost a certain perception of depth. Although its actual effect was minimal, even on the left, Key's formula eroded the movement to bring women into the marketplace and began to define women in more traditional ways, setting limits to the potential range of growth. Even here there was no systematic attempt to ground an affirmative concept of difference historically or socially, rather than biologically. As it manifested itself in Germany at the turn of the century, the affirmation of difference appeared more like a Bernsteinian revision of feminist theory than a feminist revision of culture and society.

NOTES

1. Mary O'Brien, *The Politics of Reproduction* (Boston: Routledge & Kegan Paul, 1981). I am grateful to Jill Lewis' lecture "Feminism and Motherhood" March 31, 1983 (Brown University). Carol Gilligan's *In a Different Voice* (Cambridge: Harvard, 1982) disclaims any attribution of value, but also emphasizes the concept of difference.

2. Katharine Anthony, *Feminism in Germany and Scandinavia* (New York: Henry Holt, 1915).

3. Anthony, p. 4.

4. That more radical aspect of her writings had its impact in the United States as well. See Mari Jo Buhle, *Women and American Socialism* (Urbana: University of Illinois Press, 1981) pp. 270, 292–95. For a different perspective on Key and a more comprehensive survey of her writing, see Cheri Register, "Motherhood at Center: Ellen Key's Social Vision," *Women's Studies International Forum* 5 (1982) 6, pp. 599–610.

5. It is difficult to translate this concept. Cheri Register uses "Misused Womanpower", and while, in German at least, *Kraft* does also incorporate some connotations of the English "power" it would not be the translation for "*power*" of the state". Similarly, in German, composites like *Frauenkraft* are rather common and would not necessarily evoke the awesomeness of "Womanpower."

6. Hedwig Dohm, *Die Antifeministen* (1902; rpt. Frankfurt/M.: Verlag Arndtstrasse, 1976).

7. Ellen Key, *Missbrauchte Frauenkraft* (Paris: Albert Langen, 1898). The preface to this work stated that it was a compilation and translation of two of Key's works: the original speech and *Frauenpsychologie und weibliche Logik,* a rebuttal to her critics, published in Swedish. Since Key lauded the translator's compilation as well as her translation, we may assume it is an accurate representation of her views. In any case it is the form in which they were received in Germany.

8. For a study of the Anglo-Saxon version of this phenomenon, see Stephanie A. Shields, "Functionalism, Darwinism, and the Psychology of Women. A Study in Social Myth," *American Psychologist,* July, 1975, pp. 739–54.

9. Cesare Lombroso and Guillaume Ferrer, *The Female Offender* (New York: Appleton, 1915), p. 151.

10. Paul Julius Möbius, *Über den physiologischen Schwachsinn des Weibes,* 12th ed. (Halle: Marhold, 1922), and Max Runge, *Das Weib in seiner geschlechtlichen Eigenart,* 4th ed. (Berlin: Springer, 1904).

11. For samples of professional acclaim of Möbius' pamphlet, see Joachim S. Hohmann ed. *Schon auf dem ersten Blick. Lesebuch zur Geschichte unserer Feindbilder* (Darmstadt: Luchterhand, 1981), pp. 158–61.

12. It would be a mistake to think that Ellen Key was the first or only woman to oppose the women's movement in public debate. Adele Crepaz, for instance, warned in 1892 of the dangers of women's emancipation on the basis of arguments similar to

those of Lombroso. Here, as elsewhere, the ideas of equality are associated with the English and American movements. Crepaz warns that these may not be appropriate for every country and worries about the future of the human race, while urging women not to betray their true nature. Instead of seeking higher education when it is not necessary, they should inspire men and participate in charity work. The only appropriate workplace for women is the home or volunteer community work. Adele Crepaz, *Die Gefahren der Frauenemanzipation* (Leipzig: Reissner, 1892). In 1901 two feminists distributed and analyzed the results of a survey which confirmed the negative effects of menstruation, childbirth, motherhood, and even celibacy on women's intellectual and artistic endeavors. To be sure, the authors stated that this irreconcilable conflict was also a necessary one, since women needed intellectual work. But their conclusion, nevertheless, confirmed the biological nature of the conflict without exploring the difficulties caused by socialization. Möbius would later laud the research. Adele Gerhard and Helene Simon, *Mutterschaft und Arbeit* (Berlin: Reimer, 1901).

13. Luise Büchner, for instance, seems to have read him and suddenly seen the possibilities for women in the public sphere. Compare Luise Büchner, *Die Frauen und ihr Beruf* (Frankfurt/M.: Meidinger, 1856) and Luise Büchner, *Uber weibliche Berufsarten* (Darmstadt: Köhler, 1872). In the earlier one she still envisages rather traditional occupations for women, but in the second she not only mentions Hippel, she has vastly expanded the types of work she finds appropriate for women.

14. Richard Evans, *The Feminist Movement in Germany, 1894–1933* (London: Sage, 1976). For discussions of women in the proletarian movement, see Jean Quataert, *Reluctant Feminists in German Social Democracy, 1885–1915* (Princeton: Princeton University Press, 1979).

15. Helene Lange, "Altes und Neues zur Frauenfrage," *Die Frau,* 2/9 (June, 1895), 536–41.

16. Lange had supported the notion of women doing social work as early as 1892, but for different reasons. Helene Lange, *Not* (Berlin: Oehmigke, 1892).

17. Helene Lange, *Intellektuelle Grenzlinien zwischen Mann und Frau* (Berlin: Moeser, 1897).

18. For a survey of the evolution of Helene Lange's position on equality in the schools, see James C. Albisetti, "Could Separate be Equal? Helene Lange and Women's Education in Imperial Germany," *History of Education Quarterly* (Fall, 1982), pp. 301–17.

19. Helene Lange, *Die Frauenbewegung in ihren modernen Problemen* (Leipzig: Quelle und Meyer, 1908).

20. Gertrud Bäumer, *Die Frau in der Kulturbewegung der Gegenwart* (Wiesbaden: Bergmann, 1904), p. 29.

21. Gertrud Bäumer, *Die Frauenbewegung und die Zukunft unserer Kultur* (Berlin: Moeser, 1909).

22. Gertrud Bäumer, *Die Frau in der Krisis der Kultur* (Berlin: Herbig, 1926), p. 5.

23. Bäumer (1909), p. 15.

24. Bäumer (1909), p. 10.

25. Bäumer (1926).

26. Bäumer (1926), p. 30.

27. Ika Freudenberg, *Die Frau und die Kultur des öffentlichen Lebens* (Leipzig, Amelang, 1911), p. 173.

28. Klara Zetkin, *Geistiges Proletariat. Frauenfrage und Sozialismus* (Berlin: Vorwärts, 1902), p. 8.

29. Klara Zetkin, "Das Weib und der Intellektualismus," *Neue Zeit* 21/2 (1902/3), p. 88.

30. Zetkin, *Geistiges Proletariat*, p. 23.

31. Lily Braun, *Die Frauenfrage* (Leipzig: Hirzel, 1901), p. 196. For a detailed description of these experiments, see Dolores Hayden, *The Grand Domestic Revolution* (Cambridge: MIT, 1981).

32. Lily Braun, "Die neue Frau in der Dichtung," *Neue Zeit* 14/2 (1895/6), 293–305.

33. Braun, *Frauenfrage*, p. 200.

34. Ibid.

35. Braun, "Die neue Frau," p. 305.

36. Anna Schapire, "Missbrauchte Frauenkraft," *Neue Zeit* 16/2 (1897/8), 535–36.

37. Ria Claassen, "Nochmals Missbrauchte Frauenkraft," *Neue Zeit* 16/2 (1897/98), 597–99.

38. Ida Strauss, *Missbrauchte Frauenkraft (Arbeiterbühne #50*, Leipzig: Lipinski, 1905?).

Women in Agricultural Work, ca. 1875.

Workers in the turnip field.

Source: Max Liebermann, Des Meisters Gemälde, G. Pauli, ed. (Stuttgart and Leipzig: Deutsche Verlags-Anstalt, 1911), p. 20.

In the dairy hut.

Source: Die Gartenlaube, no. 34, 1875, p. 576.

Traditional "Women's Work"—Sewing and Lacemaking, ca. 1880.

The lacemaker.

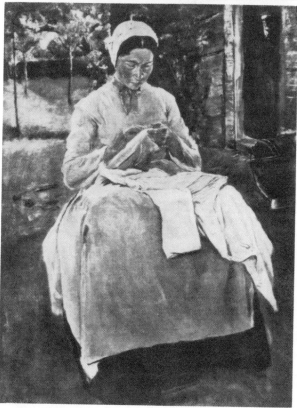

Seamstress.

Source: Max Liebermann, Des Meisters Gemälde, G. Pauli, ed. *(Stuttgart and Leipzig: Deutsche Verlags-Anstalt, 1911), pp. 48, 49.*

Spinning and Weaving.

Spinsters, ca. 1880.

Source: Max Liebermann, Des Meisters Gemälde, *G. Pauli, ed. (Stuttgart and Leipzig: Deutsche Verlags-Anstalt, 1911), p. 41.*

In the weaving mill, turn of the century.

Source: Die Gartenlaube, *no. 6, 1901, p. 157.*

Domestic Servants.

In front of the servant hiring hall, Berlin, 1875 (above).

Source: Die Gartenlaube, *no. 6, 1875, p. 100.*

Three servants, turn of the century (left).

Source: H. Zille: Bilder aus meiner Bildermappe, *G. Flugge and M. Köhler-Zille, eds. (Rudolstadt: Grei-fenverlag, 1969), p. 217.*

Women, Work, and Family in Turn-of-the-Century Berlin.

Homeworker making dolls.

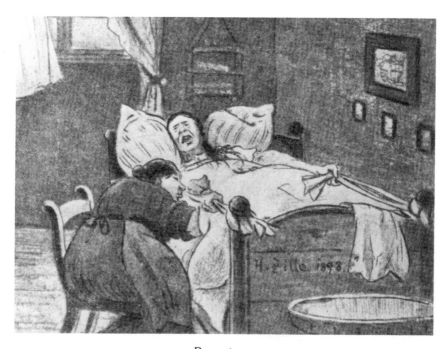

Becoming.

Source: Heinrich Zille: Ernstes und Heiteres aus seinem Leben *(Rudolstadt: Greifenverlag, 1960), pp. 8, 176.*

Women in Petty Commerce and White-Collar Work, Turn-of-the-Century Berlin.

Fishmarket on the Potsdam Canal.

The office of the Berlin hospital.

Source: Die Gartenlaube, *no. 29, 1901, p. 813 and no. 3, 1901, p. 80.*

Factory Women.

Around 1900 (left).

Source: Foto Marburg

During World War I (below).

Source: K. Bauer, Clara Zetkin und die proletarische Frauenbewegung *(Berlin: Oberbaumverlag, 1978), p. 147.*

Feminisms

"THAT GIRL IS AN ENTIRELY DIFFERENT CHARACTER!"[1] YES, BUT IS SHE A FEMINIST?

OBSERVATIONS ON SOPHIE VON LA ROCHE'S *GESCHICHTE DES FRÄULEINS VON STERNHEIM*

Ruth-Ellen B. Joeres

The pinpointing of feminist thought in literary works from centuries other than our own is fraught with many problems, not the least of which have to do with the pitfalls of anachronism and ambivalence. The former plagues us, because an investigation of any past era is bound to involve the danger of incorrect assumption not only about historical facts, but even more about past attitudes and subjective reactions that we simply cannot verify with any certainty.[2] The latter is equally bothersome, because we as feminist critics, not liking what we find, may well experience considerable frustration that will cloud our vision. To paraphrase Ruth Yeazell, despite our wanting to read women's fiction from the past with the pleasure felt at such public assertion of women writing, we are bound to find ourselves disturbed by the narrow circle of influence we see mirrored in the lives of female characters.[3]

The multiple methodologies and points of view that are accommodated under the general heading of feminist criticism only complicate the issue further. Thus, for example, one can clearly distinguish the extremes of both an optimistic and a pessimistic school of thought among feminist theorists, yet conclude by seeing validity and possibility in both. The pessimism that says it finds nothing but limitation and repression in women's past, conditions that clearly affected an already slow and often uneven progress toward emancipation and equality, can find its verification in considerable textual evidence. At the same time, the optimism that acknowledges the validity of such pessimism nevertheless goes beyond that apparent dead end. It examines how women learned, often subversively, to assert themselves despite their oppression and thus gained and imparted an important sense of their power. Both schools, however, may well use the same texts for their proof. The pessimists see equality in male society as the necessary given, as the ultimate, but not yet attained goal for women; the optimists, while agreeing, also show women gaining power from their uniqueness as women quite apart from male society, developing as human beings not entirely determined and controlled by the patriarchy. In all probability, the pessimists are liberal, the optimists conservative. Nevertheless, the search for accuracy and enlightenment, complicated by the biases of the feminist critic who by definition and intent will not distance herself from the material—and who so often is in search of her own history—is thus made all the more problematic.

An added complexity of defining feminism and then of locating evidence of it in the past is the absence of the word itself until comparatively recent times. Certainly in the case of Germany, were we to confine ourselves to a study only of those years in which the word has actually been in use, we would scarcely be able to go farther back than the present century.[4] Feminism, if viewed most generally as a combination of self-awareness and the resulting self-assertion among women, would in any case hardly seem to be characteristic of German women before the onset of the first formal efforts toward equality in the nineteenth century. Hedwig Dohm as an example of such thought comes immediately to mind; in fact, Janssen-Jurreit has said that except for her writings, all the other products of that first generation of socially critical German women writers consisted merely of "a feeble collection of the provincial literature of upper-class daughters."[5] Despite that, I can see valid reasons for investigating some of those provincial daughters, Luise Dittmar, Louise Otto, Louise Aston, Fanny Lewald, Johanna Kinkel, among others. But Louise Otto's acknowledgement of the influence of earlier writers on the shaping of her own philosophy of equality[6] indicates that it would be inaccurate, were we to trace the concept of feminism back to its origins, to assume that it was only as of the 1840s that German women began to express a concern with their self-image and their role in the larger context of society. Publishing itself is an assertive action: an exploration of earlier women writers would thus help to tell us more about how women viewed themselves before the organized women's movement, and how in fact they may have influenced the formation of that movement. To this end, I shall offer a reading of an eighteenth-century German novel that has only recently caught the attention of feminist critics.

In a 1981 discussion of an eighteenth-century American text, Annette Kolodny detailed two specific concerns of the feminist critic that are appropriate for any discussion organized around literary and social history: "(1) How do contemporary women's lives, women's concerns, or concerns about women constitute part of the historical context for this work? and (2) What is the symbolic significance of gender in this text?"[7] The interdisciplinary nature of her questions is apparent: the social and cultural circumstances that determined the writings of the female chroniclers of a past era are as significant as the less easily established information, what Yeazell calls our need to "read [a text] metaphorically."[8] We can no more judge literature in isolation than we can confine our study of the past to historical accounts of Great Men and Significant Events, and our use of every available source, from quantitative data to the less obvious symbolic aspects of a work of literature, is an imperative step in forming a portrait of past generations—especially in regard to the tracking of the elusive women in those generations.

Sophie von La Roche's *Geschichte des Fräuleins von Sternheim* (The Story of Miss von Sternheim), published anonymously in 1771 but almost immediately attributed to her, has been called the first German *Frauenroman* (woman's novel) by literary historians, and because of that label has not been allowed to fall into the oblivion assigned to so many writings by German women in previous centuries.[9] Acknowledged favorably by the younger male writers of La Roche's day (notably Goethe, Herder, and Merck), the novel was published under the aegis of another male, Wieland, who took it upon himself to edit the text. Although it is a fiction that, as Wieland reports in his preface, Sophie von La Roche was not aware of his plans to have the book appear, it is also clear that without his strong support and influence, *Geschichte des Fräuleins von Sternheim* might well have remained in manuscript. It is a novel that has noticeable connections to the philosophical, literary, and social context of its age: it employs the epistolary techniques of Samuel Richardson, it echoes sentiments expressed by contemporary thinkers such as Rousseau and Kant, and it reflects aspects of rationalism, sentimentality, and pietism. Accordingly, it has been designated by critics as a work that was to influence the development of the sentimental novel,[10] as an imitative, conservative reassertion of the status quo,[11] or as a permissible literary structure in which a woman writer was allowed to assert herself at a time when the relaxation of the rigidly defined letter form and the acceptance of the epistolary novel as a valid subgenre were in vogue.[12] No one has accused it of possessing feminist tendencies; indeed, Sophie von La Roche herself is so utterly straightforward in her message of female limitation and her apparent acceptance of woman's traditional role that any other interpretation would seem Procrustean. Yet there is enough that is unusual about the novel and its principal character to make another look at it appropriate. Whatever dangers of anachronistic error or ambivalent uncertainty may arise, a discussion of *Fräulein von Sternheim* can offer insights that may ultimately help to explain the development of German feminist thinking in the following centuries.

Sophie, the heroine of the novel, is the daughter of a military officer and a slightly melancholy woman who, because she dies in childbirth while her daughter is still young, plays little more than a symbolic role in Sophie's development. The father also dies before his daughter reaches maturity and can be safely delivered into the care of a husband. Her precarious state is recalled by her later in reporting the words of an English friend: "a female of your class and charm must either move in with close relatives or be under the protection of a worthy man." (250) Initially, she is given into the care of a pastor, whose daughter Emilie is the eventual recipient of Sophie's thirty-one letters that make up the bulk of the novel; then she is sent to an aunt and uncle at the court of D, where an intrigue is begun to make her the mistress of the Prince, thereby facilitating a sphere of influence for the aunt and uncle, who are in financial difficulties. In the process, Sophie makes the acquaintance of two Englishmen: Seymour, a good, yet weak man who has been ordered by his uncle to keep his distance from Sophie while the attempts to win her for the Prince are in progress; and Derby, the evil wisecracking young Lord who is intrigued and attracted by the innocent charm of the girl and decides to use that vulnerability to his own advantage to win Sophie for himself. He succeeds when the unsuspecting Sophie is informed that she is indeed the victim of an immoral plot; in her desperation to escape, she agrees to marriage with Derby, unaware that the ceremony is a sham performed by his disguised and equally evil servant John. After forty days in a village where Derby has confined her while he continues his revels, she is abandoned by the now bored ex-suitor who, finding her frigid and bland, tells her of the invalidity of their marriage before he leaves.

A period of recovery at the house of Emilie is followed by Sophie's establishment of a school for poor girls that is financed by an old, wealthy woman who has taken her in, and by a journey to England as the companion of another woman at whose English estate Sophie organizes another school on a similar model. There she is wooed by a middle-aged Englishman who has almost won her over when Derby, now married to the Englishwoman's niece, gets word of her presence. In fear of her exposing him, he has Sophie abducted and taken to a remote section of Scotland to pine away and die in the imprisonment of warders who once before had watched over the death of another of Derby's victims, a young woman who was brought there with his and her illegitimate child. The readers are led to believe that Sophie does indeed die after John reappears to offer her a last chance to rescue herself by returning to his master, who has tired of his new wife. For when Sophie refuses, choosing death over life with Derby, John shoves her into a dank cellar where she is confined for a time, and then, in her last letter fragment, tells of her waning strength and details the conditions of her will and her wishes for her burial. When Seymour and Lord Rich, Sophie's older suitor and the brother of the younger man, come to Scotland to find her, however, having been sent by a dying and remorseful Derby, their discovery that she has died and their sad pilgrimage to her grave are interrupted. Sophie's warders admit that her death is an invention of the Lady who has rescued and taken her and the illegitimate child of Derby to her estate to recover. The novel ends happily, with Sophie married to Seymour, the mother of two sons, the younger of whom has been given into the care of Lord Rich, with Rich himself ensconced in a house on their estate, and with Sophie's continued efforts at educating poor girls. Derby, whose plea to Sophie that she come and forgive him his sins is rejected by her in a show of uncharitable but independent strength, is dead, and Sophie's world is in harmonious equilibrium.

Sophie La Roche's own life story is in many ways equally reflective of the acquiescence and submissiveness which a pessimist feminist critic would immediately point to in the fictional namesake. Despite what amounted to an education that went beyond the normal training for girls in the eighteenth century, La Roche still acceded to her father's wishes when it came to the choice of a husband by not marrying the man she had initially chosen and by becoming instead the wife of her father's choice. The publishing history of her first novel also involved less than an assertive move on her part; Wieland's prefatory comments may exaggerate the central importance of his role, but he was nonetheless responsible for the book's appearance. And despite the general acclaim with which the volume was greeted, the review most often cited includes a telling statement that illustrates the special, non-literary status accorded her novel: "But the gentlemen [critics] err if they think they are judging a book—it is a *human soul*. . . ."[13] The book does not agitate against acceptable ideas either in its form or in its overt message. Indeed, the often moralizing nature of epistolary novels, their effort to teach appropriate social behavior, might well explain La Roche's novel's popularity in a patriarchal society that liked to see its women trained in ways pleasing and beneficial to men.

Yet not all is as it seems. Sophie von La Roche herself was far from being undistinguished or usual: when one realizes that in 1789, eighteen years after the appearance of her novel, less than 20 percent of the 23 million inhabitants of the German state were literate, and out of that number certainly far less than half were women,[14] it is clear that La Roche was unusual even within her privileged class.[15] Her character Sophie is also different in spite of the unanimity of most critics, contemporary and current, who have dismissed her in the manner of Ian Watt's generalizing description of the post-Pamela heroines he claims were in vogue until the end of the Victorian era. Watt's depiction of such a model as "very young, very inexperienced, and so delicate in physical and mental constitution that she faints at any sexual advance," as "devoid of any feelings toward her admirer until the marriage knot is tied,"[16] simply does not correspond to Sophie, who never faints,[17] who shows open affection for her later husband Seymour, first as a friend, then as a potential mate, and who is a difficult challenge for the villainous Derby precisely because, as he complains, she "loves intellect and knowledge." (101) To write her off, as Caroline Flachsland did in a letter to her fiancé Herder as "my complete ideal of a female: soft, gentle, charitable, proud, virtuous, and betrayed"[18] is witty, but not entirely accurate. To label her variously, as more recent critics have done, by echoing Richardson and calling her "persecuted innocence,"[19] or glorifying her as "a person open to everything that is beautiful and noble and able to realize the harmonious balance of all the powers of her spirit and soul"[20] is to provide ultimately unsatisfying, stereotypic answers to a figure whose complexity is thereby ignored. To equate Sophie Sternheim with Lessing's tragic and passive Miss Sara Sampson, as Wolfgang Martens has done, and to typify them both as "the Richardsonian girl who is all too soft, absolutely bashful, modest, angelically soulful and probably an innocent sufferer"[21] borders on the derogative opinion that sees women in general, whether as writers or characters, as inferior objects whose thoughts and activities are childlike. There is considerably more to both Sophie von La Roche and her character Sophie than any of these descriptions implies. Even the abbreviated plot summary given above provides evidence of nuances and strengths that neither Ian Watt nor the critics of La Roche's novel have encompassed within their assessments of the possibilities open to eighteenth-century heroines.

What helps to explain the discrepancy between the comments of Watt and other critics and the portrayal in La Roche's text may well be the novel's date of appearance. Karin Hausen has convincingly argued that the latter third of the eighteenth century saw the establishment and defining of *Geschlechtscharaktere* (acculturated sexual role-typings) that would provide prescriptive guidelines for socially acceptable behavior for men and women from that time until well into the present century.[22] If Hausen's thesis is correct, then La Roche wrote and published her book in an era in which the defining of the role and responsibilities of women was marked by a growing tendency to depict women in general as passive recipients, as keepers of the hearth, as mothers, and as defenders of culture. According to Hausen, once the home as center of work and life activities had been replaced by the new perception of it as a retreat from the world at large where work was now located, a search for new ways to legitimize what was already the traditionally narrow sphere of women's activities occurred. *Geschichte des Fraüleins von Sternheim* appeared when the new designation of a woman's sphere was still in flux, and the resulting portrait of its principal character provides evidence of that state of change: the strong woman who has a clear sense of her far from modest place in life, but who represents as well some of the uncertainties of her existence in the midst of a waning ideology that allowed her a degree of freedom and possibility, and the new way that would culminate in the German classical pedestalization of her, thus removing her effectively from all arenas of public action. The following discussion will keep Hausen and the critical questions of Kolodny in mind in its effort to review La Roche's novel.

Geschichte des Fraüleins von Sternheim is a work that frequently repeats words and phrases both as structural motifs for the novel as a whole and as characterizing labels for its principal figures. The word most often attached to its heroine is *Erziehung* (education); emerging from the duality of *Geist* (intellect) and *Herz/Tugend* (heart/virtue), which represent the outward manifestations of her upbringing, and *Eigenliebe* (self-love), an inner strength, it shapes and dictates her entire existence. In all of its forms, this determining education goes far beyond the passivity and limitation of the Richardsonian heroines: Sophie is said from the outset to be well educated, trained by her father in all aspects of philosophy, in history, and in languages (she is fluent in English and on one occasion speaks Italian), as well as in the expected areas of music (singing and lute), dancing, and the economics of running a household (42). Her dying father declares that his first and most important task has been Sophie's " 'appropriate and blessed education' ";[23] when she is left an orphan at nineteen to tend her grandmother, the latter's words are deliberately chosen to paint a portrait of a less than passive woman: " 'You have the *intellect* of your father. . . . You are *left on your own* and shall commence the realization of your *independence* with the exercising of *charitable acts* for your grandmother!' "[24] *Geist,* defined in a 1796 lexicon as "the simple substance that is bound up with the human body and that is blessed with the power to think and to will . . . most often applied to the powers of the intellect,"[25] provides Sophie with the concrete knowledge for her life; the charity mentioned by her grandmother can be associated with the heart and virtue that are often in evidence as the outward philanthropic manifestations of Sophie's education, the practical moral imperatives that she carries out in her care and assistance of those less fortunate. There is no evidence here of the sex-determined split described by Hausen in her depiction of the new sexual role-typings.[26] Instead, by representing both sides of the duality, Sophie Sternheim seems to echo the early rationalist urging that women become knowledgeable in the aesthetic and pragmatic spheres of life.[27]

Sophie's progression through difficult situations is noticeably marked by her dependence on both aspects of her education. From the outset, the emphasis is on a woman alone, placed against the evils and intrigues of the world, defended essentially by no one and dependent on her own acquired knowledge and capabilities. There is clearly no time for fainting or, for that matter, for dying: thus Sophie responds to the first major blow that occurs when she is made aware of the plot to align her with the Prince by immediately confronting him and demanding his permission to leave the court. When the invalidity of her marriage is revealed to her, she can within hours express her grief in a letter; once she has reached the protection of her friend Emilie, she can recover rapidly and while doing so, find the strength to teach her goddaughter to read. Even in the darkest moment of her life, when she seems to have reached a level of utter powerlessness, when she has been abducted and finds herself in a raw place where not even the language is comprehensible to her, she turns to her intellect as well as to her heart: she learns the dialect, trains the children of her warders to read and perform handiwork, and writes letters and diary entries so that her fate may be recorded and not entirely forgotten. Her reaction to great distress is intellectual as well as moral; in every case, she recovers by using the knowledge she has attained and her sense of what is good to react positively and assertively to counteract each challenge. To claim, as Peter Hohendahl does, that she never questions the system that creates the poverty that she tries to ameliorate, to say, as he does, that she lives by the "basic color of the axiom of success . . . : he who is poor is also morally suspect,"[28] is too facile.

Although Sophie begins with the ample inheritance of her parents, she assigns (at least for three years) the profits from that estate to her aunt and uncle when she flees with Derby, and she then undergoes progressive financial deterioration in her dependence on the two women who take her in, ultimately identifying herself completely with the poor: "I am really a part of the circle of the poor and serving." (234) The difference between her warders and herself is seen by her to be a matter of intellect, not class; the contrast between them is that of upbringing: "There is no difference between us," she comments, "but how many of their soul's abilities have been and remain dormant!" (266) Even the larger social sensitivity that Hohendahl finds lacking in her is not entirely absent; on observing the weak character of her warders, in fact, she observes: "Hideous fate of poverty—it seldom has enough heart to stand up against the force of the oppressive rich!" (274) Despite the limitation on the spheres of activity open to Sophie Sternheim, she clearly makes up for it with countless forays, both mental and physical, beyond the boundaries normally imposed upon the women of her era.

In keeping with the pedagogical aims of the novel is Sophie's discussion on several occasions of the importance of her education. In only one instance is the message unambiguously oppressive: a lengthy report on the educational philosophy of an unnamed Mr. **, who echoes Rousseau by assigning women to primarily nonintellectual pursuits, concludes with Sophie's calling the time she spent with him one of the most fortunate occurrences of her life.[29] The modern feminist reader/critic can find only modest encouragement in the fact that the entire text of Mr. **'s remarks is given in the indirect subjunctive, thus placing responsibility for it on Mr. ** and not on the preached-to Sophie. At the same time, the novel frequently speaks of Sophie's love of reading and writing. When, for example, her aunt, jealous of the books that distract Sophie's attention from her, has them removed, the girl's response is not quiet acceptance but renewed and intensified activity. Describing the disappearance of what she calls her "best friends," she comments: "A nasty joke that will not help her at all! Because now I'll write all the more. I don't want to buy new books, since my stubbornness would just anger her." (67)

There are other examples of this combination of overt obedience (praising and apparently reinforcing Mr. **; not asking for more books) and inner assertion, if not revolt (modifying the impact of Mr. ** by having him speak the words; renewed stress on writing). Although Sophie's first plan to assist a family that has fallen into poverty is improved on by a male mentor, it is essentially her idea that is used. A second plan, worked out during her stay with the German woman, is formulated and carried out by Sophie alone. Two conversations with a young widow on the advantages of remarrying also present a double-edged message: although in the first, Sophie urges the widow to remarry, in the second she has accepted the woman's reluctance as valid and is willing to suggest an alternative and presumably equally useful course of activity, namely that of educating the daughters of the widow's friends and relatives. It can hardly come as a surprise that Sophie speaks out against purely intellectual activity for women, yet the language she employs is less than absolute. When the widow asks if she should encourage her charges to be "scholarly," Sophie's response, although firmly negative, still indicates that intellectual women exist, albeit in minute numbers. (232) While accommodation and pragmatic purpose are placed above individual self-assertion, at the same time there is no passivity, no retreat on Sophie's part.

The voices of a novel are all those of its author. La Roche did not create only Sophie, but also the widow. It is worth noting that the first conversation has the widow express her desire for freedom ("I want to enjoy my freedom." [217]) and point out the restrictions on the rosy picture of love and marriage that Sophie paints. Although she listens and comments favorably on much that Sophie says, the widow remains determinedly antimarriage and concludes "but my neck has been so wounded by the first yoke that even the lightest silk ribbon would hurt." (221) Sophie herself, having not won her debate with the woman, wonders at her own rigorous defense of marriage, and the portrayal of the widow, whose views are clearly not those of the novel's heroine, is not a negative one. The perception of marriage as a self-contained, economic unit is clearly no longer valid. Now that its meaning and purpose are in flux, it is understandable that Sophie and the widow could begin to perceive of alternate routes to take in spite of the growing rigidity and containment that were to mark the new role determinations for women.[30]

Sophie Sternheim is nineteen when she is put on her own resources and expected to live according to the education that she has been given. She is approximately twenty-four at the novel's conclusion. Her sustained level of activity is all the more astonishing for the relatively short span of time: in a period of five years she has managed to educate countless poor girls, to retrain two families in the art of living, to set up two schools on two continents, and even in the depths of her despair to teach the children of her landlord (in the village where Derby has placed her) and of her warders to read and to perform useful tasks.[31] She credits the practice of her intellect and virtue with her own salvation. As she declares in her final ecstatic letter:

> Knowledge of the intellect, goodness of the heart—experience has proved to me even at the edge of my grave that you alone compose our true earthy happiness! My soul depended on you when my sorrow wanted to lead it to despair. You shall be the support of my happiness; I want to lean on you in the serenity of my well-being, and to ask eternal Providence to make me capable of becoming an example of appropriately exercised power and wealth at the side of my noble, generous husband! (297)

Sophie's method of recognizing her limited sphere of activity, but using that sphere to the fullest, represents a dubious victory, but one worth noting. The fact that she concentrates her efforts entirely on women and on the family as an institution worthy of attention is also not to be overlooked: it is clearly women who are improved because of her actions, and that overt attention to her sex was certainly not lost on her readers.

Education is, however, not entirely based on overt actions, on the philanthropy that constitutes an acceptable realm for women even in the late eighteenth century. Sophie is not simply a public figure who, as one critic states, has made a career of her good deeds.[32] Although letter writing presupposes the existence of a dialogue, its very nature also tends to impart a sense of intimacy, the opportunity to reveal inner thoughts that might not necessarily be expressed out loud. Sophie Sternheim's channeling of her energies into open, public aid for her sex is enhanced by her need for the intimate friendship of women, a need she fills by the letters to Emilie: as she tells her friend on one occasion, "I write you about the part of my soul that I cannot reveal here [in England]."[33] The letters provide a forum not only for the detailing of Sophie's many public activities, but also for an evaluation of the inner self and the ways in which she defines and perceives that self. The pessimist feminist critic might point out that the essential passivity and lack of clear self-identity that one finds in Pamela and

Clarissa are also present here: thus Sophie denies her female self so completely that she dons male clothing in order to flee with Derby (79–80), and then changes her name emblematically to Madam Leidens (Madame Suffering) after Derby's departure. The two occasions on which she employs nature metaphors to describe herself seem bereft of personal power: there is the "sad winter of my fate," (208) the way in which she describes her life with the German woman who has befriended her. And there is the tree to which she compares herself after her move to England: having been damaged and having needed rest, it is only just now beginning to stir in its depths, sending forth "fresh but small branches of charity and usefulness." (240) Although there is eventually a brief restoration of her real name (292), Sophie replaces it almost immediately with the name of another, her new husband Seymour, and the last nature metaphor is reserved for him, who in the words of his brother is "a lovely but powerfully rushing stream that carries many pure specks of gold in its center." (295) Sophie is a passive, indeed a damaged tree, while her husband is the moving force of a stream, of rushing, fruitful water.

The picture, however, is not complete. The inner side of Sophie's nature is frequently bound up with the term *Eigenliebe* (self-love) which, in contrast to the egoistic *Selbstliebe* (selfish love) is defined in a contemporary lexicon as "the love of one's self . . . in a positive sense, since self-love tends to be happy in its natural state, which is the basis of all physical and moral life."[34] Sophie's effort to understand and define the word's place in her life is a strong motif of the novel. A particularly revealing passage in which it plays a role is the one fantasy that Sophie allows herself to engage in shortly after her arrival at court. Since her negative observations of the empty life she sees around her have created a need for "moral reflection," she turns to her inner self and feels that self increasingly invigorated by the "principles of my education." (93) But in contrast to those aspects of her upbringing that have involved her in the outward tasks of doing good, her words here concentrate on the useful pleasures of fantasy, on imagining from her limited vantagepoint how things might be were the world educated as she has been:

> My fantasy places me in turn in the positon of those whom I judge,
> then I measure the general moral duties that our Creator has assigned
> to every human being, whoever he may be, according to eternally
> unchanging laws, according to the potential of each and the intention
> he has to use that potential. In this fashion I was already a prince, a
> princess, a government minister, a lady-in-waiting, a favorite at court,

the mother of these children, the wife of that man, once even a powerful mistress—and in every case I found a chance to practice good and
to impart wisdom in many ways, without having the characters or the
political circumstances become unpleasantly monotonous. (93–94)

Despite the clearly rationalist bias to her thinking—the unchanging
universal laws that are acknowledged and thereby validated as the
determinants of social class and position—there is also the role playing
in which Sophie engages, as well as the manner in which she describes
such dreams as "these fantastic journeys of my self-love" that in turn
serve to strengthen "my knowledge of myself."[35] The use of *Eigenliebe*
is an indication of self-awareness, and its frequent appearance in the
course of the novel concentrates the reader's attention on its importance as an element of Sophie's view of herself. Her self-love is at
times a positive force: shortly after referring to its "delicious nature"
(134) for example, Sophie can conclude that, supported by the inner
love of self, she cannot be harmed by whatever overtures the Prince
may make toward her. But it can also be untrustworthy: Sophie pro-
phetically describes it as "erring" (184) after Derby has taken her to
the village, and when he leaves her, she comments: "Self-love, you
have made me miserable." (194) With a growing awareness and consciousness, however, she can also redefine the term once she has gone
to live with the German woman as "polyplike: all its branches and
arms can be removed, even its main trunk can be injured—it will still
find ways to send out new growth." (204) At this point the word begins
to take on a far larger significance, for Sophie aligns self-love, as she
now perceives it, with "the charitable love of one's neighbors," which
she describes as "bound up completely with my self-love." (204) Here
the philanthropic, active love of others is related to the inner strength
and conviction of self-love, with each complementing and aiding the
other: Sophie's outwardly-directed activities are thus seen as not only
an obedient performance of what she has been taught is correct, but
also as a way to help her own self. The assertion of public tasks—
whether educating girls or writing—is given validity and importance as
a revelation and function of self, even of the limited self of a woman
who, faced with boundaries, can thereby begin to stretch the edges of
those boundaries. Indeed, an early comment that begins by reinforcing the need for controls concludes with the thought: "But who knows
whether even the overstepping of boundaries does not have its cata-
lyst in the desire to increase our perfection?" (96)

It is significant that the final mention of *Eigenliebe* occurs after

Sophie's marriage to Seymour, where it is tied to the knowledge that she has stressed throughout her travails. Here too the relationship of outwardly-directed and inner love is apparent:

> My knowledge, the support of my suffering self-love and the method by which I could experience some pleasure now and then, is to be consecrated to the service of human life; is to be used for the happiness of those who live near me and for the revelation of every single hidden misery of my fellow humans, so that I can find every great and small loving way to help. (297)

Sophie Sternheim successfully combines her active determination to aid those less fortunate with a self-aware love, an assertion that is possible precisely because she loves that self. As to determining whether her success makes her a hero, we need to turn to feminist criticism and those scholars like Lee Edwards who have attempted to broaden the definition of heroes to encompass women. And Sophie Sternheim is indeed recognizable in Edwards's statement that "heroism involves both doing and knowing, . . . the pattern of action that characterizes heroism exists to support an underlying de-velopment and growth of consciousness. Action, then, exists not for its own sake but as a support or, more accurately, as a symbolic expres-sion of underlying psychic structures."[36] Edwards's assertion that "heroism depends on the transforming and transcendent qualities that link social change to love and individuation for both men and women"[37] also is applicable to a woman whose self-love is reflected in the outward loving acts toward others. La Roche's message is limited in its potentiality; nevertheless, the assertion of self in a female charac-ter who neither faints nor succumbs, and who, despite her marginal position in society at large, effects positive change while contributing actively to her own self-worth, who thinks as well as feels, is worthy of note.

Having dealt in the manner of the mostly optimistic feminist critics with the meaning of the specifically female hero of La Roche's work, I find it imperative that I also acknowledge my ambivalence by illustrat-ing briefly how the same text is easily open to more than one interpre-tation. In her study of femininity, Silvia Bovenschen speaks at length of the many forms of censorship that act on us, apart from the usually understood political controls that affect men and women alike.[38] Sophie von La Roche was a victim of such censorship even if she does not overtly acknowledge it. The confining prescriptive comments of Wieland in his preface—his assumption that the novel may well be greeted harshly, his reference to the "twenty little sour tones" he has discovered in the text (6), to La Roche's problems with form and method of writing (8), and his comments on women in general, "who are not professional writers" (10)—as well as the controlling mechanism of his footnotes and his clarifying additions to the text itself, are only the most obvious control. The far more subtle presence of ideas indicating the pressure of a dominant male society on the self-expression of a female author creates a struggle in any present-day reader to discover any power specifically emanating from the author as woman. Sophie Sternheim may well assert herself in successful ways, but the skeptic in me then asks whether the final result is to her benefit—or merely an acknowledgement of her acceptance of the male perception of what she should be.

A single example will suffice to illustrate this dilemma. When Sophie admits to Derby that "she notes with pleasure whenever her intellect and her figure are favorably commented upon. . . ." (191), she suddenly seems very ordinary, a woman who is exhibiting the vanity of which women have often been accused, or perhaps embodying the assertion of Rousseau in the fifth book of his *Emile* that "society's opinion is the grave of virtue for men, but for women it is their throne."[39] The need for Sophie Sternheim to accrue the acceptance and blessing of male society by being pleasing to it is interiorized and so obvious to her and to her creator La Roche that it need not even be explicitly stated. John Berger could well have used the La Roche novel to illustrate his assertion that woman, born "within an allotted and confined space, into the keeping of men," must be able to see in two directions: "She has to survey everything she is and everything she does because how she appears to others, and ultimately how she appears to men, is of crucial importance for what is normally thought of as the success of her life. Her own sense of being in herself is supplanted by a sense of being appreciated as herself by another."[40] Sophie may well be a hero, an ideal figure who, however, knows that the given of her life is her ability to be acceptable to men, who will in any event dominate her life. Whatever positive characteristics we may find in her depiction must always be judged in the light of their being observed by both the fictional characters around her and the real-life men who controlled and organized La Roche's life and writing. As Berger continues:

How a woman appears to a man can determine how she will be treated. To acquire some control over this process, women must contain it and interiorize it. That part of a woman's self which is the surveyor treats the part which is the surveyed so as to demonstrate to others how her whole self would like to be treated. And this exemplary treatment of herself by herself constitutes her presence. . . . Men look at women. Women watch themselves being looked at. . . . The surveyor of woman in herself is male; the surveyed female. Thus she turns herself into an object. . . .[41]

Whether it is Bovenschen's subtle censor who is in control or Berger's self-conscious censorship of the surveyed and surveying woman, the effect is bleak. La Roche may impart encouragement to her female readers by presenting a hero who is strong and assertive, but the controls on that hero provide a powerful shaping of her message. It is the limitation of Sophie Sternheim's existence that most contemporary readers would have registered: the novel ends, after all, with a marriage, with the reaffirmation of an institution that involves the subjection of the woman to legal and social dependence on her male mate. Sophie functions independently for all but the final pages of the novel, yet her reward for such active independence is her willing surrender of power to a man whose superiority she seems not to question.

In light of that, can I claim that there is a feminist message in Sophie von La Roche's novel? Any such assertion would, of course, have to go beyond the stress on the limitations of both character and author or the acknowledgement of Wieland's overt interference as well as La Roche's own homilies on the confined role of women. What remains, however, is the very obvious strength of the novel's main character. Sophie Sternheim is clearly to be viewed as a success, able to face the most severe of odds. Her education, that harmony of intellect and virtue that complements her self-love, provides her with the power of self-realization in her fight for existence. Her particular emphasis on the importance of educating and aiding women is not to be slighted: if she is to serve as a hero for her sex, then it is significant that she can not only handle every degree of problem on her own—without fainting or waiting for a male to rescue her—but that she can also assist less fortunately-endowed women, a message of particular significance for her female readers. Here they were not faced with the uncertain image of Pamela, or of a Clarissa, who followed one standard course of tragic heroines by dying—or even of a German creation who was to appear in the following year, Lessing's Emilia Galotti, who unlike Sophie would already give up when confronted with the symbol of Sophie's first challenge, the lust of the aristocracy.

La Roche's heroine does not fulfill Derby's cynical prophecy that she will either die or flee (158). Although she occasionally experiences emotional uncertainty and physical illness or accident, her way of confronting the trials placed upon her involves continued useful activity, a genteel, yet determined spirit of confrontation, and a strong sense of purpose. There is no other character in La Roche's novel, male or female, who can rival her in intellect or heart; indeed, the men who woo her are more like the passive heroine described by Watt, capable only of helpless observation of her struggles. In this instance, the final vignette of the novel is symbolically, if not realistically, significant. The potential problem of a triangle—both men love and want her—is resolved in what amounts to converting the dilemma into an advantage for Sophie. It is true that she chooses the younger man, but the older brother is not discarded, does not find another wife, but remains on the estate to educate the second son, his namesake, clearly a child who is at least figuratively his and Sophie's offspring. The menage à trois allows both men to benefit from Sophie's wise presence, while giving her the pleasure of both of them: the mature love and respect of her brother-in-law are complemented by the youthful joys of her original love. Polygamy—at least theoretically—is the utopian vision with which the readers are left, but the patriarch who usually rules is replaced by a matriarch. Marriage is not the end for Sophie, does not reduce her to the obliging conformity, the role of the Other, that it normally signifies for women, but allows her rather to carry on her useful activity and particularly to attend to members of her own sex.

If feminism is to be viewed as a possibility long before any formal move was underway for the emancipation of women, indeed long before the word itself came into use—if we can be permitted, as the optimists urge, to view the power in women while also taking into account their essential powerlessness—then it can be asserted that evidence of prefeminist thought is to be found in as ostensibly conservative a novel as *Geschichte des Fräuleins von Sternheim*. Sophie von La Roche herself, encouraged by her first success, went on to write and publish other novels (including one with a character who is outspokenly critical of men[42]), to edit and publish the autobiography of Friderika Baldinger, who wrote of problems between women and men,[43] and to publish the journal *Pomona,* which Schumann has described as "the only journal of the time that consciously viewed itself as a challenge to the women's journals edited by men and that for the first time reflects a change in the self-perception of the woman."[44] Sophie Sternheim is, according to male thought, an appropriate figure, obliging, moral, humble to a level of occasional self-deprecation, and utterly pliable; such traits make her ultimately welcome to the society in which she has to live. At the same time, whatever else is at stake here, from the pedagogic aims of rationalism, to the emotional extremes of sentimentality and the urging for self-examination of pietism, Sophie von La Roche shows subversive intent by also making her heroine a successful survivor on her own terms, a self-loving figure who shares that self with other women. It is no doubt a minor victory, but it is a message that brings with it in this first *Frauenroman* an encouraging initiation for the role of women authors in German prose writing.

NOTES

1. Sophie von La Roche, *Geschichte des Fräuleins von Sternheim. Von einer Freundin derselben aus Original-Papieren und anderen zuverlässigen Quellen gezogen herausgegeben von C. M. Wieland* (Munich: Winkler, 1976), p. 121. This modern reprint of La Roche's 1771 novel has been supplemented by an epilogue and a selected bibliography by Günter Häntzschel. The citation is taken from a letter written by Derby, the novel's villain, about the title figure. All translations from the German in my essay are my own. Where possible, page numbers from this text will be provided in the body of the article.

2. Ian Watt, *The Rise of the Novel* (Berkeley, Los Angeles: University of California Press, 1965), p. 154, provides a comment on the problems of applying social history to literary interpretation.

3. Ruth Yeazell, "Fictional Heroines and Feminist Critics," *Novel* VIII, 1 (Fall, 1974), p. 29.

4. See Richard Evans's contribution to this volume for a discussion of the difficulty of establishing a historically valid meaning for the concept of feminism.

5. Marieluise Janssen-Jurreit, *Sexismus. Über die Abtreibung der Frauenfrage* (Frankfurt: Fischer, 1976), p. 13. This text has recently been published in English translation in an abridged version: *Sexism: The Male Monopoly on History and Thought* (New York: Farrar, Straus and Giroux, Inc., 1982).

6. An essay by Louise Otto on the writer Agnes Franz appeared in Otto's journal *Neue Bahnen* XXIX, 8 (1 April 1894), pp. 59–61. An abridged version is to be found in a modern reprint in Ruth-Ellen Boetcher Joeres, *Die Anfänge der deutschen Frauenbewegung: Louise Otto-Peters* (Frankfurt: Fischer, 1983), pp. 256–57.

7. Annette Kolodny, "Turning the Lens on 'The Panther Captivity': A Feminist Exercise in Practical Criticism," *Critical Inquiry* 8, 2 (Winter 1981), p. 345.

8. Yeazell, p. 32.

9. Although the term is used by Renate Möhrmann in her brief discussion of La Roche's novel (see *Die andere Frau. Emanzipationsansätze deutscher Schriftstellerinnen im Vorfeld der Achtundvierziger-Revolution* [Stuttgart: Metzler, 1977], especially pp. 21–23), it was Christine Touaillon who popularized the designation in her *Der deutsche Frauenroman des 18. Jahrhunderts* (Vienna, Leipzig: Wilhelm Bräumuller, 1919). She deals at length with Sophie von La Roche; see particularly pp. 69–206.

10. See Adolf Bach, "Sophie von La Roche und ihre Stellung im deutschen Geistesleben des 18. Jahrhunderts," *Zeitschrift für Deutschkunde* 40 (1926), pp. 165–82 for a general discussion of La Roche and her most famous novel. Bach is one of the

few earlier critics to acknowledge La Roche's indirect influence on the development of the women's movement in the nineteenth century (p. 170).

11. Peter Hohendahl, "Empfindsamkeit und gesellschaftliches Bewusstsein. Zur Soziologie des empfindsamen Romans am Beispiel von *La Vie de Marianne, Clarissa, Fräulein von Sternheim* und *Werther,*" *Jahrbuch der deutschen Schillergesellschaft*, 16. Jg. (1972), pp. 176–207.

12. See Silvia Bovenschen, *Die imaginierte Weiblichkeit. Exemplarische Untersuchungen zu kulturgeschichtlichen und literarischen Präsentationsformen des Weiblichen* (Frankfurt: Suhrkamp, 1979), esp. pp. 190–200.

13. Quoted in Adalbert von Hanstein, *Die Frauen in der Geschichte des Deutschen Geisteslebens des 18. und 19. Jahrhunderts. 2. Buch: Die Frauen in der Jugendzeit der grossen Volkserzieher und der grossen Dichter* (Leipzig: Freund & Wittig, 1900), p. 130.

14. Sabine Schumann, "Das 'Lesende Frauenzimmer': Frauenzeitschriften im 18. Jahrhundert," in Barbara Becker-Cantarino, ed., *Die Frau von der Reformation zur Romantik: Die Situation der Frau vor dem Hintergrund der Literatur- und Sozialgeschichte* (Bonn: Bouvier, 1980), p. 140.

15. According to Hanstein (in the first volume of his history of women, *Die Frauen in der Zeit des Aufschwunges des Deutschen Geisteslebens* [Leipzig: Freund & Wittig, 1899], p. 210), Sophie von La Roche could read at three and had finished the Bible by the age of five.

16. Watt, p. 161.

17. Sophie does briefly lose consciousness when she is pushed into the cellar by Derby's servant, but it is the result of injury and not a manifestation of the fainthearted nature ascribed to women in Sophie's day.

18. Heinrich Düntzer und Ferdinand Gottfried von Herder, eds., *Aus Herders Nachlass. Ungedruckte Briefe . . . ,* 3. Band (Frankfurt: Meidinger Sohn und Comp, 1857), pp. 67–68.

19. Marion Beaujean, "Das Bild des Frauenzimmers im Roman des 18. Jahrhunderts," *Wolfenbüttler Studien zur Aufklärung* III (1976), p. 15.

20. Bach, p. 173.

21. Wolfgang Martens, *Die Botschaft der Tugend. Die Aufklärung im Spiegel der deutschen Moralischen Wochenschriften* (Stuttgart: Metzler, 1968), p. 369.

22. See Karin Hausen, "Die Polarisierung der 'Geschlechtscharaktere'—Eine Spiegelung der Dissoziation von Erwerbs- und Familienleben" in Werner Conze, ed., *Sozialgeschichte der Familie in der Neuzeit Europas. Neue Forschungen* (Stuttgart: Klett, 1976), pp. 363–93. This article has become a classic of sorts and is now available in English in Richard Evans and W. R. Lee, eds., *The German Family* (London/New Jersey: Croom-Helms/Barnes & Noble, 1981), pp. 51–83. Also very useful in the matter of sexual role assignations among eighteenth-century German women are: Barbara Duden, "Das schöne Eigentum. Zur Herausbildung des bürgerlichen Frauenbildes an der Wende vom 18. zum 19. Jahrhundert," *Kursbuch* 47 (März 1977), pp. 125–40; and the early chapters of Dagmar Grenz's fascinating study of children's literature for girls in the eighteenth and nineteenth centuries, *Mädchenliteratur. Von den moralisch-belehrenden Schriften im 18. Jahrhundert bis zur Herausbildung der Backfischliteratur im 19. Jahrhundert* (Stuttgart: Metzler, 1981).

23. La Roche, p. 43. See also Hausen, pp. 385–90.

24. La Roche, p. 47. Italics mine.

25. Johann Christoph Adelung, *Auszug aus dem grammatisch-kritischen Wörterbuche der hochdeutschen Mundart*, 2. Theil (Leipzig: Brietkopf & Härtel, 1796), p. 433.

26. Hausen provides many examples of the growing split in the assignation of characteristics that occurred in the late eighteenth century. Duden augments those examples and includes a chart of virtues assigned to women and men (p. 138).

27. Martens, p. 523.

28. Hohendahl, p. 198.

29. La Roche, p. 109. Mr.** is a nod to La Roche's editor Wieland.

30. See Hausen, esp. pp. 375–82.

31. At times Sophie's determination to remain active borders on the farcical. During the latter days of her imprisonment, for example, when her paper begins to run out, she makes plans to sew into canvas the words she feels she must record (p. 270).

32. See Fritz Brüggemann's introductory essay to his edition of *Geschichte des Fräuleins von Sternheim* (Leipzig: Reclam, 1938), p. 14.

33. La Roche, p. 241. See also p. 243 for a further comment on the value of friendship among women: Sophie, in stressing how much she needs Emilie, indicates that it is only with her friend that she can be open and honest.

34. Adelung, 1. Theil (1793), p. 1316.

35. La Roche, p. 94. At a later point in the novel, Sophie actually acts out her fantasies by assuming the roles of the members of a family whom she is assisting (pp. 211–16). There is a frequent use of the term *Eigenliebe* in this passage, indicating once again the tie between inner-directed and outward love.

36. Lee R. Edwards, "The Labors of Psyche: Toward a Theory of Female Heroism," *Critical Inquiry 6* (1979), p. 39.

37. Edwards, p. 45.

38. Bovenschen, p. 200–20.

39. Jean-Jacques Rousseau, *Emile oder über die Erziehung* (Stuttgart: Reclam, 1970), p. 733.

40. John Berger, *Ways of Seeing* (London: BBC/Penguin, 1972), p. 46.

41. Berger, pp. 46–47.

42. Published initially and anonymously in *Iris* (1775–1776), these *Frauenzimmer-Briefe* later appeared in two volumes under the title *Rosaliens Briefe an ihre Freundin Mariane von St.* Von der Verfasserin des Fräuleins von Sternheim*. The two most intriguing figures are Madame van Guden, who seems androgynous, and Frau Grafe, who is openly and wittily antagonistic of men.

43. Sophie von La Roche, ed., *Lebensbeschreibung von Friderika Baldinger von ihr selbst verfasst* (Offenbach: Ulrich Weiss und Carl Ludwig Brede, 1791). I am grateful to Sally Winkle for providing me with a copy of this text. Christine Touaillon includes several startlingly open and critical citations from Baldinger in her text.

44. Schumann, p. 151. Indicating the sort of limitations I too have seen, however, she goes on to say: "That phenomenon occurs within the framework of convention and tradition; feeling, grace, and intellect are the poles between which a woman's existence unfolds."

"AND THIS SHIELD IS CALLED—SELF-RELIANCE"

EMERGING FEMINIST CONSCIOUSNESS IN THE LATE EIGHTEENTH CENTURY

Ruth P. Dawson

Feminist consciousness—the awareness of women's oppression and the vigorous demand for change—first began to assume its modern aspect in the late eighteenth century. It came soon after the newest ideology of sexual character and separate spheres had gained acceptance, with its vision of women as supplementary to men. Women's characteristics and activities were to supplement the characteristics and activities of men, not to duplicate them, as Silvia Bovenschen has shown.[1] Evolving during the period when the private and public worlds were being increasingly separated, this ideology meant assigning women to the private and excluding them from the public, in effect eliminating them from the best opportunities for meaningful work and good pay, restricting them to housekeeping and jobs which could be carried out in the home. The very earliest documents of modern feminism, such as Mary Wollstonecraft's *Vindication of the Rights of Woman* (1792), were partly in reaction to this confining dogma. In Germany in the early 1790s three important feminist advocates emerged. One, a man, was the most outspoken and definite and is the best known today. The others, both women, were more tentative and less consistent, and have gone almost completely unrecognized in the history of feminist thought. Two of these writers considered the important issue of women and work.

Über die bürgerliche Verbesserung der Weiber (On Improving the

Status of Women) is Theodor Gottlieb von Hippel's extraordinary feminist manifesto.[2] Hippel's radical act of thought was to apply the ideas of the enlightenment to women precisely as they had been applied to other groups, particularly slaves. While the model of supplementarity occasionally influenced his thinking, he was more interested in pointing out that, in fact, despite any rhetoric to the contrary, his culture and society first postulated that women were innately inferior and then forced women to conform to that view. He examined the arguments on inferiority, attempted to show how women's character and behavior (particularly their weaknesses) were shaped by their lot and advocated drastic and rapid change. Along with improving their education, one of Hippel's key demands was to give women opportunities for meaningful activity, which he recognized as an important aspect of successful self-definition. Seeing too that women as a group had been damagingly excluded from meeting this important human need, he demanded change: "When will activity of one's own choosing ever cease to be the royal prerogative of the men! When will women attain that human right to perform work not for bread, not in the hope of selling something, but wholeheartedly and as a labor of love! When, O when!"[3] Women were working already, Hippel knew, but the occupations available were so limited as to preclude real choice.

He advocated the admission of women to key professions. Not only were they well qualified to be teachers, but virtually all forms of government jobs—except, he thought, probably soldiering—should be available to them. That they were also profoundly interested in medicine and suited for medical careers was shown, he argued, by the fact that they had persisted in practicing medicine even when it was forbidden to them.[4] Depriving women of these opportunities was harmful to them:

> Let us be honest! Every means by which human beings can distinguish themselves has been taken from the women. A conspiracy among their enemies debases this sex as deeply as an unavenged insult does a husband, expelling it to the class of servants and menials by means of the bugbear that the limits of its feminine modesty might otherwise be transgressed—when in truth it is only so that we may remain secure from their challenge to a duel.[5]

Women had been excluded, Hippel said, because men did not want to compete. But society would benefit by a change in this situation. In law, for example, women would reform the current obscurantism and reject the reliance on force on which legal decisions depended until then.

Such ideas about women's contribution were not entirely futuristic dreams of course because, as Hippel pointed out, women already had records of accomplishment in many areas. He named women who had headed governments from classical times until the present, he talked about women scholars throughout Europe and considered women writers from England to Germany. Hippel is quite definite about the fact that their motivation for achievement was the same as men's. It was neither necessary nor appropriate to judge talented women's behavior as compensation for failures in feminine roles; these women were simply following their natural talents.

Work is only part of Hippel's program for women. He wanted to improve their education and their civil rights as well, and he expected the benefits to affect men, women, and the state itself:

> In short, if the state were serious about employing this great and noble half of its population in a useful way; if it felt the important obligation to treat those equally and according to their rights whom nature herself had created equal, and to restore their rights along with personal freedom and independence, as well as with the merit and honor of citizenship, the weal and welfare of the state will everywhere begin to increase. If the state were to open to women its council chambers, its courts, lecture halls, commercial establishments, and its places of employment; if it were to grant to the presumably stronger male the monopoly of the sword only when it cannot, or does not, wish to keep from butchering people in the attainment of its ends; and if, moreover, the state does not draw a distinction between the sexes and chooses rather to follow the wishes of nature and what ought to be the desires of bourgeois society as well—that is, if society is not to be ashamed of its origins in nature—then not only will weal and welfare of the state everywhere begin to increase, but people will multiply like willows at the side of a brook, and humanity will approach its true destiny with great and rapid strides.[6]

Hippel wished to realign condition and consciousness on the basis of sexual equality.

Altogether it is an extraordinary vision, especially when compared with other contemporary views. Even writers who emphatically stressed their belief in the basic equality of men and women were often unwilling to accept all the consequences that Hippel advocated. An anonymous essay that appeared in Wieland's monthly, *Der Teutsche Merkur,* for instance, stressed equality of the sexes and graphically depicted the current oppression of women, all as part of an argument for the abolition of marriage. The essay, which was translated from English, was given a misleadingly anthropological title, "On the Advantages of the System of Gallantry and Inheritence among the Nayre"[7]; the "Nayre" are mentioned only in a note, not in the essay itself. The essay argues for giving women full responsibility for raising children but no new way at all to earn a living. To get money women should simply inherit it. In fact, the author—to every appearance a man—writes paeans about the accomplishments men could anticipate in their professions when unencumbered by wives and families.

This essay on the Nayre appeared in the *Merkur* in 1793. Both Hippel's *Bürgerliche Verbesserung* and Mary Wollstonecraft's *Vindication of the Rights of Woman* had appeared the year before, their timing coinciding because both writers had been deeply moved by the same events in the French Revolution, especially the exclusion of women from citizenship.[8] Impelled by other forces, two other writers in Germany, Marianne Ehrmann and Emilie Berlepsch, were also developing feminist ideas in those years; they were becoming conscious of their oppression as women and were beginning to advocate fundamental changes in their condition.

Marianne Ehrmann was a journalist, one of the earliest German women in this profession.[9] For five years, from 1790 almost until her death in 1795, she published a monthly magazine for women, the first three years appearing under the title *Amaliens Erholungsstunden* and the next two as *Die Einsiedlerinn aus den Alpen*. As a true disciple of enlightenment, Ehrmann's purpose was grand: "to the best of my ability, to nurture, enlighten, and ennoble the reason, heart, and curiosity of my female friends." The task was necessary because of women's present deplorable condition: "I want to cry when I see our sex eternally being led like a toddler, completely without culture, merely sensual or infected by some nonsense. . . ."[10] And to a large extent Ehrmann blamed these conditions on the men who were satisfied to tolerate and even encourage female ignorance instead of assisting women to improve themselves. "Oh yes! You men are the most responsible for this. You have to first stop praising *lead* and *iron* to women's faces as if they were *gold* so that by this lie you can weasel sensual advantages. That is the crux of the matter!"[11] Exactly like Mary Wollstonecraft, Marianne Ehrmann suspected that men were content to leave women with their minds undeveloped because uneducated women were sexually more docile.

When she received an anonymous letter telling her she overestimated her female readers and had not yet identified all their faults, she responded with vigorous sarcasm:

> I have my reasons for not putting *all* female errors directly on display at once: I did not want to make the triumph of *your flawless sex* so complete. You already nag at us enough and I am afraid you are tempted to *dispense with us* altogether! In any case it has often been mysterious to me how these perfect sons of Adam can busy themselves so thoroughly with such imperfect beings as we are.[12]

Ehrmann saw misogyny but was not quite able to name it.

Education was the central issue on which she concentrated her efforts to better women's condition. Through her stories, essays, and satirical dialogs, she wanted to improve women's manners and morals and wanted to give women the prod they needed to change. When she urged women to take charge of their own education and improvement, it was partly because she was so disillusioned with what men demanded. In a slightly different context she had exclaimed to the anonymous letter writer, "speaking frankly, everything that comes from you lords of creation is suspicious to me! All the more because we poor women don't know anymore how we are supposed to satisfy you insatiable men."[13] She was particularly irked by the criticism because her professed position was to concede superiority to men, still seeking major improvements in education and in women's general status. She seems to have hoped that as long as she accepted female inferiority her demands would not be threatening.

Ehrmann also professed to accept the concept of women as supplementing men. She frequently mentioned women's destiny *(Bestimmung)* as something different from men's, and on the delicate topic of education, she wished to avoid the dreaded label of scholar *(Gelehrte),* since that kind of learning was reserved for males, suggesting that she was a thinker *(Denkerin)* instead.

Ehrmann originally indicated that she was hoping to educate women only to a specific level, "until we have attained the mental level which makes us into lovable wives, tender mothers, reasonable companions, worthy housekeepers and good Christians."[14] These were the traditional roles permitted to women. And yet she herself was well aware that for many women who had to support themselves other options were important too.

Marianne Ehrmann may be the earliest German woman writer— aside from novelists and writers of tales like La Roche—to discuss alternate occupations with her readers, even though she does so in a negative way. After all, as she had said from the start, she herself was earning a living—"my meager piece of bread"—by writing.[15] It was not a condition she recommended, but from her own experience she realized that there were women who had no choice whether to work or not. She explicitly discouraged others from trying careers, but in the process gave a reasonable and realistic assessment of the difficulties women faced. The two occupations she discussed, acting and writing, are the two areas in which she had personal experience.

On the topic of acting, she indicated the many different skills an actor or actress needed, endorsed the call for acting schools, and then warned women, especially adventuresome girls, about the difficulty of acting as career for them. In fact, she said there were so many unpleasant aspects to the work, especially the dangers of poverty and seduction, that she discouraged any woman from trying it who was not forced to by "almighty necessity."[16] In other words, despite the general inadvisability of becoming an actress, circumstances may justify such a step. Precisely what these unhappy circumstances are, Ehrmann does not say. She herself had gone on stage after her first husband abandoned her.

Marianne Ehrmann was one of a striking number of eighteenth-century women writers who were divorced. They include, for example, Elise von der Recke, Susanne Bandemer (twice), Sophie Albrecht, Sophie Friederike Seyler, Juliane von Mudersbach, Augusta von Goldstein, Johanne Friederika Lohmann, and Johanna Elisabeth Gregorius, as well of course as Anna Louise Karsch, whose divorce in 1748 was the first in Silesia, and both Karsch's daughter, Caroline Klencke, and granddaughter, Helmina von Chezy (in 1801). Early in the 1790s, while Ehrmann and Hippel were writing, a number of women obtained divorces, including Elise Bürger (1792), Dorothea Margarethe Liebeskind (1793), Charlotte Diede (1794), and Karoline von Wolzogen (1794). Afterwards came the famous Romantics, especially Dorothea Schlegel, Caroline Schelling, Sophie Mereau, and Sophie Bernhardi. No wonder the English writer of the "Nayre" article extolled the ease of divorce in Protestant Germany, but especially in Prussia, where, he said, marriage was considered a simple contract that could be revoked by mutual agreement of the partners, leaving them both as free to remarry as if they had been left widowed.[17]

Accessibility is not, however, respectability. As of the early 1790s the women involved were not discussing divorce in their writings, and articles about them avoided the topic. Strangely, Hippel said nothing about divorce in *Bürgerliche Verbesserung;* perhaps it was a controversial topic which he feared might detract from the effectiveness of his other arguments. In any case, for women, divorce could not be a particularly valuable option until they had ways to support themselves outside of marriage.

Although in her discussion of acting as a career Marianne Ehrmann did not explicitly mention her experience on the stage—much less the divorce that effectively sent her there—on the topic of writing, she could of course hardly avoid acknowledging her own activity. She explained her career several times, always including references to necessity and unusual circumstances, such as the fact that she was childless and her husband was also a writer. She used the very title *Amaliens Erholungsstunden* (Amalia's hours of recreation) to reinforce the ingenious claim that her writing was done entirely in her leisure time. Altogether, she thought, as a serious occupation for women, writing is only for the few. Whether it was a privilege or a bane was a matter Ehrmann felt differently about at different times.

Ideology plays an important role in her ambivalent feelings about writing as a profession and is her primary reason in another passage for discouraging volunteers:

> I for my part do not advise any woman, unless fate has selected her for it through a combination of many circumstances to venture into *this* career. First, it would lead our sex as a whole too far from our destiny, and, second, it is connected with so many difficulties, which barely *one* woman in a hundred is able to surmount!

In addition to the ideological objection she goes on to stress the artistic, psychological, and sociological difficulties a woman writer confronts.

> From the artistic side, which is not always easy to attain, as well as from the side of one's disturbed peace of mind, this is really the saddest female occupation on earth. Art demands so infinitely much in order to be able to write *well* and *usefully,* and the many public attacks, the bitter critiques, the prejudice which braces itself against woman's writings, the jealousy which tries to besmirch them, the personal attacks against woman writers, usually denying them all domestic virtues—these are things which far outweigh the little bit of incense and satisfied vanity.[18]

It was not a promising image. Ehrmann is clearly describing her own struggle to write well and the pain and humiliation inflicted on her as a woman in an unconventional career. Nevertheless, Ehrmann's lament shows that the tactic of defining herself as an exception by no means completely exempted her from ideological demands and may in fact have prevented her from seeing the fundamental injustice of the ideological restrictions on women.

Sandra Lee Bartky comments:

> Women have long lamented their condition, but a lament, pure and simple, need not be an expression of feminist consciousness. As long as their situation is apprehended as natural, inevitable, and inescapable, women's consciousness of themselves, no matter how alive to insult and inferiority, is not yet feminist consciousness.[19]

Marianne Ehrmann, still firmly under the influence of Rousseau and battered by a disapproving world, was disturbed more about the degree of inferiority than the fact. Emilie Berlepsch was bolder in an essay she wrote on marriage that appeared in two parts in the *Teutscher Merkur* in 1791.

Masquerading under an innocuous title, "Some Characteristics and Principles Necessary for Happiness in Marriage" (*"Einige zum Glueck der Ehe nothwendige Eigenschaften und Grundsätze"*), the essay begins with general advice. The first five pages contain utterly conventional instruction on the importance of subordinating oneself to one's husband, accepting his moods, not contradicting his mistakes, and so forth. Meekness and orderliness, *Sanftmut und Ordnung*, are the two cardinal virtues she recommends here. According to Wieland's introductory note, the essay, which had lain in a drawer for ten years before Berlepsch consented to its publication, was originally designed as private advice to a sister who was getting married. But the tone quickly changes. Since writing those pages, the sister had died and Berlepsch herself had separated from her husband and perhaps divorced.[20] From these experiences and from the ferment of the French Revolution, she had acquired new ideas about the roles and rights of women. Emilie Berlepsch began to ponder the psychological cost of submissiveness to women and the cause in husbands of derogatory behavior toward wives.

She recognized the pervasiveness of misogyny in her world and its extensive influence, "the bad consequences of this misogynist tone for society and manners."[21] This destructive attitude saturates men's wit, their social gatherings, and even their scholarship. Their relations with women inevitably suffer. In particular, Berlepsch stressed the effect of misogyny on marriage, something she thought was not widely recognized.

Misogyny is especially potent because women's education has made them extremely vulnerable to male judgments and misjudgments: "Our education teaches us to be entirely dependent on the judgments of others, makes applause and admiration the highest goal of our efforts and turns the effort to please into our primary duty." The situation means that even the least slight can jeopardize a woman's self-confidence: "Thus it is very natural that at the most minor wound or refusal of anything that we believe we deserve or have a right to demand, we feel ourselves anxious, insulted, and robbed of an important part of our existence." The symptoms are a catalog of female ills: "Mental and physical weakness . . . melancholy or frivolity . . . depression and foolishness of various sorts."[22] And the best women, Berlepsch believes, are the most endangered.

The problem then is significant, but what is the cure? Berlepsch has no suggestions of how to deal with misogyny except defensively. For this her argumentation is detailed and direct in rejecting the traditional solution, which she herself had originally advanced, and in proposing a new one.

> Now if the danger is so great and so urgent, then how much care we must apply to escape it! If even the best men have not remained entirely unaffected by the widely disseminated poison of injustice toward us, then how necessary is a means of self-preservation which, even though it does not completely alleviate the evil itself, at least is capable of removing its destructive influence. Meekness alone is not sufficient, although vehement resistance is certainly infinitely more damaging. To be sure, it, enduring meekness, will preserve peace and decency outwardly, but it will not be able to deter the inner grudge, the enervating loss of courage, and the soul's gradual decline into discord, and loud complaints will then have the effect that a strong blast of wind has on a slowly devouring flame. There is only one shield which can guard the soul and protect its delicate sensitivities against harm; and this shield is called—self-reliance.[23]

Berlepsch's prose is clear and straightforward. She lacked Hippel's wit but avoided the cumbersome style that plagued Wollstonecraft.

Berlepsch realizes that having a self-reliant spirit is contrary to everything young women are trained to be.

> I know that this characteristic is hard for the young—and especially the female—heart to acquire. It likes so much to cling to everything, judges itself only according to the value that others attribute to it, and certainly feels more deeply and warmly than any male heart is able to do; Rousseau is right when he says that *our true self is not entirely in us.*

Berlepsch is aware that urging women to practice independence con-
tradicts the prevailing view of women as supplementary to men and
she knows that Rousseau's mighty name will be raised to refute her.
"But this is precisely what we have to combat; precisely this is the
source of our vanity, our weakness and many of our sufferings." Acknowledging the power of Rousseau's argument, she answers with
forceful rhetoric: "No, we must, we must learn to stand alone. We
must make our way of thinking, our character so honorable in our own
eyes, that the judgement of others does not distract us from our own
considered and just verdict about ourselves."[24] This is a program of
progress that women are still laboring to fulfill two hundred years later.

Berlepsch goes on to reject explicitly the androcentric view of
women as supplementary to men: "The principle that simply for the
sake of men, to please them, to be respected, praised, and preferred
by them, women should try to acquire endearing characteristics, talents, and information—this principle, drilled in by mothers and governesses and only too often praised by men themselves is valid, in my
opinion, only for the Orient." She calls on the new political idea of
human rights to justify her own position: "We who—at least in many
respects—enjoy and share with men the same inalienable human
rights, why should not we also preserve our inner spiritual lives independently and individually?"[25] She is gingerly approaching the claim of
full equality, within, as she makes it clear elsewhere, the great whole of
society.

Berlepsch's article was supposed to be about marriage, but her
consideration of women's predicament as wives led her to a far
broader analysis of the ideas that influence the behavior and training
of both men and women. By advocating independence, she would
change women's education, change the marriage relationship, and
potentially give women new opportunities for work. Nevertheless, she
thinks of women's expanded responsibilities but keeps them essentially within the limits convention permitted to women.

> The woman is no longer just the housekeeper of the man and bearer
> of his children; she is also an educator and a participant in his often
> very complicated affairs and has her own sometimes not unimportant
> role in society. If she is to act prudently and independently, then she
> must be able to think freely and on her own, that is, not be a machine
> which simply depends on the will of the man. In everything which
> does not concern his prosperity, his honor and the well-being of his
> children, he must not arrogate to himself any ruler's right. The woman
> must know that this is not permissible, must know that she, supported
> by her own reason, has to walk many a rough, steep, or slippery trail.

> When she knows this, she will work to train her understanding, sharpen her critical facility, strengthen her character.[26]

Even while advocating women's rights, Berlepsch accepts a separation of male and female responsibilities. Although she wants women to know that their husbands do not have absolute powers, the men are still unquestionably dominant. Rather like Marianne Ehrmann, she seems to say in several places that being second rate could be acceptable to women if they were handled right.

Does this deference disqualify Ehrmann and Berlepsch as feminists? Mary Wollstonecraft took similar positions. She did not directly assert that men and women are equal, complaining instead that men have increased female inferiority, "till women are almost sunk below the standard of rational creatures."[27] Wollstonecraft also seemed to envision women in roles that basically complemented men's:

> Would men but generously snap our chains, and be content with rational fellowship instead of slavish obedience, they would find us more observant daughters, more affectionate sisters, more faithful wives, more reasonable mothers—in a word, better citizens. We should then love them with true affection, because we should learn to respect ourselves; and the peace of mind of a worthy man would not be interrupted by the idle vanity of his wife, nor the babes sent to nestle in a strange bosom, having never found a home in their mother's.[28]

The improvements Wollstonecraft, Ehrmann, and Berlepsch advocated would enable women to carry out their traditional responsibilities more effectively. To a lesser extent Hippel agreed with this view too. Thus modern feminism as it was first emerging in the late eighteenth century demanded change but still accepted much that was traditional.

Even with this foundation in traditional values, Emilie Berlepsch was not confident enough of her radical ideas to be consistent about them, a fact which diminishes the impact of her essay. In the second part, for example, she recommended reading as a way to learn independence, but said the wife should let a man, usually her husband, select her books for her.[29] Sustaining a radical vision is difficult, as the essay shows.

Of the two German women who wrote critically and at length about women's condition, only Ehrmann explored the implications work might have for women, and even she did not see work as part of human self-definition, as Hippel had done. With so small a sample of writers under discussion it is difficult to explain differences among them on the basis of gender, and yet one wonders why the women writers did not perceive the broader implications of work. To some extent it may reflect women's lack of experience with the satisfactions that work could offer. Berlepsch had no personal experience with it at all except for writing, and Marianne Ehrmann's work had led her into painful conflict with society. For a man such as Hippel, who was a prominent lawyer in the government of Koenigsberg, working was or could be quite different. "Activity," Hippel had observed, "is the spice of enjoyment, and enjoyment is the spice of activity."[30] Ehrmann's experience was fraught with too many disappointments for her to make such a statement.

Probably, however, another constraint on the minds of women writers was more important: their tremendous desire for respectability. Marianne Ehrmann had complained that popular prejudice denied women writers every domestic virtue. Surely this is the reason for her rapturous enthusiasm for writing on the topic of housework: "Ever since I first took up the pen to dedicate the fruits of my recreational hours to Germany's daughters, I have not begun any article with more intense pleasure than this little essay about the art of housekeeping."[31] Housework was a touchstone in the ideology of supplementarity. The seemingly progressive author of the essay on abolishing marriage had explained the division of roles clearly: "Even though both sexes are equal, still it is not absolutely necessary that both are destined for the same occupations. The man is destined for an active life and the woman for a domestic one."[32] The repetition of the word "destined" (bestimmt) shows that this was not simply a convenient division of labor but a matter beyond individual inclination or control. If a woman deviated from her prescribed occupations, her femininity was jeopardized, and femininity as a social construct is inseparable from respectability. No wonder Ehrmann anxiously continued her remarks: "The art of housekeeping is, as all my readers will know, the *first* and most important occupation of the female sex. It makes me much happier when someone in the circle where I live recognizes me as a good housekeeper than as an acceptable writer, because writing can only rarely, in very special conditions, be reconciled with the art of housekeeping." She is more concerned with defending herself in conventional terms than in changing the rules and prescriptions that restrict women. In part she is arguing that writing among women is not dangerous since so few women do it; but even more, she insists that she can be both the housekeeper that society requires her to be and the writer that her special circumstances permit.

Considering the overwhelming propaganda in the late eighteenth century about housekeeping as women's primary destiny, it is remarkable how little attention Hippel, the thorough analyst of women's condition, devoted to the topic. Still, he does not omit it entirely. He alludes to the tedium of women's work and to the higher prestige it enjoyed in ancient times, as shown in Homer, for instance. He pointed out casually that even Jesus gave preference to Mary over the exclusively domestic Martha. As for the time- and energy-consuming work of raising children, he said that was as much the father's responsibility as the mother's.[33] Never does he treat housework as a reason to exclude women from any opportunity.

For women writers of his time, however, housekeeping was both a distraction from writing and a problem of reputation. Since women who took the time to be writers were presumed to be poor housekeepers, they were by that fact alone rebelling against their natural destiny and thus disrespectable. The quest for an exception from the general disrepute of course interfered with each woman's ability to argue certain other points. Thus, if she argued, as women writers from La Roche to Ehrmann tried to do, that she never let writing distract her from her primary work as homemaker, then she was unlikely to promote other forms of activity that might cause a new conflict or distraction.

Perhaps these women writers in their reticence to reexamine the issue of work were simply being practical. If Ehrmann had not been so exposed to her public, she might have been less conservative. But she was exposed in two ways, first because her identity was known; her style of journal, the *Personalzeitschrift,* common in the eighteenth century, was carried to a large extent by her reputation and recognized name. Others might contribute to the *Erholungsstunden* anonymously, but what Ehrmann wrote there was always under her own name. Although Berlepsch, on the other hand, had intended anonymity, she may well have anticipated recognition, and Wieland's notes in fact make her identity unmistakable.[34] The two men, Hippel and the Nayre author, by contrast, both succeeded in concealing their names completely. The author of the "Nayren" article is still unknown,[35] and Hippel's secret was revealed only after his death in 1796. Probably if Hippel had had to assume public responsibility for the ideas in his book, he would never have written it. But Ehrmann in particular was exposed to public misapprobation in a second way too, because she was producing a magazine, trying to get it accepted month after month by as large an audience as she could reach. She could not afford to alienate readers.

What if she had been free from these constraints? In 1794, an article satirizing women writers appeared in *Flora*, the journal which the publisher Cotta had devised to replace *Amaliens Erholungsstunden* when he deposed Ehrmann as editor. "Last Testament of the Husband of a Learned Woman" seems out of place in the very proper *Flora;* until this piece appeared, the editors had stuck faithfully to their promise never to publish anything which could possibly offend the moral sensibilities of delicate female readers. In this case, the editors did not apologize but promised to publish a rebuttal if one were submitted. One was, and it seems plausible that Marianne Ehrmann was the author.[36] If so, it was her first change in years to write about a topic that was of enormous importance to her without worrying about reprisals from her audience.

Whoever wrote it, "About My Husband's Last Testament" does appear to be by a woman. It takes a very interesting view of women, and touches the topic of work again. After a scathing critique of the unnamed man who wrote the first piece (or, as she claims, hired someone to compose it for him), the author vigorously asserts male and female equality. She does this by ceremoniously invoking the spirit and words of two famous seventeenth-century women, the scholar Anna Maria Schurmann and the poet Sybilla Schwarz, citing passages in which each claims the intellectual equality of men and women.

Knowing that most men will disagree with her position, the author proceeds to deride some of the usual charges against women:

> Hand them over to me, those *prejudices*, you men! and shame on you for your triumphant smiles.
>
> If the *male body* exceeds the *female* in *strength*, must *your spiritual powers* therefore also be greater? Then the healthy person would be more intelligent than the sick one and the youth have more understanding than the old man.
>
> Or can we control our *emotions* less? Are we by nature *less constant, less attentive?* Is our *temperament* less suited for study?—No, no! *physically* you can still call us the *weaker sex;* but the *soul* is neither male nor female.[37]

So why are women not more advanced? In part, the author blames jealous men for crippling talented young women with moralistic inhibitions that prevent them from participating in unconventional activities. Through their deliberate obfuscations about modesty, men deliberately direct girls away from the gold and silver mines she considers meaningful activity to be.

Also, their own concern for respectability stifles talented women; the author reconstructs the thoughts that send bright young men back to the spinning wheel. She points out their awareness that if they are brilliantly educated they will be displayed like menagerie animals and treated as if they were ashamed of their girl friends and were trying to sneak over to the men's side. The experience of being an oddity was daunting indeed. In all this, the author does not quarrel with the idea that domestic matters are women's responsibility; she claims only that they do not exclude women from other areas of activity.

In her view, then, women are capable of far more than they were doing. In fact, the range of professions that might be appropriate to them is suggested when the author summons the spirits of extraordinary learned women from the past, mostly from classical times. Along with famous names like Sappho, she apostrophizes less known women too—such as Hypathia, who gave public lectures on philosophy; Agnodicea who, dressed as a man, dedicated herself to medicine; and Aristip's daughter, Arate, who continued teaching for twenty-five years after her father's death.[38] With each name she broadens the spectrum of female achievement, often suggesting too the struggle of these women against prejudice or their forgotten contributions to the work of men.

The writer wants to end intimidation and open new opportunities to women:

> Yes, friends! We may claim for ourselves to men what Father Klopstock claimed to the people who were overfond of foreign culture:
>
> > They have high genius!
> > We have genius, like them!
> > That makes us their equals!
> >
> > They penetrate science
> > Into its deepest marrow!
> > We??——[39]

The comparison with Klopstock is well chosen. Because he was a hero of German literature in the eighteenth century, his name urged acceptance of her cause. And because his cause had won, she suggests hers would also. In fact, in some respects women had won already, as she claims in the last paragraph of her polemic: "Forward then, you women and girls! Keep conquering with your native charm the well educated man-thing, and through your wisdom and goodness force respect even from the most desolated misogynist. For any setback, our secret comfort is this: men imagine they rule but are—our slaves!"[40]

These concluding words hardly look convincing in light of the preceding evidence, but they should be understood in terms of their intent, to strengthen women's determination, no matter what obstacle and discouragements they encounter. Cloaked in anonymity, the essay strikes a militant note that other writings by women in these years do not match.

The late eighteenth century marks the emergence of the first feminist writers in Germany, especially one famous man, Theodor Gottlieb von Hippel, and two long neglected women, Marianne Ehrmann and Emilie Berlepsch. All three recognized the oppression of women and as a result advocated major changes in women's status and women's relations with men. Education, marriage, and—with varying degrees of insight and conviction—work were the major topics in this new consciousness, a consciousness so modern that the writing of these thinkers can still stir us today.

NOTES

1. Silvia Bovenschen, *Die imaginierte Weiblichkeit: Exemplarische Untersuchungen zu kulturgeschichtlichen und literarischen Präsentationsformen des Weiblichen* (Frankfurt: Suhrkamp, 1979), pp. 163–64.

2. Ruth P. Dawson, "The Feminist Manifesto of Theodor Gottlieb von Hippel (1741–96)." in *Gestaltet und gestaltend, Frauen in der deutschen Literatur*, ed. Marianne Burkhard *(Amsterdamer Beiträge zur neueren Germanistik 10)*, (Amsterdam: Rodopi, 1980), pp. 13–32.

3. Theodor Gottlieb von Hippel, *On Improving the Status of Women*, ed. and trans. by Timothy F. Sellner (Detroit: Wayne State, 1979), p. 110.

4. Hippel, p. 161.

5. Hippel, pp. 112–13.

6. Hippel, p. 165.

7. "Über die Vortheile des Systems der Galanterie und Erbfolge bey den Nayren," *Teutscher Merkur* 1793, 2, 160–99 and 242–57.

8. At the end of his translation, in "Appendix: Rausenbusch-Clougn on Hippel and Wollstonecraft," Sellner discusses the question of timing of the two works and of possible influence. Hippel, pp. 219–21.

9. Edith Krull, *Das Wirken der Frau im fruehen deutschen Zeitschriftenwesen*, (Charlottenburg: Rudolf Lorentz, 1939), pp. 236–76; Sabine Schumann, "Das 'lesende Frauenzimmer': Frauenzeitschriften im 18. Jahrhundert," in *Die Frau von der Reformation zur Romantik*, ed. Barbara Becker-Cantarino (Bonn: Bouvier, 1980), pp. 156–58.

10. Announcement cited in Krull, pp. 238–39.

11. Marianne Ehrmann, *Amaliens Erholungsstunden*, 1791, 2, 267.

12. Ehrmann, 1791, 2, 269.

13. Ehrmann, 1791, 2, 266.

14. Cited in Krull, p. 238.
15. Krull, p. 238.
16. Ehrmann, 1792, 4, 16.
17. "Über die Vortheile," pp. 176–77.
18. Ehrmann, 1792, 3, 141.
19. Sandra Lee Bartky, "Toward a Phenomenology of Feminist Consciousness," in *Feminism and Philosophy,* ed. Mary Vetterling-Braggin, Frederick A. Elliston, and Jane English (Totowa, N.J.: Littlefield, Adams, 1981), p. 25.
20. The date of the Berlepsch divorce is obscure. Even the meticulous *Neue Deutsche Biographie* (II, 95) omits the information in its entry on Friedrich Ludwig Berlepsch (Emilie has no separate entry).
21. Emilie Berlepsch, "Ueber einige zum Glueck der Ehe nothwendige Eigenschaften und Grundsätze," *Teutscher Merkur* 1791, 2, 83.
22. Berlepsch, pp. 75–76.
23. Berlepsch, p. 89.
24. Berlepsch, pp. 89–90.
25. Berlepsch, pp. 90–91.
26. Berlepsch, pp. 100–101.
27. Mary Wollstonecraft, *Vindication of the Rights of Woman* (London, 1792; rpt. New York: Penguin, 1975), p. 179.
28. Wollstonecraft, p. 263.
29. Berlepsch, pp. 131–32.
30. Hippel, p. 59.
31. Ehrmann, 1790, 2, 125.
32. "Über die Vortheile," p. 249.
33. Hippel, pp. 134, 172.
34. Ruth Dawson, " 'Der Weihrauch, den uns die Maenner streuen': Wieland and Women Writers in the *Teutscher Merkur,*" in *Christoph Martin Wieland 1733–1813: North American Scholarly Contributions on the Occasion of the 250th Anniversary of his Birth,* ed. Hansjoerg R. Schelle (Tuebingen: Max Niemeyer, forthcoming).
35. Since his article has not been picked up in scholarly discussions, the question of authorship has received little attention. Hans Wahl, however, is certainly incorrect in attributing this piece to Mary Wollstonecraft: *Geschichte des Teutschen Merkur. Ein Beitrag zur Geschichte des Journalismus im achtzehnten Jahrhundert* (Berlin, 1914; rpt. New York: Johnson Reprint, 1967), p. 223; and Dawson, "Weihrauch."
36. "Lezter Wille des Ehemanns einer gelehrten Frau." *Flora* 1794, 1, 290–98. "Über den Lezten Willen meines Ehmanns." *Flora* 1794, 2, 78–88. Both the original attack and the response are signed with initials, the man's piece with J.F., and the woman's piece with E. The man's signature does not match the name of Theophil Friedrich Ehrmann, but the woman who writes the rebuttal says her husband did not actually compose the piece, hiring instead "the biggest Misogynist and satirist in our city" to do it for him (81). Indeed, the "Last Testament" is written in sufficiently general terms that no particular biographical traits of either man or woman are identifiable there. Although he says his wife made him read her "odes, songs, elegies, romances, and tearful stories," this list could have been selected for its generalizing effect rather than as an accurate reflection of a particular woman's work. Indeed the note of the editors of *Flora* shows that they did not understand the "Last Testament" as an attack on a specific woman; they invited any champion of women to reply. The response that appeared, however, is quite different.

The author describes herself as a former actress who met her husband while she was on stage; these details correspond to the Ehrmann biography. She blames jealousy for the man's attack on her, not as a husband but as a competing writer. T. F. Ehrmann as a geographer, prolific writer, translator, and compiler, could have felt himself as such a competitor. He certainly fit the description of a man who rambled through all four corners of the world—in his study. Whether he also managed to keep four presses running at once is uncertain, but he was at that time in the midst of producing a thirteen-volume work, which he finished in five years. In addition to such biographical details, other evidence also makes the Ehrmanns plausible authors of these polemics. The direct, vigorous, and biting language of the woman's piece is certainly reminiscent of much of Marianne Ehrmann's work. The ideas are more explicitly radical than what Marianne Ehrmann wrote in her magazines, but not in actual contradiction to her writing there. Nevertheless, it seems extremely peculiar for Ehrmann and her husband to air their disagreements in the very journal that was set up to ease them out of business with Cotta—and that was in fact their present competition. Furthermore, while Ehrmann had disagreed in print with her husband's ideas on women's education, this contentious exchange was far more extreme and estranged. Available information on the Ehrmanns, whose biographies have never been explored in detail, offers no other evidence of discord between them.

37. "Über den lezten Willen," p. 82.
38. "Über den lezten Willen," p. 84.
39. "Über den lezten Willen," p. 87.
40. "Über den lezten Willen," p. 88.

DISCIPLINE AND DAYDREAMING IN THE WORKS OF A NINETEENTH-CENTURY WOMAN AUTHOR: FANNY LEWALD

Regula Venske

This essay examines Fanny Lewald's biography in its contradictory as well as its reconciliatory aspects to show some of the basic contradictions of women's "condition and consciousness"—which was often "self-consciousness"—in the nineteenth century. My analysis of Lewald's biography is not meant as a biographical sketch; rather, I would like to understand her in her exemplary character as a middle-class woman writer of nineteenth-century Prussia, whose ideal of emancipation was closely intertwined with the historical and ideological place of women in nineteenth-century society.

I begin with an introduction to three of her novels, showing some of the basic contradictions of this author. After brief reference to the theoretical context of my analysis, I turn to the major material and economic restrictions which influenced Fanny Lewald as a writer before I discuss the even more relevant internalized emancipatory difficulties: the influence of male teachers and supervisors on Lewald's writings, and her "interior censorship", a basic factor for understanding the contradictory structure of Lewald's literary imagination, as an expression of forbidden fantasies as well as well-behaved daydreaming, as rationalization and disciplining of her imagination.

Since the concept of "disciplining of imagination" and disciplining of the senses is a basic concept of bourgeois emancipation as well as bourgeois everyday life, we can revise our critical approach to Fanny Lewald in this light and postulate a new critical and historical reception of this author.

In 1855, Fanny Lewald published a novel entitled *Adele*. As a girl, Adele, the main character, was in love with a mediocre poet, Hellwig, who deceived her into thinking of him as an unappreciated genius. After he left her to marry a rich woman, Adele was totally heartbroken. In her disappointment, she turned to writing. In opposition to her weak and yielding parents, who have given in to all her whims, the only one to criticize her is her cousin Samuel; but he cannot prevent her from publishing a novel about "The Poet's Genius" in which she reveals her love to Hellwig. The novel causes a scandal, and Adele has to suffer from the gossip and sanctions of her provincial environment. Only later in the novel, after her father has been forced to sell his factory and has died of his subsequent grief, and after she has moved to the capital with her mother and has had to earn their living herself, does she succeed in taking her literary activities more seriously and finally earning a living by writing. In the beginning of the novel, her writing shows only her capricious character, and she is deservedly criticized.

For example: before her first novel is due to be published, Adele is suddenly overcome

> by a feeling of discomfort, a fear of the public. Her motivation to write had not been that free and easy spirit and creative genius which, not being affected, are communicative and innocent. Her poetical work was the result of a personal grief which she had wanted to communicate only to one single man. Succumbing to her immoderate passion, she had thought only of herself and of him as she projected onto paper the image of her vague and confused relationship to Hellwig. "How will he react?"—that had been the thought which filled her mind at every moment of her writing. Now for the first time she asked herself, "What are the readers going to say?", and a deep anxiety came over her.[1]

It is important to note that Fanny Lewald, who herself had used her first novel to reveal her secret love and her sufferings to her cousin Heinrich Simon under the cover of fiction, here denounces Adele's egocentric and "immoderate desires."

At the end of the novel, Adele marries her cousin Samuel, a rather dry and pedantic theologian, who has throughout the novel helped her develop a more rational and self-controlled character.

In 1858, another novel was published by Fanny Lewald in which we again find a portrait of a professional woman. In this case, however, the pianist Leontine is not the main character of the novel, but only one of the *Travel Companions (Die Reisegefährten)* who share the reader's attention. As a character, Leontine exhibits all the negative character traits which Lewald usually attributes to femmes fatales; partially of Spanish descent, she is torn between grandioseness and depression, she is sensual, pleasure-seeking, indefatigable, nervous, and ruled by an excessive imagination. Already in the beginning of the novel, we find another travel companion, the calm and harmonious Anna, repelled by Leontine's hectic and excited way of being. Leontine's profession as a pianist functions only as accessory to her character; by no means is it to be taken seriously. Her first performance in this novel allows the author to reason about Beethoven's genius; in her last performance she is exposed to ridicule and is shown as someone "who brings her profession into disrepute."[2] Her art serves only as a means to her (womanly) ends, and has to be seen in sharp contrast to the way in which the author depicts a male artist in this novel, a sculptor named Walther, whose creative and productive work is appreciated in its seriousness: "Proud and self-confident, he moved among his productions like a sovereign. . . ."[3]

In the end, Leontine dies under dubious circumstances—there are hints of a possible suicide. Her death should be understood at least as a well deserved punishment, as a consequence resulting from the self-idolatry, restlessness, and torn passions of this woman, who has been denounced from the beginning as an *ächte Südländerin,* a true Southern European woman.[4]

Let us now turn to a third example, another novel by Lewald which again illustrates her ambivalent feelings about feminine professionalism. In 1873—after her pamphlets *Osterbriefe für die Frauen* (Easter-Letters to Women) and *Für und wider die Frauen* (For and Against Women),[5] in which she demanded women's right to work had been published—she wrote a novel entitled *The Redemptrice.* Motto of this three-volume novel is redemption by love; its main characters are Hulda, the beautiful daughter of a parson, and Baron Emanuel, who was good-looking in his youth, but whose face is deformed because of smallpox; there lies a curse on his family according to which one of its members will always be crippled until the family line is redeemed by "young and fresh blood."[6] Before Hulda's love can absolve Emanuel of his loneliness, the lovers have to undergo various tests and trials. After their first attempt at engagement has failed, Hulda becomes a famous and celebrated actress. In her reasons for becoming an actress, we can see an autobiographical hint. Lewald once expressed in her autobiography that she herself had wished to be an actress and to be able to confess her hidden love under the cover of the mask.[7] In spite of the many temptations which Hulda is surrounded by in her profession, she manages to lead a chaste and honest life. When in the end of the novel Baron Emanuel finally proposes marriage to her, it is not only she who redeems him from the curse of his ugliness and self-doubts, but also he who rescues her from the intrigues and temptations of an amoral profession; thus her thankful remark: "If you knew from which kind of world you have abducted me, you would consider it to be a deliverance."[8] The novel's motto "Love redeems and binds" has thus come true on a second level of meaning.

I have referred to these three novels here at some length for a specific reason: critics have mentioned them in order to appreciate Fanny Lewald as a "pioneer of the women's movement"[9] who treated the problems of working or professional women not only in her political manifestos, but even in her literature.[10]

But a close reading of these novels leads us to doubt the seriousness with which these problems are dealt. In the case of Adele and the pianist Leontine, we see the author denouncing the seriousness of the women rather than taking their problems seriously. And although Hulda as a character is at least portrayed with sympathy, her acting is only an intermediate solution after her engagement has failed (similar to Adele's writing after she has been deserted by her lover), and she is more than happy to give it up as soon as possible.

What was it that caused a woman again and again to express her postulates for "emancipation for work, for serious work,"[11] and at the same time to portray some of her women characters in a degrading, dishonoring manner, in opposition to an "ideal of manly dignity"?[12]

The contradiction between professed emancipatory goal and aesthetic conservatism and triteness has to be seen not only as a contradiction between the different genres of her writing (journalistic vs. literary writing), but it reveals contradictions in her emancipatory postulates as well as a fundamental contradiction in the structure of her literary writing itself. The contradiction between theoretical demands and literary practice finds its cohesion and continuity in the context of the author's everyday life.

> I cannot repeat too often the happiness I felt in working, the pleasure I experienced in my writing. The moment I sat down at my writing desk and reached out for my copybooks, a magic wand removed me from all my sorrows, all my troubles and cares. I was happy and free and felt power and courage. . . .[13]

For Fanny Lewald, writing meant independence and autonomy from the demands of everyday life, as expressed in this quote from her autobiography. However, the demands and restrictions of everyday life penetrated her writing on several levels and have to be analyzed as major conditions of her writing. In fact, the category 'everyday life' in general could be viewed as the central category useful to explain the living conditions and conditions of production of women writers.

The extensive discussion of the concept of "everyday life" which has taken place in the past years in the social sciences—whether from a Marxist, a phenomenological, or ethnomethodological point of view—could thus be adapted for literary analysis. It is at this point that I see the possibility to integrate social and literary history: "everyday life" being understood both as a social historical concept as well as an aesthetic level and metaphor. Here, I would like to refer to the concept of "everyday life," according to Agnes Heller, as the total activity of individuals for their reproduction necessary for social reproduction.[14] In the comprehensive context of everyday life, we have to see the reproduction of human beings who have to function as social beings, their individual reproduction as the commodity of labor-power, leading to a total disciplining of their senses.

Thus, criticism of everyday life is both a criticism of alienation as well as an ethical concept: for the individual human being, it is not enough to denounce the status quo, but one also has to be willing to overcome it, to express the desire to change it; there has to be concern for one's own emancipation.

According to Heller, it is true for the majority of people that the unity of their personality has to be constituted in everyday life. This statement could be extended with regard to women, whose place in bourgeois society is more reduced to everyday life and who, according to their role and functions, suffer more from its restrictions and reductions: woman's place is at the core of everyday life. The way women's everyday life is organized in bourgeois society is marked by contradictions and ambivalences; they are subjected to a double alienation. For women, everyday life means an exile, as well as a mystification. Consider, for example, the supposed ahistorical character of everyday life which has long implied that women have no histories, this being an ahistorical viewpoint itself which only reproduces the subjective mystification of everyday life.

> For all the dinners are cooked; the plates and cups washed; the children sent to school and gone out into the world. Nothing remains of it

all. All has vanished. No biography or history has a word to say about it. And the novels, without meaning to, inevitably lie.[15]

The profane character of women's everyday life has to be taken into account when analyzing women's literature and their conditions of production. Taken as a metaphor, there is Gutzkow's denunciation of women's literature as "knitting entertainment" (Strickstrumpfunter-haltung)[16]; the knitting-kit represents both the discipline of women's creativity as well as the vain daydreaming that accompanies their forced industriousness. Discipline and daydreaming—how can women succeed in transcending the ambivalent structure of everyday life?

It cannot be discarded in an act of wishful thinking—with the help of a magic wand, as Fanny Lewald put it. The ambivalence of discipline and daydreaming may well permeate the aesthetic structures of an author's writings itself, and in all cases, it constitutes the level of social and individual reality with which a woman writer has to cope.

The material conditions of women's literary production have been summarized very precisely by Virginia Woolf: "a woman must have money and a room of her own if she is to write fiction."[17] The necessity for a woman artist to have her own Werkstatt had already been pointed out by Lu Märten in her materialist analysis about Die Künst-lerin (The Woman Artist), written in 1914, published in 1919.

Gisela Brinker-Gabler has characterized Fanny Lewald's life as the story of a woman who as a writer conquered a "room of her own."[18] Taken in its metaphorical sense, this statement has to be questioned; on a pragmatic level, though, it can be clearly illustrated by Lewald's autobiography, in which she describes her euphoric feelings after she has moved to Berlin: "Here there is room enough to become something!"[19] While living in her parents' house, she had suffered from its protective but claustrophobic environment, and had had the feeling "as if I lacked the space to move, as if I could not raise my arms without bumping against something, as if, being watched by the others, I lost my ability to move."[20]

How strongly she felt about the importance of one's own room can be seen also in the fact that she "gave room to this sentiment" several times in her novels.[21] In her novels, Lewald hinted at a further difficulty for women writers: women's (well justified) fear of publicity, which has to be seen in connection with their seclusion from the public sphere. In order to please her father, Lewald had to publish her first novels and novellas anonymously. After her first two novels had been published, she dropped the veil of anonymity. It is interesting that it was not her rational father—who by that time admitted the convenience of the step—but her younger sisters who implored her not to reveal her identity. Leward criticizes her sisters and their irrational fears: "and in this point they were driven by dark and inexplicable fears . . ."[22]. These obscure fears, however, were much more far-reaching than Lewald herself realized, and will still have to be considered in their metaphorical sense.

One of the major restrictions of women in the past century was of course their "illiteracy," or rather, as in Lewald's case, "malliteracy." Fanny Lewald visited a coeducational private school until she was fourteen, and her education can be considered quite satisfactory for a girl of her time. Nevertheless, she expressed her ardent envy of her brothers who could continue with school and later with university education, while she had to while away her time with idle occupation. In comparison to men, for example her later husband, the scholar Adolph Stahr, her lack of literary knowledge therefore has to be taken into consideration. Since Stahr was to become her private tutor in many respects, one could extend Virginia Woolf's term "educated man's daughter"[23] into "educated husband's wife." I will comment on Stahr's fatal role as a teacher for Lewald later; for the present, I should like to mention another handicap for women writers which resulted from their confinement to the private sphere: the scarce opportunities for professional, paid work for middle-class women at the time: "To teach English or give piano lessons, to become a governess or lady companion, that's what it always comes down to in the end."[24]

To a middle-class woman, writing meant one of the few possibilities of occupational work which could be performed while still avoiding public engagement. One should therefore not only consider the factors which prevented women from writing, but also those which forced mediocre women to write for want of other possibilities. An entry in Lewald's diary betrays her wish to have been a doctor, and her daydreaming about the excellent doctor she would have become, with her character traits of "self-control, sense of duty," and her "imperative calmness and assuredness."[25] The question whether she would have been a better doctor than writer in any case points to the often hypothetical nature of women's studies.

Last but not least, in close relationship with education and professionalism, one has to consider the economic and financial aspects. Discriminatory behavior of publishers in many cases forced women to increase the quantity of their writing, in turn affecting the quality of their literary production. The extensive "output" of Lewald's literary work was certainly caused to some degree by her need for *Brodar-*

beiten as she herself called her "writing as a trade."[26] Nevertheless, she was quite well-off in the later years of her life; in her diary, she once compares her position to that of an average small capitalist, and there is complacency in her statement that she and her husband are "well-balanced in our earnings and have succeeded in making plentiful provision for our old age."[27] Economic restrictions played a role in the beginning of her literary career and the decision to leave her parents' home. Her father considered her financial earnings a blemish, and probably as a threat to his patriarchal position, and made her conceal the fact from her sisters until his death.

In her autobiography, Fanny Lewald describes the feelings of pleasure she found in her ability to support herself after having lived as an "old maid" for years in her parents' house. There is a moving anecdote in which she speaks of her joy after she has received her first salary: she wanted to buy a present for her mother (a silver knife for butter and cheese), but her joy was diminished by the fact that she could not have it engraved, as her brother had done with his first present to their parents, since nobody was to know of her earnings.[28] In summation, one can conclude that Lewald's material conditions were relatively satisfying, although she was not as well-to-do as her great idol Goethe. But aside from the economic and material difficulties which a woman writer has to face, one also has to consider the emancipatory difficulties which can result in "material" damages as well. Let us therefore consider the interior dimensions of restrictions and the process of everyday life discipline.

The basic term to be applied to Fanny Lewald here is "interior censorship," or "autocensorship." Whereas in 1845 Fanny Lewald had defended herself in an assertive manner against the political censorship which had been applied to parts of her novella *Der dritte Stand* (The Third Estate), she did not recognize the danger of the interior censorship which might restrict an author's expressions as well. On the contrary, she even demanded in her diary that an author must "exercise the strictest censorship and self-government upon himself."[29]

The auto-censorship which Lewald had in mind was characterized by the imprint of her male teachers and models, by the "valiant men . . . from whom she received various sorts of instruction," as she expressed herself with regard to the novelist Adele.[30] And in *The Redemptrice*, we hear a stage manager utter his pride about having educated Hulda: "how we cut the rough diamond."[31] Who were the "valiant men" and teachers who molded Lewald's identity as a writer?

Here one has to mention her former teacher, a theologian, von Tippelskirch, who once commented on her imagination:

> The imagination of this student—this gift of God which is both magnificent and dangerous—may afford her as much pleasure and happiness in times to come as harm, if she does not succeed in curbing it by means of the strictest reason and morality![32]

In an early novella, Lewald adapted her teacher's definition almost literally but she dropped the 'good' side of imagination and only referred to its dangerous side. I will return to this aspect of her denouncing her own imagination later on.

I also should mention Lewald's brother, a lawyer, who would check her writing for correct syntax and grammar. Fanny used to admire his precise and methodical—judicial—way of thinking. In a certain way, this brother acted as mediator of a more complex process of self-disciplining: Betty Gleim, in her compendium on female education published in 1810, had already seen a general function of teaching grammar to young girls as a mode of channeling their thoughts and feelings according to the logic of grammar, according to discipline and order.[33]

Later in Lewald's life, her husband Adolph Stahr, who seems to have been a pedantic philologian, took over her brother Otto's role and functioned voluntarily as teacher and as "oracle of instruction"—a derogatory term coined by Brandes.[34] He was responsible for Lewald's change of literary ideals—she turned away from the nasty and frivolous Heine in favor of Goethe, the settled, complacent, majestic Goethe of the nineteenth-century German bourgeoisie.

When Fanny Lewald first met her future husband in Rome in 1845, she was still an admirer of Heine's, until one day Stahr reprimanded her taste: to him, a woman approving of Heine was like a "beautiful white garment with a blemish."[35] In the years to come, the couple Lewald-Stahr—"the four-legged, two-sexed inky animal" was a term coined by Gottfried Keller to express his disrespect[36]—was to visit Heine in Paris more than once. In a discussion between Heine and Lewald about the possibility of a radical change only after Christianity has lost its power, Stahr did not hesitate to correct and pacify Lewald's opinions:

> Stahr, however, shook his head. "Don't take Fanny's words as seriously as they may sound," he said. "In discussions, she is sometimes a victim of woman's habit of dealing with something in a rash manner, without thinking about it, and without knowing what she has actually done, and what she now has to stand up for—although in her heart she knows better!"[37]

Since Stahr knew Lewald's thoughts better than she did herself, he had no scruples about supervising her correspondence and moderating her opinions there too, if he thought it necessary.[38] He was by no means an "inspiring muse," but, as Lewald appreciatively commented, "in every sense a teacher, an educator, and a model."[39] His tutelage has to be interpreted as a far-reaching impediment to Lewald's development of an identity of her own, and it had fatal consequences for her writing. After her marriage, Lewald's opinions, not only those on marriage and family life, changed drastically. The couple had had to wait for years before they could marry because Stahr had to obtain a divorce from his first wife, mother of his five children. During that time, Fanny wrote some spirited polemics against the bourgeois institution of the family. After her marriage, however, she had to admit that "harmony with convention can be very sweet as well."[40] The question has to be asked whether the change in Lewald's writings after 1853—usually attributed to the historical situation after the failed 1848 revolution—should not be seen in connection with her relationship with Stahr. In any case, the opinion that, in her married life with Stahr, Lewald enjoyed sufficient independence for her own energy and dominance[41] is too optimistic and superficial a viewpoint. On the contrary, one has to notice the dominance of this vain and pedantic pedagogue, and Lewald's lack of courage or ability to overcome "the perpetual admonitions of the eternal pedagogue—write this, think that": an ability which Virginia Woolf considered as prerequisite for authentic women's writing.[42]

Fanny Lewald's relationship with Stahr could be interpreted as the masochistic way in which women choose their partners: selecting intuitively the one who will most likely prevent one's potential from coming true—potential whose realization causes fears, of course. For example, Stahr criticized her early novels and called them "pathological novels" since she had used her writing as a catharsis of her feelings. It is a pity—and a loss to her body of writing—that Lewald accepted this judgment and attempted to write in a more detached manner, at a distance from her own feelings and experiences.

"The four-legged, two-sexed inky animal"—Lewald-Stahr's relationship, or symbiosis—has to be understood also in terms of love and competition as the typical problem of literary couples. Fanny Lewald, who had probably the stronger character, nevertheless was forced to attest to Stahr's superiority. The way in which she would compliment him on his taste and style not only betrays "feminine diplomacy," but has to be taken more seriously: she did in fact believe in male superiority.

The most profound and the most subtle aspects of Lewald's auto-censorship were of course a heritage from her father, a wine merchant and representative of the "enlightened bourgeoisie." Fanny Lewald grew up in Königsberg, a town in East Prussia, at that time still known best for its most famous citizen, Kant. When she was eight years old, her father explained Kant's concept of the categorical imperative to her. Indicative of her father's rational, patriarchal—yet assuredly liberal—attitude of education is the following passage in her autobiography:

> No child can have had more unnecessary fears than I had, I think. I had been afraid of certain impressions, such as the crowing of a rooster, or the loud sounds of a trumpet, and my father inured me to these fears—which had brought me out of my senses during the first few years of my life—by deliberately keeping roosters in the yard, and by always taking me to the changing of the guards. His way was a homeopathic treatment which may not be recommended in all cases, but which was quite successful with me, for my sensitiveness soon came to an end.[43]

The self-discipline which Fanny Lewald was forced to acquire had considerable impact on her writing. For example, her father was always strictly opposed to all expressions of imagination and sensibility, and as a writer she later found it difficult to overcome his prescriptive attitude.

Renate Möhrmann has pointed out that Lewald's first novel, *Clementine,* was written under the mind control of her father. Möhrmann considers this novel to be Lewald's argument with paternal authority which she needed in order to come to terms with his influence and to be able to formulate more independent viewpoints.[44] I, however, would like to see her father's influence—which resulted in thematic preferences as well as in an internalized stylistic attitude— much more extensively examined. In the beginning of her literary career, Lewald needed his comfort and support; he even served as a motivating force to her writing: "I anticipated my name as known and appreciated by the best of the land, I anticipated my father's pride in me. . . ."[45] Fanny Lewald wrote in order to please her father, and this structure was to last even after her father's death.

Even her most ardent and radical criticism of family life, of patriarchy and paternal love's despotism, is in the end always reconciled with her respect and admiration of paternal strength. These contradictions and ambivalences within Fanny Lewald herself should not be ignored, or even "solved," by literary criticism. They constitute the double aspect of Fanny Lewald's concept of emancipation.

In Roman law, "emancipation" meant the release of a slave or adult son from tutelage of the paterfamilias. With reference to this aspect, Renate Möhrmann has interpreted Lewald's biography as "emancipation in the literal sense of the word."[46]

One could see a formal release in the fact that Lewald's father allowed his daughter—then almost thirty years old—to become a writer. Fanny Lewald describes how her father at first was reluctant to "set her free"—at that point she would still have been willing to renounce her projects if he had wished her to do so. But finally he gave his blessings to her plans:

> "Well, then be a writer! . . . May God bless you!" With these words said, he left the room, and I was so moved that tears were streaming down my face. I did not feel more solemn when I vowed marriage to my husband for the rest of my life. . . .[47]

If we understand "emancipation" beyond the formal sense, in a figurative sense, we have to deny that Fanny Lewald succeeded in freeing herself from her father's hands. She always remained "my father's daughter"[48] instead.

She idealized her father and, accordingly, paternal or patriarchal principles and thoughts throughout her life. In her novels, there are plenty of examples of her idealized vision of virile strength and dignity, and her denunciation of "feminine weakness" and "nervous state of mind." A crude instance of such a sympathetic way to identify with her male hero and at the same time to degrade the woman character can be seen in her early novel *Eine Lebensfrage* (A Vital Question), which deals with the moral decision of divorce. Whereas Möhrmann appreciates this novel in the sense that it leads beyond feminism by treating its moral subject as a "human problem," rather than as a woman's problem—I should like to suggest a different viewpoint. In choosing a male hero who suffers from a bad marriage (and an intolerable wife), Fanny Lewald betrays some of her own wishes and fantasies: mediated by the novel structure and its point of view, the author reveals herself as lover superior to "the other woman"; the negative woman character in the novel has become the author's rival. At the same time, the male hero has become an ideal. In her autobiography, Fanny Lewald admitted with regard to this novel that she had a certain "tenderness for the new hero of my imagination."[49] This structure is typical of her novels. Psychologically, Lewald's idealized view of her father, of course, has to be seen against the background of a problematic mother-daughter relationship. Fanny Lewald did not find a model of feminine development and education in her mother; her mother in turn was envious of her daughter's activities and opportunities, which she herself had stimulated and approved of. Fanny Lewald internalized these conflicts and contradictions and directed them against herself:

> There were moments in which I literally felt alienated from my mother. However, as soon as such a sentiment arose in me, bitter regret and the most severe self-accusation followed. . . . [I] cursed everything in myself which was not like her, everything in my nature which did not fit in with hers.[50]

Her feelings resulted in depression, self-doubt, the fear of not being loved by her mother, by her sisters, and later by her cousin, Heinrich Simon. Although some of the conflicts were obviously caused by her father's behavior, she exempted him totally from her criticism. The result of her idealized concept of her father was an inability to face conflict, as well as a lack of self-assurance. The roots of this structure can be seen very well in the following quotation, which follows a passage in which Lewald has described how her father first wished to maintain their "patriarchal relationship" but finally voluntarily renounced his rights in order "to win the love of independent human beings." The children's independence, however, was not very convincing:

> Such arguments as the one mentioned above between my father and myself took place only seldom; they therefore hurt me and convinced me all the more. And when my father in the end kissed me and called me his dear eldest child, I would be so deeply overcome by my errors and mistakes and so convinced that I had to change and please everybody, that I would then embark upon the fight against myself very seriously. And my reward was my self-conquest and every token of love and satisfaction which my family expressed toward me. . . .[51]

"Fight against myself," "self-conquest," and "self-control"—to which sacrifices did these internalized paternal qualities lead Fanny Lewald?

> No enemy is to be feared in the same way as one should be afraid of one's own imagination. One fights every external enemy with vigor and energy, and spiteful glee and the pleasure of victory are auxiliaries in the fight. But who fights as seriously against himself, as against somebody else?—Who does not feel pain when overcoming the spoilt child in himself? And yet, one's inner enemy is the most dangerous one, for nobody knows our vulnerable points as well as we do ourselves. . . .[52]

Fanny Lewald tried to rationalize her fears and her imagination in her writing. Many novels express as main concern the process of self-disciplining and the necessity of rational development for the main character. But not only the topics chosen represent self-control, self-discipline, and self-denial; also in their aesthetic quality, her novels page after page reveal a process of the disciplining of the senses, a disciplining of imagination, a disciplining of such aesthetic categories as for example time and space. Lewald internalized the disciplining character of everyday life, and her literary works can be interpreted according to the ambivalent structure of everyday life as an expression of daydreaming and at the same time the disciplining, or even punishment, of this same daydreaming. As she internalized the necessity of self-discipline, of the comprehensive disciplining of the senses, she renounced the imaginative dimension according to which only the "permanence of art" can be constituted, and at the same time was more and more forced to deny her own experiences, to ignore her individuality. There is her renunciation of "feminine weakness and literary sentimentality,"[53] and there is her idealization of a "firm and fully developed handwriting, as if written by a man: These upright, firm, regular lines and letters, such clarity of handwriting—I had never found in a woman. It seemed an impossibility to me, to write a lie, or hypocrisy, in such letters."[54]

Along with her constant disciplining of imagination, this is another reason for her failure as a writer and for the literary triviality of most of her writing. Her adoption of a male handwriting makes her writing trite. Lewald once postulated that a woman writer should be criticized without prejudices and without indulgence, that she should be granted equal rights with her male counterpart. The fault of Lewald's egalitarian concept, however, was to ignore the different conditions—and as a consequence, the differing consciousness, and self-consciousness—of women writers. This concept remained an abstract formula, since it denied the historical differences that existed for male and female authors.

Robert Prutz once attributed "einen männlichen Faltenwurf" to Lewald's style of writing. This image of a "male cast of drapery"[55] which envelops her writing implies two things: First, it implies the vision of a covered, hidden female body underneath a man's garments. If the male drapery has to be regarded as a strategy of protection of the woman writer, her true emancipation would take place only after it were no longer necessary for her to seek shelter, to hide and to deny herself, under the cover of male formality—similar to the metaphor of dropping one's veil, which could be applied also to a woman author's use of anonymity, or a male first-person narrator. The cast of drapery, understood as the model, or stencil, implies also that the woman's language is disciplined, stencilled, according to the negative male pattern.

Just as the disciplining of her own imagination and her own feelings was central to Lewald's literary writing, it was also the central aspect of her emancipatory theory and ideals: "the emancipation for a serious performance of one's duties, for serious responsibility, and therefore for equal rights, which should be afforded the individual by serious work amongst serious workers."[56]

This goal implied the comprehensive disciplining of all the senses and an adjustment to the bourgeois concept of everyday life. It is a kind of emancipation which could take place very well only within the family, within the private sphere, and did not necessarily mean a challenge to the organization of bourgeois society at all: "And there is sufficient work to do for the woman, outside the family, and even more so within the family, if only one enables the woman to comprehend what this work consists of. . . ."[57]

Lewald considered occupational work for women as an intermediate solution for the unhappy (i.e., unmarried) women; the concept also worked for the institution of the family. What it really came to in the end, was the "Process of Civilization," the conquest of nature (also human nature) that went along with the industrial revolution and the development of bourgeois society. Emancipation in this sense was the retarded imitation of a historical process—progress—that middle-class men had already undergone. Fanny Lewald's biographical development—from Kant's Königsberg to Bismarck's Berlin—can be understood only in terms of the dialectics of Enlightenment, the dialectics of bourgeois rationality. It is a concept of emancipation and progress which emphasizes rational control over (human) nature, over emotions, "irrational" imagination, and so forth. The rationalism (and irrationalism) of the Enlightenment has been analyzed by twentieth century philosophy as a tragic concept, a Janus-faced historical concept which produced and disciplined utopian thinking at the same time. Max Horkheimer and Theodor Adorno saw women only as objects of rationalism; Fanny Lewald's example shows, however, that women were not only subjected to this historical development, but were also "subjects," participants, in the process.

Emancipation in Lewald's case meant the wish to adopt the bourgeois man's alienation, an adjustment to everyday life, the predominance of self-control, rationality, discipline vs. (literary or emancipatory) imagination. It was emancipation confined to, and not transcending, bourgeois everyday life. Her concept of emancipation and discipline led to her literary failure, but it was effective as a historical concept which is still valid and indeed not yet overcome today. I would like to end my essay therefore by briefly considering how we can learn from the history of a woman such as Fanny Lewald, and how we can understand her critically.

The critical reception of Fanny Lewald took place in different phases. In the 1920s and early 1930s, along with the post-World-War-I women's movement, there were some dissertations on her, in which she was viewed as an author in the Young Germany movement and as the "German George Sand." In the following years, as the continuity of tradition was disrupted by Nazi fascism, the author seems to have been forgotten.

Not until the 1960s did a revival of interest take place which, along with the student revolt, concentrated at first on Lewald's role as contemporary of the 1848 revolution in Germany. In 1967, her novel *Jenny,* in which she demanded freedom and equal rights for the Jews in Prussia, was reprinted in East Germany. In the 1970s, finally, Fanny Lewald was reclaimed by the women's movement. In its first phase, the emphasis of women's studies in West Germany was on the rediscovery of forgotten women and past history, with a concentration more on "positive", and positivistic, research and investigation, rather than on the development of a critical feminist theory. As the primary concern was the rediscovery, and often enthusiastic appreciation, of forgotten heroines, of pioneers and role models of women's liberation, "negative," or contradictory aspects, which did not seem to fit in with one's emancipatory desires, were often neglected, or even ignored.[58]

Feminist criticism today should nevertheless beware of ready-made emancipatory concepts, of "instant emancipation." We should no longer search for Great Women in History, but investigate also the weakness and contradictions of women's histories. If we understand historical women's biographies in their exemplary character, our main concern will be to investigate structures of condition and consciousness, rather than to create new heroines. We have to accept the historical texts in their triviality and triteness. They *are* trivial and trite—just like women's everyday life. If we seek to transcend this structure of everyday life and its alienation in our society, we have to read the texts as material and potential for our learning. Our task then is not to conserve the past like a museum, but to make past hope come true.

NOTES

I would like to thank Alan Kramer, Hamburg, for linguistic advice.

.1. Fanny Lewald, *Adele.* Braunschweig: Vieweg, 1855, p. 79f.

2. "Ihren Beruf in gewissem Sinne entweihend." F.L., *Die Reisegefährten.* Berlin: Otto Janke, 1865², vol. II, p. 185.

3. Ibid., vol. I, p. 247.

4. Ibid., vol. I, p. 15.

5. F.L., *Osterbriefe für die Frauen.* Berlin: Otto Janke, 1863; *Für und wider die Frauen. Vierzehn Briefe.* Berlin: Otto Janke, 1870.

6. F.L., *Die Erlöserin.* Berlin: Otto Janke, 1873, vol. I, p. 83.

7. F.L., *Meine Lebensgeschichte.* Gekürzter Abdruck der Originalausgabe (abbreviated edition), ed. by Gisela Brinker-Gabler, Frankfurt/M.: Fischer Taschenbuch Verlag, 1980, p. 181.

8. F.L., *Die Erlöserin,* vol. III, p. 449.

9. Gisela Brinker-Gabler, "Einleitung" (introduction). In: F.L., *Meine Lebensgeschichte,* p. 9.

10. Ibid., p. 25.

11. F.L., *Meine Lebensgeschichte,* p. 151.

12. Ibid., p. 110.

13. F.L., *Meine Lebensgeschichte.* Berlin: Otto Janke, 1861–1862, vol. III, 1, pp. 60–61. (Passages omitted in the 1980 edition are quoted according to the original six-volume edition; otherwise, I refer to the more easily accessible paperback edition.)

14. Agnes Heller, *Das Alltagsleben: Versuch einer Erklärung der individuellen Reproduktion.* Ed. by Hans Joas. Frankfurt/M.: Suhrkamp Verlag, 1978, p. 24.

15. Virginia Woolf, *A Room of One's Own.* New York/London: Harcourt Brace & World, p. 93.

16. Cited from: Karl Gutzkow: *Liberale Energie.* Ed. by Peter Demetz, Frankfurt/M., Berlin, 1974, p. 267.

17. Virginia Woolf, *A Room of One's Own,* p. 4.

18. Brinker-Gabler, "Einleitung", p. 12.

19. F.L., *Meine Lebensgeschichte* (original edition), vol. III, 1, p. 107.

20. Ibid., p. 108.

21. See, for instance, F.L., *Die Familie Darner.* Ein preußischer Roman aus napoleonischer Zeit. Bearbeitet und mit einer Einführung versehen von (ed.by) Heinrich Spiero. Königsberg i. Preußen: Gräfe & Unzer Verlag, 1925, p. 34, 92

22. F.L., *Meine Lebensgeschichte,* p. 237.

23. Virginia Woolf, *Three Guineas.* London: Hogarth Press, 1952, p. 265.

24. F.L., *Für und wider die Frauen,* p. 31.

25. F.L., *Gefühltes und Gedachtes* 1838–1888. (Diary) Ed. by Ludwig Geiger, Dresden/Leipzig: Verlag von Heinrich Minden, 1900, p. 207 (7 July 1875).

26. Cited from: Marieluise Steinhauer, *Fanny Lewald, die deutsche George Sand.* Ein Kapitel aus der Geschichte des Frauenromans im 19. Jahrhundert. Diss. phil. Berlin 1937, p. 115.

27. F.L., *Gefühltes und Gedachtes,* p. 161 (11 Sept. 1871).

28. Cf. F.L., *Meine Lebensgeschichte* (original edition), vol. III, 1, p. 6.

29. F.L., *Gefühltes und Gedachtes,* p. 214 (30 Jan. 1876).

30. F.L., *Adele,* p. 181.

31. F.L., *Die Erlöserin,* vol. III, p. 24.

32. F.L., *Meine Lebensgeschichte* (original edition), vol. I, 1, p. 237.

33. Cf. Gottfried Kößler, *Mädchenkindheiten im 19. Jahrhundert*. Gießen: Focus-Verlag, 1979, p. 56.

34. "Belehrungsorakel." Georg Brandes, "Fanny Lewald." In *Deutsche Persönlich-keiten*. Ges. Schriften Bd. 1, München 1902, p. 347.

35. F.L., *Zwölf Bilder nach dem Leben*. Berlin: Otto Janke, 1888, p. 200.

36. "Das vierbeinige zweigeschlechtige Tintentier." Cited from: Marta Weber, *Fanny Lewald*. Diss. Zürich, Rudolstadt 1921, p. 41.

37. F.L., *Zwölf Bilder nach dem Leben*, p. 235.

38. Steinhauer, *Fanny Lewald*, p. 26.

39. F.L., *Zwölf Bilder nach dem Leben*, p. 201.

40. F.L., *Gefühltes und Gedachtes*, p. 30 (6 März 1855).

41. See for instance Brinker-Gabler, "Einleitung," p. 21.

42. Virginia Woolf, *A Room of One's Own*, p. 78.

43. F.L., *Meine Lebensgeschichte* (original edition), vol. I, 1, p. 90f.

44. Renate Möhrmann, *Die andere Frau*. Emanzipationsansätze deutscher Schrift-stellerinnen im Vorfeld der Achtundvierziger Revolution. Stuttgart: Metzler, 1977, p. 132.

45. F.L., *Meine Lebensgeschichte*, p. 196.

46. Möhrmann, *Die andere Frau*, p. 127.

47. F.L., *Meine Lebensgeschichte*, p. 204.

48. F.L., *Meine Lebensgeschichte* (original edition), vol. II, 2, p. 151.

49. Ibid., vol. III, 1, p. 210.

50. Ibid., vol. II, 2, p. 89f.

51. Ibid., p. 83.

52. F.L., *Gefühltes und Gedachtes*, 4. März 1838.

53. Cf., for example, F.L., *England und Schottland*. Reisetagebuch. Braunschweig: Vieweg, 1851–1852, vol. II, p. 307.

54. F.L., *Graf Joachim*. Berlin: Otto Janke, 1859, pp. 155, 158.

55. Robert Prutz, *Die deutsche Literatur der Gegenwart. 1848–1858*. Leipzig 1870², vol. II, p. 258.

56. F.L., *Meine Lebensgeschichte*, p. 258.

57. Ibid., p. 151.

58. Thus Renate Möhrmann, in *Die andere Frau*, concentrated on the period of the 1848 revolution and discarded Lewald's later works as "of no more interest to the literary historian" (p. 154). Brinker-Gabler's new edition of Lewald's autobiography is itself an emphatic interpretation in which some of the most eloquent parts have been omitted which hint at Lewald's process of self-disciplining, her ambivalences about specific feelings and thoughts, and the subsequent rational control, or denial, of this ambivalence. Obviously, these abbreviations have to be seen in connection with the editor's wish to appreciate Fanny Lewald's pragmatic, and rational, sense of emancipation.

For a critical feminist approach which combines literary history and theory, see Sigrid Weigel: "Der schielende Blick. Thesen zur Geschichte weiblicher Schreib-praxis." In Sigrid Weigel and Inge Stephan: *Die verborgene Frau: Sechs Beiträge zu einer feministischen Literaturwissenschaft*. Berlin: Argument-Verlag, 1983, p. 83f.

ON A FEMINIST CONTROVERSY
LOUISE OTTO VS. LOUISE ASTON

Hans Adler

Liberation and emancipation movements always involve a shift of position. The spatial metaphor of movement in this case takes into account the fact that values which were static become dynamic, that what was marginal becomes central, and that what was taboo is offensively made accessible. However, this refocusing also means that a new, or at least changed background is created, against which the object or aim of the liberation or emancipation movement starts to gain some kind of shape and relevance. There are two reasons why this background is blurred. The first is because the observer has not focused his attention on it, and the second is because it is, from a synchronic and diachronic point of view, heterogeneous. From a synchronic point of view the background can be imagined as a universe of discourse, comparable to a model of the real universe, with only temporarily fixed points. From a diachronic point of view the background itself is also changing space whose transparency as regards its mode of representation depends not least on epistemological options and the standpoint of the observer.

Thus in order to fully characterize an emancipation movement, three parameters must be considered: the aim and object of the emancipation movement, the background against which it stands out and away from which it moves and finally, the standpoint of the observer. Here, I intend only to deal with the first two parameters, the aim and object and the background of the emancipation movement. To be more precise, I shall examine the connection between the two, with the aim of obtaining information which is as historically reliable as possible about the conflict between the potential for innovation of what was proclaimed about the (new) freedom in the early women's emancipation movement and its traditional and limited character.

Many studies which examined material in the euphoric atmosphere of the rediscovery of the history of the women's emancipation movement were quick, too quick, to use epithets mixing classification and evaluation, such as "radical" or "progressive." The former asserts the emancipatory position's fundamental break (innovation) with the "background"; the latter implies, at best, an assumption/knowledge of historical progress and its direction. At worst, the term "progressive" is based on the assumption that the observer's position is the best that could have been achieved. In order not to imitate such studies, I shall place the emphasis of my observations not so much on the potential for innovation of the emancipatory concept, as on its determinedness. In short, emancipation will be shown as an attempt to release oneself from traditional fixations. The writings of Louise Otto and Louise Aston will be examined to see how far they can be "used" as sources to place these writers in the emancipation movement and to see which aspects of the texts reveal the extent to which the emancipation movement was determined by tradition, i.e. reveal its historical profile.

A Polemic for Freedom and Sin

In number 21 of the first year's issue of Louise Otto's *Frauen-Zeitung* there is an unsigned review of a small volume of poetry by Louise Aston, her *"Freischärler-Reminiscenzen"*.[1] It begins by regretting that the following criticism should be made at all but states that it is indispensible in the cause of women's solidarity and beyond that in the cause of all democrats in order to fend off all "impure elements". After making a few remarks about aesthetic shortcomings in the poems and about the function of the poet in politically turbulent times, the writer makes a specific critique of the poem "Den Frauen." Three of the seven verses (verses 1, 4, 7) are quoted to support the writer's arguments, but this is done in such a way that the polemic core of the poem does not become clear. On the contrary, the impression is created that the lyrical self has become irretrievably addicted to a sexual mania and tries to pass this uncontrollable weakness off as a strength.

> Ihr richtet streng, der Sitte heil'ge Vehm',
> Und schleudert auf mein Haupt das Anathem!
> Mögt ihr zu Boden stürzen eure Kerzen
> Und schlagen an die Brust, so tugendreich:

Ich fühl' es mächtig in dem tiefsten Herzen,
Daß meine Sünde eurer Tugend gleich.

Der Unschuld Lilien mögen euch umblühn,
Das Roth der Schaam auf euern Wangen glühn;
Wie Schwäne sich auf stillen Fluthen schaukeln,
Gefühle still durch eure Seele ziehn;
Wie Falter neckend durch die Blumen gaukeln,
Der Liebe Wünsche leis' vorüberfliehn!

Quält euch ein flammend Sehnen fessellos,
Mögt ihr entsagen stolz und seelengroß;
Mögt still verzehren eure heiße Jugend,
Auskämpfen ritterlich den heil'gen Krieg,
Und mit dem Vollmachtsbriefe eurer Tugend
Dem Tod, der Hölle nehmen ihren Sieg!

Ich achte dennoch eure Tugend nicht,
Verwerfe kühn eu'r heiliges Gericht!
Seid des Gesetzes Hort, der Sitte Rächer,
Des frommen Glaubens treuer Genius!
Es lebt ein heil'ger Geist auch im *Verbrecher*.
Der Freie sündigt, weil er sünd'gen muß!

Das Leben auch verlangt sein mächtig Recht,
Verlaßt des starren Wortes todten Knecht;
Aus edlem Feuer flossen meine Sünden,
Aus Drang des Herzens, glüh'nder Leidenschaft.
Für sie würd' ich schon hier Vergebung finden,
Die Zeugen meines Werthes, meiner Kraft.

Entsagen ist der Nonne Stolz und Ruhm,
Beglücken ist des Weibes Heiligthum,
Ihr wollt mühsam die Ewigkeit ergründen,
Mir lächelt sie aus jedem Augenblick;
Ihr wollt das Glück in eurer Tugend finden,
Ich finde meine Tugend nur im Glück.

Wenn mich der Liebe Flammen heiß umsprühn,
Will ich in sel'gem Feuertod verglühn;
Doch aus den Gluthen steig' ich neugeboren,
Wie sich der Phönix aus der Asche schwingt,
Geläutert ward mein Wesen—nicht verloren,
Zu neuem, heil'gem Liebesglück verjüngt.

Without much ado the writer's criticism is concentrated on the last line of the fourth verse: "Der Freie sündigt, weil er sünd' gen muß" (the free person commits sins because he is forced to do so). The argumentation used against this maxim-like line is, however, significantly, explicitly not morally based. On the contrary, it is asserted that this line is "unphilosophical and nonsensical," for sin is—"both according to Feuerbach and also according to Luther"—lack of freedom.

> If the free person does something which, seen from a limited standpoint, is "sin," but he himself has left this standpoint, then for him it is not sin, but freedom and justice. If, however, the free person commits an act which is *from his point of view* a sin and which cannot be reconciled with *his* free opinion, with his moral law, then this is for him a sin, but then he has stopped being a free person and has become a slave of his own sensory nature and of a foreign law.—It is very simple. I fear that L. Aston, although she calls herself a free person, is, in fact, not free at all.[2]

What to the critic seems "very simple" refers to a subjective concept of sin which she applies to acts arising from the noncongruence of volition and conscience. The free person—and thus the person free of sin—is therefore the person who acts in accord with intention and conscience. When intention and conscience are not in accord, this person is not free. This "unfree" person is, however, not capable of acting either, and is, in this sense, not the subject, but rather the object of forces which lie outside himself and his intention. Or to express it differently, we are talking here about the moral subject and his freedom, precisely that area, therefore, in which the criticism should *not* take place.[3]

Louise Aston's poem draws its polemical quality from the fact that she rejects the claim of a morality based on religion to a right to discipline the individual. In the fight against this morality, she goes so far as to suggest a "reversal" of the system of values, so that the old "evil" becomes the new "good" and the old "good" becomes the new "bad." If, in the middle of the nineteenth century, this reversal is scandalous (even if not quite new in that century[4]), it becomes threatening when, at least tentatively, the religious foundation is withdrawn from morality and decency. This is precisely the case in Aston's poem. After initial provocation by the ironically expressed criticism of hypocrisy, the irritation in the critique reaches its climax where "sin" is extolled as the duty of the free person. Since the Christian religion does not supply any arguments with which to support Aston's maxims, Louise Aston introduces another argument, which she calls "life."[5] Like Georg Büchner's Marion in *Danton's Death,* Louise Aston is searching for a premoral area of life in which reward for renunciation of instinctive behaviour is unknown.[6] The release of the individual into an amoral vacuum, which allows the unrepressed development of the individual into a subject always means, however, that institutionalized forms of repression are attacked or rejected. If this deterministic element is used to help us define emancipation, then we must, in every concrete case, always point out the specifically historical form of repression against which any particular struggle is being carried out. In the first half of the nineteenth century and later the struggle was, as is well known, against public bodies, whether those of the church,[7] politics, or business, which were entirely occupied by men. In the discussion quoted above, however, it is not the intention to put forward certain desiderata for a women's movement faced with a world controlled by men, but to clarify within the women's movement itself the direction of the struggle. Ruth-Ellen B. Joeres rightly points out the ideological homogeneity of the contributions to the *Frauen-Zeitung* under the guiding hand of Louise Otto[8] from which can be concluded that Louise Aston had been excluded from the whole "Louise-Otto-Group." Louise Aston had not been excluded because she had inveighed against "Die Frauen" or because she provoked the public by wearing trousers and smoking cigars. Nor was it because she had been expelled from Berlin, nor because she had actively taken part in the events of March, 1848. Louise Aston had been excluded because she represented a hedonistic and atheistic concept of emancipation. Expressions used in Aston's poem[9] suggest that she saw herself as a dissident or perhaps as a heretic. Since, however, the *Frauen-Zeitung* could not accept the analogy: inquisition/papacy vs. heresy, philosophy was the roundabout reason given for Aston's exclusion. It cannot be denied that the result—her intellectual incapacitation, as it were—was, in spite of its 'logical objectivity', based on and originated in religion.

For Louise Aston, only a break with the religious part of one's background could guarantee the success of emancipation. For Louise Otto and her *Frauen-Zeitung,* religion was an indispensible part of humanity. In her view, emancipation did not consist of breaking with the requirements of religious belief, but required rather that women find their place within a (reformed) religion. In order, therefore, to analyze both the literary and nonliterary sources of both positions, we must take into consideration—without making prejudicial value judgements—how far the text is determined by the religious ideas on which it is based, which is not the same as recording those passages in the texts which deal with religious topics. This is an area of literary-historical research that, as far as women's literature is concerned, has so far received too little attention.[10]

The significance of this area of research can be judged from two observations:

> 1. Religious socialization has a decisive role to play in establishing quasi-irreversible norms. Since this means of regulating behavior primarily characterizes nonpublic life, and since women in the nineteenth century were, with few exceptions, limited to this area, religious norms were among those norms which to a great extent determined what women were and were not allowed to do. In brief: religion determined freedom, and it did this in such a way as not to be accessible to rational analysis by the person concerned.

> 2. Both the results of religious socialization and the effect of religion *on* and *in* institutions determined political behavior and political life in numerous states of the German Confederation in the first half of the nineteenth century. The extreme agitation and uncertainty of political leadership concerning religious problems and disputes, which is not easy for contemporaries of the latter part of the twentieth century to understand, is an indication of the significance of religion for that era. For the Prussian Minister of Education Eichhorn, the observation that the "close connection between civil order and religious order"[11] was a basic tenet which fundamentally influenced his political decisions.

For both reasons given above, we see that religion provides a tool by which those in power can effectively maintain discipline over the individual and society. In other words, in the nineteenth century atheism or the criticism of religion were subversive factors. It is in this light that the texts of Louise Aston and Louise Otto are to be viewed and placed in a historical perspective.

Freedom from Religion: Louise Aston

When in February 1851 the notorious *Regierungsrat* Eberhardt[12] came upon the name Louise Aston in the Dresden Ministry of the Interior in the course of an investigation, he immediately asked the chief of police of the free Hanseatic city of Bremen for cooperation. The latter speedily but not exhaustively gave him information about Aston, and Eberhardt then turned to the no less notorious chief of police of Berlin Hinckeldey.[13] He sent the "secret files"[14] on Louise Aston to Dresden. These files contained evidence against Louise Aston and had led to her expulsion from Berlin.

The first item held against her was her contact with extremist "literary figures." Among those were the following: Bruno and Edgar Bauer (and his financee, whose nickname was "Mirabella," the feminine form of Mirabeau), Max Stirner, Franz Buhl, in short, most of those Young Hegelians in Berlin, who as the "free ones" had gained a certain degree of fame.[15] The fact that they believed that the historical power of "absolute spirit" alone could have practical effects and that they were partially inclined to anarchism, did not seem to the authorities to be much of a threat. On the other hand, what did seem a threat was the fact that the members of this "clique had named themselves *atheists* as did their head, *Bruno Bauer.*"

Then there is a quotation from a statement taken down after questioning in March, 1846, signed and approved by Louise Aston:

> I don't believe in God and I smoke cigars, that's perhaps why I'm an abomination for many ladies. I intend to emancipate women, even if it should cost me my heart's blood; I consider marriage to be the most immoral institution since I don't consider lasting love to be possible within it. If a man gets married he must be an imbecile. Belief in God and the institution of marriage must cease if we are to be happy.[16]

The statement goes on to name places where Louise Aston stayed after her expulsion and finally, Hinckeldey writes that she left Berlin on March 23rd, 1851 for Bremen.[17] Without any concrete reason, Louise Aston continued to attract the attention of the police.[18]

In outlining this chronique scandaleuse, it is not my main intention to give more precise details via newly revealed documents concerning the difficult phase of this woman's life between 1846 and 1850. It is, rather, my intention to make clear the assumptions and the background against which the behaviour of this woman seemed to be deviant, threatening, and criminal. Renate Möhrmann's judgement of the matter is, in a historical sense, incorrect:

> The offences with which she [Louise Aston] was charged—it should briefly be recalled that at the time of her expulsion (March 1846) she had not made an appearance in political life or had published articles in the press—were entirely within the private sphere.[19]

In her apologia, Louise Aston emphasized that her views deviated from those of official religion but were in agreement with modern philosophy[20] and she partly recognized what was going on in this expulsion affair: "My affair seemed to pass over from the area of law to that of theology, a change of faculty in which my cause gained in heaven, but obviously lost on earth."[21]

In Aston's expulsion, as in other actions against undesirable persons, it is clear that the religious factor played a decisive role. Since, however, religion determined people's views and thus placed limits on every form of behaviour, it is not possible to divide "private" from "public" behaviour. Consequently, most states in the period before 1848 had no scruples in influencing the views of their subjects for the purpose of maintaining "law and order" or in seeking out deviations whenever they appeared, in order to correct or render harmless "those who had been misled." In the period before 1848 religion had the disciplining function of mediating between the private and the public spheres. Although Louise Aston appropriately writes about a "change of faculty," she does not seem to have correctly understood that in her time law was not conceivable without the Christian faith. The Cologne mixed marriage dispute, the fear of Jesuits in Saxony, the conflicts concerning German Catholicism, the "Lichtfreunde" and the "free communities," to name but a few examples, are all clear evidence that politics and religion also stood in a similar relationship. In this connection the *Holy* Alliance and Frederick William IV's idea of a Christian-Germanic state should also be mentioned. Friedrich Sengle made the general comment:

> Order . . . is [for the period from 1815–1848] a theological concept, and the hypothesis being put forward here is, therefore, that *theological thinking continues to mould structures of behaviour, even in this age in which secularization and negation of Christendom appears in various forms.*[22]

In her novel, *Aus dem Leben einer Frau*,[23] Louise Aston has her heroine experience much of what she herself experienced. In this sense this novel does indeed have the character of a "confession," as the author emphasizes in the foreword. As it is, she strives to make her "social drama"[24] authentic and topical:

> Life is fragmentary, art should try to create a whole! These pages, whether fact or fiction, belong to life, and make no claim to artistic worth! Therefore they are fragmentary, like the whole of the modern world.[25]

If we disregard the topos of the fragmented world, which was taken from German Romanticism, the author is completely up-to-date in her demand for authenticity and especially with her idea that when depicting social problems, closeness to life and direct portrayal are preferable to artistic detachment and spirituality.[26] In spite of these programmatic statements, in spite of the high proportion of biographical elements, it should not be forgotten that Louise Aston did not choose the form of a diary, report or chronicle, but that of a novel. And this novel cannot, like a roman à clef, simply be reduced to a nonliterary substratum.

The main character, Johanna, a parson's daughter living in an apparently idyllic vicarage, leaves her family after a bitter quarrel, after having been married against her will to the factory owner Oburn. Her married life is a time of torment during which, however, she gains insight into the social situation of the factory workers and carries out charity work on their behalf. When Oburn gets into financial difficulties he tries to force Johanna to earn money as a prostitute. She flees to the capital city.

> That was the first phase of her marriage, rich in those kinds of conflicts which move people at this time. . . . She saved her better self from brutal violence . . . she saved the sanctity of her marriage by destroying it![27]

For our purpose, the reasons given for the way Johanna acts in difficult situations are interesting. After being forced to get married Johanna comes to a decision:

> I cannot pray—so I shall curse. There is no God of love; why else should I be suffering: if the grace of heaven is not for all, like its rain and its sunshine; if its blessings do not descend on me and my pain: then it is nothing but a dream of the happy, who clothe their sweet privilege in such beautiful images. I no longer have the wish to swear by these dreams. Reality has destroyed my dreams, the reality of this world and its iron power! Well, I shall recognize it and fight it for every foot of earth that I want to turn into paradise.[28]

For Johanna pain is the reason for her to doubt the existence of a loving God; the "unjust" distribution of grace is her reason for doubting the existence of a just God. She exposes the promises of grace and happiness as an illusion of the privileged, by means of which they surround themselves with their privileges. She renounces these illusory promises and turns away from hope of a hereafter to an active improvement of this life. She breaks with the church. In doing so, she frees herself completely from her parent's authority, an act whose significance becomes clear when one realizes that, according to Luther's teaching children should be brought up in such a way that "it is to be pointed out to them that their parents take God's place here on earth."[29] At least the "idea" of a connection between the social, political, and divine orders, which the Holy Alliance and its supporters were trying so hard to maintain, could be severely shaken by criticism of this kind, especially if it became widespread. It may be true that "the Prussian state . . . felt insulted as a man"[30] and "that the dogmatism of the church was to guarantee the eternal monopoly of power by men."[31] But both can only be seen clearly in their historical context against the background of their religious superstructure. It was not Louise Aston's intention to remove certain men from office, and she was only to a limited extent interested in reducing certain male privileges. Her main intention was to expose and destroy the structures which made possible and legitimized those privileges in the first place. For her the real scandal was that the whole person—the humanitarian ideal that had been formulated since the Enlightenment, idealistic philosophy and the literature of the German Classicism—was being offended against, was being diminished and was being used for purposes which lay outside itself. In Louise Aston's view, women's emancipation was, in the final analysis, emancipation of the whole person, regardless of sex. Her struggle for the liberation of women is, in the end, a struggle which she, as a paradigm, as it were, of the oppressed, is carrying on; Louise Aston sees an offense against herself as an offense against the whole species. Thus, on the one hand, the great extent of her attack can be explained, and on the other, the pathos of her attempt to bridge the gap between the problems of the individual and the species can be accounted for.

To summarize briefly, it can be said that those components of Louise Aston's position which are critical of religion and are subjectivistic fix her place within the emancipation movement. The former appear both in direct form as explicit attacks on and criticism of religion and indirectly in the form of criticism of a double morality supported by religion or as exposure of the way religious means are used to enable social misery to be tolerated and legitimized. In her criticism of religion, Louise Aston makes a direct, frontal (and thus very unprotected) attack on structural relationships which, because of the long tradition in which they have developed, had hardened and settled and had taken on an aura of unchangeableness, whether as something "natural" or as something "God-given." A consequence of this fusion—with the extensive results we have outlined, from far-reaching effects in political life to the development of "conscience" and consciousness—is the strengthening of the assumption that the usefulness of these relationships ought not to be subject to a rational analysis, but that it is appropriate to condition human beings to accept precisely these structures. Arguments and reasons for a morality based on religion are replaced by the simple observation that it exists and that its relevance is recognized. The evidence of this sensus communis, which was in large part also valid for the first half of the nineteenth century,[32] resulted in the fact that critics of this state of affairs had to be outsiders. The more (French Revolution) or less (philosophy, political theory, structural changes caused by economic factors) spectacular disturbance of basic ideological assumptions which had resulted from various shocks since the Enlightenment meant that, in Europe after the Napoleonic Wars and again, to a greater extent, after 1830, critical outsiders were classified as criminals (e.g., Büchner, Weidig) or as muddleheads. The latter is, basically, the case in the critique of Louise Aston in the *Frauen-Zeitung* review. The fact that religiously-based criticism uses the global reproach of 'absurdity' seems to be an indication of the quasi naturalness of the religious basis of the criticism.

When compared with the claim to totality of the religious framework of knowledge, Aston's attempt at emancipation is spontaneous and subjective. In the hope of gaining proselytes for the "new" evidence by the gesture of provocation, the old evidence of the sensus communis is opposed by what she claims to be the new evidence of a personality, born to develop freely. Thus a twofold relationship to the background "religion" arises. The *method* of consolidation is similar to religion, but in the *matter* the method is used against religion. In any case, its relationship to religion (and to the church) is one of the decisive factors in determining the scale of emancipatory endeavours.

Freedom in Religion: Louise Otto

Louise Otto was a Christian and in the second half of the 1840s was an active supporter of German Catholicism, as can be seen in many of her journalistic writings. She openly admitted this. Ernst Bloch's assertion that Louise Otto was a "red democrat"[33] contrasts strangely with this, since the impression might arise that she could be counted among the socialists or possibly the atheists of the time. Even if one takes into consideration the fact that German Catholicism considered a "coalition" with socialist groups in the period before 1848 to be a possibility, it would be wrong to place Louise Otto in close proximity to Marx and Engels, Weitling, or Moses Heß. Her German Catholicism was— together with her hatred of Jesuits—oriented toward ecumenism and nationalism; the Christian virtues formed a basic minimum consensus.

In forming a judgement of Louise Otto, a distinction must be made between contemporary assessments and those made in retrospect. She was described by contemporaries — according to the standpoint of the speaker—as a "demagogue"[34] and as a "courageous, patriotic

German girl."[35] For a long time the authorities regarded her persona non grata.[36] From a historical perspective she has, for the 1840s, been judged to be a "socialist,"[37] to be an advocate of violent revolutionary change,[38] to be a "near-materialist," of a Marxist type.[39] All these characterizations have one thing in common: they take no, or scarcely any, account of Louise Otto's religious views.

Louise Otto's characterization of Edgar Bauer, who was counted among the Berlin atheists I have listed above, shows how biased those attempts at classifying her as a socialist were. In 1844 she wrote the following about Edgar Bauer in *Der Wandelstern:*

> He belongs to a party founded on praiseworthy principles that ran so confusingly along its path that it would have had itself to blame for its own destruction, had not the power of its opponents destroyed it. I mean the party of the *Deutsche Jahrbücher* and the *Rheinische Zeitung.* There was nothing to fear from these periodicals because they could not be understood by most people; nothing to fear from this direction, because it carried the seed of death within itself, in its own pleasure in destruction and subversion. It would have destroyed itself from within sooner or later, if it hadn't been destroyed from without. . . .[40]

With a certain skill, which is apparent throughout Louise Otto's journalistic writings, she recognizes criticism as being legitimate but sees in it the "seed of death" if it has no firm or constant base. The fact that her criticism of Edgar Bauer is extended to the opposition periodicals *Deutsche Jahrbücher* and *Rheinische Zeitung*[41]—which were suppressed in 1843 and, moreover, were widely read—is characteristic of Louise Otto's firmly-held position. It should be noted, though, that she is not basically concerned with concrete political or social issues which were objects of disagreement. She is concerned, in general, with the methods used by Bauer, the *Jahrbücher* and the *Rheinische* to acquire knowledge or to make statements which were relevant in practice. The "seed of death" is, in principle, the removal of taboos which precedes the complete maturity of mankind. For Louise Otto the problem was not that she had needed prejudices or had considered them necessary; on the contrary, as a whole her work was dedicated to breaking down these barriers. The problem for Louise Otto was the potential decentralization of her own general framework of ideological orientation.

In Louise Otto's writings, it is conspicuous how her endeavours for emancipation are situated within a framework of reference which does not even allow "innovation vertigo" to arise. For one thing, there are quite concrete fixed points, such as family, house, home, country, state, nation, femininity, etc. For another, however—and this is what concerns us here, the *rocher de bronze*—religion appears as an un-shakeable framework for all human activity and planning, but without a great deal of justification and, occasionally, at first glance, not recog-nizable as such. This is the case even when religion appears only as a rhetorical (and thus unanalyzable) culmination point in a hierarchy of arguments, as it does in the following climax:

> The house is, by preference, the area in which women are active, but it is the duty of all human beings to improve themselves spiritually, it is a holy command of nature, indeed a command of our Christian religion, to us all—and should it be wrong to follow this command?[42]

And it is the case even when the Christian demand that life at a time of industrialization and of increasing influence of science should be lived in a manner pleasing in the sight of God—work, she wrote, was the "password of the century"—is realized by equating work and prayer:

> Let no one revile the present age in which people work more than pray, for prayer can no longer be *degraded* to become work, but work can be *exalted* to become prayer, and in the end a whole life can become a prayer.[43]

According to Psalm 90:10, which was criticized by Louise Aston, life can be magnificent, can be worship, when it has been toil and work. This religion framework, with the specification that a loving and not a vengeful God is in control,[44] is the most general precondition for Louise Otto's statements and acts.

As I have already explained elsewhere in reference to her novel *Schloß und Fabrik*,[45] this religious framework quite decisively deter-mines the structure and composition of Louise Otto's literary texts. Here, it is less interesting whether religiosity is introduced explicitly as a topic or as subject matter in the text. More interesting is the question of how far religiosity conditions literature as a *form of perception*. A further historical example which we shall draw on here is Louise Otto's novella *Arm und Reich*.[46]

The poor, young painter Edgar gets a commission from a noble married couple living on a lonely estate. The luxury and waste on the estate contrast sharply with the poverty of the painter. When his mother writes to tell him that she is hopelessly in debt, Edgar steals eleven Taler from a drunken Baron while he is lying asleep in his room at night. He justifies this theft to himself by pointing to the injustice of the excessive waste by the nobility:

> He fell to his knees and thanked God: "You gave me the sign that I asked for, to show that You were not deserting us!" he cried. He was so excited, his feelings were so confused that he happily began to pray.[47]

The theft is discovered, a servant is accused, Edgar's conscience stirs:

> The nocturnal sophism [that the waste of the rich is a justification for the poor to steal] . . . would no longer hold up in the clear light of day. . . . His numbed conscience now found its tongue. . . .[48]

By means of a mediator, he gains an audience with the Countess, who is ready to be merciful instead of punishing him:

> Edgar entered, pale as death . . . in the presence of the Countess he looked down.
> "You have done wrong—" Ferdinande began seriously, and then she stopped.
> "I can feel it!" said Edgar, "and may God forgive me for it, I myself will never forgive myself for having made myself lose my pride in being able to resist any temptation. . . ."[49]

The Countess forgives him the deed and gives him fifty Taler for his suffering mother, not least to prove to him that the poor's mistrust of the rich is based on prejudice. Thus ends this episode within the whole novella, which concludes quite horribly with murder, madness, and death by duel.

In connection with my topic, the circumstances of the theft and the rehabilitation are important and significant. In order to be able to do justice to the meaning of the theft in this form, one has to remember that the novella was published in 1845. A year before, the uprising of the Silesian weavers had suddenly made people aware that increasingly deplorable social conditions existed in the states of the German Confederation. These conditions resulted from freedom of trade, new industrially applied technologies, and an international economic boom which had also extended to the German states. The slogan which was applied to these bad social conditions was the "social question," and a veritable flood of suggestions for remedying the matter and of descriptions of the causes and extent of these conditions dominated quite a large part of the market for literature until the middle of the century—

the so-called social literature.[50] The title *Arm und Reich* has to be read in this historical context.

At night Edgar steals from the rich nobleman, assuming that his act is pleasing in the sight of God since he is taking something needed by someone from someone who does not know how to use it sensibly anyway. What seems like an act of poetic justice to the figure Edgar, is immediately judged with some skepticism as "confusion," and a short time later the deed is shown in its true light: Edgar's attempt to overturn or weaken existing legal conditions and distribution of wealth by appealing to the all-embracing justice of God, proves to be, when looked at in daylight, "nocturnal sophism" and dubious confusion of the mind. The diabolic prompting to carry out the theft in God's name shows how closely faith, the concept of property, and law and order are linked together in this story: there can be no radical change in one area without the others being affected—in other words, these areas support and protect each other. It is not the theft alone, but above all the reason for it which is important for the author, in order to show that to solve social problems outside the Christian maxims of behaviour is a step into the dark, into murky waters, into chaos. Its correlate in the life of the individual is madness. But then the immanent rationalism of the criticism of waste and those who waste ceases to be applicable.[51] Accordingly, a solution of the social question is not striven for because of economic considerations, but from the point of view of Christian moral teachings. The countess decides to be merciful by forgiving and helping the painter. It should be noted that the "remission" occurs in a kind of confession scene, which could have begun with a *mater peccavi*. The countess has the power of forgiveness because she has (limited) legal sovereignty over her possessions. That it is in this story a woman who appears as reconciler, is due, on the one hand to the construction of the plot of the whole story (which does not concern us here), and on the other, to the fact that she, the woman, is, in this point, completely in keeping with the ideas of the author, that is, of the historical person Louise Otto, as are other of her female literary figures.[52]

Louise Otto's position within the emancipation movement of the first half of the nineteenth century—and this position should have become clear in spite of the few and brief examples quoted—cannot be determined without taking into account her conditioning by religion. In doing so it is immaterial *which* Christian religion dominates in each particular instance. What is decisive is *that* her acts and thoughts are based on an orientation towards the Christian faith. Also, it is relatively unimportant for the analysis of the historical sources whether this close tie with the Christian faith is conscious or is largely un-reflected ("internalised"). The unreflected bond with Christianity can only be reconstructed by means of knowledge of the context which gives historical profile to what the author considers "taken for granted," "natural," or "evident."

To add a further short example: in the "Programm" of the first edition of the *Frauen-Zeitung* Louise Otto makes the following appeal:

> We must muster our forces in order to support the work of the re-demption of the world, first of all by spreading the great thoughts of the future: freedom and humanity (which basically mean the same) to all those groups which are accessible to us. . . .[53]

Of course, one could consider the "redemption of the world" to be pure pathos and the formulation of her aims "freedom and humanity" to have simply been taken over from her revered Schiller. But both of them should be thought of as a whole and taken seriously: "world-redemption" should be read to include connotations of the messian-ism which leads to great harmony and should be considered as a religious term in spite of having the character of a pathetic cliché. And "her" (Louise Otto's) Schiller is—as for many people in the Germany of the period before 1848—still a construct made up of idealism, humanity, and Christianity. It must be doubted that she followed or would have followed Schiller's dialectical interpretation of the Fall of Man as man's first step to freedom.[54]

In any case, terms with wide semantic extension should—from a methodological point of view—be treated as an incomplete form of the syllogism, the *enthymeme*, when their use is not specified, when their meaning is taken for granted. In the case of the enthymeme, premises are not explicitly given, nevertheless decisions are based on them: "These premises, however, which do not need to be named, and which, therefore, do not need to be tested, are the gateway for irra-tional, affected associations."[55] I shall modify this remark of Karl Eibl in light of the reconstruction of historical sources: the unspoken premises, that which is "taken for granted," traditional ideas which have become quasi-natural, what seems plausible—because of evidence and not effort of argumentation—to someone who is in agreement, all this is the sphere of the traditional, that which is effective en bloc simply because its existence is accepted. This can be called "irrational," one can also say it is "historically proven." Louise Otto's commitment to religion and Louise Aston's attempt to break away from religion are both examples of such premises. Religion as one of the important social determinants of the nineteenth century must be considered in writing the history of the feminist movement. The fact of the close nexus of women's role, women's religious education, and, finally, the religiously conditioned ideology of women of that time has in any case been greatly underestimated until now.

Postscript

After I completed this essay, two important publications germane to my topic appeared:

Ruth-Ellen Boetcher Joeres. *Die Anfänge der deutschen Frauenbewegung: Louise Otto-Peters.* Frankfurt: Fischer, 1983.

Germaine Goetzinger. *Für die Selbstverwirklichung der Frau: Louise Aston.* Frankfurt: Fischer, 1983.

Just recently I was also made aware of two reprints of texts by Louise Aston. Karlheinz Fingerhut edited and provided useful commentary to both, neither of which is mentioned by Goetzinger:

Louise Aston. *Aus dem Leben einer Frau.* Stuttgart: Akademischer Verlag Hans-Dieter Heinz, 1982.

Louise Aston. *Ein Lesebuch. Gedichte, Romane, Schriften in Auswahl (1846–1849).* Stuttgart: Akademischer Verlag Hans-Dieter Heinz, 1983.

And finally, I need to share the following dubious document that I discovered while doing research at the Biblioteka Jagiellońska, Cracow, in the fall of 1984. It consists of a small slip of paper, 10.9 × 13.9 cm., with writing on both sides. The text is as follows:

Louise Aston.

When Madame Aston was banished from Berlin, Rudolf Gottschall suggested to her that she pass herself off as a writer to provide a pretext for staying in Berlin. Within a few days he wrote *Wilde Rosen* for her, which was then published under her name. Later on he wrote *Meine Ausweisung aus Berlin* for her. Madame Aston's friend Scepansky wrote *Aus dem Leben einer Frau* for her, basing it partly on her own stories, and Gottschall corrected it and made some additions. Some of the poems published in 1850 in the collection *Freischärler-Reminiszenzen* were composed by Gottschall, the rest by Hiersemengel. The latter also wrote a play for her, but it was not performed. The novel *Lydia* and a later novel, both published under the name of Madame Aston, are by Max Schasler. This would-be author thus did not write even a single line on her own; everything was written by her friends. She remunerated these friends with love or money: Gottschall was rewarded with love, Schasler with money, since she shared the honorarium with him. It is at the moment unclear whether Hiersemengel received love or money.

When she married Dr. Meyer [sic] later in Bremen, she made a
stipulation that she be allowed vacation time every year to do what she
wished to do. Once she used this free time to take a trip with her old
friend Scepansky.

The origin and the author of the note are not clear; the only certainty is that Karl August Vernhagen von Ense did not write it. It is
possible, however, that his cousin Ludmilla Assing was the author. No
decision can be made here on whether the allegations are true or not.
To verify them or not would at most provide information about their
author; the historically relevant position of the *texts* remains untouched.

I would like to thank the director of the Biblioteka Jagiellońska's
Department of Modern Manuscripts in Cracow, Mrs. Elżbieta Burda,
for her gracious assistance and support.

NOTES

I wish to thank David Beal, Ruhr-University Bochum, for translating this article.

1. *Frauen-Zeitung* No. 21 of 8 September 1849, page 5 f. (hereafter FZ) about
Louise Aston: *Freischärler-Reminiscenzen. Zwölf Gedichte* (Leipzig: E. O. Weller 1850
[sic]). The review is also included in the selection from the FZ: *"Dem Reich der Freiheit
werb' ich Bürgerinnen." Die Frauenzeitung von Louise Otto.* Ed. and commented by
Ute Gerhard, Elisabeth Hannover-Drück and Romina Schmitter (Frankfurt/Main: Syn-
dikat 1980), p. 146 f. I quote from the originals. The first four verses of the poem were
first printed in: *Der Freischärler. Für Kunst und sociales Leben.* Redigirt von Louise
Aston. No. 2 of 8 November, 1848, p. 5 (title page). Differences between the two are
unimportant.

2. FZ, p. 6.

3. "This subjective or 'moral' freedom is what a European in particular calls
freedom. In virtue of the right thereto a man must possess a personal knowledge of the
distinction between good and evil in general: ethical and religious principles shall not
merely lay their claim on him as external laws and precepts of authority to be obeyed,
but have their assent, recognition, or even justification in his heart, sentiment, conscience, intelligence, etc." *Hegel's Philosophy of Mind.* Translated from the Encyclo-
pædia of the Philosophical Sciences with five introductory essays by William Wallace.
(Oxford: Clarendon Press 1894), p. 113 f.

4. The criticism of Heine's "frivolity" and of parts of his reception of Saint-
Simonism takes up such points.

5. Parallels can be made with Heine here, too: "Life is neither a purpose nor a
means to an end; life is a right. Life wants to assert this right against the paralyzing
death, against the past, and this assertion is the revolution." Heinrich Heine:
Verschiedenartige Geschichtsauffassung written in 1833. In H. H., *Sämtliche Schrif-*

ten. Ed. Klaus Briegleb. Vol. III, ed. Klaus Pörnbacher. (Darmstadt: Wissenschaftliche Buchgesellschaft 1971), p. 23. For the same reason one can refer to George Büchner: "Nature does not proceed by pursuing an aim . . . , nature in all its manifestations is directly *self-sufficient."* Georg Büchner: "Ueber Schädelnerven" (1836). In: G. B.: *Sämtliche Werke und Briefe.* Vol. 2. Ed. Werner R. Lehmann (München: Hanser 1972), p. 292.

6. Regarding Marion see Reinhold Grimm: "Coeur and Carreau. Über die Liebe bei Georg Büchner." In: *Georg Büchner I/II.* Ed. Heinz-Ludwig Arnold (München: Edition Text und Kritik 1979), p. 311 f. Cf. also: Hans Adler: Georg Büchner. Dantons Tod. In: *Deutsche Dramen. Interpretationen zu Werken von der Aufklärung bis zur Gegenwart.* Vol. 1: Von Lessing bis Grillparzer. Ed. Harro Müller-Michaels (Königstein/Ts.: Athenäum 1981), p. 148 f.

7. In connection with the church as an institution, for example, the attractiveness of the protestant "Freie Gemeinden" and of German Catholicism for the women's movement of the period before 1848 should be noted. "The particular reason why some of the well-known speakers of the feminist movement had joined the nondogmatic religious communities was the fact that women had equal rights in the Free and German-Catholic communities." Jörn Brederlow, *"Lichtfreunde" und "Freie Gemeinden." Religiöser Protest und Freiheitsbewegung im Vormärz und in der Revolution von 1848/49.* (München und Wien: Oldenbourg 1976), p. 67 (Studien zur modernen Geschichte. Vol. 20).

8. Cf. Ruth-Ellen B. Joeres: "Louise Otto and her Journals: a Chapter in Nineteenth-Century German Feminism." In: *Internationales Archiv für Sozialgeschichte der deutschen Literatur* (IASL). Vol. 4 (1979), p. 109. Cf. further remarks of Louise Otto's and Ernst Keil's concerning Louise Aston in : Twellmann, Margrit: *Die Deutsche* [sic] *Frauenbewegung. Ihre Anfänge und erste Entwicklung. Quellen 1843–1889* (Meisenheim am Glan: Hain 1972), p. 88 f. (Marburger Abhandlungen zur Politischen Wissenschaft. Vol. 17/II). It appears that M. Twellman is scarcely acquainted with Louise Aston's texts.

9. For example "Anathem," "heil'ges Gericht," and the biblical allusions and quotations.

10. For an institutionalised form of religious practice, see Catherine Prelinger's contribution to this volume.

11. Eichhorn in a letter of 13 January, 1847 to the Prussian Minister of the Interior (quoted from Brederlow (Note 7), p. 56).

12. Eberhardt was the publisher of the *Allgemeiner Polizei-Anzeiger,* a continually updated collection of details on wanted persons—anyone with a reputation of having critical or opposition opinions.

13. Regarding Hinckeldey, see Dieter Langewiesche: " 'Staatsschutz' und politischgesellschaftlicher Wandel in Deutschland 1848 bis 1914." In: *Literarische Geheimberichte. Protokolle der Metternich-Agenten.* Ed. Hans Adler. Vol. 2. 1844–1848 (Köln: Informationspresse-C. W. Leske 1981, (Materialien zum Vormärz. Vol. 6)), p. 218.

14. Cf. Hinckeldey's letter to Eberhardt of 5 March, 1851, Staatsarchiv Dresden, Ministerium des Innern 459, fol. 156r (hereafter: StA Dresden MdI).

15. Regarding the "Freien" see Karl Marx and Friedrich Engels: *Die heilige Familie, oder Kritik der kritischen Kritik. Gegen Bruno Bauer & Consorten* (1845). In: MEW, Vol. 2. Auguste Cornu: *Karl Marx und Friedrich Engels. Leben und Werk.* Vol. 2. 1844–1845 (Berlin: Aufbau-Verlag 1962), p. 23 f. *Literarische Geheimberichte. Protokolle der Metternich-Agenten.* Vol. 1. 1840–1844. Ed. Hans Adler (Köln: Informationspresse-C. W. Leske 1977, (Materialien zum Vormärz. Vol. 5), p. 151 f.

16. StA Dresden MdI 459 fol. 156/1r.

17. Letter of 24th March, 1851, StA Dresden MdI 459, fol. 157r.

18. We have the copy of a document of 26 March, 1857, in which the following is reported: "The notorious Louise Aston, now married to Dr. Meyer [sic], whose husband has found permanent employment in Odessa is staying at present in Berlin, and she plans to return to Odessa." StA Dresden MdI 459, fol. 170r.

19. Renate Möhrmann, *Die andere Frau. Emanzipationsansätze deutscher Schriftstellerinnen im Vorfeld der Achtundvierziger Revolution* (Stuttgart: Metzler 1977), p. 145.

20. Cf. Louise Aston: *Meine Emancipation, Verweisung und Rechtfertigung* (Brüssel: Vogler 1846), p. 45. Cf. also Aston, *Aus dem Leben einer Frau* (Hamburg: Hoffman und Campe 1847): "German philosophy has the task of finding the true nature of these phenomena [the bad social conditions], of understanding their real significance and of placing them in the development of the spirit. . . . The work of the thinkers will not and cannot be in vain. The power of thought will and must conquer the world." (p. 130, 132 f.).

21. Aston: *Meine Emancipation*, p. 26 (quotation taken from Möhrmann: *Die andere Frau*, l.c. (Note 19), p. 147).

22. Friedrich Sengle, *Biedermeierzeit. Deutsche Literatur im Spannungsfeld zwischen Restauration und Revolution 1815–1848*. Vol. 1 (Stuttgart: Metzler 1971), p. 64.

23. Aston: *Aus dem Leben einer Frau* (see note 20).

24. Ibid., p. 31.

25. Ibid.

26. Regarding the discussion of the problem at that time, see Hans Adler, *Soziale Romane im Vormärz. Literatursemiotische Studie* (München: Fink 1980), p. 13f.

27. Aston: *Aus dem Leben einer Frau* p. 154. She did not write about further phases of her marriage as she announced she would.

28. Ibid., p. 26 f.

29. Martin Luther, *Werke*. Vol. 30, 1. Abt. (Weimar 1910; reprint Weimar and Graz 1964), p. 147. Michel Foucault: *La volonté de savoir* (Paris: Gallimard 1976 [Histoire de la sexualité. Vol. 1]), p. 132; Foucault denies the "representational function" of the family, but sees in the "dispositif familial" a supporting function in the manipulation of power.

30. Möhrmann (see note 19), p. 147.

31. Ibid.

32. Cf. a short investigation of one example: Hans Adler, "Sukzession und Konsequenz. Skizze zum Verhältnis von Narration und sozialer Frage im 19. Jahrhundert." In: *Lendemains* 30, 1983.

33. Ernst Bloch, *Das Prinzip Hoffnung* (Frankfurt/Main: Suhrkamp 1977 [E.B.: Gesamtausgabe. Vol. 5]), p. 690. Bloch's handy phrase has become the subtitle of a very mediocre, compilatory account: Cordula Koepcke, *Louise Otto-Peters. Die[!] rote Demokratin* (Freiburg: Herder 1981 [Herderbücherei. Vol. 855]).

34. Dresdener Tageblatt, 17 August, 1846, p. 389 b. Quoted from Helmut Kirchmeyer, *Situationsgeschichte der Musikkritik und des musikalischen Pressewesens in Deutschland dargestellt vom Ausgange des 18. bix zum Beginn des 20. Jahrhunderts. IV. Teil. Das zeitgenössische Wagner-Bild*. Vol. 3: Dokumente 1846–1850 (Regensburg: Bosse 1968 [Studien zur Musikgeschichte des 19. Jahrhunderts. Vol. 7]), p. 106.

35. *Sächsische Vaterlands-Blätter* No. 142 of the 5th September, 1843, p. 634 b (editor's note).

36. I have, until now, not been able to find any archive documents for the repres-

sion by the censor, as described in Auguste Schmidt and Hugo Rösch: *Louise Otto-Peters, eine Dichterin und Vorkämpferin für Frauenrecht. Ein Lebensbild* (Leipzig: Voigtländer 1898 (Biographische Volksbücher 17–20)), p. 30, 58. The documents in the Staatsarchiv Dresden referring to Louise Otto were almost completely destroyed in the war. Documents which are available to me indicate that Louise Otto was being persecuted up to 1858. In the *Anzeiger für die politische Polizei Deutschlands auf die Zeit vom 1. Januar 1848 bis zur Gegenwart. Ein Handbuch für jeden deutschen Polizeibeamten.* Ed. **-r* (Dresden: Liepsch und Reichardt 1855; Reprint Hildesheim: Gerstenberg 1970), on p. 50 Louise Otto is listed as "democrat and comrade of Kathinka Zitz, Louise Aston, Johanna Kinkel etc.".

37. Schmidt/Rösch (see note 36), p. 57.
38. Vera Wulff, "Eine Nachtigall im Winter." In: *Neues Deutschland* No. 46 of 22nd February, 1958 supplement, s.p.
39. Cf. Hedda Zinner: *Nur eine Frau. Roman* (Berlin [8] 1960), p. 282—the obscure episode in which, by reading the *Rheinische Zeitung,* Louise Otto is made to doubt her own basic idealistic views.
40. Otto Stern (pseudonym of Louise Otto), "Ein Blick auf 1844." Second article. In: *Der Wandelstern.* Blätter für Unterhaltung, Literatur, Kunst and Theater No. 7 of February, 1843, p. 815a.
41. Cf. note 39.
42. Louise Otto, "Frauen und Politik." (Conclusion). In: *Sächsische Vaterlands-Blätter* No. 188 of 25th November, 1843, p. 815a.
43. Louise Otto: Ueber weibliche Erziehung. In: *Sächsische Vaterlands-Blätter* No. 174 of 31 October, 1844, p. 706a.
44. Two years before the FZ appeared we find the following lines:

> Dem Reich der Liebe will ich Bürger werben,
> Als Priesterin ihm leben und ihm sterben!

("I will win citizens for the empire of love which I will serve as priestess and die for.") In: Louise Otto, "Schlußgesang." (1847.) In: L.O. *Lieder eines deutschen Mädchens* (Leipzig: Wienbrack 1847), p. 226 (in the original text spaced). These are the final programmatic lines of the volume of poems. Cf. the motto of the FZ: "Dem Reich der Freiheit werb' ich Bürgerinnen!" ("I will win women citizens for the empire of freedom!")
45. Cf. Adler: *Soziale Romane im Vormärz* (see note 27), p. 115 f.
46. Louise Otto: *Arm und Reich. Novelle.* In: L.O.: *Aus der neuen Zeit. Novellen und Erzählungen* (Leipzig: Wienbrack 1845), p. 181 f.
47. Ibid., p. 229 f.
48. Ibid., p. 233.
49. Ibid., p. 249.
50. Among other examples regarding fictional literature are: Erich Edler: *Die Anfänge des sozialen Romans und der sozialen Novelle in Deutschland* (Frankfurt/Main: Klostermann 1977 [Studien zur Philosophie und Literatur des 19. Jahrhunderts. Vol. 34]); Otfried Scholz, *Arbeiterselbstbild und Arbeiterfremdbild zur Zeit der Industriellen Revolution. Ein Beitrag zur Sozialgeschichte des Arbeiters in der deutschen Erzähl-und Memoirenliteratur um die Mitte des 19. Jahrhunderts* (Berlin: Colloquiúm 1980 [Historische und Pädagogische Studien. Vol. 11]); Adler: *Soziale Romane im Vormärz* (see Note 26).—Regarding the revolt of the weavers see Lutz Kroneberg and Rolf Schloesser (eds.), *Weber-Revolte 1844. Der schlesische Weberaufstand im Spiegel der*

zeitgenössischen Publizistik und Literatur (Köln: Informationspresse-C. W. Leske ²
1980 [Materialien zum Vormärz. Vol. 7]).

51. For the very vehement criticism of utilitarian behaviour in Louise Otto's novel—
Schloß und Fabrik see Adler: *Soziale Romane im Vormärz* (see note 26), p. 146.

52. At the same time it should be noted that Louise Otto did not have a tendency to
gloss over or glorify her women figures. Compare, for example, Amalie in Schloß und
Fabrik or Rosalie in *Arm und Reich.*

53. Louise Otto, *Programm.* In: FZ No. 1 of 21 April, 1849, p. 1. Uncertainties
about how to classify this point of the program, when the religious background is not
taken into account, result in Margrit Twellmann's work: *Die deutsche Frauenbewegung. Ihre Anfänge und erste Entwicklung 1843–1889* (Kronberg/Ts.: Athenäum
1976 [first 1972]), p. 20 f.

54. "This fall of man from instinct, bringing the morally evil into the Creation but
only to make possible there the morally good, is unmistakably the greatest and most
auspicious event in the history of Man; this is the origin of his freedom, here, long ago
the first foundation-stone for his morality has been laid." Friedrich Schiller, "Etwas
über die erste Menschengesellschaft nach dem Leitfaden der mosaischen Urkunde
1790." In F.S., *Sämtliche Werke* in 12 vols. Vol. 10 (Berlin: Bibliographische Anstalt
n.d.), p. 257. Compare also under this aspect Louise Aston's poem "Den Frauen."

55. Karl Eibl: "Ergo todtgeschlagen: Erkenntnisgrenzen und Gewalt in Georg
Büchners 'Dantons Tod' und 'Woyzeck.' " In: *Euphorion* 75 (1981), p. 415. Regarding enthymeme in more detail see H. Schepers "Enthymem." In *Historisches Wörterbuch der Philosophie.* Ed. Joachim Ritter et al., Vol. 2. (Darmstadt: Wissenschaftliche
Buchgesellschaft, 1972), column 528 f.

THE NINETEENTH-CENTURY DEACONESSATE IN GERMANY
THE EFFICACY OF A FAMILY MODEL

Catherine M. Prelinger

German women entered the official mainstream of Protestant philanthropy for the first time through the institution of the female diaconate,
the *Diakonissenwerk,* at Kaiserswerth outside of Düsseldorf early in
the decade of the 1830s. By mid-century the institute at Kaiserswerth
conducted a thriving and multifaceted enterprise consisting of a hospital, an orphanage, a nursery school, and a hostel for former female
prisoners, facilities which also administered nearly one hundred and
fifty nurses in the field and where some three hundred teachers had
been trained.[1] Since that time the institution has enjoyed an uninter-
rupted history to the present day. Because charity has become synonymous with women's work it is easy to lose sight of the distinctiveness of
the German experience, one which had not previously embraced
women in any significant way. Charity was in fact a male preserve in
Protestant Germany[2] and the female diaconate, or deaconessate (I use
the terms interchangeably), was a work of innovation. Theodor Fliedner (1800–1864), a clergyman, and his first wife Friedericke Münster
(1800–1842), were responsible for this reversal of historical precedent.[3]

This paper will develop two principal themes. The first, deriving
from the early decades of the institution, argues that the Fliedners'
success reflected the effective adaptation of the model of the traditional family—*das ganze Haus*—as the basis for institutional administration and development. I will suggest that by incorporating the ideal
of the patriarchal family into the structure of the deaconessate,

215

Theodor Fliedner was able to recruit large numbers of women into the service of the institution, women whose existence was threatened by the declining traditional economy. My contention here is that the family model was not necessarily imposed on these women but rather that it satisfied reciprocal if very different needs. The images and controls of the patriarchal family also made it possible for these women to enter unfamiliar and potentially threatening situations. By the same token, the novel institution was able to gain credibility and acceptability in German society. Having demonstrated the efficacy of the surrogate family as an institutional model, I will go on to suggest a second theme, namely that the institute at Kaiserswerth was in a position after the revolution of 1848 both to challenge and to coopt certain of the demands and the rhetoric of the so-called bourgeois women's movement. The unlikely amalgam was feasible in part because both initiatives drew on an essentially religious set of assumptions which, however different their ultimate goal, shared a similar language and conceptual structure. The suggestion of a link at this level resonates with some of the work developed elsewhere in this collection, notably that of Hans Adler.[4]

The founding of the deaconessate was fueled from two sources: one, the acute rivalry between Protestants and Catholics in the Rhineland where Catholics predominated but Prussian Protestants governed; the other, the Awakening and the wish to supplement in some fashion the deficient spirituality of Friedrich Wilhelm III's Evangelical—or united—Church of Prussia. Fliedner correctly anticipated hostility from both contemporary Christian confessions. Consequently he confined his initial experiment to the nursing office, rightly perceiving that the introduction of a female diaconate centered on the care of the sick would be most readily tolerated by the public: there was universal agreement that conditions in contemporary hospitals were deplorable. With these considerations in mind, Fliedner purchased the largest house in Kaiserswerth in 1836 to serve as a hospital and deaconess home, so far having little notion of how or where his deaconesses would be recruited.[5]

The first deaconess was the sister of a missionary, daughter of—and assistant to—a physician whom Fliedner recruited through his clerical network: an ideal candidate.[6] Thereafter, however, recruitment to Kaiserswerth depended in a large measure on what was in fact a coincidence of religious and social goals articulated by Fliedner and the needs of a precarious segment of German womanhood: young single women to whom the traditional economy no longer offered a secure existence. Their struggle for survival, both spiritual and material, is recorded in their *Lebensläufe,* the self-biographies which they were required to submit as part of the admission's procedure. An examination of these statements illuminates one side of the formula which insured the success of the family model, the operational ideology that became so crucial a part of the deaconessate. All of the women who originally applied to Kaiserswerth were deeply touched by the Awakening. They perceived themselves to be sinners reborn in Christ. They were deeply concerned to live out the consequences of personal spiritual regeneration.

At the same time, the statements of deaconess candidates, in case after case, reflect a struggle with feelings of frustration and rage against parents and siblings or employers who were themselves victims of circumstance. The demographic revolution which overburdened the rural economy in Germany, increased the population by 38 percent in thirty years, set a previously stable population wandering, and dramatically elevated the rate of illegitimacy, also stimulated enrollment at Kaiserswerth because single women were the most vulnerable of all.[7] Most—though not all—of the early probationers at Kaiserswerth were from rural families. Many had already been in domestic service. Virtually all came from large families and had lost one or both parents. Many had either raised or been raised by siblings. Some of their siblings had succeeded in marrying; they had not. Some ascribed their circumstances to the loss of a family farm, to inadequate education, to early placement in domestic service. Disobedience to an employer or a parent is often the antecedent of what is then described as a struggle with the Devil or the Enemy. The Enemy or Devil in these accounts is finally subdued in the appearance of Jesus.[8] For these women, Kaiserswerth offered not only a chance to legitimate their conversion and atone for their understandable sense that life had dealt them ill; it also provided them with a livelihood, a home, and a surrogate family. Marie Handel described her earlier situation and conversion as follows:

> In the year 1834 my beloved father died. I stood there completely without faith. Why? Because I had no Savior. Indeed often I experienced his calls and appeals but I always avoided him and soon after my father's death I sought my pleasure again among the children of the world. As I had to leave my former position, according to God's will, I came to the house of the tax commissioner Kinzelbein where from the very first day the Lord sent great and heavy burdens to test me. . . . Indeed they befell me ever more furiously and I believed I couldn't endure them any longer. There I stood and said, dear God, how can I endure it any more. I received the answer: Long ago I wanted to draw you to me with love but you distanced yourself ever

more from me; now the Lord had to silence the scourge over me. From here on I promised my dear savior to be faithful and to live for him, . . . for he had so wonderfully sought me.[9]

For whatever reason—death, poverty, competitive claims on their property—the families of these women had found them neither husbands nor an adequate means of support at home. The familial structure and imagery which the deaconessate at Kaiserswerth increasingly elaborated clearly resonated well with the needs of these young women and, I would argue, was crucial in attracting them.

The community as it developed at Kaiserswerth resembled a Catholic order in its autonomy from the parish structure of the church; in their appearance and in their obedience to a rule, deaconesses were separated from the laity. A training program comprising both practical and spiritual instruction preceded a period of probation. Successful completion of probation, recognized by the ritual of consecration anticipated a commitment of five consecutive years of service in assignments to be determined by the institution. Service was either renewed for another five years or terminated at the wish of the individual deaconess. Those who remained attached to the institution were entitled to perpetual care when they retired.[10] The institutional routine was strenuous, including as it did care of the sick both day and night, school lessons, and frequent worship. As Sophie Eberle, a probationer, wrote to her parents: "The powers of both soul and body are perpetually in motion."[11] And Florence Nightingale, for whom Kaiserswerth also provided an early source of instruction, wrote to her sister: "Until yesterday I never even had time to send my things to the laundry."[12] The rigor of training was, however, mitigated by the sense of sisterhood which Theodore Fliedner, his wife, and the deaconesses themselves sought to cultivate.

In the house order Fliedner specified: "All the deaconesses in the institution constitute a family in that they live together united as sisters through ties of genuine love."[13] Deaconesses addressed one another as Sister. Friedericke Bremer, the Swedish feminist novelist, visited the training center at Kaiserswerth in 1846 and marvelled at the climate of sisterly community prevailing there. She had never seen, she wrote, "such a collection of enthusiastic, friendly, satisfied expressions."[14] Florence Nightingale wrote to Sister Sophie Wagner, the head deaconess, when she departed in 1853: "What Sister Katherine [the deaconess who accompanied her as far as Cologne] cannot describe to you is the great grief with which I parted from all my dear sisters and especially from you my honored and beloved Sister Sophie. I will think of you *every* moment and of all your goodness and patience and kindness towards me I can never forget you."[15] The sense of sisterhood—indeed of daughterhood—also sustained these women in the field. It provided a psychological insulation which permitted them to take risks and assume responsibilities otherwise inconceivable. This is what Amalie Richter wrote back to Fliedner from the journey which took her and two others through Germany and Austria to Triest and ultimately to Smyrna in 1853:

> At the end of the day's heat we all wept together and wished longingly to have our dear Herr Pastor with us. But fortunately we all three did not lose our heads. On the same evening we continued to Gloggnitz. An excellent coffee that we took strengthened us for our night tour that we had to withstand and about which we were all anxious. A crowd of rabble: Polish Jews, Austrians, Slovenes [*Krainer*], etc. climbed into third class and it moved us painfully to see how the poor were swindled from various sides. For awhile we had the coach to ourselves so we sang "Grace be with all" in three part harmony.[16]

Conscious efforts were made to enhance the sense of dependence of the sisters in the field with Fliedner and his wife at the motherhouse.

For even more salient to the character of the German deaconessate and its reinforcement of family norms than the concept of sisterhood was the incorporation of the marital and parental hierarchy of the patriarchal family into the authority structure of the institution. The patriarchal family—*das ganze Haus*—was a functional concept, a productive unit which constituted both public and private space. Functions divided along gender lines. The woman upon marriage became the helpmeet of her husband according to his will and his occupation. She and the women of the household conducted certain of its functions; authority over the household—wife, children, servants, all of whom were considered part of the family—resided with the father.[17] When Theodor Fliedner made his marriage proposal to Friedericke, he explicitly told her that, in the case of disagreement, "a wife must defer [to the husband] by human and divine right. If the word is to have any meaning, the wife must be subject to her husband." For, as he continued, "there is a peculiarity of mine which should not go unmentioned, namely the right of the man to be master in his house. [This] is one I am firmly accustomed to exercising."[18]

Friedericke was made superintendent of the deaconess institution not long after Theodor purchased the motherhouse. As superintendent she had the responsibility for the internal administration of the hospital, for household management, for liaison with the physician and for supervision of the deaconesses. She reported weekly to the Inspector, as Theodor was known. In the community of the deaconessate the superintendent was called Mother, the Inspector, Father. Friedericke often accompanied deaconesses to their posts in the field; once they were there, she corresponded with them, and sent them their clothing and pocket money. Neither private nor public—not even altogether internal rather than external—her responsibilities were functional.

The office of superintendent thus embodied the qualities of the wife's role in a patriarchal marriage, and in this form it was perpetuated both at Kaiserswerth and elsewhere as the motherhouse form of administration was replicated at other deaconess centers in Germany. The centrality of the familial function and imagery to the operation of the institution is manifest in Fliedner's sixth annual report for 1842, where he announced his forthcoming marriage to Caroline Bertheau a year after Friederick's death. Acknowledging the contribution of the committee constituted in the absence of a superintendent, he observed that

> it could in no way substitute for the absence of a woman's eye and heart, that with the keen glance of mother love and wisdom comprehends all operations of the institution with wifely tact, organizes and controls all woman's work, who with the Undersigned conducts the woman's education of the many aspirants and helps to preserve the parental relationship of the motherhouse for the sisters laboring away from it. The more anxiously the Undersigned was frequently questioned both orally and in writing by the many insightful male and female friends of our institutions about the filling up of this hole, the more he deems it his duty to convey here the happy report [of his forthcoming marriage].[19]

Under the aegis of Caroline the deaconessate moved in the direction of a greater division of function between Superintendent and Inspector. From her accession date the significantly more sentimental expressions of dependence on the part of deaconesses in the field, of "childlike trust" and "childish love." Word quickly spread among potential candidates that "it is best if one attaches oneself, particularly to the wife of the pastor, in a truly childlike fashion."[20] From 1842 also dates the founding of the orphanage at Kaiserswerth, an institution specifically intended to supply recruits for the deaconessate— genuinely parentless daughters for the surrogate family.

The surrogate family imagery was instrumental in gaining general acceptability for the deaconessate. Municipal and ecclesiastical officers who administered poor houses and hospitals as well as families who required attendants for the sick conducted their communications and negotiated their contracts exclusively with Theodor Fliedner, much as negotiations with a household head for an apprentice or a servant were conducted. Hence, at the most critical level, the introduction of the deaconessate required no change in societal attitudes.[21]

The deaconessate gradually came to enjoy external recognition and material success. Fifteen years after its founding, in 1851, the budget had increased fourfold over the first year to nearly thirty thousand Prussian thaler and there were approximately three thousand individual contributors, among them members of most of Germany's Protestant royal families. Shortly after the accession of Friedrich Wilhelm IV the deaconessate was formally recognized as a corporation with a legal and ecclesiastical relationship to the Prussian church in the province of Rhine-Westphalia. It enjoyed extensive franking privileges, interest-free loans and a normal enrollment of more than two hundred deaconesses. Fliedner was invited by the king to counsel him on the creation of a deaconess order under his personal patronage at Bethanien; he and Johann Hinrich Wichern, founder of the Inner Mission, were brought into the monarch's confidence and remained in a close advisory capacity to this project.[22]

The prosperity of the deaconessate during the decade of the 1850s and thereafter, like that of the Inner Mission and of the monarchy itself, reflected the successful strategy of reaction in which all of the institutions supporting the established church and state collaborated to contain the revolution. In the case of the institution at Kaiserwerth there was an additional, not always explicit, agenda directed not simply at the spirit of revolution in general but very specifically at the goals of the women's movement with a strategy which combined both challenge and cooptation.

There had always been a teaching program at Kaiserswerth; it had been eclipsed by the centrality of nursing, and the emphasis on consecration for the diaconate over training for lay women. Two services were available to lay teachers. One, the teachers' conference, was convened for a few days each year for confessional nursery school personnel to discuss their common concerns. The second pedagogical service was a training seminar. Originally organized on an informal basis, the seminar prepared women for nursery school teaching in the confessional organizations of their own communities. They used the nursery school attached to Fliedner's rectory as a practice area. By 1843 a total of 149 women had participated in the program. The following year a parallel seminar was opened for elementary teachers which trained them to teach traditional elementary disciplines as well as basic female vocational skills such as sewing and knitting. By 1847, Fliedner started fund raising for a new facility for the teaching program, one to which both the king and queen of Prussia contributed.[23]

It was on the basis of this foundation that Fliedner launched the vigorous promotional campaign for teachers which became the principal thrust of all promotional literature published at Kaiserswerth in the wake of the revolution. His response to what he viewed as the lack of cultivation and morality displayed by the revolution, the "uncontrolled rebellion against godly and human laws,"[24] was to propose a system of education which would penetrate every village of the realm and instead of starting with five- or six-year olds, would take children of two and three. He described the seminars at Kaiserswerth and the qualities necessary for admission: knowledge of Christian salvation combined with a Christian way of life, an inexhaustible love of poor children, cheer, and good health. The course, of six months duration, embraced training in children's play, stories, especially Bible stories, singing, simple language and arithmetic exercises, sewing, and teaching method. He developed a similar prospectus for the seminar in elementary and vocational teaching. By 1855 Fliedner incorporated language training into his program and extended its duration to two years so that women could qualify as well for posts in the upper girls' schools.[25] The recruitment effort was aimed both at lay women and women preparing to be deaconesses.

What is interesting in these proposals is neither the content of the programs nor the qualifications for admission—these had been published in annual reports before—but rather the rationale of the program, a rationale which reveals the impact of contemporary events. Fliedner defended both separate education for girls and the introduction of women teachers into girls' schools, a practice so far exceedingly limited, on the grounds that "womanly modesty, morality and discipline, love of cleanliness, a sense of order and sensitivity" could be better instilled by female than male teachers, and that women fostered a greater closeness to the church than male instructors do.[26] In 1857 Fliedner took up the issue of prejudice against female teachers in the schools and developed a historical argument in their favor, invoking leaders of the Reformation.[27] Focusing on the professional aspirations of unmarried women, Fliedner invited single women and widows to apply to the program at Kaiserswerth. "A good number of Christian young women may want to come," he wrote, "who feel an inner calling to give themselves over to the delightful business of instruction in the world of children, . . . and at the same time to make themselves into useful members of society."[28] Appeals to patriotism, to vocational and social utility, even to domesticity are something altogether new to the literature of the deaconessate. The use of the concept *christlich-mütterlicher Sinn*[29] (Christian maternal instinct) was, in fact, very close to the language of Friedrich Fröbel. Fröbel was the theorist of the kindergarten and mentor of the women promoting early childhood education under the aegis of the revolutionary women's movement in 1848–49. At the women's college in Hamburg, the *Hamburger Hochschule für das weibliche Geschlecht,* the most nearly feminist institution created by the revolution, Fröbel theory and method provided the core curriculum. There seems to be considerable justice to both the claims and the warning lodged by Louise Otto's *Frauen-Zeitung* in 1850 that the deaconess movement was usurping their rhetoric for the purpose of diluting the women's movement.[30]

Fliedner's tactic was one of *both* cooptation and challenge. In a prospectus on nursery teaching he openly attacked Friedrich Fröbel. He specifically objected to Fröbel's insistence that neither Bible stories nor fairy tales be included in the early childhood curriculum. Fröbel, for his part, rejected confessionalism of all kinds: he abhorred the doctrine of original sin; he rejected the concept of personal immortality on the ground that it was premised on the duality of spirit and physical nature which he repudiated, and also for pedagogical reasons: the teacher's responsibility was to help the child deal with the realities of this world, not to train it for the next. As Fliedner correctly put it: "According to his [Fröbel's] opinion, children's hearts are all pure and guiltless and have no need for a Savior." Fliedner found it impossible "to come to any kind of reconciliation with such enemies of godly revelation." He referred with biting sarcasm to the hallmarks of the Fröbel system, the block, ball, and cube, as childish rather than childlike; these were the devices on which Fröbel constructed a theory of cognition and movement for children.[31] The Fröbel kindergartens were proscribed by the Prussian government in 1851[32] and Fröbel himself died in 1852, a broken man. Early on, in Theodor Fliedner's book of verses and songs for children, the author declared that since so many children were destined to die between the ages of two and seven, it was better that they be prepared for eternity in a knowledge of their Creator and Savior than with songs of blocks, balls, and cubes on their lips.[33] Fliedner did not openly attack the women who developed Fröbel's program as part of their commitment to the revolutionary women's movement but he voiced his disdain in unmistakable code words when he observed, in his eighteenth annual report of 1854, that employers could expect the teachers trained by the deaconessate to be "exempt from any urge to be in vogue, [*Modesucht*]."[34]

The concerted push into teaching inevitably attracted a broader constituency to Kaiserswerth, the warnings from Otto's *Frauen-Zeitung* notwithstanding. The term *Lehrdiakonisse,* or teaching deaconess, appears for the first time in 1849. In 1853 there were nineteen teaching deaconesses among the 140 consecrated deaconesses. They often joined nursing deaconesses in the teams sent abroad.[35] The social composition of the deaconessate correspondingly changed. A statistical analysis of the status of families from which deaconesses were recruited in the postrevolutionary years documents a significant modification of the earlier rural constituency. According to the account compiled by the archivist of the institution, under the administration of Julius Disselhof (1865–1896) who followed Fliedner as Inspector, the sisterhood consisted of the following categories: 16 percent were daughters of clergy, teachers, high officials, and landowners; 33 percent, of master artisans, merchants, and middle-ranking officials; 32 percent of artisans and miners; 15 percent of peasant origin; and 4 percent of working class parentage.[36] While there are virtually no daughters of the academic class, the new bourgeoisie, or the proletariat, there is great variety to the representation of the traditional classes. A number of women from prominent Prussian aristocratic families entered the deaconessate as well, women such as Agnes and Johanna von Scharnhorst and Charlotte Gräfin von Schwerin. Certainly the heavily peasant character of the earlier deaconessate is gone.

But the Kaiserswerth constituency broadened in a much more substantial way. Women entered into training at Kaiserswerth who had no intention of becoming deaconesses. Florence Nightingale and Agnes Jones from England belong to this category, but nearer to hand were such distinguished names as Helene von Bülow, Marie von Rantzau, Adelheid Bleibtreu, and Franziska von Lepel, to mention just a few.[37] Access to this new and often vocationally oriented constituency did not, however, induce the institution to abandon familial rhetoric or structure. Clearly it was welcome even among the new breed of deaconesses and trainees. Nightingale's story is a familiar one, and many German women document similar cases of parental disdain and educational deprivation. Henriette Bleibtreu described the opposition her family raised to her attendance at Kaiserswerth and her memory of a "long, unlucky, unclear and useless life. . . . My parents were always so occupied in diverse ways that they were unable to concern themselves with our education." Agnes von Scharnhorst described the constant change of residence her father's professional life required and the consequent "unbroken loneliness" of her own girlhood: "all instruction I obtained, I obtained by myself."[38] The familial promise of Kaiserswerth continued to offer an alternative. Even the women from whom one might expect the greatest sense of autonomy—those deeply committed to their vocational goals or those whose spirit of independence from the institution took the form of the decision to marry, reveal in their comments the persistent hold of the surrogate family. In a letter to Caroline Fliedner, Margarethe Geib writes that "the thought of leaving my profession is truly very difficult for me, for it is a valuable and blessed calling"; nevertheless, she wants to marry and because she wishes both the permission and the blessing of the Fliedners, she sets out to describe her situation "ganz offen und kindlich" (with complete and childlike openness).[39]

What Theodor Fliedner accomplished in the last decade of his directorship—he died in 1864—was to graft the language and concept of women's professions onto the already existing imagery of the surrogate family. Similarly he coopted the concept of the bourgeois mother from the rhetoric of the women's movement and neutralized it by depriving it of any implication of a separate or autonomous sphere. For the attraction of the new motherhood to women of the revolutionary women's movement was its implicit moral hegemony. Fliedner expropriated the new language of motherhood but reincorporated the concept into the safer structure and context of the traditional household.[40] Thus it was possible to maximize the appeal of the institution at Kaiserswerth, to embrace both polarities of female experience: the need for intimacy and protection on the one hand and the need for independence and challenge on the other.

It has been customary to speak of liberal movements in Imperial Germany becoming feudalized, the bourgeois women's movement among them,[41] stunted as it was by alienation from the socialist feminists. It is perhaps not too farfetched to speak of the embourgeoisment of the institute at Kaiserswerth, the usurpation and neutralization of many of the goals of the revolutionary women's movement in such a way as to appeal, not to the true stalwarts of the movement—many of them were in exile anyway—but rather to women who might have been pulled in either direction. The repression of the women's movement for the time being left the conservatives uncontested. The movement emanating from Kaiserswerth was able to orchestrate the connection between female experience and feminist consciousness at will; the goals of the women's movement lived on in a way which was certainly unanticipated and unintended.

NOTES

1. *Das zweite Jahr-Zehnt der Diaconissen-Anstalt zu Kaiserwerth am Rhein in einem Abdrucke des 11.-20. Jahresberichtes vom. 1. Januar 1847 bis 1. Januar 1857* (Kaiserswerth: Buchhandlung der Diakonissenanstalt, 1857), pp. 2, 13.

2. The absence of a Protestant tradition of female philanthropy in Germany was intrinsic to the nature and development of the Lutheran Church. Martin Luther himself cast out the role of good works from the process of Christian redemption. In his insistence on the value of the family on the one hand and the centrality he gave to the Word of God as articulated by the male clergy on the other, Luther left very little scope for the development of women's public service. The repudiation of celibacy on Luther's part and the dissolution of celibate orders eliminated the very institutions in which the charitable dimension of Christianity had been practiced. The clerical marriage on which Luther laid great emphasis came to absorb many of the functions of charity to itself and in this sense acted as a deterrent to serious charity by lay women. Gerhard Uhlhorn, *Die christliche Liebestätigkeit* (Neukirchen-Moers, Kreis Moers: Neukirchener Verlag, 1959), p. 729; Wilhelm Liese, *Geschichte der Caritas,* 2 vols. (Freiburg i.B.: Caritasverlag, 1922), 1, pp. 240–56. There was a somewhat different tradition in the Reformed Church; see "Erneuerung des apostolischen Diakonissen-Amtes vor und nach der Reformation des 16. Jahrhunderts," *Armen- und Krankenfreund* 1, 4 (1849), pp. 13–14; "Das Diakonissen-Amt in der Reformation-Zeit," ibid., 6 (May–June, 1854), pp. 4–5. During the War of Liberation women, inspired by the combined forces of pietism and patriotism, were active in war-connected works of charity and created valuable precedents for the deaconess movement; see "Eine freiwillige Krankenspflegerin in den Befreiungskriegen," ibid., 17 (1865), pp. 77–78. This periodical, first issued by the deaconessate at Kaiserswerth in 1849 as a quarterly, became bimonthly in 1851, and after 1860 was paginated by the year. Hereafter cited as *AuKF.* Male forms of wartime charity tended to survive into the postwar years in a way that female philanthropy did not, giving the charitable enterprise of the first decades of the nineteenth century its particularly masculine cast; Uhlhorn, pp. 708–29. The needs of a large organization such as Johann Hinrich Wichern's *Rauhe Haus* in Hamburg with its lay brotherhood for extensive linen services engaged a number of women and one by-product was the trivialization of female charity; see Fliedner Archiv, Briefe der Schwestern, Pfarrer usw. betr. Aufnahme, Franziska Lehnert to Pfarrer Fliedner, 28 April 1836 [read 1837]. Hereafter cited as FlAr. I should like to express my deep appreciation to Sr. Ruth Felquentreff, Archivist of The Fliedner Archiv.

3. The best biographies are Martin Gerhardt, *Theodor Fliedner. Ein Lebensbild,* 2 vols. (Düsseldorf-Kaiserswerth: Buchhandlung der Diakonissenanstalt, 1933–37); and Anna Sticker, *Friedericke Fliedner. Von den Anfängen der Frauendiakonie. Ein Quellenbuch,* 2nd ed. (Neukirchen-Vluyn: Buchhandlung des Erziehungsvereins, 1963). The authors were successive archivists of the institution. Sticker provides a welcome antidote to Gerhardt's treatment of the deaconessate as a monument to Theodor Fliedner's life.

4. See my "Religious Dissent, Women's Rights, and the *Hamburger Hochschule für das weibliche Geschlecht* in mid-Nineteenth Century Germany," *Church History* 45, 1 (March 1976), pp. 42–55, in which I develop the religious context of mid-century feminism; and Hans Adler, in this collection.

5. FlAr, Theodor Fliedner to Elizabeth Fry, 2 Dec. 1839. For another example of Fliedner's anti-Catholicism, see his correspondence with Friedrich Klönne, a fellow

pastor near Cleve who also proposed a female diaconate and who shared Fliedner's hostility to Catholics; Georg Fliedner, *Theodor Fliedner. Durch Gottes Gnade Erneurer des apostolischen Diakonissenamtes in der evangelischen Kirche*, 3 vols. (Kaiserswerth: Buchhandlung der Diakonissenanstalt, 1908–12), 2, p. 8. On the connections between the practice of charity, private worship and opposition to the state church, see Uhlhorn, pp. 704, 711, 718. Theodore Fliedner, "Kurze Geschichte der Entstehung der ersten evangelischen Liebes-Anstalt zu Kaiserswerth," *AuKF* 8 (Jan.–Feb. 1856), p. 4, in which he describes the urgent need for nurses; Sticker, *Die Entstehung der neuzeitlichen Krankenpflege* (Kaiserswerth-Stuttgart: W. Kohlhammer, 1960), pp. 13–19. See also Catherine M. Prelinger and Rosemary S. Keller, "The Function of Female Bonding," *Women in New Worlds*, 2 vols., ed. Keller, Louise L. Queen, Hilah F. Thomas (Nashville: Abingdon Press, 1982), pp. 318–27.

6. "Bilder aus dem Diakonissen-Leben: Gertrud Reichardt, die erste Diakonisse der Neuzeit," *Kaiserswerther christlicher Volkskalender* 99 (1940), pp. 36–37.

7. Donald G. Rohr, *The Origins of Social Liberalism in Germany* (Chicago and London: University of Chicago Press, 1963), pp. 12–19; Mack Walker, *Germany and the Emigration 1816–1885*, Harvard Historical Monographs 56 (Cambridge: Harvard University Press, 1964), pp. 1–174; Edward Shorter, "Sexual Change and Illegitimacy: The European Experience," *Modern European Social History*, ed. Robert Bezucha (Lexington Mass., Toronto, London: D.C. Heath, 1972), pp. 231–69.

8. Henriette Brüning's father had been a pastor as was her brother; Caroline Brandt's brother was a pastor. Rebekka Müller's brother was a surgeon (meaning?); the father of Marie Schäfer was a farmer and vineyard owner; Sophie Wagner's father was a draper; Christine Klett's, a day laborer, was too poor to give her travel money to get to Kaiserswerth. FlAr, Briefe der Schwestern, alphabetically arranged. There was a cluster of early deaconesses from rural Württemberg where the revivalist preaching of the Hofacker brothers, Ludwig and Wilhelm, was important; Sticker, *Friedericke Fliedner*, pp. 202–13. One suspects that the Devil was often a sexually harassing master or subjective feelings of sexual temptation. A young woman was dismissed for her confession of an earlier sexual encounter; she wrote home to her mother: "O mother, forgive your evil daughter Elise von Morsey. I am dissolving this name with tears and putting Elise Sinner in its place," ibid., p. 353.

9. FlAr, Briefe der Schwestern, Marie Handel, [*Lebenslauf*], Stuttgart, 12 May 1840.

10. The evolution of Fliedner's conception of the institution is traced in Gerhardt, 2, pp. 9–56; statutes and other documentary instruments are to be found in Fliedner, G., 3, pp. 51–98, 141–75. The expectations for admission and service of deaconesses and the house rule are given in convenient form in the appendix of Sticker, *Friedericke Fliedner*, pp. 358–62.

11. FlAr, "Sophie Eberle an ihre Eltern," letter no. 1, Kaiserswerth, 19 Feb. 1854, typescript transcribed by the current archivist, Sister Ruth Felquentreff. (pp. 329–30) also gives the day's schedule; a valuable appendix is her discussion of room and board monetary equivalencies, pp. 335–39.

12. Cecil Woodham-Smith, *Florence Nightingale, 1820–1910* (New York, London, Toronto: McGraw-Hill, 1951), p. 60.

13. Georg Fliedner, 3, p. 161.

14. Friedericke Bremer, "Kaiserswerth am Rhein 1846," *Deutsches Lesebuch für die oberen Klassen der höheren Töchterschulen*, ed. Ferdinand Seinecke (Hannover: Ehlermann, 1850), p. 389.

15. Quoted in Sticker, *Florence Nightingale Curriculum Vitae* (Düsseldorf-

Kaiserswerth: Diakoniewerk, 1965), pp. 14–15.

16. FlAr II, Tagebücher und Briefwechsel mit Schwestern, Minna Grosse: Amalie Richter to Liebe Mutter und lieber Herr Pastor, Trieste, 8 Dec. 1853.

17. There are many good descriptions of the traditional household of which the classic is Otto Brunner, "Das ganze Haus und die alteuropäische Oekonomik," *Neue Wege der Verfassungs- und Sozialgeschichte* (Göttingen: Vandenhoeck und Rupprecht, 1956), pp. 40–45; the role of women is addressed specifically in Joan W. Scott and Louise A. Tilly, "Women's Work and the Family in Nineteenth-Century Europe," *The Family in History,* ed. Charles Rosenberg (Philadelphia: University of Pennsylvania Press, 1975), pp. 145–78; on the lack of distinction among biological family members and servants, see Heidi Rosenbaum, "Zur neueren Entwicklung der historischen Familienforschung," *Geschichte und Gesellschaft* 1, 2 and 3 (1975), p. 222.

18. Quoted in Sticker, *Friedericke Fliedner,* pp. 13–15.

19. *Das erste Jahr-Zehnt der Diakonissen-Anstalt in einem Abdrucke der zehn ersten Jahresberichte* (Kaiserswerth: Buchhandlung der Diakonissenanstalt, 1847), p. 91.

20. FlAr II, Bonn Schwesternbriefe, Maria Plattfahs to Herr Pastor und Frau Pastorin, 26 June 1859; Berlin Marthahof Schwesternbriefe, Elise Teckemeier to "Lieber Herr Pastor und liebe Mutter," 30 Dec. 1861; FlAr, "Sophie Eberle an ihre Eltern," Kaiserswerth, 19 Feb. 1854.

21. Sticker, *Die Entstehung,* pp. 282–328, gives examples of contracts and correspondence entailed by both engagement in private families and city hospitals.

22. *1. Jahresbericht über die Diakonissen-Anstalt zu Kaiserswerth* (Kaiserswerth: Buchhandlung der Diakonissenanstalt, 1837), pp. 24, 13–22; *15. Jahresbericht (1851),* pp. 61, 28–61; "Grundsetze des Rheinisch-Westphälischen Vereins für Bildung und Beschäftigung evangelischen Diakonissen," *10. Jahresbericht (1846),* p. 56.

23. *Das zweite Jahr-Zehnt,* pp. 13–8, 22; *Das erste Jahr-Zehnt,* pp. 107–108, 132, 161, 51; Gerhardt, 2, pp. 356–57.

24. "Notwendigkeit der Kleinkinderschulen, und Einrichtung des Seminars für Kleinkinder-Lehrerinnen zu Kaiserswerth," *AuKF* 1, 1 (1849), pp. 21–22.

25. Ibid., pp. 22–27; "Wirksamkeit und Werth der christlichen Elementar- und Industrie-Lehrerinnen, und Einrichtung des Seminars für dieselben," *AuKF* 2 (June 1850), pp. 1–14; *Das zweite Jahr-Zehnt,* p. 228.

26. "Wirksamkeit und Werth," p. 2.

27. "Die Bemühungen des Reformators Johannes Bugenhagen zur Errichtung von Mädchenschulen," *AuKF* 9 (Jan.–Feb. 1857), p. 30.

28. "Wirksamkeit und Werth," p. 13.

29. Ibid., p. 3.

30. See my "Religious Dissent, Women's Rights, and the *Hamburger Hochschule,*" pp. 42–55; *Frauen-Zeitung* 2, 43 (26 Oct. 1850), p. 8.

31. "Notwendigkeit der Kleinkinderschulen," p. 7.

32. Karl Müller, *Kulturreaktion in Preussen im 19. Jahrhundert* (Berlin: Verlag für Kulturpolitik, 1925), p. 8.

33. Theodor Fliedner, *Lieder-Buch für Kleinkinder-Schulen und die untern Klassen der Elementar-Schulen mit Melodien, Gebeten, Bibelsprüchen. . . .* "Vorrede," quoted in Gerhardt, 2, p. 336.

34. *Das zweite Jahr-Zehnt,* p. 197.

35. Sticker, *Theodor und Friedericke Fliedner: Von den Anfängen der Frauendiakonie* ([Neukirchen-Vluyn] Neukirchener Verlag des Erziehungsvereins, [1965]), p. 62; *17. Jahresbericht (1853),* p. 2; *Das zweite Jahr-Zehnt,* p. 198.

36. Sticker, *Experiment und Tradition in der 140-jährigen Geschichte des Diakoniewerks Kaiserswerth*. Promotionsansprache . . . Sonderdruck aus der Deutsche Krankenpflegezeitschrift 12 (1972), p. 12. In my own survey of the Pflegerinnen-Buch for the years 1852, 1856 and 1860 which listed all women who entered as probationers, the figures are comparable but it should be noted that of the roughly fifty or sixty women who were admitted yearly, some twenty list themselves either as orphans or did not designate their parents' occupation. I counted altogether fourteen pastors' daughters, forty-two daughters of men attached to the government, twenty-four artisans, ten artisan masters, three landowners, three who listed themselves in ways that suggest the peasantry, four who called their fathers workmen, three who listed themselves as in service, two who called their fathers merchants—one a manager, one a manufacturer, and one a *"Bürger."* FlAr, Das Pflegerinnenbuch 1836–62. Verzeichniss der Diakonissen und Probeschwestern I. Probepflegerinnen 1849–61.

37. *10. Jahresbericht (1846)*, p. 7; *13. Jahresbericht (1849)*, p. 8; *17. Jahresbericht (1853)*, p. 12. Von Bülow was a member of the Mecklenburg aristocracy who ultimately introduced the deaconess organization in her home duchy; von Rantzau was made superintendent of the new motherhouse, Bethanien, in Berlin; Bleibtreu ultimately headed the motherhouse in Jerusalem; von Lepel established a home for wayward girls in Potsdam.

38. FlAr, Rep II Fg. 3; Lebensläufe, Henriette Bleibtreu, Agnes von Scharnhorst.

39. FlAr, Rep II Fg. 4: Heiraten von Schwestern 1841–64: Margarethe Geib to Caroline Fliedner, 23 April 1856 and April 1856. Her fiancé, a Pfarrer Krebs, also wrote to Theodor Fliedner April 1856 and 8 May 1856.

40. Wulf Wülfing, whose work appears elsewhere in this collection, has drawn my attention to the existence of a publication by Fliedner's successor, Julius Disselhof, *Luise, Königin von Preussen oder eine Geschichte von grosser Freud und tiefem Leid*, 3rd ed. (Kaiserswerth: Verlag der Diakonissen-Anstalt, 1910). Wülfing's own work on the mythologization of Queen Luise, the Prussian queen during the War of Liberation, demonstrates that by this means Luise was transformed into the ideal of bourgeois motherhood as the century progressed. By associating her name and legend with the enterprise at Kaiserswerth, Disselhof presumably completed the process begun by Fliedner of concurrently assimilating bourgeois values to the ethos of the deaconessate and draining them of potentially oppositional content. I am grateful to Wülfing for his very interesting contribution.

41. Richard J. Evans, *The Feminist Movement in Germany 1894–1933*, Sage Studies in 20th Century History 6 (London and Beverly Hills: Sage Publications, 1976), p. 26. Judging from conversations at the conference Condition and Consciousness in Minnesota, however, I gather that Evans no longer considers the manifestations of the women's movement during the 1848–49 period so politically radical but accepts the position I have always held, namely, that it was deeply imbued with religious assumptions.

GENDER AND CLASS IN WORKING-CLASS WOMEN'S AUTOBIOGRAPHIES

Mary Jo Maynes

The distance between the goals of working-class women and feminists of middle-class origins that has troubled the contemporary women's movement is not without historical precedent. Many studies of the "first wave" of feminism of the turn of the century have suggested a similar problem. The German women's movement was certainly no exception.

The aim of this essay is to use workingwomen's autobiographies as a way of approaching the larger issue of distance between working-class women and women's movements both historical and contemporary. Autobiographical accounts written by German-speaking women workers usually attest to an awareness of their special oppression as women and of difficulties faced by women because of their gender. In many cases, the autobiographical urge apparently flowed from a strong need for self-expression normally left unfulfilled in the normal course of a woman's life. These autobiographies can even be construed as a sort of propaganda, aimed at publicizing not only, or even primarily, each woman's personal story, but also the broader story of the injustice routinely done to women of the working classes.[1] Still, it would be a distortion to characterize these accounts, or their authors, as feminist. This, simply put, is the problem this essay will address.

First, it will be useful to describe the genre under consideration here, as well as the specific autobiographies that form the basis of my analysis. The special character of working-class autobiographies must be taken into account in any attempt to interpret them or to use them as a historical source.[2] The limits of their usefulness to the historian are all too obvious and need not be dwelt on here. They are highly selective accounts, and by no stretch of the imagination can they be read as systematic or representative in the sense that social historians usually like their sources to be. Autobiographers are by definition extraordinary people, and their interpretations of their lives cannot be accepted uncritically. For the historian, reference to other sorts of evidence must constantly serve to place the autobiographer in a social-historical context, to question the intentions of the autobiographer and the process whereby her autobiography came to be written and published, and to prevent the over- or misinterpretation of the evidence of a single life account.

What autobiographies offer—above and beyond the enrichment of quantitative data and detail about how individuals actually worked out the problems of everyday life—are two possibilities not directly opened by structural evidence: first, they offer insights into the ways in which some people made sense of their societies and their own lives, a normative dimension beyond the potential of most social-historical evidence; secondly, they offer an alternative vantage point from which to critique the apparent givens, the assumptions on which social-historical analysis and its categories usually rest.[3] To be sure, social historians commonly attempt to find indirect routes to this sense-making operation by drawing inferences about intentionality from patterns discerned in aggregate data. But for some sorts of questions, particularly for questions about the connections between evolving historical conditions and evolving consciousness, the direct testimony of autobiographies (and analogous sources like life histories and oral histories) can be particularly telling.

The interpretation of these sources is never simple. Even autobiographers who restrict themselves to fairly straightforward narratives of life events have gone through a process of selecting certain events for inclusion and exclusion, a selection process that rests not only on their aims in writing their life history, but also on their understanding of historical causation as it operated in their own life. The historian cannot assume that the autobiographer is an impartial judge of the logic of her own life course, but can read the autobiographical testimony as an indication of the notions of social and historical dynamics.

Beyond this, autobiographies need to be interpreted in a literary context as well. The autobiographer, despite her originality, subscribed to a set of literary constraints in writing about her life. The implicit rules governing the genre affected what she would and would not report, how she reported events, the language employed and so forth. In addition, the place of the autobiography as a literary product also helped to determine its likelihood of being published. In all of these regards, the working-class autobiography must be distinguished from autobiographies and other literary works produced by individuals from the educated classes who wrote under the conscious influence of literary models. Nevertheless, the historical use of working-class autobiography must be informed by the literary history of the genre.

It seems useful to distinguish at least three subgroups within the broad category of working-class autobiography.[4] First, there were socialist autobiographies written with fairly concrete political aims in mind: to testify about the misery of the proletarian existence and to suggest to workers ways out of that misery.[5] A second kind of autobiography was published with the encouragement of bourgeois editors and seemed aimed at reaching a middle-class audience concerned with the plight of workers or simply curious about life in the depths of society.[6] Finally, there are a few autobiographies of women who rose out of the working class and whose life stories document the struggle involved in that process.[7] I would like to suggest in the following discussion that by distinguishing among autobiographies according to their apparent intended audience and aim as "intentional" writing, one can discern patterns of variation in what is reported. This method of juxtaposition of subgroups of autobiographies cannot solve all of the methodological problems inherent in the social-historical use of autobiographical testimony, but it can at least call attention to those substantive areas about which there are systematic differences in what is reported and suggest ways of reading and interpreting different kinds of autobiographies.

The analysis that follows is based on the accounts of about twenty women autobiographers born in German-speaking countries between the 1840s and the 1880s. All of them had parents who were manual workers and/or themselves became workers. Among the socialists, Adelheid Popp came from an Austrian weaving family, and she herself worked in factories from childhood on. Ottilie Baader's father was a factory worker in Frankfurt an der Oder and later in Berlin, as she herself was. Her mother died when Ottilie was a child. Anna Mosegaard was an orphan sent into domestic service at the age of thirteen. Most of the women who contributed short autobiographical essays to the *Gedenkbuch* (Memory Book)—the 1912 publication that commemorated the twentieth anniversary of the founding of the *Arbeiterinnen-Zeitung* (Women Workers' Newspaper) of Vienna—were from families of home weavers or factory workers. (These include Anna Altmann, Anna Boschek, Sophie Jobst, Anna Maier, Anna Perthen, Amalie Pölzer, Aurelia Roth, and Amalie Seidl.) A few others (Betti Huber, Marie Sponer, and Marie Beutelmayer) had petit bourgeois fathers whose early death or negligence forced their daughters into factory work.

The nonsocialists came from similar social backgrounds. Kathrin, the author of *Dulden* (Endure) was the daughter of itinerant factory workers. The author of *Im Kampf ums Dasein* (In the Fight for Existence) had a mother who glued paper bags—first in the factory and then later at home. The job of her father was never specified, but he apparently also worked in a factory. She herself became a waitress in a large city. Angela Langer's father was a shopkeeper in a small Austrian town but he went bankrupt in her early adolescence. She herself was a servant, and her mother eventually became a charwoman in Vienna in order to feed her family. Lena Christ was the illegitimate daughter of a cook. She was raised in rural Bavaria by her maternal grandparents, and rejoined her mother in Munich when she married.

Whatever can or cannot be said about the autobiographers as a sample of German-speaking women workers, one thing at least is clear: they were *atypical* in their urgent need to tell their story, to tell it publicly, and to tell it for a reason. In many cases, this need is an extension of other forms of telling, of a painful process of finding a public voice that had shaped the lives of these autobiographers. A great number of these accounts include descriptions of some process of finding a voice—either literally coming into speech at a public gathering, or figuratively finding a voice through literary expression in revealing personal writing.

Finding the *Mut* (nerve or courage) to speak publicly is practically a convention in the socialist accounts.[8] Quite a few of the Austrian socialist women who wrote in the *Gedenkbuch* made their public "coming-out" a centerpiece of their memoirs. Amalie Seidl, for example, was a sixteen-year-old factory worker in the fall of 1892 when she heard Anna Boschek speak at a women's meeting in Vienna. She recalled:

> The fact that a young girl trusted herself to speak made a great impression on me and awakened in me the wish to be able to speak too; but I did not dare. But on May 1, 1893 I tried it anyway at a large meeting of dyers in Mariensaal in Rudolphsheim. Then the strike came and I had to talk.[9]

She is here referring to a strike that ensued at her factory when she was fired for agitational activity. Her coworkers walked out in sympathy and went to her home, where she then gave an informal speech in front of her house.

Marie Sponer began her political life agitating for better conditions at the factory where both she and her mother were employed. They were paid the same low wages that were the rule for women workers nearly everywhere, but in addition, Marie reported, she was the victim of sexual harassment. At one point, she was threatened with the loss, not only of her own job, but also her mother's, if she did not comply with the demands of her supervisor. All of her experiences made her begin to "reflect on her condition," reflections which were informed by readings at the local worker's educational society. She was involved in early efforts to organize women workers, and to build for them their own educational societies. She recalled:

> About this time, several women lecturers came from Vienna. . . . Among us there were also comrades who would have liked to speak, but none of us could find the courage. We all were afraid of a public appearance. When comrade Popp was here for the second time, we said to each other: one of us has to speak. But since no one volunteered, we elected Hermine Roscher. I would have given anything to have been able to do it, but I just could not bring myself to. But Comrade Popp encouraged me so much that I promised to say a few words. I listened attentively to the lecture and got many ideas from it. Then I asked to say something. Once I had spoken, further words came easily. It went better than I had expected. . . . After the meeting, Comrade Popp told me that I had spoken very well and should do it more often. From this time on, I spoke at large and small assemblies.[10]

Adelheid Popp, the inspiration to so many Austrian women socialists, also acquired her ability to tell her story in public slowly and with great difficulty. She began to read the working-class press as a young woman, and even to discuss it at work, much to the disapproval of her supervisors, who would shake their heads and say, "That girl speaks like a man!"[11] Popp thought of herself as exceptional, more like a man than a woman. Her interest in politics was an anomaly, she presumed. "The social question, as I understood it then, I took to be a man's question and politics was the concern of men."[12] Then, she read an article in the workers' paper about the middle-class women's movement, and this opened her eyes to a new insight:

> At home, I stood up on a chair and gave a speech as I would have done it if I had to talk at a meeting. "A born orator," was the verdict of my brother's friend. . . . "If only I were a man," was my usual reply. That a girl could do anything in the socialist movement or in political life in general, was something I did not yet realize. I had never heard or read about women at meetings and all of the invitations in "my newspaper" were addressed only to the male workers, to the men.[13]

Popp finally did ask her brother to take her to a meeting, where she was the only woman in attendance. At her second meeting, the speaker's words reminded her of her own childhood and she came to a realization:

> I knew that too; I could also recount that! But still, I did not dare say a word, I did not have the nerve to contribute anything. I thought of that as unfeminine and only appropriate for men. And besides, at the meeting, only men were considered—none of the speakers addressed himself to women.[14]

Then, on a Sunday afternoon, she decided to go by herself to a meeting. Despite the fact that the branch of industry that was its subject employed a large number of women, there were only nine women in attendance and 300 men. The absence of women was striking and led one of the speakers to address the issue of organizing women workers, who he claimed were undercutting men's wages. Popp heard his words as a personal attack. He pointed to "the backwardness, the few needs and the satisfaction with their lot of women workers as crimes that brought all the other evils in their wake." Then, continued Popp in her recollection of the meeting:

> I had the feeling I had to speak. I imagined that all eyes were on me. They were waiting to see what I had to say in defense of my sex. I raised my hand and asked to say something. Someone shouted "Bravo" even before I opened my mouth, the effect of the very fact that a woman worker wanted to speak. As I mounted the steps to the podium, my head spun, and I felt as if I would choke. But I got control of myself and gave my first speech. I spoke of the sufferings, the exploitation and the spiritual deprivation of women workers. At the end, I referred back to this last point, because it seemed to me to be the basis for all the other forms of backwardness and for the other characteristics so damaging to women workers themselves.[15]

The result of the speech for Popp was profound. She recalled: "I went home in a trance. An indescribable feeling of happiness transported me. It seemed to me as if I had conquered the world."[16] One final—and equally telling—testimony comes from Ottilie Baader. She describes her need to overcome, not only self-doubt, but also the hold of an authoritarian father:

> I experienced in my own life the conditions of dependency in which women, even working women, stood with respect to the male mem-

bers of their families. Despite the fact that for quite a while I had been the sole support for our small household, I was always regarded by my father as a daughter who had no need for an opinion of her own, who was supposed defer to him, unconditionally, in every matter.[17]

When Baader asked to accompany her father to meetings, he at first discouraged her, but finally took her along. Then, she got up the courage to announce to him that she was going alone to a meeting:

> I had learned through my reading to form my own opinions, but I was not permitted to go to meetings alone. Eventually, that no longer satisfied me. . . .
> All of a sudden I had an energetic moment and declared: "This evening I am going to go to the meeting of the shaftworkers!" My determination must have completely surprised my father. He remained completely silent and let me go alone to the meeting.
> At this meeting I spoke for the first time.[18]

The juxtaposition of Baader's speech with her father's silence is all too expressive. Long before coming to employ the self-revelatory and hortative autobiographical form, Baader, like other socialist women, had gone through the difficult passage from silence to witness in her own life. These accounts of the liberating effect of public speech certainly have feminist overtones. It is interesting to note that many of these first speeches were either delivered to assemblies of women or else in the absence of the male family members who usually accompanied the women to meetings. The accounts suggest that the difficulties involved in speaking were particularly women's difficulties. In this sense, the autobiographies these women wrote can be interpreted as a product of the experience of and need for public self-expression.

The nonsocialist autobiographies are more difficult to characterize as a group in terms of what they reveal about connections between autobiography and other forms of self-expression. Two were written by women who saw writing, if not speech, as important for their self-definition. Angela Langer wrote poetry and novels, although her literary career was cut short by her early death. Lena Christ also wrote several novels set in the rural Bavaria in which she had spent her few relatively happy early years. According to Langer's account in her autobiographical novel, her poetry writing was a constant symbol of her superiority over the status into which life had thrown her. This is made especially clear in the account of her friendship with a patron and critic who cannot seem to forget that she is a domestic servant, whatever her talent. For Christ, the writing of novels followed her deliverance from her miserable early life and marked a departure from those years. There is a suggestion in both of these women's lives that finding a literacy voice was part of a process of considerable duration, a process integral to each woman's development and certainly connected closely to the autobiographical urge.

But some of the other nonsocialist autobiographies seem to owe their publication more to the determination of editors than to their authors. Although it would be unfair to dismiss them as elicited documents, it is harder to see them as logical products of a need for self-expression that had long been an integral part of the described life. Both cases, significantly enough, were autobiographers who published anonymously. In the case of the autobiography entitled *Dulden*, the author of the preface noted that the book would afford the reader "a glimpse into the life of the lowest popular classes, the relatives of an alcoholic . . . as it cannot be described with such fearful clarity in any other written record."[19] Similarly, Dr. G. Braun noted in his foreword to *Im Kampf ums Dasein* that this autobiography would show

> how seduction, need and misery in [the described] milieu so quickly paves the way to hell, but why we still do not have the right to condemn these unfortunates who from a moral standpoint are raised differently, think differently and act differently. It is indeed, made impossible for them to act morally. They are the victims of horrifying social circumstances.[20]

If these two memoirs can be regarded as propaganda pieces, the causes they champion are apparently more the causes of their editors than of their authors.

The intent here has been to suggest the variety of motives which could lie behind, first the writing, and then the publication, of these autobiographies. The connections between the autobiographical account and the life it attempts to describe can never be overlooked. The authors of different types of memoirs chose to recount different sorts of experiences, and their choices were to some extent a consequence of their intentions in writing and the place that the writing of an autobiograpy held in their lives. I will turn now to some illustrations of how this variation shows up in the depiction of several aspects of the lives of German working women.

The autobiographies provide especially rich documentation in areas which are of particular concern for historians of women.[21] These include: the nature of family relationships—especially mother-daughter and father-daughter relationships, the character of the female networks in which women lived and which were so crucial to their survival, networks that included coworkers, sisters and other female relatives, mistresses (in the case of domestic servants), and, more rarely, women friends. The autobiographies also describe and characterize relationships with men—bosses, potential husbands and lovers, potential seducers, political comrades, and, much more rarely, male friends. They also suggest the autobiographer's own sense of a "normal" life trajectory as well as routes of escaping a fated trajectory through education, rebelliousness, political activity, or luck. They suggest sources of self-esteem that sometimes enabled these autobiographers to see themselves as others did not see them and, in most cases at least, to maintain a kind of integrity despite the odds against that.

And those odds were substantial. From childhood on, the lives these women led were exceedingly harsh. Six of the accounts are dominated by memories of paternal brutality or negligence. Marie Beutelmayer's complaint was a fairly mild one—she simply claimed that her father had no use for her and gave her nothing but "a little bit of talent" and "existence." But for others, paternal drunkenness and violence was a routine part of life, often coming to a peak on payday when the father returned home late and drunk and short of pay. Adelheid Popp dwelt on the violence of her dreaded father; Aurelia Roth reported that she was still, at the time of writing her memoir, unable to forgive her father for his alcoholism and negligence, even though, as she pointed out, "he was always good when he was in a sober condition."[22] In only one case, however, was there a report of a mother actually leaving her husband. In this instance, in *Im Kampf ums Dasein*, the mother endured a long period of neglect and brutality and only left her husband after he beat her for reproving him for making sexual advances to her own sister.[23]

This last example raises explicitly the connected issue of how sexual relations within the families of autobiographers were portrayed. In this area, in particular, the differences among different types of autobiographies seem clear. The socialist accounts, while they do not shrink from reporting violence between the parents, are silent or evasive about issues of sexuality in the family. It is left to "Kathrin," the author of *Dulden*, to report a father's incestuous sexual advances, to Lena Christ to report abuse with sexual overtones at the hands of her mother. In fact, the whole question of abuse of children is again raised primarily by the nonsocialist writers—Lena Christ, and the two authors of *Im Kampf* and *Dulden*—all of whom recall beatings and other forms of violent punishment.

It seems to me that there is a tendency in the socialist accounts to stress only certain kinds of family problems. Socialist women did not shy away from pointing out how male violence against a dependent wife could ensue from inadequate pay and the alcoholism that so often accompanied poverty, but the nonsocialist accounts are far more severe in their depiction of the psychological life of the working-class family. The most brutal childhoods, the most oppressive parents, the most profligate sexuality, indeed, the single account by an autobiographer of infidelity and brutality on the part of her *own* husband, were published by nonsocialists.

There is a possible logic to this pattern. On the one hand, certain kinds of sordid stories probably appealed to a middle-class audience prepared to believe the worst about working-class life. On the other hand, socialist women would have had a different stake in their portraits. They certainly would want to portray the damage done to family life by poverty and insecurity, but they probably would not want to imply that the working-class family was unsound in its very essence. While this reticence is understandable in the political context, the implied silence about many issues concerning violence or sexual abuse or conflict within the family blunts a potentially strong feminist critique which also might have been derived from the family experiences of the autobiographers.

I think that this implied silence is even more strongly suggested by way of a contrast with the handling of the issue of sexual harassment on the job. In this regard, and in contrast with the depictions of family life, there is far more similarity across the board. Women who spent part of their lives as domestic servants routinely reported the danger of potential seduction or rape by their employers. For example, in her article in the socialist women's newspaper *Die Gleichheit* (Equality), Anna Mosegaard reported her outrage at reading in the bourgeois press of the threat to the morality of children that the employment of servants represented. She then went on to recount a series of experiences she had had as a young servant. She had left three posts in a row after being the victim of unwanted sexual advances. Angela Langer also recounted the experience of being driven from a well-paid post as a governess because she refused to comply with her employer's sexual demands.[24]

Stories of this sort are common stock in literature and were much discussed in accounts of servants' conditions. Less well known, but apparent in the autobiographical accounts of both socialist and nonsocialist factory workers, is the phenomenon of sexual harassment at the factory. The author of *Im Kampf,* for example, reported on the situation of a pregnant coworker in a shoe factory:

It was known that a high-ranking employee of the factory had gotten her in this state, but he did not intend to marry her, which made the girl very unhappy.

   Now, because he had to drop her, he looked for a new victim for his desires and he cast his eye upon me, but didn't have any luck because I refused him sharply. The result of this was that soon I was back on the street.[25]

Adelheid Popp describes a nearly identical situation from her experiences. She reported that nearly all of the women workers in a factory where she worked when she was fifteen were crazy about a certain travelling representative of the firm. When she finally met him, he gave her what he called a "fatherly kiss." The next day, Popp recalled:

I was overwhelmed with reproaches by one of my coworkers, a young blond girl who had always seemed to me to be the most agreeable of all. She charged me with supplanting her in the affections of the travelling salesman; he had loved her, she claimed amid tears and sobs, and now it was all over because of me.[26]

Popp's reaction was to flee the situation, to leave the job and not return since:

I sensed an unnamable fear of unknown dangers. . . . They also told me that one of the workers was always in good graces with the traveling representative, but that the chosen one always changed. When somebody new came along who pleased him better, she took over from her predecessor.[27]

The point here is that all of the autobiographers apparently considered it appropriate to discuss the problem of sexual harassment on the job, and the terms in which they discussed it were similar. The relative silence on sexual matters at home that seems to characterize the socialist autobiographies is highlighted.

If the socialist women autobiographers chose to emphasize certain aspects of the condition of the woman worker and ignore others, in such a way as to perhaps blunt a possible feminist interpretation of their experiences, that choice would follow from their adoption of a socialist critique. Even as it would have been improper to exaggerate the psychological or physical brutality in working-class family life, so it would have been subversive of the cause to emphasize the conflict of interest between men and women in those families. Both tendencies would have undermined the political purposes for which the autobiographies were published. I am not arguing that these choices were conscious, or that they resulted from the adoption of a "party line" from which the autobiographers preferred not to depart. It was a more subtle and varied process than that, and seems rather to be the result of the very contradictory position of women within the socialist movement. Jean Quataert has aptly characterized German socialist women of this era as, at best, "reluctant feminists," whose position on women's issues was always taken in the context of the socialist movement and its strategies.[28] Some socialist women reflected in depth on the issue of women's special oppression, and consciously made their decision that socialism was the movement most likely to produce real improvements in women's conditions. Ottilie Baader, for example, although she spent her life organizing women and agitating on behalf of them, had little patience with the nonsocialist women's movement, and spurned efforts at reconciliation of women across class lines.[29] Adelheid Popp published her autobiography with the explicit aim of encouraging "those countless women workers who are perishing with a heart full of longing for activity, but shrink back because they don't feel they have the capacity to do anything."[30] But for her as for Baader, involvement in the socialist movement brought both personal satisfaction as well as the activity she felt was most beneficial to all working women.

Still, there are hints in other socialist memoirs that are much more troublesome. There are all too often phrases that suggest that women's activities in the socialist movement were shaped largely by the regard of socialist men, and that many women within the movement had internalized the misogynist critique of women workers that lay just under the surface of some socialist claims. There is a sense of this in Marie Beutelmayer's account of the "progress" of Austrian socialist women:

> Since 1910, there has no longer been a women's educational society in Linz. It has outlived its usefulness, and "New life blossoms from the ruins." Today we have the women's political organization, which with all its strength leads the common struggles together with the men for better living conditions and political rights. Everything, everything is different now. And our male comrades look with pride upon the women's movement. . . . And if fate is good to us, I believe that we will make the Upper Austrian Women's Movement into a part of the movement that will be worthy of the whole Party.[31]

The sentiment behind this statement is also revealed by Anna Perthen:

> Socialist thinking strides ever forward and will waken even the most indifferent woman worker from her sleep, and then she will join her

struggling sisters. The male comrades can help in this, if they would take their wives and daughters to meetings more frequently and give them workers' newspapers to read.[32]

These comments suggest an acquiescence to the view that had startled Popp into speech—that working women were politically backward and hostile to their own liberation, as well as damaging to the cause which promised to improve the condition of the whole working class.[33]

To be sure, in the context of their times, the socialist parties of late nineteenth- and early twentieth-century Europe were far more progressive on women's issues than other parties were. And the programs they and the socialist labor unions advocated would indeed have helped women workers in basic ways. Furthermore, the socialist movement was open to women, did offer them political and organizational skills and educational opportunities virtually without parallel elsewhere. I am not suggesting that the strategy of working in the socialist movement to improve the conditions of women workers was mistaken. But the testimony of the autobiographers does suggest that involvement in the movement did place women in a problematic position, did pressure them to subsume women's problems under the more general problems of workers, and perhaps even kept them from recognizing or admitting that their life courses were shaped by differences which were associated with the dynamics of gender.

However problematic was the position of women in the socialist movement, at least one result is clear: socialist women autobiographers did tend to regard their situation in collective terms and see collective solutions to their problems. Naturally, the nonsocialist female autobiographers were not involved in collective activities, but more profoundly, their very ways of regarding their situation led them to emphasize the individual or personal character of their problems (and occasional triumphs). And the solutions they suggest, or in some cases, the downright despair of finding a solution, also reflect this basic difference.

Angela Langer, perhaps in part reflecting her petit bourgeois origins, constantly suggests in her autobiographical novel that she maintained a sense of superiority over the coworkers or other women of her class with whom she was categorized. She constantly seeks to improve herself, through, for example, English lessons that distance her from a friend employed with her as a domestic servant. Significantly, the real lessons she took from the middle-class tutor, according to her account, were lessons in how to shed her common manners and pass for a lady. An educated male friend she meets later also reinforces the notion that the best escape from her lot is through self-improvement; her relation-ship with him teaches her that she will not be taken seriously as long as she remains a servant. His temporary interest in her as a patron and critic of her writing offers her an opportunity to see a way out of a life as a servant. The author of *Im Kampf* also improves her lot through the intervention of a male friend, but in a very different sort of relation-ship. She becomes the mistress of a man about whom she maintains discrete silence, claiming perhaps too assertively that her new found respectability (he sets her up in a small apartment and a small busi-ness) is a real triumph.[34]

For the author of *Dulden* and for Lena Christ, there really are no solutions. These women portray themselves as victims without will or prospect. Both considered suicide (Christ eventually did kill herself). At the point at which Christ ends her autobiography, her brutal hus-band has been committed to an asylum, her children institutionalized, and she herself is hospitalized in search of a "release from all her misery." She has survived, but even her survival seems not to be of her own doing: "Life held fast to me, and tried to show me that I was not that which I had so often held myself to be—superfluous."[35]

Of all the lives I have discussed, Christ's was described in the most brutal and despairing terms. Survival under the circumstances in which many of these autobiographers lived *was* an accomplishment. Sur-vivors' accounts are instructive. So are the more optimistic accounts which tell of at least small triumphs—over timidity, despair, over the arrogance or brutality or simple lack of understanding on the part of husbands and fathers and comrades, bosses, and even mothers and sisters. As sources of insight into women's abilities to survive, to do what had to be done, and even to rebel in the face of very trying conditions, these autobiographies are quite suggestive. They illustrate different paths to self-definition followed by working-class women, and show a great deal of variation in the degree to which these women saw their condition as unjust, and saw it as something that could be changed.

I think it is fair to say, however, that gender oppression was not regarded as primary by any of the female autobiographers. Whether socialist or apolitical, whether writing for a working-class audience or a middle-class one, whether positing collective or individual solutions to their problems, or no solution at all, these autobiographers all seem to agree that it is mostly because they are poor and reliant on their labor that they suffer. It is the poverty of their families that is the source of their troubled lives as children and adolescents. It is because the need to earn money drives them early on to take jobs they often don't like, working for bosses who harass and exploit them, that they feel there is injustice in their lot. While their identity as women is certainly central to their accounts of their life courses, they do not regard solidarity with women, across class lines, as a possible or desirable tactic for improvement. (Most, indeed, ignore the "women's movement.") And we need not agree with their analyses, or accept them uncritically, to find in these accounts potent evidence for the distance between "women's issues" as defined by the (essentially middle-class) "women's movement" of the turn of the century and the issues of concern to the working women whose reflections on and accounts of their own lives have survived.

NOTES

This essay was originally prepared for presentation at "Condition and Consciousness: An International Conference on German Women in the 18th and 19th Centuries," held at the University of Minnesota in April, 1983. The research on which it is based was supported through grants from the Graduate School and the Office of International Programs of the University of Minnesota and the American Philosophical Society.

1. For interesting discussions of the differences between working-class and middle-class autobiography, see W. Emmerich, *Proletarische Lebensläufe: Autobiographische Dokumente zur Entstehung der Zweiten Kultur in Deutschland* (Reinbek bei Hamburg: Rowohlt, 1974) Bd. I, pp. 11–39; U. Münchow, *Frühe deutsche Arbeiterautobiographie* (Berlin: Akademie Verlag, 1973); and E. Dittrich and J. Dittrich-Jacobi, "Lebensläufe nach aufsteigender Linie? Autobiographie als Quelle zur Sozialgeschichte der Erziehung," (Unpublished Working Paper, 1979).

2. Working-class autobiography has been the subject of much interest among social historians recently. There have been a number of important studies of the history of the genre, as well as some discussion of the use of autobiographical data for historical study. In addition to the works cited in the previous footnote, see K. D. Barkin, "Autobiography and History," *Societas*, 6, 2 (1976), pp. 83–108. W. Fischer, "Arbeitermemoiren als Quellen für Geschichte der industriellen Gesellschaft," *Soziale Welt* 9, 3–4 (1948), pp. 288–94; J. Fout, "Writing Social History from Working-Class Women's Autobiographies: Rewards and Problems," (unpublished conference paper presented at the meeting of the American Historical Association in December, 1982). Some of the more useful models for the use of autobiographical literature have come from English historians. See, for example, D. Vincent, *Bread, Knowledge and Freedom: A Study of Nineteenth-Century Working-Class Autobiography* (London: Europa, 1981). There have also been several anthologies of autobiographical excerpts published. Some of those bearing on the subjects raised in this essay (in addition to the Emmerich edition already cited) include: U. Münchow, *Arbeiter über ihr Leben* (Berlin: Dietz, 1976); R. Klucsaritz and F. G. Kürbisch, eds., *Arbeiterinnen kämpfen um ihr*

Recht (Wuppertal: Peter Hammer Verlag, 1975); J. Burnett, ed., *The Annals of Labor: Autobiographies of British Working-Class People, 1820–1920* (Bloomington, Ind.: Indiana University Press, 1974); and M. L. Davies, ed., *Life as We Have Known It, by Cooperative Working Women* (London, Vicago Press, 1977[2]).

3. My thinking about the use of autobiographies has been guided by work of historians with somewhat analogous sources—life histories and oral histories. The idea of using life histories to evolve a critique of the terms of analysis employed in studies using other kinds of sources is developed in a series of as yet unpublished papers by Susan Geiger and Riv-Ellen Prell, in particular, "Toward an Analysis of the Use of Women's Life Histories in the Study of Societies and Theories of Social Organization," presented at the meeting of the Society for Cross-Cultural Research, Minneapolis, February, 1982; and S. Geiger, "Reconceptualizing the Use of Life Histories for the Study of Women," presented at the International Conference on Research and Teaching Related to Women, Montreal, July–August, 1982. On oral history, see P. Thompson, *The Voice of the Past* (Oxford: Oxford University Press, 1978); and, especially useful, Popular Memory Group, "Popular memory: theory, politics, method," in R. Johnson, et al., eds., *Making Histories: Studies in History-Writing and Politics* (Minneapolis, Minnesota: University of Minnesota Press, 1982), pp. 205–52.

4. A somewhat analogous general argument is made by W. Emmerich, pp. 22 ff.

5. The autobiographies of this sort which will be discussed here include: Anonymous (A. Popp), *Jugendgeschichte einer Arbeiterin* (München: Ernst Reinhardt Verlag, 1909); O. Baader, *Ein steiniger Weg: Lebenserinnerungen* (Stuttgart, Berlin: Dietz Verlag, 1921); and the collection of brief memoirs edited by A. Popp, *Gedenkbuch: 20 Jahre österreichische Arbeiterinnenbewegung* (Wien, 1912).

6. The clearest examples of autobiographies of this sort are: E. Bleuler, ed., *Dulden: Aus der Lebensbeschreibung einer Armen* (München: Ernst Reinhardt, 1910); and G. Braun, ed., *Im Kampf ums Dasein: Wahrheitstreue Lebenserinnerungen eines Mädchens aus dem Volke* (Stuttgart: Verlag Karl Weber, s.d. (ca. 1908).

7. Angela Langer's *Stromaufwärts. Aus einem Frauenleben* (Berlin: C. Fischer Verlag, 1913) is a slightly fictionalized account, but certainly follows a model of linear development in its description of the author's life course. Lena Christ's autobiography *Erinnerungen* (München: Albert Langer, 1921) is much more problematic in form. It certainly resembles the two autobiographies cited in the previous note in its focus on the sordidness and misery of her early life. But it was apparently written once she was an established novelist and seems more a genuine effort to exorcise a past that lay behind her than a sensationalist account designed to shock the bourgeois conscience as the other two seem to be.

8. Here, the need to compare the autobiographies of socialist women with those of socialist men is apparent. I suspect that the emphasis on finding a voice would not be so central in the latter, and I intend to examine that issue. This essay is the first analysis of a large set of working-class autobiographies—of men as well as women, and from France as well as Germany—that I have been collecting as part of a project designed to study the impact of the extension of primary education to the European working classes.

9. A. Seidl., "Der erste Arbeiterinnenstreik in Wien (1893)," in W. Emmerich, ed., p. 235.

10. M. Sponer, "Aus Nordböhmen," in A. Popp, ed., *Gedenkbuch,* pp. 143–44.

11. A. Popp, *Jugendgeschichte,* p. 64.

12. A. Popp, *Jugendgeschichte,* p. 67.

13. A. Popp, *Jugendgeschichte,* pp. 60–70.

14. A. Popp, *Jugendgeschichte*, p. 73.

15. A. Popp, *Jugendgeschichte*, p. 80.

16. A. Popp, *Jugendgeschichte*, p. 81.

17. O. Baader, p. 23.

18. O. Baader, p. 29. Jean Quataert cites these passages about Baader's relationship with her father in the context of her analysis of the motives and effects of joining the socialist party for women in "Unequal Partners in an Uneasy Alliance: Women and the Working Classes in Imperial Germany," in M. Boxer and J. Quataert, eds., *Socialist Women: European Socialist Feminism in the Nineteenth and Early Twentieth Centuries* (New York: Elsevier, 1978). pp. 120–21.

19. E. Bleuler, ed., p. 1.

20. G. Braun, ed., p. 8.

21. For a detailed account of a variety of topics of interest to social historians and women's historians that are addressed by the evidence of autobiographies, see the conference paper by John Fout cited above.

22. M. Beutelmayer, "Aus Oberösterreich", in A. Popp, ed., *Gedenkbuch*, p. 70; A. Roth, "Eine Glasschleiferin," in A. Popp, ed., *Gedenkbuch,*pp. 52–54; A. Popp, *Jugendgeschichte*, pp. 1–5.

23. G. Braun, ed., pp. 35ff.

24. A. Mosegaard, "Die 'unsittlichen' Dienstboten?", in R. Klucsaritz, and F. G. Kürbisch, eds., *Arbeiterinnen kämpfen um ihr Recht*, pp. 97–98; Langer, pp. 112ff.

25. Anonymous, *Im Kampf*, p. 75.

26. A. Popp, *Jugendgeschichte*, p. 35.

27. A. Popp, *Jugendgeschichte*, p. 37.

28. For Quataert's important work on the place of women in the German socialist movement, see, in addition to the article cited earlier, her book *Reluctant Feminists in German Social Democracy, 1885–1917* (Princeton: Princeton University Press, 1979). Although Quataert is prepared to use the term "feminist" to describe many of the middle-class and working-class women who were active in the socialist movement, her careful analysis of the ideas about women and the programs of the Social Democratic Party make clear the constraints on, as well as the support for, feminist awareness that work in the movement involved. See also K. Honeycutt, "Socialism and Feminism in Imperial Germany," *Signs*, 5 (1979) pp. 30–41, who offers a similar analysis of the contradictory position of women in the German socialist movement. For a recent, fuller study of women in the German Socialist movement, including a detailed local study, see H. Niggemann, *Emanzipation zwischen Sozialismus und Feminismus* (Wuppertal: Peter Hammer Verlag, 1981). For Austria, see I. Lefleur, "Five Socialist Women: Traditional Conflicts and Socialist Visions in Austria, 1893–1934," in M. Boxer and J. Quataert, eds., *Socialist Women*, pp. 215–60.

29. See one account in O. Baader, pp. 61ff.

30. A. Popp, *Jugendgeschichte*, p. 95.

31. M. Beutelmayer, p. 74.

32. A. Perthen, "Der Anfang in Bodenbach," in A. Popp, ed., *Gedenkbuch*, p. 116.

33. It should be noted that both of these statements issue from women in the Austrian Socialist movement. For a description of the special character and problems of Austrian socialist women in this era, see I. Lefleur, cited above.

34. A. Langer, pp. 72ff., 124ff.; Anonymous, *Im Kampf*, pp. 180 ff.

35. H. Christ, p. 301.

THE CONCEPT OF FEMINISM
NOTES FOR PRACTICING HISTORIANS

Richard J. Evans

In this brief essay I am not concerned with making any dogmatic statements about what feminism is or is not. Rather, my purpose is to explain and to try to justify my own usage of the term, and, more generally, to think out loud about some of the problems which any use of the term in a historical context necessarily involves. Anyone who writes about the history of feminism must arrive at some working definition of the term, if only for the merely practical reason that there has to be some criterion for deciding what to include and what to leave out. At the very least, therefore, I hope that by making my own practice in this respect explicit, I will help other historians working in this field to think more carefully about their own, even though it might be different from mine.

The first problem that arises in discussing the concept of feminism is the word itself. However simple and self-explanatory the word may seem, it is in fact a relatively recent term, at least in its current usage, for its meaning has changed over time, and at a different rate between countries. Its original meaning, which still appears as one of the definitions given in the *Concise Oxford English Dictionary,* was the "development of female characteristics in a male person." It only entered English in its modern sense ("advocacy of women's rights on grounds of equality of the sexes," according to the same dictionary) in the 1890s, from the French *féminisme.* As E. J. Hobsbawm has remarked, the appearance of a new word in the political vocabulary of a society is often a sign that a new political movement or ideology has entered the public arena,[1] and certainly as far as England and America

247

are concerned, the arrival of "feminism" in the 1890s paralleled the coming of age of the feminist movement. Interestingly, however, the term *Feminismus* in German continued to retain its old meaning of "female qualities in a man," or "effeminacy" right up to the 1960s, when it can still be found defined exclusively in the sense in the *Wahrig Deutsches Wörterbuch,* for example.[2] It was in this sense, too, that the word was often used in political debate, for example by the far-right magazine *Hammer,* in an attack on Chancellor Bülow issued in its pages in 1909:

> Feminism is a sign and at the same time a cause of the decline of a people. It destroys manly feelings and capabilities, it dilutes, weakens and finally exterminates the people. . . . Prince Bülow is the leading personality in Prussia and the Empire, [but] his policies contain an element that, if not feminism itself, is at least closely related to it. Only a statesman who does not pursue a policy of compromise or opportunism, but ruthlessly and single-mindedly follows the aim of securing the future of his people—a second Bismarck—only such a statesman could rescue our people from the morass of degeneration.[3]

By contrast, leaders of the German women's movement such as Gertrud Bäumer, Marie Stritt, and Anita Augspurg never referred to themselves as *Feministinnen* or the doctrine they believed in as *Feminismus.* Usually they chose some circumlocution which employed the concept of a women's movement *(Frauenbewegung)* or a women's suffrage movement *(Frauenstimmrechtsbewegung).* The rhetoric of a movement *(Bewegung)* was itself borrowed from the labour movement (or "social movement" as it was sometimes called) and implied of course a more or less coherent body of oppressed people moving toward the final goal of equality and emancipation. Sometimes, however, more radical women such as Augspurg referred to themselves as *Frauenrechtlerinnen* or women's righters, to use a clumsy but reasonably precise translation of the word.[4] This in turn was used against them by those who thought a concentration on equal rights indicated a narrow and legalistic approach to the problem of women's oppression; thus Clara Zetkin, the socialist women's leader, frequently wrote savage condemnations of the *Nur-Frauenrechtlerinnen* and their *Frauenrechtlerei,* contrasting what she regarded as their exclusive concern with legal rights with the broader, more comprehensive approach of the socialist doctrines which she herself advocated.[5]

Thus in describing these women and the organizations they led as "feminist," one is using a word which they themselves did not employ. In itself, there is nothing particularly wrong with such a procedure; not even the most committed of historicists would argue that one should only use about the past the concepts that the past used about itself. If we tried to do this, we would in any case soon get into difficulties. The term "women's movement," which these women themselves preferred, may sound neutral, but in practice it was given a wide range of definitions. Gertrud Bäumer, for example, argued that the women's movement consisted of a general spread of "specifically female influences" through society; these influences centered on motherhood and included patriotism and a commitment to the collective identity of the Volk.[6] Thus Bäumer denied that pacifist groups or organizations supporting the legalization of abortion or the encouragement of family limitation were part of the 'women's movement', and indeed the histories of the German women's movement written in the years of Bäumer's ascendancy, up to 1933, went a long way toward suppressing the fact that such groups had existed at all.[7] Again, Bäumer used her definition of "female influences" to argue that a woman who "limits herself to house and family" was "under certain circumstances acting in this way more in accordance with the ideals of the women's movement than if she goes into any male profession."[8] This very broad description helped paper over some of the differences within the *Bund deutscher Frauenvereine* and conceal the increasing heterogeneity of its member organizations. But it was also flexible enough to be used against groups like the *Bund für Mutterschutz,* or, later, the Women's International League for Peace and Freedom, which Bäumer disliked, while continuing to cover groups like the German-evangelical Women's League which Bäumer broadly approved of.[9] Here too, therefore, it is difficult for the historian to treat the term "women's movement" as a neutral concept, or to accept the way in which it was used in the past. Whatever we do, therefore, we are forced in the end to work out our own set of definitions.

This leads me to a second point, relating to the problem of ideology and the historicity (or lack thereof) of feminism. By this I mean, first, whether feminism can be said to be an ideology with a specific, irreducible core of concepts and beliefs at its centre, however many variations there may be on secondary issues. Secondly, there is the related question of whether, if it is not an ideology, feminism has existed throughout history in various forms or whether, if it is an ideology, it has only existed at a specific period or periods. There is a parallel here with a similar problem in the history of socialism; some writers take any argument for the sharing of resources for the common good to be socialist. It was for a long time conventional for historians of socialism to begin with Plato or the Old Testament and trace the development of collectivist doctrines up to Thomas More's *Utopia* and beyond, before leading on to the great flowering of socialist thought in the eighteenth and nineteenth centuries. An example of this kind of approach is Alexander Gray's book *The Socialist Tradition: Moses to Lenin.*[10] Here the parallel is with those who argue that any assertion of women's rights or female equality in history can be defined as feminist. Hence in the 1920s Léon Abensour began his history of feminism in classical times.[11] In this view, feminism is a permanent aspect of the human condition.

It has now become accepted by historians of socialism that the term should properly be applied only to a specific body of doctrines originating in the "Utopian socialists" of the late eighteenth and early nineteenth centuries. Here new elements came into play which had not been present before: the Industrial Revolution, the emergence of the factory system, the growth of the proletariat and the elaboration of a novel ideology—individualism—to justify and legitimate the new capitalist ethics of the free market untrammeled by law or custom. Socialism in turn, while drawing on older traditions, was developed as an intellectual response to these novel developments.[12]

The idea that feminism is a specifically modern doctrine has not found such wide acceptance, however. Present-day women's historians, like the socialists of the late nineteenth century, are eagerly searching the past for forerunners. They are attempting, in part, to establish a pedigree for the women's movement of the present day. At a similar stage in the socialist movement, writers such as Kautsky and Engels were also searching the distant past for "socialists" of one kind and another. This search has now been admitted to be largely unhistorical. The same, I believe, can be said about the search for feminist forerunners. Women have always protested against their oppression in some way, and the place of women in society has attracted the attention of writers and thinkers throughout the ages. Until the end of the eighteenth century, however, it is not possible to discover any continuous or organized campaign for women's rights, merely isolated individuals or groups. Moreover, there is a constant temptation to read back into the past the concerns of the present and to reclaim as feminist women whose ideas were a great deal less radical than their reputations would lead us to suppose. By selecting those parts of the thought of someone like Mary Wollstonecraft which resemble present-day concepts of feminism and omitting those which do not, we run the risk of distorting our view of her thought in its totality and so misunderstanding important aspects of it by taking them out of context.

My plea, therefore, is for a historical view of feminism. The danger of looking for feminism everywhere in the past and celebrating the discovery of feminism in Ancient Greece or in the Reformation is that by doing so we abolish time and resurrect the useless notion of a permanent battle of the sexes. Only by understanding the limitations of past struggles can they be transcended, and these limitations can only be understood by viewing them in their historical conditions. To put it another way, if feminism is an eternal aspect of the human condition not tied to specific historical circumstances, then so is patriarchy, and if this is so, then patriarchy cannot be abolished. If patriarchy is historically determined, however, then so is feminism.

An alternative way of looking at this question might be to say that *organized* feminism only emerged in the late eighteenth and nineteenth centuries, and that this is something that has to be explained, but that it was the rise of feminist *organizations* that has to be explained since there were already in existence clear feminist *doctrines* or *ideas*. To some extent this is undeniably true; yet these ideas rested on other themes of equal rights in law, of the primacy of reason in the organization of state and society, of the self-determination of the individual—which were themselves relatively new, and certainly did not go back much beyond 1700. So doctrines which can reasonably be called feminist all date in my view from the eighteenth century at the earliest.

In reaching any definition of an historical concept one pays a certain price. If one opts for a very broad definition of feminism, the price paid is a difficulty in making necessary distinctions. A useful touchstone for such definitions is an organization such as the German-evangelical Women's League *(Deutsch-evangelischer Frauenbund)*, which played an important role in the German women's movement from 1908 to 1918 but which publicly opposed female suffrage and had close ties with the German Conservative Party, which supplied much of the driving force behind the leadership of the German League for the Prevention of the Emancipation of Women *(Deutscher Bund zur Bekämpfung der Frauenemanzipation)*.[13] It seems reasonable to say that the German-evangelical Women's League was not feminist. Indeed, this seems a necessary distinction to make. If on some criteria it has to be accounted feminist, then those criteria must be wrong, at the very least they are very unhelpful. If—to take one very broad definition— feminism is the process of women gaining control over their own lives, then it was feminist, for the women who belonged to it were certainly doing this, in however limited a way. The German Evangelical Women's League was also feminist if we define feminism as the attempt by women to improve the circumstances and conditions of their own lives, for the League's members undoubtedly believed they were doing this by belonging to it. Neither of these concepts of feminism seems to me, therefore, to be adequate.

What was new about the doctrines of female equality and emancipation propounded in the late eighteenth and early nineteenth centuries was above all the fact that they argued that women were oppressed because they were women, not for some other reason (e.g., because they were Protestants or Dissenters). Indeed, the feminist philosopher Janet Radcliffe Richards has recently defined feminism, helpfully, as "the idea that women suffer from systematic social injustice because of their sex."[14] This, she claims, has the advantage of including very many women in the category of "feminist": "the broad definition of feminism allows feminism to survive the failure of any particular set of theories about the position of women, and to adopt it is therefore to make it much easier to take a flexible attitude to particular feminist theories." Feminism is thus "a movement for the elimination of sex-based injustice," without implying in itself how that injustice is caused or how it might be rectified.

I am rather doubtful about the use of the word *social* in this definition, unless it is taken at its widest possible definition; in the nineteenth century, and indeed still today (even if to a lesser extent), women also suffer legal, economic, and political injustice because of their sex. On the other hand, the inclusion of the word *systematic* seems particularly useful in dealing with the difficult problem of socialist women and whether or not they can legitimately be called feminist.

At one time I was inclined to go further and argue that what distinguishes feminists from other people is their belief that the *most* important and systematic inequalities that women suffer are due to their sex, and that therefore all women have a common interest in rectifying them. This certainly was the view in many countries before the First World War. Socialist women such as Clara Zetkin, Alexandra Kollontai, and Louise Saumoneau violently opposed it. Even though they believed that women were unjustly treated, they also held that the men and women of the proletariat had more interests in common than the women of the proletariat and the bourgeoisie.[15] In Russia the word *feministka* was current before 1914; it was reserved by all for the largely liberal, middle-class movement of women who concentrated on rectifying the injustices to which the female sex was subjected. For socialist women, such issues were always secondary in the end to the destruction of capitalism and bourgeois rule. Thus Richard Stites remarks quite correctly that feminism was only one component in a larger women's liberation movement which included nihilist and later socialist and communist women's organizations as well. These latter, which receive full treatment in Stites's book, are never referred to as "feminist." Similarly, Charles Sowerwine, in his study of the French socialist women's movement, maintains the same distinction between "feminism" and "socialism." Much of his work is devoted to explaining why "the alliance between feminism and socialism" failed, why "the feminists were unable to attract a mass following and the socialist women shrank from feminist positions."[16] One should not regard socialist women's movements and "bourgeois" feminist organizations as two arms of the same "feminist" movement; they disagreed fundamentally and spent as much time attacking one another as they did fighting for women's rights. Without an appreciation of the depth of this division it is very difficult to reach a balanced view of the history of the socialist women and their organizations.[17] Socialist women like Zetkin simply did not accept most of the arguments of the feminists: for Zetkin, capitalism and the bourgeoisie, to whom the feminists belonged, were the real enemy; the goal, a socialist society, would establish female equality, to be sure, but that was not its main purpose.

Yet I am not so sure now whether this problem is not taken care of by the word *systematic* in Radcliffe Richards's definition. Zetkin and the socialists tended to believe that women's oppression was an incidental by-product of capitalism, and that different groups of women were oppressed in different ways. They also tried frequently to argue that reforms that would remove the oppression of middle-class women would not benefit the majority of women (e.g., Married Women's Property legislation). The only kind of oppression that was in their view *systematic* (caused by a system) was capitalist oppression of the proletariat. This also deals satisfactorily with the problem of other groups and individuals who only supported one aspect of the women's campaign (e.g., the vote) for reasons of their own—for example, the temperance movement. Finally, it suggests a fine but viable distinction between socialists who saw capitalism as the cause of women's oppression but argued that it oppressed some women more, or even rather, than others, and nationalist feminists who believed that women were systematically oppressed because of their sex in many countries, but saw their own situation as caused in particular by the domination of a foreign power. Czech women in the Habsburg Monarchy, for instance, argued they were denied their rights as women by the Habsburgs, and would achieve them if Bohemia achieved self-determination; but they never, to my knowledge, denied that Austrian women were equally oppressed.[18] Socialist women, on the other hand, were often inclined to deny that bourgeois women were oppressed in any serious sense at all.

Clearly, there will always be borderline cases such as these in which reaching a decision on whether the concept of feminism applies or not is a debatable one. The core of the feminist movement has always consisted of those who place the combating of women's subordination and oppression at the centre of their concerns. But perhaps we can also describe as feminist those who believe women are systematically oppressed as women, but who do not necessarily regard this as the only or even the most important form of injustice. John Stuart Mill, after all, can fairly be described as a feminist, but feminism, though important to him, was only one of a great many other concerns.

A further problem is raised by the tendency of historians to construct typologies of feminism. Here, if we are not careful, the proliferation of different definitions of subcategories of feminism, all very different from one another, may dissolve the concept of feminism itself altogether. One simple typology of feminism which has gained wide currency is William L. O'Neill's division of feminists into "social feminists" and "hard-core feminists." "Social feminists" he defines as women not primarily concerned with equal rights but still active in social reform movements organized by themselves. "Hard-core feminists" he describes as female suffragists, that is, women who fought for the right to vote in legislative elections.[19] This is a useful distinction in some respects. I would suggest, however, that it is based too narrowly on the American model, where women demanded the vote from very early on. It seems to have no place for women who fought for equal rights other than the vote—for example, in the criminal law (over the question of prostitution), in control of the property and income within a marriage, or in admittance to higher education and the professions. O'Neill, I think, is right to draw a distinction between suffragists and the rest, but I don't think he draws it precisely enough.

As Richard Stites has pointed out,[20] there was in Europe a general progression from an early phase of feminism, "usually concerned more with charity, self-help, and the improvement of educational, professional and legal status than with securing the vote," and a later phase, in which the vote occupied "a central place in the feminist struggles." In Germany these two types or phases of feminism were referred to respectively as moderate and radical, but both of them put women's rights, however conceived, first, and other issues of social and political reform second.[21] "Social feminism," as O'Neill defines it, is therefore a rather misleading concept, unless one redefines it to mean feminism that sought the redress of the injustices women suffered in the social rather than the political sphere. In my view, it is not enough to refer in this context to social feminism as consisting in "practical social reforms to improve the circumstances of women's lives,"[22] because the central notion of injustice done to women because of their sex is not present. Moreover, there is the problem of who is to define why the circumstances of women's lives need improving; after all, even the Nazis believed they were doing this, but it would be unreasonable to call Hitler a social feminist.

Other kinds of feminism which appear in conventional typologies are socialist feminism, Catholic feminism, domestic feminism, Jewish feminism, or Nazi feminism. Socialist feminism I have already discussed. As for Jewish feminism, as Marion Kaplan has shown, the women of the Jewish Women's League, though they attempted to enlarge women's role within the Jewish community, did not seriously question women's role in society at large.[23] Nor did the Catholic Women's League. Domestic feminists went even further, arguing that women be paid to do the housework, thus strengthening the conventional division of labour and accepting the ideology of "separate spheres" that lay behind it. Nazi feminists, few though they were, seem to have accepted Nazi doctrines about the place of women in society in their "separate sphere" and simply argued for more power in the Nazi movement for themselves; here too there was no suggestion of accepting the doctrine of full equal rights.[24] Equal rights and separate spheres are mutually contradictory doctrines; the only principle on which it is possible to base an argument for equal rights, or for the elimination of sex-based injustice, is the principle of the equal rights of women as human beings, as individuals.

The concept of feminism in which I have operated in my own work has contained three basic requirements of feminism, namely:

the belief that women suffer systematic social and political injustice because of their sex

the idea that this injustice is more important than other kinds of injustice that women suffer through belonging to other groups (e.g., a religious minority, an oppressed nationality or an exploited social class)

the determination that therefore all women, considered socially, economically, and politically, should assert their common interest in removing the injustice which they suffer because of their sex.

A socialist would disagree with the second and third, for example, while other women's organizations would disagree with the emphasis on injustice. This allows for a variety of accounts of what the injustices

are and how they are caused. Classical feminism, for example, considered legal inequalities in the public sphere—denial of rights over
property, exclusion from universities and professions, lack of civil rights
up to and including the vote—to be the most important. A feminist
today might place more emphasis on economic inequalities or inequalities in the private sphere (domestic role, sexuality, and so on).[25]
Indeed, the historian should perhaps pay some attention to the dominant orientation of feminist ideology in the period studied. For example, between about 1910 and 1920, in almost all countries in which
there was a feminist movement, it concentrated overwhelmingly (indeed perhaps to an excessive degree) on the vote as the most important injustice from which women suffered. So groups who opposed
votes for women in this context were thus taking a decidedly anti-
feminist stance in a way they would not have been doing fifty years
earlier, when the vote in most European countries was an impossibly
radical demand. Thus historical distinctions can be made which are
obscured by a broader kind of definition.

Nevertheless, I would not deny that the advantages of a relatively
precise and narrow definition of feminism are bought at a certain price.
In particular, it has the disadvantage of excluding from the category of
feminist many people who supported some feminist aims (such as the
vote), and others who believed that some women did suffer from
some kinds of injustice because of their sex, even if this injustice was
not systematic and did not apply to all women. Without being a feminist it was possible, for example, to believe that prostitutes were unjustly treated, but it required a generalization of this injustice, as a
symbol, before it became a feminist issue. Still, on balance I would
continue to defend my own practice, as historian of organized feminism, in applying these criteria. Whether or not they can usefully be
applied by students of feminist ideas, or feminist literature, must be for
them to decide.[26]

NOTES

1. E. J. Hobsbawm, *The Age of Revolution 1789–1848* (New York, 1962), p. 17.
2. Gerhard Wahrig, *Deutsches Wörterbuch* (Gütersloh, 1968), p. 1240: "Femi-
nismum (m; Gen-; Pl.-men) *weibliches Wesen beim Mann (bes.Homosexuellen) zu
feminin* -nistisch (Adj.) *auf Feminismus beruhend, weibisch.*"
3. Zentrales Staatsarchiv Potsdam, Reichskanzlei, 2266: copy of Justizrat
Schnauss, "Die Gefahren der Frauenbewegung," *Hammer* No. 158 (15 Jan. 1909).
4. Thus Anna Pappritz in her diary entry for 17 May 1899 (Helene Lange Archiv,
Berlin, Box 16).

5. Numerous examples in Clara Zetkin, *Ausgewählte Reden und Schriften* (East Berlin, 1953), Vol. I.

6. Gertrud Bäumer, "Was bedeutet in der deutschen Frauenbewegung 'jüngere' und 'ältere' Richtung?," *Die Frau*, 12/6, March 1905, pp. 321–29.

7. See, for example, Agnes von Zahn-Harnack, *Die Frauenbewegung— Geschichte, Probleme, Ziele* (Leipzig/Berlin, 1928).

8. Bäumer, loc.cit.

9. Archiv des Bundes deutscher Frauenvereine, Berlin, 16/II/1: Protokoll der Sitzung des Gesamtvorstandes, 11 March 1910, 13 March 1910.

10. Published in London, 1946.

11. *Histoire générale du féminisme dès origines à nos jours* (Paris, 1921), beginning in classical times.

12. George Lichtheim, *A Short History of Socialism* (London, 1970).

13. See my book *The Feminist Movement in Germany 1894–1933* (London/ Beverly Hills, 1976).

14. Janet Radcliffe Richards, *The Sceptical Feminist: A Philosophical Enquiry* (London, 1980), pp. 11–19.

15. Richard Stites, *The Women's Liberation Movement in Russia: Feminism, Nihilism and Bolshevism, 1860–1930* (Princeton, 1978); Charles Sowerwine, *Sisters or Citizens? Women and Socialism in France since 1876* (Cambridge, 1982); and, for Zetkin, my article "Bourgeois Feminists and Women Socialists in Germany 1894– 1914: Lost Opportunity or Inevitable Conflict?," *Women's Studies International Quarterly* vol. 3 (1980), pp. 355–76.

16. Stites, pp. xvii, 191; Sowerwine, pp. xii, 184.

17. Compare, for example, M. Boxer and J. Quataert (eds.), *Socialist Women: European Socialist Feminism in the Nineteenth and Early Twentieth Centuries* (New York, 1978), and my review in "Women's History: the limits of reclamation," *Social History*, vol. 5 (1980), No. 2, pp. 273–81.

18. See my book *The Feminists* (London/New York, 1977).

19. W. L. O'Neill, *The Woman Movement: Feminism in the United States and England* (London, 1969), p. 33.

20. Stites, p. xvii.

21. This does not of course exclude the fact that they considered that the attainment of female equality would bring about other changes in public life, for example stricter sexual morality, a decline in alcoholism, or even an end to war.

22. O'Neill, p. 33.

23. Marion Kaplan, *The Jewish Feminist Movement in Germany* (Westport, Conn., 1979).

24. Jill Stephenson, *The Nazi Organization of Women* (London, 1981).

25. Herrad Schenk, *Die feministische Herausforderung: 150 Jahre Frauenbewegung in Deutschland* (Munich, 1980).

26. In the general introduction to their recent most useful collection of documents on *Women, the Family and Freedom*, Susan Groag-Bell and Karen Offen deal with the problem of defining feminism by simply avoiding it altogether.

Unless they are used by the historical authors themselves, we are deliberately avoiding the terms *feminist, anti-feminist, feminism,* and *anti-feminism* to characterise challenges and dissenting ideas put forward against entrenched and prevailing points of view on women's position. We aim to circumvent current misunderstandings about the evolution of historical demands made on women's behalf during the last three centuries; most of these misunderstandings arise from present-day efforts to eradicate notions of inherent sexual characteristics and the sexual division of labour, and to celebrate the individual.

> Many of these notions remained unchallenged, however, by eighteenth- and nineteenth-century advocates of women's rights who described themselves, and were in turn described by their contemporaries, as *feminists*. Instead, we have tried to clarify the societal context of those dissenting ideas generally subsumed under the categories of "the emancipation of women," "women's rights movement," etc. as required to pinpoint the specific economic, moral, or political reform and the organised efforts they and their male supporters undertook to achieve them. [p. 2 note 3]

In effect, therefore, Bell and Offen are saying that anyone who described herself as a feminist was a feminist. Given the fact that linguistic usage has changed over time, and varied between countries, this is a confusing procedure, to say the least. The use of terms such as *the women's rights movement* does not obviate the need for some general theoretical definition, since there were disagreements on which organizations, theories, and individuals should be counted as belonging to the women's rights movement, and what the emancipation of women actually consisted of. At the very least, the procedure adopted by Bell and Offen demands some definitions of precisely what "entrenched and prevailing points of view on women's position" were, and hence some criteria for deciding what views and ideas can be characterized as dissenting from these entrenched positions. Such a characterization does not differ in effect from a definition of feminism according to the principles discussed in the present essay.

Women Writers of Germany.

Sophie Laroche.

Fanny Lewald.

Madame Aston.

Source: Bayerische Staatsbibliothek, Munich.

Louise Otto, Early Leader of the German Women's Movement.

As a young woman.

As a political leader.

Hedwig Dohm, early leader of the German women's movement.

Source: Bayerische Staatsbibliothek, Munich.

"The spiritual children of a female writer"—E. Marlitt surrounded by her fictional creations.

Source: Die Gartenlaube, *no. 4, 1875, p. 69.*

Ellen Key, Swedish feminist writer and source of controversy in the German women's movement.

Source: Die Gartenlaube, *addition to no. 18, 1901, p. 2.*

Women and Politics.

British satire of an emancipated German housewife.

Source: The Graphic, *1882.*

Proletarian women's meeting.

Source: I. Weber-Kellerman, Frauenlaben im 19. Jahrhundert (Munich: Beck Verlag, 1983), p. 192.

Clara Zetkin and Rosa Luxemburg, prominent socialist women.

Front page of the socialist women's newspaper, showing censorship.

Source: K. Bauer, Clara Zetkin und die proletarische Frauenbewegung *(Berlin: Oberbaumverlag, 1978), pp. 12, 82.*

Women's Words and Women's Self-Definitions

INSIDE ASSIMILATION
REBECCA FRIEDLÄNDER'S
RAHEL VARNHAGEN

Deborah Hertz

Almost two centuries ago in Germany, Rahel Varnhagen was a much-admired, much-discussed phenomenon. During the last decade of the eighteenth century and again during the third decade of the nineteenth century, she was at the center of Berlin's social and intellectual life.[1] Varnhagen was not the only Jewish woman in central Europe to entertain and befriend the era's most prominent male intellectuals. A tiny circle of rich Jewish women in Berlin achieved stunning successes as mediators of high culture and as pioneers in social assimilation. Their successes at the outset of the long process of Jewish emancipation were all the more remarkable because social triumphs on this scale largely eluded their counterparts in subsequent decades.[2] But Rahel Varnhagen earned her renown not just because her salon was popular or because her lovers were prestigious noblemen. Varnhagen attracted admirers for the quality of her mind as well as for her social skills. Although she was not well educated and she rarely published her writing, both her conversation and her letters earned her praise for her originality, her honesty, her expressive powers, and her aesthetic judgement.[3] After her death in 1833, the posthumous publication of many of her letters kept her memory alive for two groups who claimed her as a pioneer in their respective struggles for emancipation. Successive generations of literary women found inspiration in these letters, and lauded Varnhagen for her "feminine" influence on Romantic high culture and for her progressive opinions on women's condition. For those German Jews who saw assimilation via mastery of high culture as the best path to emancipation, Rahel Varnhagen was an obvious model. Most who struggled to become assimilated were ambivalent about the personal costs of leaving Judaism and Jewry. She, too, had clearly been ambivalent about the calculated opportunism which was often required for successful social integration. In Heinrich Heine's words, Rahel Varnhagen had "fought for the truth, suffered, battled, and even lied for it." Her oft-cited deathbed admission that she was in the end proud and not ashamed to be Jewish insured her place as one of the first complex, modern "non-Jewish" Jews.[4]

Yet neither the feminist nor the Jewish preoccupation with Rahel Varnhagen continued in the decades following the second world war. Not only did Nazi successes virtually obliterate Jewish life in Germany; in so doing, Nazism called into question the assimilationist strategy and thus Rahel Varnhagen's fitness as a model for twentieth-century Jews. The feminist constituency for an interest in her was also diminished. When literary feminists did appear, their initial focus was on published, "professional" female authors rather than on female "dilettantes" whose fame rested merely on their personal impact and letters. Then, too, the continuing obscurity of Rahel Varnhagen in the decades following the war was also due to the declining fascination of the romantic era for literary historians. The one book that did arouse some interest in Varnhagen was the biography of her written by Hannah Arendt before the war but first published in 1957. The book was well received critically, but its tone was abstract for a biography. Arendt's interpretation of Varnhagen as ultimately having been more of a rebellious "pariah" than an opportunist "parvenu" was exciting. But alone, and because of its anomalous style, her book did not bring Varnhagen to the attention of a very wide audience, either in the United States or in Germany.[5]

But all of this has changed now. As the immediate, paralyzing traumas of the Holocaust have receded, German interest in the Jewish past has revived. Having already rediscovered prominent published women authors, literary feminists are paying increasing attention to female intellectuals who had a less direct relationship to the reading public.[6] And so the time has come for a postwar generation to repossess Rahel Varnhagen. The 1983 celebration of the sesquicentennial of her death was the occasion for rather grand pronouncements of her true importance. One critic complained that although "until now the title of honor 'author' has been denied her, this is unfair." For, in the words of another, Varnhagen's letters and aphorisms are "perhaps the richest treasure of German literature." Indeed, she is now hailed as "the greatest female author among the Germans."[7]

Considering the new estimation of Rahel Varnhagen's significance, it is all the more disturbing that her letters have been so difficult to obtain. To begin with, many letters were omitted or tampered with when they were first published in the nineteenth century. It was not until the 1960s that a four-volume, annotated selection of her letters was published. And it is only now, in 1984, that a ten-volume reprint of all of her hitherto published letters will finally be available.[8] Even more importantly, now that Rahel Varnhagen's papers have been discovered intact in Poland, the new interest in her can be matched with a new, complete set of Varnhagen's corpus. The necessity of going back to the original letters was urged by Arendt, whose work with the full set of Varnhagen's diaries and letters convinced Arendt that Rahel's husband, Karl August Varnhagen von Ense, had tampered with the texts when he edited her letters for publication after her death in 1833. Whole segments of her correspondence were never published, sentences and paragraphs were omitted from those letters which were published, and the identity of recipients of the letters was deliberately disguised.[9] Yet Arendt's plans to supplement her biography with a selection from unpublished letters never came to fruition. A century after Varnhagen's death, in 1933, she left Germany, leaving the original letters behind. She would never see them again.

Rahel Varnhagen's letters were a small part of the enormous Varnhagen Collection, which originally belonged to the Rare Manuscript Division of the Prussian State Library in Berlin.[10] In 1942, most of the Division's holdings, which included original Beethoven and Mozart scores, were moved to a variety of depots in eastern Germany, which was then believed to be the safe front of the war. After 1945, the location of the lost Manuscript Division remained unknown, and none of its precious holdings was ever returned to East or West Berlin. When Arendt published her biography of Varnhagen in 1957, she believed that the Varnhagen Collection, along with the rest of the Manuscript Division, had been lost. By the time her biography was reissued in 1974, Arendt had reason to believe that the Varnhagen Collection might have survived, but she had been unable to gain access to it. Since then, a long search by many Western scholars has finally succeeded in locating the collection and tracing the history of its odyssey. It was housed during the war in a monastery in the small hamlet of Grussau in Silesia. The collection was eventually moved to Krakow, and has been there, at the Jagiellonian Library, since 1946. The German Democratic Republic has publicly demanded that all the material now in Krakow be returned to East Germany, but Polish officials have thus far been unwilling to do so. The eventual fate of the Varnhagen

Collection and the other precious material from the Berlin State Library remains unclear.

One major set of letters which Varnhagen von Ense kept almost completely from publication were those which his wife wrote to the novelist Rebecca Friedländer between 1805 and 1810.[11] Only one side of the correspondence survived; Friedländer's replies to Varnhagen were burned at some point. Partly because few of these letters were ever published, Friedländer's name (later changed to Regina Frohberg) and her work have fallen into complete obscurity. The letters Rahel Varnhagen wrote her in these years are of great interest, however, not so much because of Friedländer's intrinsic importance as an individual, but rather because of her sociological similarity to Rahel Varnhagen at the time that they were written. Both women were born into wealthy and acculturated Jewish families, but neither settled into conventional Jewish marriages. Both women suffered the pain of voluntarily moving to the edge of acculturated Jewish society in Berlin without achieving any immediate success in entering the highest levels of gentile society. Intermarriage with gentiles was often the mechanism for female assimilation in this era, and a Jewish woman's failure to succeed at intermarriage meant triple pain—as a Jew who had chosen exile from the Jewish world, who was also excluded from gentile society, and as a woman deprived of love and marriage. Varnhagen was ultimately successful in the struggle to assimilate; because she was intelligent and sensitive, her own version of the female-specific assimilation process is an important one. Assimilation by intermarriage was thus a nuanced, difficult process, one which involved distancing oneself from kin while carefully cultivating a new social network. It is crucial to reconstruct in which ways Varnhagen interpreted the changes in her own life as legitimate personal emancipation and in which ways she interpreted her assimilation as a betrayal of the Jewish world.

In this essay, the newly available letters Varnhagen wrote to Friedländer in her life's loneliest years are examined to take us "inside" the assimilation process, to reconstruct how one articulate Jewish woman at the time viewed her own troubles achieving emancipation. The range of themes covered in the letters is broad, and only two of these themes can be touched on in what follows. A major theme of the letters is how Varnhagen felt about her intense friendship with Rebecca Friedländer. Thus I concentrate here on how their common fate of being stranded between two worlds drew the two women together for comraderie and support. But the writing of letters, the very same medium that was so crucial in forging the private bond between the two women, was also a quasi-public activity which could contribute to winning fame and a professional career. So the second theme I examine below is what Varnhagen herself has to say in the letters to Friedländer about publishing her writing.

But before turning to interpret the very subjective letters, it is imperative to briefly survey the objective social universe in which the two women lived. That the two women could even come close enough to gentile society to feel the pain of periodic rejections by its representatives was itself an unusual accomplishment due largely to the altogether unique position of Berlin Jewry in this era. Whereas in most European Jewish communities only a few families were wealthy, in Berlin somewhere close to half of the 3200 members of the community were wealthy, including the city's very richest men. The astonishing wealth of the tiny community was a consequence of King Frederick the Great's maxim of obtaining the greatest economic service from the fewest number of Jews. Such services were needed in a Prussia where an overly strict mercantilism, the crown's unwillingness to let commoners grow wealthy enough to challenge the nobility, unlucky geography, and the absence of German national unity all hindered the development of a vigorous gentile bourgeoisie.[12] The daughters born into such families enjoyed the sumptuous homes, silk dresses, French tutors, hairdressers, and trips to nearby spas made possible by their fathers' money. What was unprecedented was that the daughters' wealth and their acculturation should have become adorned with a prize no amount of money could buy: a degree of social acceptance by the cream of Berlin society. Between 1780, when Henriette and Markus Herz first opened their salon, until 1806, when French troops occupied Berlin, ninety-eight individuals—including princes, diplomats, and the avant-garde intelligentsia—attended sixteen salons, nine of them hosted by Jewish women. Varnhagen was the most famous of these Jewish salonières, Friedländer the most obscure.

One might well expect Varnhagen's letters to Friedländer to be exceptionally forthright, not only because of the general similarity in the two women's backgrounds, but also because in the years when the letters were written the two women's social and emotional situations became even more directly parallel. When the correspondence began in 1805, Varnhagen (then still Rahel Levin) was thirty-five, single, and living in the attic apartment of the family home in the center of Berlin, on the Jägerstrasse. Some very happy times as a family member, as a lover, and as a salonière were behind her. It was not that her relationships in any of these three regions of her emotional landscape had ever been altogether unproblematic. Yet when viewed from the sharp, painful loneliness which began in 1805, her previous life looked rich and satisfying indeed. She was born in Berlin in 1771. Her early years as a child and an adolescent in the Levin household were, to be sure, difficult ones. Her father, a prominent jewelry merchant who enjoyed entertaining amusing nobles and actors, was a moody autocrat. His daughter Rahel was a frail child who nonetheless tried to stand up to her father. Over the years of her life at the Jägerstrasse household, she had difficulties with her mother and with two of her brothers who managed her inheritance. Still, there was a strong family bond, and Varnhagen would later show loyal devotion to her mother when she became ill in 1809.

Sometimes, family strife was caused by Rahel's new gentile friends. The 1790s had been a decade of great social success for Varnhagen. In these years, while still living at home with her mother and brothers, she slowly began to make herself into a person of intellectual competence. She hired tutors to work on French, English, and mathematics; she improved her German (Western Yiddish was her native tongue) through correspondence with a young Jewish medical student at Göttingen. And so, having mastered the requisite languages, in the summers at spas she made the acquaintance of free-thinking noblemen and noblewomen who became her champions, and, in the winter in the city, brought their friends by to meet her. These social successes, to be sure, were not crowned by success at intermarriage; Varnhagen had two unhappy love affairs with nobles between 1795 and 1804, and in both cases the men declined to marry her.[13]

Of all the losses from which she suffered in the first years of the new century, none was simultaneously more acute and less personal than the gradual disappearance of her salon circle. To begin with, salons were fragile, evanescent institutions. They tended to appear in preindustrial European cities where there was peace, prosperity, a tiny intelligentsia, an absence of meritocratic intellectual institutions, an intellectually motivated and urbanized nobility, and where wealthy women's intellects were valued by themselves and others. Salons hosted by Jewish women and frequented by gentile guests required even more prerequisites. For Jewish salons to appear and endure there had to be wealthy Jews whose wives and daughters were acculturated as well as gentiles who had financial, erotic or ideological reasons to visit them. The very existence of Rahel Varnhagen's salon between 1790 and 1806 was thus due not solely to her impressive personal qualities, but also to the convergence of the various factors which caused all sixteen of the city's salons to appear in Berlin in these years. To be sure, the heady success she achieved as the city's most well-known salonière was also due to her widely-praised intellectual and social talents. She established a devoted following among a circle of young men who would later constitute Germany's intellectual leadership, including Wilhelm and Alexander von Humboldt, Johann Fichte, Ludwig Tieck, Friedrich Schlegel, and Friedrich Schleiermacher. Progressive nobles who were not publishing intellectuals, like Gustav von Brinkmann and Wilhelm von Burgsdorff, brought their prestigious noble friends along when they visited the Jewish salons. But the utopian heterogeneity of the salon circles did not endure. Just as the sheer magnetism of Rahel Varnhagen's personality did not create her salon to begin with, her charm alone could not hold her salon together when the times changed radically in Berlin. As political efforts in France turned from internal reform to foreign conquest and as Prussia finally joined the coalition resisting such conquests, imitation of French culture, including salon attendance, became less popular among Berlin's intelligentsia. And so, by the time the correspondence with Rebecca Friedländer began, Varnhagen was bereft and alone. Neither privately nor publicly had the dream of assimilation been fulfilled.

On the surface, Rebecca Friedländer's life had been less traumatic than her friend Rahel's had been. She was born Rebecca Salomon in 1783. Her father, Jacob Salomon, was a jewel merchant serving the Prussian court in Berlin. The Salomons, some of whom changed their name to Saaling, tended to marry into prominent Jewish families. Rebecca's uncle Salomon Bartholdy was married to Bella Itzig, a daughter of the premier Jewish family in Berlin. Their daughter Lea Bartholdy married Moses Mendelssohn's son Abraham, and was the mother of Felix Mendelssohn-Bartholdy, the composer.[14] Friedländer herself married Moses Friedländer in 1801, when she was eighteen. Moses Friedländer was the son of David Friedländer, a banker and colleague of Mendelssohn's who was the author of a controversial 1799 pamphlet proposing that the Jewish community convert en masse to a rationalized version of Christianity. Yet the marriage quickly soured, and by 1804, Friedländer was divorced and living alone in an apartment in the home of another prominent Jewish family, that of Amalie and Jacob Herz Beer. Luckily, divorcing a banker's son had not left her in poverty. For although her father had not possessed an "oversize" fortune, it was divided evenly among all of the six siblings, and each inherited enough to "live without cares."[15] Her cares may not have been financial, but she did have cares nevertheless. She was often unhappy. Her woes fell into the two central areas of life, love and work. When the correspondence began, Friedländer was in love with Count von Egloffstein. This relationship went badly, as did the one with von Egloffstein's successor, Count Frederic d'Houdetot, a French field officer stationed in Berlin. Her literary efforts also caused her considerable frustration. Her first novel, published in 1808, was poorly reviewed, and her second, a roman à clef only thinly depicting her friend Varnhagen's salon, caused considerable trouble in the friendship. Later, she would convert and adopt her pen name, Regina Frohberg, but she never did remarry.

A decade's more experience with doomed love affairs with noblemen, meddlesome brothers, and the literary scene had made Varnhagen rich in relevant experience. She confided in, consoled, and advised her younger friend. Although for almost all of these five years the two women were living in the same city only three miles apart, for some periods Varnhagen wrote almost daily, when the weather was poor, when she had a migraine, or when lack of a carriage made a visit impossible. Frequently, the topic of her letters turned to the details of how things stood between the two friends. Hannah Arendt, who judged the letters to have been so important because of what they revealed about Varnhagen's Jewishness, gave no hint that one of the major topics of the letters was her extensive analysis of the state of the friendship with Friedländer. Varnhagen was often affectionate, sometimes angry; previous visits and letters were pored over in enormous detail. Discovering this theme is a surprise, for Arendt's comments on Friedländer suggest that she was not a very important friend to Varnhagen, that her chief significance lay merely in her sociological similarity to Rahel in these lonely years. In Arendt's words, the two women's "real solidarity" lasted only until Friedländer's "stupidity became too apparent to her [Varnhagen]." In Arendt's view, the cause of the breakup of their friendship was not just that Friedländer was "insufferable, unnatural, *pauvre* by nature in her pretensions," but in the novel that she published in 1810, under the name of Regina Frohberg. According to Arendt's account, the book, intended as "a picture of a German salon . . . compromised both herself and her entire circle of acquaintances, since no one at the time had any difficulty dubbing in the real names." Quoting Varnhagen to the effect that "she [Friedländer] is a greater fool than I thought," Arendt summed it all up by concluding that Varnhagen then proceeded to "cut off relations with her."[16]

Arendt's negative view of Friedländer was, to be sure, shared by others who had the advantage of knowing her personally. Rahel Varnhagen's brother Ludwig Robert wrote a most unflattering poem about her, found among the letters in Krakow. He portrays her as a person utterly lacking in authenticity. He described Friedländer as "honorable, when you deceive, deceptive when you believe." He concluded by condemning her intellectually as well: "silly when you read books, sillier still when you write them."[17] Nor did Friedländer's nephew, the writer Paul Heyse, have much positive to say about his aunt. He attributed her success as a salonière merely to her pretty face and her "worldliness." Heyse wrote of his shock when, as a fourteen-year-old, he happened upon his aunt while she was staying on the bottom floor of the Heyse home in Berlin. In the darkened room she sat "for the entire day all dressed up with white kid gloves," and "let her fat, pockmarked maid make her tea."[18]

Others may have found Friedländer comical and unworthy of Varnhagen. Yet these letters do not show that Varnhagen herself felt this way, and they definitely contradict Arendt's claim that Varnhagen did not relate "anything particularly secret" to Friedländer. Varnhagen concluded a May 1807 letter: "do understand the friendliness of this letter. It is that. Such a rush of truth, a reverence. No one ever spoke to me in this way."[19] She frequently wrote about the balance between her affections for Friedländer and Friedländer's affections for her. Earlier in 1807 she wrote that "today, especially, I would have liked to see you and shown my love."[20] By 1809, to be sure, the mutuality of their affections was in doubt. She admonished her friend: "you are not so necessary to me, as I may be to you, so it goes in friendship: but you are not in love with me!"[21] Quite frequently, her tone was physically intimate. She concluded an 1806 letter: "I embrace you for a quarter hour."[22]

Interpreting the meaning of these passages is a tricky business. This was an era in which language was often flowery and overblown. Even without seeing these letters, Kay Goodman suggested in 1980 that the nature of the relationship between the two women should indeed be characterized as a lesbian one, although not necessarily in the physical sense.[23] Surely these and other passages in the letters could provide additional evidence for Goodman's provocative claim. But there are good reasons for refraining from use of such controversial labeling altogether. Lillian Faderman's term "romantic friendship" would seem a better label than lesbian for this relationship.[24] There is rarely evidence to show that romantic friendships were actually sexually consummated, however lavish the language and however much time was spent together in intimate settings. Others have supported Goodman in arguing that by denying the women the label "lesbian" one is depriving the contemporary homosexual movement of its heroes in the German past.[25] Yet without some explicit evidence in the letters of erotic experience, use of this label would seem unwarranted and imprecise. Even Varnhagen's most ardently passionate claims do not provide evidence for going beyond the double assertion that this was a deeply affectionate friendship and that previous biographers minimized its importance in Rahel Varnhagen von Ense's life. The question of whether Karl August Varnhagen found the openly declared romance of the friendship embarrassing in the terms of his own day, and therefore censored the letters for that reason, must remain a mystery for now.

Similarly, more research is necessary before making a final decision on whether the 1810 publication of *Schmerz der Liebe*, Friedländer's second novel, really caused the end of the friendship. The novel, whose characters were all aristocrats with high titles, was a story of competition for love, worry about misalliance, rebellion against arranged marriage, and enjoyment of luxury. The narrative unfolds by the reader's overhearing the conversations at one Gräfin von Aarberg's salon and reading the letters exchanged by the characters. The novel, like Friedländer's other novels, received a pretty devastating reception. Her publisher, to be sure, advertised that her "touching situations" and "striking character sketches are totally the work of the feminine feeling for delicacy," and that her new book would count on receiving the "approval of the elegant reading world."[26] But her nephew Heyse portrayed her as lacking any talent at all, and considered it a riddle how her "wretched products could have found a publisher at all."[27] Karl August Varnhagen von Ense published an utterly damning review of three of Friedländer's books in 1811 under a pseudonym, August Becker. He began by blaming the rush of mediocre women's writing on their participation in intellectual interchanges, which led some of the women to believe that they themselves were intellectuals. In his opinion, their tales of private life and of love should not have been allowed to emerge from "the secrets of hidden hours."[28] He had nothing, absolutely nothing good to say about Friedländer's books. In his view, the characters were thin, the plots simple minded, the dialogue stilted. He concluded by wishing that the author would enjoy "in other circles all of the happy success which is denied her in this one."

Granted then, her work may not have been very good. But was Arendt correct that it caused the end of the friendship? The letters suggest that this was not the case. In May of 1810 Friedländer was apparently considering withdrawing the novel from the publisher, although the printing had begun. Varnhagen herself urged Friedländer not to withdraw it, and stressed that its author should look on her novel as a stranger would. "That is what I would do also . . . it [the novel] can hurt me as much as someone in China; because it pains you so much, we will forget this altercation even faster than I would normally."[29] In August, she recounted how her other friends had been asking her for her reaction to the book; she told them that she did not want to withdraw the novel from the publisher, as it could not hurt her. The friends claimed that Friedländer should have withdrawn it behind Varnhagen's back, but she reported to Friedländer that her response had been that "a play of fantasy should be permitted." She did admit that "the incident is annoying," but counseled her friend: "don't make anything out of it. Every author is bound to be attacked."[30]

Varnhagen's sympathy for her friend's plight did not originate in her own experience with publication. Her very reluctance to publish has in fact been hailed by some literary historians. These scholars' enthusiasm for her position on the fringe of the literary establishment follows from their own relativism about the division between craft and high art.[31] Were Rahel Varnhagen's letters a work of literature? Did she see them as such? Friedländer's literary situation at the time makes the letters to her a fitting source to answer both of these questions. Comments about publishing penned by one brilliant "dilettante" to one mediocre "professional author" are useful in questioning whether traditional categories of literary work ought to be abolished. This period is precisely the right one, moreover, for investigating the relationship between women's letters and women's literature. The last two decades of the eighteenth century were a glorious epoch for a letter-writing culture. This was a time when the content and style of letters was less bound to formula than ever before. Simultaneously, letters played a more important role in the lives of intellectuals than they would in the subsequent century. Newspapers were infrequent and censored in Germany, a country also lacking a capital city. New intellectual disciplines and new kinds of literature were born in these years from letters. Travelers' letters grew into anthropological observations and books of travel reportage; the epistolary novel grew into the psychological novel; scholars' correspondences came to be published in fledgling scholarly journals.[32] But at the very same time that the stuff of private communications found new outlets as public, published commodities which could be sold for a profit, the culture of letterwriting itself became more public. It was Rolf Engelsing who aptly called writing letters in the eighteenth century a "half-public" activity.[33] Letters were often read aloud; they were sometimes sent on to a third person; their style and contents could become known to important strangers; they could also be published. This was a setting in which the distinction between private and public was not as fixed or as comprehensive as it would subsequently become. Letters offered a chance to express oneself and to become famous, all without leaving home.

In their "half-public" quality, letters were very much like salons. Both institutions offered intellectual women a stage which they lacked in later decades, when intellectual life became more formal. Letters and salons both allowed women, who remained excluded from educational and employment opportunities, to participate in the literary culture. The importance of letters in the literary culture was due partly to the fact that in the eighteenth century literature was a young and decentralized enterprise for which formal training was not required. But letters and salons could also play a central role then because wealthy homes in these years were still public places. Letter writing and salon participation were two ways that talented women could become famous without leaving home or publishing their words. If the women's role in public life was even more restricted because they were Jewish, letters were an especially important medium. In this way Rahel Varnhagen's success at letters and at salons was a testimony to her own talents as much as a testimony to the structure of literary possibilities at the time.

The question of which letters were public and which were private seems to have depended greatly on the letter. Sometimes it apparently was understood that sharing the letter was expected, even wished. On Christmas Eve of 1806, Varnhagen announced that she was writing especially clearly so that Friedländer could read the letter aloud to her guests.[34] Sometimes she wrote her friend of her plans to share Friedländer's letters with a third person, or instructed her to convey her impressions of a third person's letter to that person.[35] Yet other letters were clearly for Friedländer's eyes alone. She was exhorted to "honor this letter with deep silence," and not share its contents "even indirectly;" another letter's contents were especially to be kept from Friedländer's sister Marianne Saaling.[36]

Many passages show that the two women understood letter writing to be a serious intellectual endeavor. Some letters contain long evaluations of books read, or short essays on topics of interest. Varnhagen occasionally stressed emotional issues connected with writing: "even if speaking and writing do not help at all, by no means should one stop speaking and writing." On another occasion she insisted, "you should write, and get it out! That does the mind, body, soul, and heart good."[37] She herself knew full well how little she could accomplish when she suffered from migraine, breast ache, or extreme nervous exhaustion. So as well as exhorting her friend to write, she sometimes admonished her not to read or write until she had rested. These comments suggest that the women understood reading, speaking, and writing letters to be intellectual work. Literary historians who have argued that letters as well as her conversation in salons should be classified as literature should be glad to see these lines. These scholars have focused on Varnhagen's oft-cited boast that "I am as unique as the greatest figure on this earth. The greatest artist, philosopher, or poet is not above me."[38] Varnhagen did explicitly link salon-style conversations, letters, novels, and memoirs as having aesthetically similar structures.[39] Her own statements expressing a kind of literary relativism, equating unpublished words with published words, has matched these scholars' own rejection of traditional definitions of high art. Silvia Bovenschen's "pre-aesthetic" category, which seems to include virtually all varieties of unpublished writing, has been presented as a way to include more women in the literary canon.[40]

While the urge to reevaluate accepted definitions of artistic creation may be a well-founded and timely one, removing the boundary between unpublished and published words altogether in the end causes more confusion than illumination. As one of the relativist literary historians has himself noted, labeling Rahel Varnhagen's letters as literature requires making endless demarcations between some letters which are literature and others which are not.[41] The letters to Friedländer provide a more specific reason for not equating unpublished with published words. And that reason is Varnhagen's own discussion of why she did not join in writing for publication. In a letter of 1807, she announced that she could do a better translation of a book than the one she had just read. She concluded: "I have talent. Should I use it? and earn something? Oh God! I know myself already! Some abilities; how I will use them—impossible! Nature did a lot for me inside; the other gods all stayed away from my cradle."[42] Her own revelation that her failure to publish was due more to her own lack of ability and temperament than to a self-conscious rejection of the medium is consistent with an older interpretation of her relationship to the printed word. It was Otto Berdrow who attributed her inability to write for publication to her lack of discipline and to her need to express herself to a specific, known individual rather than to an abstract, unknown reader.[43] All this suggests that while we work to insure that gifted women's words are not forgotten simply because they were not published in a traditional literary form, we should also pay attention to the role that individual temperament played in individual decisions not to publish.

In the past scholars have often selected the "most important" dimension of Rahel Varnhagen mainly on the basis of their own ideological passions. Traditional literary historians have seen her as the muse of the era, feminists have claimed her as a women writer, and pro- or antiassimilationist Jews have blamed or praised her according to how they saw her own relationship to her Jewishness. But the meaning of Rahel Varnhagen's life cannot be grasped if it is separated into compartments. All research into the world of the Berlin salons shows that Jewish women then and there possessed both opportunities for assimilation and concomitant sadnesses not shared by the Jewish men of the era. Although Varnhagen rarely referred to Jews directly in these letters, the love advice she pressed on Friedländer and her complaints about her lack of access to good society can only make sense when interpreted in light of the fact that they were written to another Jewish woman. The intimacy of her friendship with Friedländer was surely also linked to the women's common ethnic and social fate. The rediscovery and reconstruction of the richly detailed world described in the letters to Friedländer should be the occasion for finally seeing the woman in a whole and integrated way. Namely, not as a Jew in general or as a woman in general, but as a Jewish woman whose social environment combined with her individual personality to allow for glamorous opportunities and also to cause great suffering.

NOTES

I am grateful to the Foundation of SUNY at Binghamton, whose 1982 summer grant facilitated preparation of the Varnhagen-Friedländer letters for publication. For helpful comments on earlier versions of this essay, I am indebted to members of the Women, Culture and Society group at SUNY at Binghamton, to members of the German Women's History Study Group in New York, to Tamara Schoenbaum-Holterman, and to Martin Bunzl.

1. It was difficult to decide what to call the persons discussed in this essay. Women and men are both referred to by their last name. Since Rahel Varnhagen is known to posterity by a name acquired after that period discussed here, she is referred to by Varnhagen rather than Levin. But preserving historically authentic names is also an important principle. Since Rebecca Friedländer's subsequent name, Regina Frohberg, is scarcely better known than the name she had at the time, she is referred to here in the same way she was referred to in the original letters.

2. For discussion of the situation of Jewish women in the ensuing centuries, all of which points to diminished success at social assimilation, see the concluding chapter of Ingeborg Drewitz, *Berliner Salons: Gesellschaft und Literatur zwischen Aufklärung und Industriezeitalter* (Berlin, 1965) and Marion Kaplan, "Tradition and Transition: The Acculturation, Assimilation and Integration of Jews in Imperial Germany, A Gender Analysis," *Leo Baeck Institute Yearbook* 28 (1983). For general background on the late nineteenth-century situation of Jews in Berlin, see Fritz Stern, *Gold and Iron: Bismarck, Bleichröder, and the Building of the German Empire* (New York, 1979).

3. An accessible collection of Varnhagen's letters was edited by Friedhelm Kemp in four volumes: *Rahel Varnhagen: Briefwechsel mit Alexander von der Marwitz* (München, 1966); *Rahel Varnhagen: Briefwechsel mit Karl August Varnhagen* (München, 1967); *Rahel Varnhagen im Umgang mit ihren Freunden* (München, 1967); *Rahel Varnhagen und ihre Zeit* (München, 1968). (Henceforth referred to as Kemp I, II, III, and IV.) An expanded, corrected edition of the Kemp edition was published in Munich in 1979, but this edition was not available to me.

4. On the feminist concern with Rahel Varnhagen in the early twentieth century, see Kay Goodman, "The Impact of Rahel Varnhagen on Women in the Nineteenth Century," in *Gestaltet und Gestaltend: Frauen in der deutschen Literatur*, vol. 10 of *Amsterdamer Beiträge zur neueren Germanistik*, ed. Marianne Burkhard (Amsterdam, 1980), pp. 125–53. See also Anna Plothow, *Die Begründerinnen der deutschen Frauenbewegung* (Leipzig, 1907), chapter 1; Lily Braun, *Die Frauenfrage: Ihre geschichtliche Entwicklung und ihre wirtschaftliche Seite* (Leipzig, 1901), pp. 90–101, and Helene Lange and Gertrud Bäumer, *Handbuch der Frauenbewegung; Erster Teil, Die Geschichte der Frauenbewegung in den Kulturländern* (Berlin, 1901), p. 21.

The Heine quote is cited in Siegfried Prower, *Heine's Jewish Comedy* (Oxford, 1983), p. 213. The deathbed quote is: "Was so lange Zeit meines Lebens nur die grösste Schmach, das herbste Leid und Unglück war, eine Jüdin geboren zu sein, um keinen Preis möcht' ich das jetzt missen." It is cited on page 3 of Hannah Arendt's *Rahel Varnhagen: The Life of a Jewish Woman* (London, 1957). One reviewer of the Arendt biography noted that Varnhagen's full deathbed citation shows a more positive attitude toward Christianity than implied by this one sentence: see Heinrich Schnee's review of the book in *Historisches Jahrbuch* 81 (1960), p. 458. (I am grateful to my colleague David Biale for reminding me of the importance of this reviewer's critique.) For a sensitive discussion of many Jewish historians' ambivalence about Rahel Varnhagen and the Jewish salonières, see Maximilian Stein, "Paul Heyse und die Berliner Salons," in Stein's *Vorträge und Ansprachen* (Frankfurt/M., 1932). For a contemporary nineteenth-century critique of Rahel Varnhagen's relationship to Judaism by Gabriel Riesser, see Konrad Feilchenfeldt, "Die Anfänge des Kults um Rahel Varnhagen und seine Kritiker," in W. Grab und J. H. Schoeps, eds., *Juden im Vormärz und in der Revolution von 1848* (Sachsenheim, 1982).

5. See Arendt, *Rahel Varnhagen*. Also of interest are Arendt's collected essays on the theme, edited by Ron H. Feldman, *The Jew as Pariah: Jewish Identity and Politics in the Modern Age* (New York, 1978); Elizabeth Young-Breuhl, *Hannah Arendt: For Love of the World* (New Haven and London 1982), and Sharon Muller, "The Pariah Syndrome," *Response* 39 (Summer, 1980), pp. 52–57.

6. For instance, see Silvia Bovenschen, *Die imaginierte Weiblichkeit: Exemplarische Untersuchungen zu kulturgeschichtlichen und literarischen Präsentationsformen des Weiblichen* (Frankfurt/M., 1979).

7. These quotations are reprinted in the Fall 1983 brochure of Matthes und Seitz (Munich), publishers of the new collected works of Rahel Varnhagen. See Uwe Schweikert, "Ich lasse das Leben auf mich regnen: Rahel Varnhagen—Ein Porträt aus ihren Briefen," *Frankfurter Rundschau* (March 5, 1983). See also Konrad Feilchenfeldt, "Rahel Varnhagen in neuer Sicht," *Neue Züricher Zeitung* (March 5, 1983).

8. The four-volume edition is that edited by Kemp; see note 3. The editors of the new ten-volume edition (see note 7) are Konrad Feilchenfeldt, Uwe Schweikert, and Rahel E. Steiner.

9. See Arendt, *Rahel Varnhagen*, p. x. On Karl August's Varnhagen's disguise of Friedländer, see also Kemp III, pp. 413–14.

10. For a survey of the collection's contents, see Ludwig Stern, *Die Varnhagen von*

Ensesche Sammlung in der königlichen Bibliothek zu Berlin (Berlin, 1911). For a summary of the search for the lost material, see Nigel Lewis, *Paper Chase: Mozart Beethoven, Bach . . . The Search for Their Lost Music* (London, 1981). My own shorter report is "The Varnhagen Collection is in Krakow," *American Archivist*, 44 (1981), pp. 223–28.

11. In Kemp, III, pp. 267–92, 18 of Varnhagen's 346 letters to Friedländer were republished. All of them originally appeared in *Rahel, Ein Buch des Andenkens für ihre Freunde* (Berlin, 1834).

12. For background on the economic activities of Berlin Jewry, see Eugen Wolbe, *Geschichte der Juden in Berlin und der Mark Brandenburg* (Berlin, 1937), Selma Stern, *Der Preussische Staat und die Juden,* 3 volumes (Tübingen, 1971). See also Henri Brunschwig's essay, "The Struggle for the Emancipation of the Jews in Prussia," which is included as an appendix to his *Enlightenment and Romanticism in Eighteenth-Century Prussia* (Chicago, 1974). For a general background on the salons in Berlin, see the Drewitz volume cited in note 2 above; Karl Hillebrand, "Die Berliner Gesellschaft in den Jahren 1789–1815," in Uhde Bernays, ed., *Unbekannte Essays* (Bern 1955); Bertha Meyer, *Salon Sketches* (New York, 1938); Mary Hargrave, *Some German Women and Their Salons* (London, n.d.). Two books written during the Nazi era, useful in spite of their ideological perspective, include Hans Karl Krüger, *Berliner Romantik und Berliner Judentum* (Bonn, 1939), and Kurt Fervers, *Berliner Salons: Die Geschichte einer grossen Verschwörung* (Munich, 1940).

13. This summary of Varnhagen's life story until 1805 is based mainly on material found in Otto Berdrow, *Rahel Varnhagen: Ein Lebens- und Zeitbild* (Stuttgart, 1902).

14. It is unclear when each of the Salomons changed their name to Saaling, and when each converted. Jacob Jacobson, in his *Jüdische Trauungen in Berlin, 1723–1859* (Berlin 1968) (henceforth, *Trauungen*), p. 440, claims that Frohberg was born "Saaling." But a poem dedicated to Friedländer to be sung at her birthday in 1786, found among Julie Heyse's papers in the Paul Heyse Collection (at the Bayerische Staatsbibliothek in Munich, Rep. VIII, 17), refers to her as "Madame Salomon." She herself could not have converted before 1801, since she married Moses Friedländer in a conventional Jewish ceremony that year, which would not have been possible if she had converted. For additional biographical information on Friedländer, see Ludwig Geiger, "Marie oder die Folgen des ersten Fehltritts, ein unbekannter Roman," *Zeitschrift für Bücherfreunde* N.F. 9 (1917), pp. 58–62.

The reason that Bella Itzig's and Friedländer's uncle, whose original name was Levin Jacob Salomon, had children named Bartholdy was that Bella Itzig had previously been married to a Bartholdy, and her second husband, Friedländer's uncle, changed his name to Bartholdy after they married in 1775. See *Trauungen*, p. 226. On the Mendelssohn-Bartholdy family, see Heinrich Eduard Jacob, *Felix Mendelssohn und seine Zeit* (Frankfurt/M., 1959), pp. 33–35.

15. Little is known about Moses Friedländer. See *Trauungen*, p. 440, and, on his attempt to be exempted from the Jewish marriage tax because his mother belonged to the Itzig family, see Karoline Cauer, *Oberhofbankier und Hofbaurat* (Frankfurt/M., 1965), p. 36. The fact that Friedländer was living in the Beer home is known because several of Rahel Varnhagen's letters of 1807 were addressed to her there. On the Beer family, see the Beer family papers in the Archive of the Leo Baeck Institute in New York City. On the division of the inheritance of the Salomon family, see Paul Heyse (her nephew), *Jugenderinnerungen und Bekenntnisse* (Berlin, 1901), p. 6.

16. Arendt, *Rahel Varnhagen*, p. 107.

17. The poem is untitled and unsigned. In Karl August's Varnhagen von Ense's

handwriting above the poem is written "Rebecka Friedländer (Frohberg)" and below the poem "Ludwig Robert." (The poem is reprinted in Geiger, "Marie," p. 58.)

18. Heyse, *Jugenderinnerungen*, p. 9.

19. Letter of 15 May, 1807. All of the letters cited here will appear in my forthcoming book: *Briefe an eine Freundin: Rahel Varnhagen an Rebecca Friedländer* (Cologne, Kiepenheuer und Witsch, 1985). All quotes are in Varnhagen's original German, which sometimes is incorrect in grammar and spelling.

20. Letter of 18 January, 1807.

21. Letter of 16 February, 1809.

22. Letter of January, 1806.

23. Goodman, "The Impact of Rahel Varnhagen."

24. See Lillian Faderman, *Surpassing the Love of Men: Romantic Friendship and Love Between Women from the Renaissance to the Present* (New York, 1981). Although at the outset Faderman's term avoids the problems of the term lesbianism, one reviewer has noted that Faderman actually equates the two terms and the two experiences. See Isabel V. Hull's review of Faderman's book in *Signs: Journal of Women in Culture and Society* 8 (Summer 1983), pp. 708–9.

25. This objection was raised when an earlier version of this essay was presented at "Condition and Consciousness: German Women in the Eighteenth and Nineteenth Centuries: An International Conference," held at the University of Minnesota in April, 1983.

26. This phrase was part of the ad for Friedländer's novel, *Die Brautleute oder Schuld im Edelmuth* (Wien, 1814), and was printed at the conclusion of her novel *Bestimmung* (Wien, 1814). The rest of her published novels include: *Louise* (Berlin, 1808); *Schmerz der Liebe* (Berlin, 1810); *Das Opfer* (Amsterdam und Leipzig, 1812); *Verrath und Treue* (Berlin, 1812); *Marie* (Dresden, 1812); *Darstellungen aus dem menschlichen Leben* (Vienna, 1814); *Das Gelübde* (Vienna, 1816); *Erzählungen* (Vienna, 1817); *Herbst-Blumen* (Vienna, 1817); *Gustav Staning* (Vienna, 1817); *Die Rückkehr* (Frankfurt/M., 1825); *Der Liebe Kämpfe* (1827); *Eigene und Fremde Schuld* (Leipzig, 1837); and *Vergangenheit und Zukunft* (Gera, 1840).

27. Heyse, *Jugenderinnerungen*, p. 9.

28. Karl August Varnhagen von Ense's review was published under the pseudonym "August Becker." He reviewed *Louise*, *Schmerz der Liebe*, and *Erzählungen*, in *Die Musen* (Berlin, 1811). The copy of the review found among the letters to Friedländer in Krakow has the name "Varnhagen" written under the name "Becker" in Karl August Varnhagen von Ense's handwriting.

29. Letter of May, 1810.

30. Letter of 9 August, 1810.

31. See the unpublished M.A. thesis by Klaus Haase, "Rahel Varnhagens Brieftheorie: Eine Untersuchung zum literarischen Charakter des Privatbriefs in der Romantik" (Munich, Ludwig Maximilian University, 1977).

32. Two good introductions to the literary profession in eighteenth-century Germany are H. Kiesel and P. Münch, *Gesellschaft und Literatur in 18. Jh.: Voraussetzungen und Entstehung des literarischen Markts in Deutschland* (Munich, 1977), and George Steinhausen, *Geschichte des deutschen Briefs* (Berlin, 1889).

33. Rolf Engelsing, *Der Bürger als Leser: Lesergeschichte in Deutschland 1500–1800* (Stuttgart, 1974), p. 296. See also Reinhard M. G. Nickisch, "Die Frau als Briefschreiberin im Zeitalter der deutschen Aufklärung," *Wolfenbüttler Studien zur Aufklärung* 3 (Wolfenbüttel, 1976), pp. 29–66.

34. Letter of December, 1806.

35. Letter of 28 March, 1810.
36. Letter of 14 September, 1806.
37. Letter of 14 December, 1807.
38. See Kemp, III, p. 262.
39. See Hase, "Rahel Varnhagens Brieftheorie," passim.
40. In addition to the book cited in note 6 above, see Silvia Bovenschen, "Über die Frage: Gibt es eine weibliche Aesthetik?" *Aesthetik und Kommunikation* 15 (1976), pp. 60–75. For a critique of Bovenschen, see Elke Frederikson, "Die Frau als Autorin zur Zeit der Romantik," *Amsterdamer Beiträge zur neueren Germanistik* 10 (Amsterdam, 1980), pp. 83–108.
41. Karl Haase, "Rahel Varnhagens Brieftheorie," p. 14 and p. 33.
42. Letter of 13 January, 1807.
43. Berdrow, *Rahel Varnhagen*, pp. 217–20.

ON TRAVEL LITERATURE BY WOMEN IN THE NINETEENTH CENTURY

MALWIDA VON MEYSENBUG

Wulf Wülfing

It is interesting to look at travel literature written by women to try and find out if women authors reflect on female problems in their literature. I choose this kind of literature on the assumption that travel literature is traditionally and per definition not hermetic, but open in every sense: open for new topics that can be treated in an open way because of its impressionistic character, with no obligation of an ending, or a result.[1] But above all, travel literature is a pragmatic kind of literature in a twofold sense: First, the reader can use it for his or her own travelling. Secondly, the "connotative function"[2] that travel literature can possess is connected with the fact that it need not belong to the fictional kinds of literature, but that the writers' own experiences when travelling can be reported: They say "I," and this "I" need not be a fictional "I". That is why editors often classify travel literature as "autobiographical writings" in their editions of collected works.

Malwida von Meysenbug is an important example of a woman who regarded travelling as a means of recognizing the signals of a new age and of affirming them by describing them especially for contemporary women. She believed that women could overcome the restrictions to which they as travellers were particularly subject. She did not want to employ class-based means to do so but rather a female self-assurance based on her belief in the equal rights of women.

Malwida von Meysenbug was born on 28 October 1816 in Kassel.

She was the daughter of a noble family of Huguenots who were closely aligned with the Court. Already in her early youth she tried, "although nursing strong scruples," to keep aloof "from the philosophical views of her family, her class, and her church."[3] In 1848 she witnessed the Revolution in Frankfurt and joined the Democrats. "Her work at Fröbel's Women's Advanced School in Hamburg was brought to an end by the closing of the school by order of the political reactionaries; when she moved to Berlin, she was banished from the country because of her contacts with foreign Democrats."[4] She went into exile, first to London where she made friends with Mazzini, Garibaldi, and Kinkel, then to Paris, where she met Richard and Cosima Wagner, and later on, Nietzsche, "whose lectures *Über die Zukunft unserer Bildungs-Anstalten* (On the Future of Our Educational Establishments) she translated into Italian."[5] Until her death in 1903, she lived in Italy, where she had frequent contact with, among others, Franz Liszt, Romain Rolland, and Franz Lenbach.[6]

Her best-known book is *Memoiren einer Idealistin* (Memoirs of an Idealist). The first part of this autobiography was published anonymously in 1869 with the title *Mémoires d'une Idéaliste (entre deux révolutions 1830–1848)*.[7] Malwida von Meysenbug gave one copy to Nietzsche, who in his letters time and time again strongly advised friends to read it.[8] On Good Friday of the year 1876 (14 April) Nietzsche wrote to the author about his reading of the *Mémoires* as if he were speaking of a revival:

> Highly respected Miss, about a fortnight ago there was a Sunday which I passed all by myself extremely close to you at Lake Geneva from the morning til the moonlit evening: with restored senses I finished reading your book, and I told myself again and again that I had never experienced a more hallowed Sunday; the mood of purity and love did not desert me, and on that day nature was the mirror image of this mood. You walked in front of me as a loftier self, as a *much* loftier self—but you nevertheless encouraged rather than ashamed me: this is the way you floated in my imagination, and I measured my life against your example and asked myself for the many things I lack. I thank you for much more than for a book. . . . How often I wanted you to be near me to ask you questions that only a higher morality and entity than I am can answer. . . . But your book is a stricter judge for me than you might be in person. What does a man have to do not to be obliged to accuse himself of being unmanly when he imagines your life, that's what I often ask myself. He will have to do everything you did and nothing more at all! But most probably he won't be able to, he will lack the safely guiding instinct of ever-helpful love.[9]

In this book that Nietzsche praises so highly, Malwida von Meysenbug tells among other topics of a journey to Ostend that she had made
after the failure of the Revolution of 1848.[10] She had recorded her
adventures immediately after the journey, had read them to friends at
the above mentioned Hamburg school,[11] and had actually considered
publishing them. On 4 February 1850, for example, she wrote to
Johanna Kinkel from Detmold:

> You have encouraged me in such friendly fashion that I dare to send
> you some pages where I go into greater detail concerning these
> ideas.[12] The pages are part of a book I wrote this last winter, and I
> report in it on a journey I made to Ostend last summer. I have tried to
> publish this small book, but I don't know yet if I'll succeed. I doubt it
> because things are unfavourable when you have no reputation yet,
> but I won't be discouraged, as I first have to be completely *convinced*
> that my talent is too insignificant before giving it up.[13]

But the book obviously was not printed during the author's lifetime.[14] It
is said that six copies, handwritten by other women, existed of the
manuscript.[15] In 1905, Gabriel Monod published a copy which is,
however, incomplete: *Eine Reise nach Ostende (1849)* (A Journey to
Ostend).[16]

Only a self-assured person can—according to Malwida von Meysenbug—describe the present time (1849) as it reveals itself to the traveller. Self-assurance is necessary, for only this feeling of mental independence produces the ability to experience new things. She talks about
this problem in the first lines of her report:

> I feel sorry for the person who has never experienced the beautiful
> feeling of independence and of reposing in herself, in the face of
> distance, of the new and the unknown and the longing caused by
> them; that feeling or rather that knowledge of the eternally unalterable
> amid the pleasure of change, of expectation, of hurrying on to new
> things worth exploration. [9]

Once a woman has acquired the necessary independence, she can
profit from two possibilities that did not exist before: she can travel on
her own, and she can enjoy the new means of transport that revolu-
tionized the perception of reality, the railway:[17]

> I don't know if many of my sisters share my taste, but with regard to
> the present safety of travel, even for single women, there is a rare
> delight in this independence, for one has a sense of strong, compelling
> inner dignity. And no way of travelling increases this delight as much as
> the railway, that doesn't even slow down one's winged longing. [10]

For Malwida von Meysenbug, however, who in 1849 travelled from Cologne to Dusseldorf, this delight was not entirely pleasurable. A year before, in the spring of 1848, she had covered the same distance. At that time the *Vorparlament* (Pre-Parliament) in Frankfurt had just ended:

> Black-red-golden flags fluttered from our train; a long row of carriages full of volunteers: young, enthusiastic men, who were going to Schleswig-Holstein, and Polish men on their way back home. At every station they were cheered by the assembled crowd. . . . And now? The people had vanished, there were only poor workers, travelling artisans on business, frequenting the third and fourth class compartments; in the other classes there were elegant people of the "privileged classes," who, with their usual indifference, looked down on the others and seemed to say: "We want quiet at any cost." [10–11]

Meysenbug's political friends had been jailed or forced into exile, a fact which makes the travelling woman think about a problem still of pressing importance today: the right to call a person a political criminal:

> As if there really were political criminals! Can it be a crime, if an oppressed, eternal sense of justice awakens in the people and rebels against a jurisdiction or a law that represents nothing more to the people than the jurisdiction or law of violence? [11]

But in 1849 hardly anybody wants to ponder on revolutionary thoughts:

> At Düsseldorf Station I got the feeling of such distance from the year before, and I felt such an aversion for the restored, kid-glove Old World, that I closed the window of the compartment I was sitting in alone, and pressed myself into a corner. [12]

Here, Malwida von Meysenbug inserts the "Geschichte, die der Eisenbahnkondukteur erzählt hat" (Story the Railway Conductor Told),[18] a story which provides a different perspective of the literary genre of travel literature. The new means of transport was not only a narrative novelty, but also a political horror of German reality. At that time, many people had hoped that the railway would have a democratic effect because it united many people of entirely different social classes in a single, very small place; they hoped, in fact, that this effect might even be so strong as to cause a democratic process that might affect all classes of society.[19] But that dream was soon destroyed by the technical measure Meysenbug spoke of above: different classes of carriages were introduced[20] and caused the opposite effect. The contrast between classes become more obvious than ever before, and the railway became a society of classes in nuce. And the only person who oversaw all of it was the conductor.

Meysenbug tells of one such conductor.

> He sighed . . . deeply . . . whenever he went down from the noble spoils of the first class along the carriages to the open carriages of the fourth class, where the industrious artisan and farmer with their faces worked to the bone and their miserable clothes stood exposed to the biting wind. [16]

One day, the conductor meets a lady, and again we come across the problem of the woman travelling on her own. For the conductor immediately asks

> where she intended to travel on her own in such stirring times.
>
> She replied that she was travelling to Frankfurt to visit dear relatives who had invited her to spend the beautiful days of the *Vorparlament* with them. "I travel without fear, too, for during such days, when a sublime feeling fills every heart, who might think of insulting a woman; that is the beautiful aspect of such moments, that they concentrate life on a higher plane and remove the pettiness of everyday existence from it. I also go third class by principle for, on the one hand, when close to the common people to whom alone I want to belong, because my heart belongs to them, I feel better and safer than in the often very dubious vicinity of the people travelling first class; on the other, I am enraged that they imposed upon the democratic institution of the railway the severe hierarchy of the Old World. I am vexed that even here, where the spirit quickly flies from one place to the other and becomes everybody's property, where individuals of the most different social groups mix and thus pave the way for the end of nationalities and the union of human beings into humanity, that here again, the one who has possessions has such immense privileges and enjoys every comfort, while the poor and needy person so totally lacks them. If the luxury of the first class were distributed among all classes to make them more comfortable, then the expenditures for the poor would also probably not have to be increased just because that sort of luxury would disappear." [20–21]

The conductor meets the lady a second time; she is now on her way back from Frankfurt and is enthusiastic: to show her solidarity with the new ideas, she has become engaged to a spokesman of the Republicans.

And of course, the conductor sees the lady a third time, in mourning: The Republican has been arrested during the battle in Baden and has been executed. And again this woman had offended public etiquette and travelled on her own. For she reports

> how, when she received the news of her friend's arrest, she hadn't been moved by any remonstrances to stay behind, and how she travelled to see him. "What did the thing *they* call etiquette mean to me at that moment? They, who force even the most sublime feeling into the confinement of their rules? The highest, the only etiquette at *that* moment was: to see him once again, to try everything to save him, and if that was not possible, to show him during his last moments the divine consolation of love." [31]

But the lady does not succeed in becoming a second Karoline Schulz, who, on New Year's Eve of 1834, managed to free the Republican publicist Wilhelm Friedrich Schulz from the Fortress of Babenhausen and to flee to Strasbourg with him.[21] Still, in the eyes of the conductor, the lady becomes a "Goddess of History," who presents him with a ring and the advice always to stay a faithful "son of the people and of freedom." (33)

Malwida von Meysenbug's "Geschichte, die der Eisenbahnkonduk-teur erzählt hat" should be discussed under three different aspects:

> as an attempt to use new means of transport as a new topic of narrative texts;
> as a story in which the railway is not only a fashionable topic, but a symptom of society in general and of the political change in 1848–49 in particular;
> as the linking of the first two aspects with the fate of a woman.[22]

In the next chapter, "Von Cöln bis Brüssel" (From Cologne to Brussels),[23] Meysenbug again discusses the problem of the woman travelling alone, and again she has actual politics in mind. This time a Polish woman is concerned:

> When we asked her why she was travelling on her own and why she had been in Germany, she revealed that her husband had fought in the Palatine while she had lived in Frankfurt. After the revolt, he had fled to Paris and now had written her to join him. [38]

The chapter focuses on the story of an ostracized woman and her dog. The woman has to make an additional payment for the dog although she is very short of money. Meysenbug describes the misery of an emigrant with impressive insight when she says: "un chien est trop cher pour l'émigration" (a dog is too expensive for exile). (40)

In every chapter, Meysenbug is an eminently politically motivated traveller who stresses again and again that she is led by a "principle," the "principle of future." (46) She thus visits the "dignified memorial to the sons of the people who died in 1830 during the Battle of Liberation" (49) in Brussels. In Antwerp, however, she attends the ecclesiastical ceremony in remembrance of the accession of the King, a Catholic event dominated by the military. While her companions are outraged at the view of the "spectacle," she reacts in a different way; "But I had my own thoughts watching it, and I felt that Catholicism contains some aspects with which the New Church, the Church of the Future, might go along." (57) Malwida von Meysenbug wishes to interpret not only Beethoven's symphonies but also a painting by van Dyck in the sense of a "Cult of Future." (58) To employ modern terminology: she proposes a "progressive" interpretation of the cultural heritage.

But when thinking about the future, she does not forget the present. In the chapter "Neue Bekanntschaften" (New Acquaintances),[24] she learns about Brussels lace. She is not interested in the esthetic-fashionable effect of the regional product, however, but in the conditions of its production:

> They talked about the cruel way the factory workers were treated and when I asked, they told me that these poor people have to sit in completely darkened rooms, where the beam of light falls upon their work by way of a single small opening, so that the light for that infinitely delicate work is concentrated.

Naturally the workers' eyes are destroyed in the process. (70) After having described the cost of industrialization, Malwida von Meysenbug professes a social program which has immense connotative function:

> No, industrialization must no longer blossom at the expense of the human being. No lover of humanity can rest until these problems are solved. Vanity must not adorn itself any longer with the bitter fruits of misery; the tear of grief must no longer drop from the tasteful products of artistic skill. [70]

Malwida von Meysenbug bluntly confesses that she is a supporter of socialism concerned mainly about women's fate. Thus, another chapter is called: "In Ostende: Die Frau des Leuchtturmwächters" (In Ostend: The Wife of the Lighthouse Attendant).[25] She talks about a woman, who, against her mother's wishes, had started to work and had made her living as a fisherwoman, but who is now weary:

> "Yes", she said, "it is starting to tire me out, I am growing older, and want to be able to rest and think about things without having to work and produce perpetually."
> How touched I was by the longing in this great and simple being; the whole secret and justification of socialism was embodied in this remark. [78]

In Malwida von Meysenbug's eyes this fisherwoman is the "daughter of nature and the sea," "a daughter of the spirit," "la femme du peuple." (80) And she ends the chapter with the appeal:

> You women of the upper classes, the so-called educated ranks: if you go to Ostend, visit the cottage near the lighthouse and observe how the nature and grace, the strength and independence of that woman and a truly feminine sense can go together so well. [80–81]

Whereas up to this point Malwida von Meysenbug illustrated her views by examples, she uses the second half of her book to review a number of conversations with different men.

She first talks to a Jesuit and again confirms her opinions concerning the state (that is to say the Republic) and religion, (86) but also the role of women in society. (89) And again she is overcome by happiness because of her own steadfastness:

> I felt overjoyed and absolutely fearless opposite that dark spirit of a past epoch; for my convictions were so unshakable and clear that my heart did not have to fear subversion for one moment. [90]

The Jesuit finally escapes from being exposed to so much "future."[26]

Malwida von Meysenbug pities another man because he still wants to "banish us [women] to a closed circle, like hothouse plants that have to be protected against rough wind and strong sun, so that one can enjoy their exquisite beauty." (123)

The last chapter of the book is about the new "position of the female sex." (130) The heading reads: "Zukunftsgedanken" (Thoughts Concerning the Future).[27] Again, a man tries to provoke the travelling woman with, among others, the following opinion: "The woman *has to be* beautiful, that's her profession, and that's the only way a man selects her." (132) Meysenbug by no means wants to "be equal with the other sex in gesture and habit, or to erase the line separating male from female life." (135) But she asks: "Where is it written that only one part of humanity may eat from the Tree of Knowledge and the other mustn't?" (137) She is obviously only concerned about mental equal rights, for she writes: "If you establish mental equal rights for women and men, you must by no means infer that women have to be professors, lawyers, statesmen, or the like." (138) In Meysenbug's opinion, the woman belongs to the family, "the Alpha and Omega" (141) which she, however, situates differently under a Socialist perspective. (142–43) That is to say: the place of the family is within a public spirit, which will be made possible by "justice of the institutions." (145) "Socialism" in her eyes is only mental equalization, for she expressly refuses "material equalization": "Only a narrow-minded Communism can demand material equalization." (148)

If we refer to the beginning of the book, which was imprinted by her enthusiasm for an open future, this restriction sounds as if Malwida von Meysenbug had revised her views. The last chapter of the book, "Schluss" (End),[28] is also strangely marked by resignation. The female traveller has to go back to Germany, something she abhors. (155) On the eve of her return, on August 27th, some friends meet. Among these people too, the eve of the hundredth anniversary of Goethe's birth sets a mechanism of consolation into motion which offers poetic thought as a substitute for failed political action. Somebody says:

> The unified Empire could not be given an emperor because of the vanity of the many different, independent states. In the empire of poetry, he, the magnificent prince of poets, has been crowned without any objection.[156]

Meysenbug herself adds:

> I didn't agree with the bitter words of displeasure about the struggle that had failed. I didn't agree with the strong accusation against the presumed originators of the deceived hopes of the Revolution. [157]

But when she thinks more fundamentally about the problem, resignation is to be found in her as well. She talks about an idea—which Heinrich Heine, too, had entertained[29]—of something like a "division of labor among the peoples," and says that "the spirit of the universe" had reserved its own task for every people. (159) In this context, she asks: "If we feel so united at the thought of the great minds of our literature, isn't that a sign that this is the real meaning of our lives?" (160) At the same point we read about the often-quoted *Dichter und Denker* (Poets and Philosophers),[30] a slogan that Meysenbug did not invent and that was often used by people like Ludolf Wienbarg[31] and

Karl Gutzkow,[32] who thought politically, but were forbidden to act in public. It is interesting that Malwida von Meysenbug thinks that this German aspect could be extended to "Slavonic elements." (161)

However, the book does not end in resignation, but with an outlook, a symbolically interpreted sunset: "I looked at the sun and a voice inside me cried longingly: To the West!" (165) Malwida von Meysenbug talks about America, several times referring to Julius Fröbel. (163–64) And her summation of the Revolution of 1848 reads as follows:

> The most beautiful, historically significant fruit of the movements of the past two years is perhaps: to have directed to the young continent the fertile stream of German life as far as intelligence, energetic action, and desire for freedom are concerned. [162]

The deep yearning for American that the travelling woman expresses here corresponds to Meysenbug's feelings after her return. Her entire family rejects her because of her convictions, and even the most inoffensive attempt to be of use is interpreted and denied as something ideologically reprehensible:

> I felt that I wanted to transmit the knowledge I had acquired to others. I began with our servant girls and went to see them every once in a while in order to convey clearer ideas to them while they were doing needlework. I told them, for instance, about the orbit of the earth around the sun, the alternation of the seasons and so on. They were delighted and said: "Oh, Miss, if only everyone were of your opinion that we poor people also enjoy learning something! How much easier would it be for us to work if we could think of such beautiful things at the same time."—In former times my mother would not only not have said anything; on the contrary, she would have been glad to see me do such a thing. Now she thought that I wanted to propagate my extravagant ideas, she reproached me for spoiling the useful work time of the girls. I replied that I wanted nothing but to fill the void of thoughts during domestic work by keeping them busy with good knowledge. She, who otherwise had never been strict as far as the servants' work was concerned, answered me unkindly. . . .[33]

Meysenbug now feels impelled to make fundamental decisions in which America plays an important role:

> For the first time I told myself quite clearly that you *have* to free yourself from the authority of the family, as painful as it may be, as soon as it leads to the death of individuality and tries to submit the freedom of thought and conscience to a certain form of conviction. Freedom of individual convictions and a life in conformity with them is

the first of the rights and the first of the duties of a person. Until then people had debarred women from their holy right and a duty just as holy. . . . I realized that it was time to lift this ban, and I told myself that I wouldn't be able to esteem myself any longer if I didn't have the courage to leave everything in order to justify my convictions by my action. When my decision was made, the only thing I thought of was how to execute it. There was only *one* thing I could do: go to America—to a young earth, where labour wasn't a humiliation as in Europe, but a title of honour by which people prove their rights in society.[34]

She writes to her mother about her decision from the Women's School in Hamburg:

The answer came, almost annihilated me, and filled me with wonder and pain. . . . I was fully entitled to break the chains. . . . But—it was my mother who hit me that way. . . . That was what mattered! I replied that I had always been able to sacrifice my *desires* to her peace of mind, and that therefore I would give up my plan to emigrate, but that I would always insist on the freedom of my *convictions.* . . .[35]

Let us finally look at a larger framework indicating whether Malwida von Meysenbug's book *Eine Reise nach Ostende (1849)* is unique in contemporary travel literature by men and women.

Since the eighteenth century the secularized bourgeoisie have defined time as a precious good which they describe by terms constituting a special concept of time: *Zukunftsbegriffe* (terms of future)[36] are invented. The numerical distance between tomorrow and yesterday is turned into a qualitative one: tomorrow will necessarily be better than yesterday.

During the 1830s, this concept of time was propagated especially in travel literature by oppositional bourgeois writers like Heinrich Heine, Ludwig Börne, Heinrich Laube, and Theodor Mundt.[37] Aristocratic writers of travel literature like Prince Hermann von Pückler-Muskau were more reserved, to put it mildly.[38] The most famous female aristocrat of the time who wrote travel literature, Ida Countess Hahn-Hahn, expressly refuses the idea of "progress" in 1842:

People say that things have improved because there is progress in our time. Oh, progress! Progress implies a higher degree of evolution! Would you call autumn a progress of nature because it begins later than spring and summer and produces yellow leaves instead of green ones? Or would you say that old age in human life is progress because it renders red cheeks pale and turns robust confidence into sickly caution? And why do you absolutely want to call the transition stage between two epochs in the history of the world progress, while in nature and in the human being you may only name it that way under certain conditions?[39]

Countess Hahn-Hahn clings to a cyclic concept of "nature" which does not know "change," which only knows the "return of the same thing."[40] It would be interesting to compare the ideas both travelling women have concerning women, because the Countess's refusal of the idea of progress affects her opinion concerning the important problem of female self-reliance. So it is really nature's fault that women are the way the Countess thinks they are:

A lack of self-reliance and power produces inconstancy. That's what nature has provided women with. Oh, pardon me, but it isn't true, and is it really a disgrace to be the way God has created you? He wanted the woman to be more dependant on the man than the other way round. No intelligent man has ever been turned into a stupid one by a stupid woman. But give the most intelligent woman a stupid man, and he will stupify her to such a degree that she will be odd or depraved after some years. Some wives and daughters have become engrossed in their husbands' and fathers' dry essays in order to please them, and they have become interested in the subjects; but never in the history of mankind has a husband or son grown fond of his wife's or mother's work. No one has ever knitted a pair of stockings in order to share everything she does.[41]

On the other hand, the emancipation of women is Malwida von Meysenbug's aim which she tries to achieve by arguing with men. By so doing, she practises and confirms female self-assurance. She is strictly opposed to adjusting the idea of emancipation to male conceptions: "From the beginning education must have woman as its ultimate object. She mustn't be educated for the home, to be a good housekeeper or cook, or for the husband." (138)

This program, which Meysenbug tried to realize with the help of Fröbel, is a fundamental one: it believes in the "principle of future." Malwida von Meysenbug, born into nobility, believes in a concept of progress, and she is a Republican.[42] So Meysenbug is an aristocratic writer of travel literature who does not agree with the political concept of her aristocratic sisters, but who rather accepts the very ideas that the oppositional bourgeois writers of travel literature of the 1830s—like Heine[43] and Börne—supported.

Malwida von Meysenbug's ideas of female nature are part of a larger concept of society that she calls socialism, a way of thinking that she regards as a necessary development of Christianity. Apart from being embedded in this more general concept of society, Meysenbug's reports of her journey refer to the concrete political experience of the years of 1848–49.Travel adventures and reporting about them are seen entirely through the experience of the failure of the revolution. The female author succeeds in some ways to establish a relation between the new means of transport, the railway, and the political events. She succeeds by seeing to it that a new literary form manifests itself: Her "Geschichte, die der Eisenbahnkondukteur erzählt hat" is a political and historical *Zeitgemälde* (painting of the time), in this context an *Eisenbahngeschichte* (story of the railway).[44]

NOTES

Translation by Angelika Wülfing, assisted by Angelika Friedrich and Dorothee Köhler.

1. Wulf Wülfing, "Reiseliteratur," *Deutsche Literatur. Eine Sozialgeschichte,* ed. Horst Albert Glaser, vol. 6: *Vormärz: Biedermeier, Junges Deutschland, Demokraten. 1815–1848,* ed. Bernd Witte (Reinbek: Rowohlt, 1980), pp. 180–94.
2. Karl Bühler, *Sprachtheorie. Die Darstellungsfunktion der Sprache.* 2nd ed. (Stuttgart: G. Fischer, 1965), pp. 25–33 ["Appellfunktion"]. See Roman Jakobson, "Closing Statement: Linguistics and Poetics," in *Style in Language,* ed. Thomas A. Sebeok (Cambridge, Mass.: The M.I.T. Press, 1968), p. 355.
3. Hiltrud Häntzschel, "Malwida von Meysenbug 1806–1903," in *Deutsche Schriftsteller im Porträt,* vol. 4: *Das 19. Jahrhundert,* ed. H.H. (Munich: Beck, 1981), pp. 116–17.
4. Ibid.
5. Ibid.
6. Ibid. See *Frauenemanzipation im deutschen Vormärz. Texte und Dokumente,* ed. Renate Möhrmann (Stuttgart: Reclam, 1978). pp. 242–48.
7. Häntzschel, p. 117. See Katherine Ramsey Goodman, *German Women and Autobiography in the Nineteenth Century: Louise Aston, Fanny Lewald, Malwida von Meysenbug and Marie von Ebner-Eschenbach,* Ph.D. diss. (University of Wisconsin [Madison], 1977 [University Microfilms 77–25, 821]), pp. 127–84.
8. Friedrich Nietzsche, *Werke in drei Bänden,* ed. Karl Schlechta, vol. 3 (Munich: Hanser, 1956), pp. 1072, 1125, 1137, 1140.
9. Ibid., pp. 1118–19. See Elsa Binder, *Malwida v. Meysenbug und Friedrich Nietzsche. Die Entwicklung ihrer Freundschaft mit besonderer Berücksichtigung ihres Verhältnisses zur Stellung der Frau* (Berlin: Mayer & Müller, 1917), p. 36 ff.
10. Malwida von Meysenbug, *Memoiren einer Idealistin und ihr Nachtrag: Der Lebensabend einer Idealistin,* vol. 1 (Berlin: Schuster & Loeffler, 1917), pp. 179–84.
11. Rudolf Kayser, "Malwida von Meysenbugs' Hamburger Lehrjahre," in

Zeitschrift des Vereins für Hamburgische Geschichte, XXVIII (1927/28), 116–28 (see p. 121).

12. Thoughts about America (see the end of this essay).

13. Malwida von Meysenbug, *Briefe an Johanna und Gottfried Kinkel 1849–1885,* ed. Stefania Rossi, Assisted by Yoko Kikuchi (*Veröffentlichungen des Stadtarchivs Bonn,* vol. 28, (Bonn: Rohrscheid, 1982), p. 33.

14. Emil Reicke, *Malwida von Meysenbug. Die Verfasserin der 'Memoiren einer Idealistin'. Mit 17 Bildern* (Berlin/Leipzig: Schuster & Loeffler, 1911), p. 36; Malwida von Meysenbug, *Gesammelte Werke,* ed. Berta Schleicher, vol. 4 (Stuttgart, Berlin, Leipzig: Deutsche Verlags-Anstalt, 1922), p. 6.

15. Gabriel Monod, "Vorwort," in Malwida von Meysenbug, *Eine Reise nach Ostende (1849)* (Berlin and Leipzig: Schuster & Loeffler, 1905), p. 7. Kosch has obviously been dazzled by the date 1849 in the title of Monod's edition, for he notes "Meysenbug, Malwida von: *Hauptwerke: Eine Reise nach Ostende 1849* (2. Aufl. 1905)" (Wilhelm Kosch, *Deutsches Literatur-Lexikon,* vol. 2 [Halle/Saale: Niemeyer, 1930], col. 1580).

16. Malwida von Meysenbug, *Eine Reise nach Ostende (1849)* (Berlin and Leipzig: Schuster & Loeffler, 1905). Future page references to the text will be provided in parentheses following the citation.
The National Forschungs- und Gedenkstätten der klassischen deutschen Literatur in Weimar possess the manuscript/copy that apparently served Monod as a draft. This is particularly evident when one compares the "note for the printer" on page 150 of the copy with Monod's edition, p. 133. This edition is generally identical with the copy. Yet there are the following alterations:

There are no headings for the different chapters in the copy with one exception: "Geschichte, die der Eisenbahnkondukteur erzählt hat" (see below).
The chapters XVI and XVII of the copy are not printed in Monod's edition.
If one takes into account the fact that the copy itself is incomplete—the chapters VII, VIII and XIX (according to the method of counting in the copy) are missing!—one can only say that the state of the text is most unsatisfactory.

17. Wolfgang Schivelbusch, *Geschichte der Eisenbahnreise. Zur Industrialisierung von Raum und Zeit im 19. Jahrhundert* (Munich: Hanser, 1977).

18. Meysenbug, *Eine Reise nach Ostende,* pp. 15–33.

19. Wulf Wülfing, *Schlagworte des Jungen Deutschland. Mit einer Einführung in die Schlagwortforschung* (Berlin: Erich Schmidt, 1982 [*Philologische Studien und Quellen,* vol 106]), p. 232.

20. Schivelbusch, pp. 67–83.

21. Wulf Wülfing, *Junges Deutschland. Texte—Kontexte, Abbildungen, Kommentar* (Munich: Hanser, 1978 [*Reihe Hanser,* vol. 244; *Literatur-Kommentare,* vol 10]), p. 99.

22. Another woman compiled a volume, *Die schönsten Eisenbahngeschichten* (Most Beautiful Railway Stories) in 1976. Among the thirty authors there is only one female author: Patricia Highsmith (*Abfahrt auf Gleis elf,* ed. Renate Nagel [Zurich and Cologne: Benziger, 1976]). Malwida von Meysenbug's attempt to open a new political and literary genre of literature for women's problems with her railway story obviously found no successors.

23. Meysenbug, *Eine Reise nach Ostende,* pp. 35–44.

24. Ibid., pp. 65–74.

25. Ibid., pp. 75–81.
26. Ibid., pp. 98–99. See Meysenbug, *Memoiren einer Idealistin*, pp. 182–83.
27. Ibid., pp. 127–51.
28. Ibid., pp. 153–65.
29. Heinrich Heine, *Sämtliche Schriften*, ed. Klaus Briegleg, vol. 2 (Munich: Hanser, 1969), pp. 655–56; vol. 3 (1971), pp. 593–606.
30. Meysenbug, *Eine Reise nach Ostende*, p. 160:

It is above all Germany, which through its poets and philosophers, helped the world to find the way out of isolation and selfishness to reach the climax of its second great cultural epoch. This was achieved by pure theory and the ideals of an existence that reveals the great thought of the world . . . : the free, harmonically structured moral state.

31. Ludolf Wienbarg, *Ästhetische Feldzüge*, ed. Walter Dietze (Berlin and Weimar: Aufbau, 1964), p. 283.
32. Karl Gutzkow, *Zur Philosophie der Geschichte* (Hamburg: Hoffmann und Campe, 1836), p. 117; see *Geflügelte Worte. Der Zitatenschatz des deutschen Volkes*, ed. Georg Büchmann, 31st ed. (Berlin: Haude & Spenersche, 1964), p. 162.
33. Meysenbug, *Memoiren einer Idealistin*, p. 184.
34. Ibid., p. 185.
35. Ibid., p. 200–201.
36. Reinhart Koselleck, *Vergangene Zukunft. Zur Semantik geschichtlicher Zeiten* (Frankfurt: Suhrkamp, 1979), p. 113.
37. Wülfing, *Junges Deutschland*, pp. 133–41; "Reiseliteratur."
38. Wulf Wülfing, "Reiseliteratur und Realitäten im Vormärz. Vorüberlegungen zu Schemata und Wirklichkeitsfindung im frühen 19. Jahrhundert," in Wolfgang Griep and Hans-Wolf Jäger, *Reise und soziale Realität am Ende des 18. Jahrhunderts* (Heidelberg: Winter, 1983 [*Neue Bremer Beiträge*, vol. 1]), pp. 371–94, esp. 372–83. The title of this essay is unclear; it was formulated by somebody else. My original title reads as follows: "Reiseliteratur und Realität im Vormärz. Vorüberlegungen zu Schemata von Wirklichkeitsbeschreibung im frühen 19. Jahrhundert."
39. Ida Gräfin Hahn-Hahn, *Erinnerungen aus und an Frankreich* (Memoirs from and on France), vol. 1 (Berlin: Alexander Duncker, 1842), pp. 158–59.
40. Gerhard Plumpe, "Zyklik als Anschauungsform in historischer Zeit. Im Hinblick auf Adalbert Stifter," in Jürgen Link, Wulf Wülfing eds., *Bewegung und Stillstand in Metaphern und Mythen. Fallstudien zum Verhältnis von elementarem Wissen und Literatur im 19. Jahrhundert* (Stuttgart: Klett-Cotta, 1984 [*Sprache und Geschichte*, vol. 9]).
41. Hahn-Hahn, *Erinnerungen aus und an Frankreich*, vol. 2 (Berlin: Alexander Duncker, 1842), pp. 96–97.
42. Anna Blos, *Frauen der deutschen Revolution 1848. Zehn Lebensbilder und ein Vorwort* (Dresden: Kaden, 1928), pp. 33–46. Christine Brückner, "Eine Oktave tiefer, Fräulein von Meysenbug! Rede der ungehaltenen Christine Brückner an die Kollegin Meysenbug," in Christine Brückner, *Wenn du geredet hättest, Desdemona. Ungehaltene Reden ungehaltener Frauen* (Hamburg: Hoffmann und Campe, 1983), p. 93–108.
43. Joachim Kröll, "Malwida von Meysenbug," *Archiv für Geschichte von Oberfranken*, vol 46 (1966), pp. 241–328 (see p. 256, note 54).
44. The titles of many books written in the nineteenth century that are considered

travel literature are metaphors which belong to the field of the picturesque: *Reisean-sichten* (Views of Travelling), Reisengemälde (Paintings of Travelling), *Reisepanorama* (Panorama of Travelling), *Reiseskizzen* (Sketches of Travelling), *Reisebilder* (Pictures of Travelling). These titles stress the aspect of the transient (Wülfing, "Reiseliteratur", p. 183). In opposition to those books, Malwida von Meysenbug's *Eisenbahnge-schichte* is a "real" story: the constellation of its characters is clearly arranged and the structure of action can even be called strict in the triple recurrence of the meeting of the two main characters.

". . . NOTHING MORE THAN A GERMAN WOMAN."

REMARKS ON THE BIOGRAPHICAL AND AUTOBIOGRAPHICAL TRADITION OF THE WOMEN OF ONE FAMILY

Gudrun Wedel

Women's Autobiographies as Source Material

The rise of the autobiography as a literary form in Germany occurred in the eighteenth century. Out of the lively interest in the fortunes and private lives of other people grew the wish to describe one's own life and to make the description known to the world. In the last two centuries, thousands of men have written and published their auto-biographies. The number of women who made their autobiographies public, however, remains very small. It has taken several years of intensive research to get at least an approximate overview of the nineteenth-century German women who wrote autobiographical works and published them.

My aim here is to show to what extent autobiographies can be used as source material about the living conditions and the inner world of women. I intend to do this by using the bio/autobiographical works of a single family and concentrating on a limited number of topics. I shall begin, however, with a short survey of the source material I have unearthed, so that the selected autobiographies can be put into per-spective.

The formal criteria for selecting the female autobiographers were date of birth—between 1800 and 1900—and the writer's affiliation to the German-speaking world. In addition, the autobiography had to have been published. I made notes on unpublished works, but did not evaluate them. In all, I have a collection of more than five hundred autobiographers comprising about eight hundred autobiographical works. Literary criteria I did not apply, such as the traditional (although in my view misleading) distinction between memoirs, autobiographies, and reminiscences, or a judgement of the author's literary merits. My aim was to describe the sources from a social-historical standpoint—that is, on a general level to deal with aspects of a history of everyday life and, on a more particular level, to reveal specific living conditions and the inner world of nineteenth-century women.

It is, however, not easy to construct a model biography *(Lebenslauf)* following any model of life stages[1] from autobiographical writings. On the one hand, the women authors are not representative in the light of statistical criteria, and on the other, the many differing aspects of their lives only document how little we still know about nineteenth-century women. Those few famous women who generally arouse a wider interest tend to be the exception rather than the rule, and extensive research has yet to be done. The various ways in which women present themselves—autobiographies, letters, and diaries, but also painted self-portraits—are certainly of major importance here. That there is increasing interest in the lives of women is evidenced by the growing amount of academic research into biographical documents.[2]

Autobiographies show that, despite the restrictions imposed on them by society, women again and again succeeded in finding and pursuing their own paths. Autobiographies also show the changes in the position of women, especially in the second half of the century, when, in the course of economic, social, and political upheavals, it became gradually necessary for middle-class women to earn their own living when they were not provided for in a marriage. At the same time, there was a growing demand for qualified labor, especially in the newly developing professions. This constellation gave women the chance to obtain jobs that up to then had been exclusively male preserve. New jobs such as teaching or nursing were basically still those which were compatible with the idea of women being wives, housewives, and mothers, but they loosened the factual and ideological tie of middle-class women to the family.

Numerous autobiographies document this change, for most women authors come from the middle class. They hardly mention, however, the so-called women's question or the contemporary women's movement. In addition, autobiographies of women playing an active part in the women's movement are comparatively rare. After middle-class women, aristocratic women form the second largest group of auto-biographers. There are only rare reminiscences of lower-class women, mostly written by servants or female workers who were involved in the working-class movement. Rural women hardly ever wrote autobiographies. This indicates that writing is closely connected with the social origins of the author: to write a book demands not only a considerable amount of education but also sufficient spare time.

Finding adequate criteria for a more detailed and correct social classification of the women authors presents a major problem. In the past, women were generally defined in terms of the social status or profession of the male breadwinner, be it father, husband, or son—a superficial and unsatisfactory method. To be sure, most autobiographers conformed to this definition, but by reporting and commenting on norms, the authors also revealed the repressive character of these norms. We can also determine the way in which the norms shaped women's consciousness and to what extent they restricted the women in their freedom of action. As long as the problem of social status definition remains unresolved, regarding women's work as a criterion for social classification offers a solution: women's work encompassing social activities as well as employment or any other sort of work. This can rarely, if at all, be found in other sources. At any rate, most women authors (more than 75 percent) did have a job, usually in one of the "feminine" professions: as teachers, doing social work of all kinds, as writers, or artists.

A woman's autobiography offers us a selected, carefully formulated and subjective view of the life of the author and the lives of other women with whom she was connected. For the evaluation of the sources, however, comparative material for control has to be consulted, if one wants to deduce general statements on the real historical situation. If we dispense with this control, we are left with subjective statements which should be evaluated only with great care. Many women authors, however, published their autobiography during their lifetime and hence were open to criticism by a contemporary and—regarding statements of historical fact—reliable readership. Conventional objections to autobiographical sources (subjectivity, mistakes, omissions, distortions, fakes) lose impact when the method of critical historical research is applied, providing that misplaced or disproportionate expectations are dispensed with. The advantages of these kinds of sources then become much clearer: autobiographies show how women from another era judged their own lives, what sort of conditions they held responsible for their decisions and actions, and how they appraised their environment.

After these more general remarks demonstrating the documentary value of autobiographies, I should like to present the autobiographical writings of a woman who is scarcely remembered today and to discuss some selected issues raised in these works. I have chosen the writer Agnes Sapper because she wrote her mother's biography, and her own biography was written by her daughter. Hence, we are in possession of reports on the lives of at least three generations of one family. But besides grandmother, mother, and daughter, we also learn about the great-grandmother and, to some extent, the grandchildren. By not choosing famous or prominent women, we also gain insight into so-called normal living conditions. But then, what is normal? Are we—judging from the present and on the basis of a rather inadequate knowledge of the past—in any way able to comment on that? When we read Agnes Sapper's introduction to her mother Pauline Brater's biography, such questions spring inevitably to mind. For Agnes Sapper begins as follows:

> Who is Mrs. Brater, or who was she? Why should we take an interest in her? Was she an artist, a scholar, a benefactress for mankind? Did she excel in any field and make herself known throughout the world? These justified questions have been the cause of considerable doubts since they must all be denied. Mrs. Brater never entered public life, she was nothing more than a German woman. Those who did not know her personally know nothing about her.[3]

But her mother's life was, in fact, not so run-of-the-mill as suggested in the introduction.

Before we turn to the lives of the women in this family, some remarks have to be made concerning the relationship between the general and the specific as described in the autobiographies. As might be expected, extraordinary events in a person's life are described in an autobiography, rather than everyday routine. Naturally, it is the author who decides what is to be communicated and what might interest the reader most, but how she describes it is very much determined by the way her friends and her social class view certain topics. This "public opinion" not only influences the selection and formulation of events and facts, but also shapes the self-image of the author. Therefore, the self-description of women in autobiographies is to some extent affected by the predominant (i.e., male) norms, although it is very difficult to establish precisely to what extent. For that reason, biographical works written for an anonymous public convey only a filtered picture. It is, however, sometimes possible to reveal this male influence by comparing the autobiography with letters which deal with "women's issues."

Without being aware of this problem, Agnes Sapper tells us how she herself was influenced by "public opinion." In her autobiography she describes in detail her work on the biography of her mother Pauline Brater. She points out how she was faced with the problem of selecting from several hundred letters those which might interest the readership.[4] For fear of being too diffuse, she omits many things even when she knows they might convey a vivid picture of the times. To illustrate the nature of these omissions, she quotes from a letter which her great-grandfather wrote to his bride, asking her to abstain from the snuffbox before marriage.[5]

Judging from a present feminist standpoint these concessions to contemporary taste are peculiar. On the other hand, they were justified at the time. After the biography had been published, a Munich newspaper printed a rather negative review of it, and Agnes Sapper, very distressed, began once more to question her way of writing:

> Thus, for the first time I experienced being strongly criticized, all the more embarrassing since this book dealt with our family. I asked myself: Should you, after all, have refrained from relating so much about your family?[6]

The principal objection was "that the wife was much more discussed than the political activity of her important husband. It should be quite irrelevant to posterity whether Mrs. Brater had at one time received a cream cake or not."[7]

Criticism did not only revolve around the fact that in a woman's biography a woman is actually the main figure but also that many unimportant and redundant details are conveyed—unimportant and redundent being characteristics specifically tied to the woman's sphere. And this contempt for the woman's world is typical of prevailing contemporary opinion. It is thus not surprising that women find it difficult to report on their own lives, especially when extraordinary events are missing. Even the writer Agnes Sapper, who was widely read in her time, is very insecure when it comes to describing her family and herself: "Most of all I was plagued by this fear [of pushing oneself into the foreground and boring others] while I was writing the biography of my mother, and it is not much different even today while I am writing these lines."[8] Her daughter Agnes Herding-Sapper confirms this. She tells us why Agnes Sapper originally wanted to have her autobiography published postumously: "Initially it had been her intention to have it published only after her death, but the thought of the many old friends not being able to read it anymore conquered her shyness at writing about herself."[9] Agnes Herding's criticism of Pauline Brater's biography is also typical of the tradition of general contempt for the everyday life of women. She says emphatically:

> And thus, a vivid picture [of Pauline Brater] is born, totally truthful, without any glossing over. But we are not reduced to the fussy prose of a woman whose life was strenuous; the important, the valuable receives attention; relieved of the contingencies of the moment, we see the true inner portrait of this personality.[10]

The Nature of the Selected Autobiographical Biographies as Sources

The works which I present here are both primary and secondary sources—a mixed form which calls for a more detailed explanation. In addition, I want to describe in what manner and from what perspective the historical facts are dealt with and the kind of sources the women authors used.

Agnes Sapper, the connecting link between the different generations of women, is the center of our interest. She wrote an autobiography under the title *A Greeting to the Friends of My Books,* which D. Gundert, the publisher of her children's books, published in 1922. In the autobiography, Agnes Sapper deals with the time from her first efforts as an author at the start of the 1880s until her seventieth birthday in 1922. Its major focus is her writing; and the autobiography was her last literary work.

In 1907, some months after her mother Pauline Brater's death, Agnes Sapper began to work on her biography. This book, dealing with Pauline Brater's life from her birth in 1822 until her death was published in 1908 under the title *Mrs. Pauline Brater. Biographical Sketch of a German Woman* by Beck in Munich.

The third work—also a biography—is by Agnes Herding-Sapper, the youngest daughter of Agnes Sapper, and is called: *Agnes Sapper, Her Path and her Effect* (Cover title: *The Life Story of the Mother of the Pfäffling Family*). It was published in 1931—also by Gundert in Stuttgart—two years after Agnes Sapper's death. The book describes Agnes Sapper's life from her birth in 1852 until her death.

Besides these two women, a cousin of Agnes Sapper, the daughter of Pauline Brater's brother Friedrich, also wrote about Pauline Brater's maiden years, but in the form of a novel: Else Pfaff: *From Pauline Brater's Youth 1845–1849*, Munich (Beck), 1931.

The first three works are very much autobiographical in character, especially (and naturally enough) the autobiography of Agnes Sapper. But in her biography of her mother, we also learn a lot about Agnes Sapper's own life, particularly about her childhood and youth, something which she does not mention in her autobiography. There are only a few autobiographical passages in Agnes Sapper-Herding's work, but our knowledge of her life can be supplemented by details given in her mother's autobiography.

Agnes Sapper's life is depicted by herself as well as by her daughter, so that we get to know it from different perspectives: in Pauline Brater's biography, Agnes describes herself as a daughter, in her autobiography as a daughter and a mother, and in her daughter's biography of her, we see her from the perspective of her daughter. In her daughter's case, the situation is similar: she writes about herself and is also described by her mother. Pauline Brater was the only one who did not write about herself, but she is portrayed several times: by her daughter, by her granddaughter, and by her niece.

These three works, therefore, belong to the border zone between autobiography and biography. On the one hand, autobiographies have a biographical character, insofar as other persons are usually described in them as well. And often these sections provide the only information we have about these persons. The scope and the quality of these descriptions will determine how close the autobiography comes to biographical writing. On the other hand, biographies take on autobiographic features if the author knew the portrayed person herself and was connected to her. Here, too, content and scope of the autobiographical passages will determine the proximity to biography. However, detailed studies regarding both aspects of this border zone with regard to contents and the comparison of a greater number of works, have not yet been done.

The oral and literary sources used by women authors fall mainly into four categories. The most important of the four is the writer's own memory and the memories of close friends and relatives who make their knowledge available to the author. Closely connected with this type of source is the second, which consists of written self-testimonies such as letters and diaries, but also of other personal sources such as family chronicles, notes on family life, note books, and housekeeping books, as well as pictures, drawings, or photographs which accompany these records. Contemporary publications such as newspaper articles and other writings form the third category. The last group of sources consists of interviews with contemporaries. Both Agnes Sapper and Agnes Herding-Sapper interviewed contemporaries and quoted their remarks in their works.

We learn about the amount and the evaluation of the manifold and various sources Agnes Sapper used in the part of her autobiography which deals with the genesis of her mother's biography. She describes how on the death of her mother she is asked to write her biography and how, after some hesitation, she only agrees to do it after the publisher, Dr. Oskar Beck, a long-standing friend of the family, approves of the project. Before she starts writing, she tries to collect as much source material as she can possibly find:

> In order to present a vivid picture of my mother and—as I told myself—at the same time of my father, I needed letters from every period of her life as well as newspaper articles and publications to visualize the political situation of Bavaria with which my father's life and activities were connected. My sister, meanwhile, was also deeply in favor of it and was able to prod my memory a lot since she had kept a diary from the age of eleven. I wrote to various relatives and friends, asking them for letters, and I promised conscientiously to return them. Soon afterwards, contributions arrived from all sides, quite a lot at that. Together with those letters which were in my personal possession there were in the end more than a thousand. A precious treasure, but frightening.[11]

This information about the letters is in itself quite remarkable, in that it shows the extreme frequency and the extent of the correspondence as well as the care with which the letters were preserved. On the other hand, this does not surprise the reader of autobiographies, for letters always provided very important source material. Letters can also be especially important as source material for feminist critical work, for example, the examination of the relationships between nineteenth-century women, a topic which Carroll Smith-Rosenberg has already researched.[12] Letters as a collection of private sources could provide material to allow us to judge whether Carroll Smith-Rosenberg's theses hold true for German conditions as well.

As far as I can see, autobiographies yield less information in this respect than letters and diaries, mainly because the former are written toward the end of one's life. There are several reasons for this slight difference: the time lag between the events and their recording, the unavoidable selection process, and the fact that the information is to be published. All this influences the author's self-portrayal so that, in the last analysis, we receive a picture of how the author wants to be seen at the time of writing rather than how she was at the time of the event.

Apart from its more general communicative function, the writing of letters is of special relevance for women. For example, friendships between women, often lasting a whole lifetime, are to a considerable degree dependent on a continuous exchange of letters. But the written exchange of events and thoughts is also of major importance for the relationship between mother and daughter. Again and again we read how often letters passed between mother and daughter and how detailed were the discussions on the problems of everyday life,[13] as well as on more general issues such as religious questions.[14] Agnes Herding-Sapper, for example, quotes from one of her mother's letters indicating the close relationship. In the following extract, Agnes Sapper writes to her daughter Anna, who is living in Paris at the time in order to finish her training as a language teacher:

> Your sixteen-page letter has made me happier than many a needlework found on a birthday table. Such an exchange of letters is a delightful compensation when one has to do without personal contact. When they are together in a lively household, a week may pass by easily without mother and daughter talking as intensively with each other as we are doing by letters.[15]

But letters not only replace conversations, they also are meant as intellectual stimuli, as Agnes Herding reports from her own experience. During the time she is training as a nurse far away from the family, her mother's letters console her and compensate for the disadvantages of her environment:

> However much Mrs. Sapper loves her daughter's occupation, she nevertheless realizes the hard privation it entails, at least during the apprenticeship, namely the abstention from intellectual stimulation. Therefore she discusses many issues in her letters which might seem unusual for a young nurse, such as political and literary questions. Furthermore, she lets her daughter participate to a large extent in her writing. This way she compensates for the lack of intellectual activity as much as possible.[16]

The Lives of Grandmother, Mother, and Daughter

The memoirs of these three women give us insights into the lives of the female members of one family during a period of over a hundred years: from the beginning of the nineteenth century until the 1920s.

They start with the birth of Pauline Damajanti Pfaff, the eighth child of a mathematics professor, Wilhelm Pfaff, and his wife Luise, in 1827 in Erlangen.[17] The parents are described as conventional people, living in modest circumstances and not putting too much emphasis on outward appearances. Of her seven brothers and sisters, Pauline gets on best with her four brothers, and the five of them grow up relatively unrestrained.

Pauline is only eight when her father dies. At that time she makes friends with a well-educated girl in the neighborhood. Luise is the daughter of the widowed official Brater. At the Braters' Pauline is confronted with a totally different way of life:

> She began to realize how a well-kept household should actually function. With amazement, she noticed that every object had its fixed place, that the place was tidied up and dusted every day and that the modest rooms thus appeared fine and comfortable.[18]

Pauline likes the Brater lifestyle and consequently tries to reproduce it, without success, in her own family.

In due course, Pauline's brothers and sisters leave the family and set up their own households. From then on, Pauline is regularly invited to visit when help is needed. In 1849, she moves to the house of her brother Hans to manage his household. He has meanwhile become assistant headmaster at a school in Nördlingen. The separation from the family is eased by the fact that Karl Brater, the brother of her friend Luise and the man she secretly loves, is mayor of Nördlingen. Both families meet very often: Karl Brater becomes more closely acquainted with Pauline and finally asks her to marry him. The marriage takes place at Easter, 1850.

Karl Brater, who in 1848 was inclined to liberal and national politics, suffers more and more under the reactionary politics of the time and has to resign in 1851. Having no fortune and no chance of ever being employed again by the State, he is forced to support the family by publishing legal and political writings. In 1851, their daughter Anna is born and, in 1852, Agnes, the second and last child. The girls grow up under modest circumstances. Their father's publishing[19] and his political commitments, which lead to frequent changes of address and bring many visitors to the house, make life varied and strenuous at the same time. It is only because of the mother's ability to improvise that family life does not suffer seriously. This is not easy, since Karl Brater's political reputation damages even the everyday management of the household, as the following example shows: Once again, another flat has to be rented. Frau Brater finds one, but the owner, having discovered who his new tenants are, withdraws his consent. He does not dare to associate with "such a subversive tenant."[20] During a stay in Munich, the two girls are induced to study and to prepare for examinations in French to enable them to take up teaching posts later on.

In 1869, at the age of fifty, Karl Brater dies of a lung infection. In the early stages of mourning, Pauline stays with her sister-in-law, but later moves in with her widowed brother Hans to manage his household and to bring up his four children. Her own daughters soon get married: Anna to Dr. Dietrich Kerler, a librarian at the university library, and Agnes in 1875 to Eduard Sapper, the mayor of Blaubeuren in Wurttemberg. Mother and daughters suffer under the separation. But Pauline visits both her daughters regularly, and they engage in an extensive correspondence. Apart from that, Pauline is fully occupied with caring for the four children of her brother, who has died in the meantime. In 1880, Pauline moves to Würzburg to live near her daughter Anna. In 1885, her youngest niece leaves home, and for the first time in her life, Pauline has to live on her own.

In addition, she now has to face the sad fact that more and more people and friends her own age are dying. She finds some consolation in travelling, making visits and writing letters, and in the fact that she is still able to manage on her own. But old age also begins to trouble her so that, in 1898, she moves in with her widowed daughter Agnes, with whom she lives until her death in 1907.

Agnes Sapper's life was uneventful. From her biography of her mother and her own daughter's biography of her, we learn some details of her early life until the first years of her marriage. She seems to have been a quiet girl, but not without imagination, and she was fond of education. Later she becomes a language teacher and finally a conscientious housewife and mother. The main topic of her autobiography is how she became a successful writer of books for teenagers. In 1818, her husband dies, and when both daughters have grown up and are able to earn their own living, a new era begins for Agnes Sapper, which Agnes Herding-Sapper describes as follows:

> The period during which she had to devote herself to the family is over. . . . She can now freely dispose of her time and strength. In her mid-fifties, she feels better, intellectually and physically more productive than in earlier decades. The very quiet and monotonous life of a widow would probably have been her lot, had not her poetic talent brought such immense happiness into her life. She had the good fortune only very few women are allowed to experience: she was able to develop further and to make use of her intellectual gifts and her

mind in an equally harmonious way. Now she could quietly dedicate
herself to her literary work.[21]

Besides writing books, Agnes Sapper maintains an extensive correspondence and travels a great deal, mainly to visit her children and
grandchildren. But she not only looks after her own family: she cares
for orphans and prisoners as well. The last part of her life Agnes
Sapper spends with her unmarried daughter Anna.

About Agnes Herding-Sapper, who was born in 1883, we learn very
little, despite the fact that her mother wrote about her, as did she
herself in her biography of her mother. Until about 1930, we can only
roughly reconstruct her life. At the age of twenty-three, she finishes a
nursing course, but gets engaged soon afterwards. In 1909, she marries the teacher Fritz Herding. For some years, they live in Würzburg
near her mother until her husband gets posted elsewhere. Occasional
visits and many letters now must replace the daily meetings. Our
knowledge of the life of Agnes Sapper-Herding ends with the description of the last hours of her mother's life in 1930.

These (auto-)biographical works offer an illuminating though limited
look at the way of life of educated middle-class (Bildungsbürgertum)
women in southern Germany. Their authors deal with topics such as
family life, children's education, and problems of household management. They describe the forms and terms of social contact, write about
their travels, and comment on the intellectual interests and opinions of
women as well as on their own occupational activities. I would now
like to extract two topics from this range of subjects which show continuity and change in the position of women: the one deals with educa-
ton and profession, the other, with the ideal of the good housewife.

Education and profession:

In the first part of the nineteenth century it was typical that women
were induced to take part in the occupational lives of their fathers and
husbands. Many people ask Luise Pfaff, a doctor's daughter, for medical advice. Her daughter, educated with her brothers, has some knowledge of the natural sciences and later helps her husband by correcting
his articles. Even at a very old age, she is primarily interested in the
political items in the newspapers; she also introduces her granddaugh-
ters to the study of astronomy.[22] This intellectual open-mindedness,
however, does not prevent her from being sceptical of her daughters'
professional training. But soon after her husband's death, the eigh-
teen-year-old daughter Agnes is able to profit from her training and to

support the family by teaching. Many years later, when Agnes herself is a widow and has to provide a living for herself and her daughters, she intends to augment her income by cooking lessons and by taking in lodgers. Like countless other women in the same position, she wants to profit from her housekeeping abilities. The thought of taking up writing again—something which she had done very successfully when she was a young housewife—and of making a living at it does not, however, enter her mind. Only when she is urged by friends does she make use of her natural talent for a profession. However, the professions which Agnes Sapper's daughters choose are in total harmony with her idea of proper employment for women: Agnes becomes a language teacher and Anna decides to take a nursing course. Although Anna practices teaching as a private tutor, Agnes gets engaged shortly after finishing her course, marries, and has children.

The good housewife:

Whether a woman was employed or not, she was expected to be an exemplary housewife. The ideal of the good housewife is a subject which we find discussed in all the biographical texts. This does not mean to say that we get a detailed insight into the organization and equipment of the various households, but we do learn from the outlook and opinions of the younger generations what was considered old-fashioned and therefore worthy of comment.

When, for example, Agnes Herding describes her mother's first household, she points out that her mother still had an open fireplace in 1875 instead of an oven.[23] Details such as this are, however, rare; reports on the predominant standards are much more common. Pauline Brater, who has been brought up by her mother Luise Pfaff to adopt an easy-going approach to the economics of housekeeping, only partially adapts herself to the pedantic ideas of her husband's family on the subject. Since she is forced to practice utter frugality, she has to do most of the work herself, but does no more than is necessary. Even when she later finds herself in economically secure circumstances after inheriting some money, she still adheres to the complicated saving system she has worked out. Some of her energy-saving methods[24] may well have been used by countless other housewives, but some labor-saving devices seem to be rather odd:

> When you looked closely at her friendly, perfectly-kept apartment, you noticed that there were small wooden blocks underneath the front legs of her closets. Why? Because that way the closet doors tended to shut

by themselves and thus it was not necessary to always lock them with the key, something which seemed to her a waste of time and energy.[25]

A housewife's duties comprise not only cooking well and keeping the house in exemplary order. Agnes Herding-Sapper emphasizes how her mother also tried her best to provide her husband with a comfortable home when he returned from his troublesome work:

> In addition, a large household in the country had to be maintained; we are told about cutting cabbage, making cider, the vegetable garden. Nevertheless, the worried housewife does what she can not to involve her husband too much in her troubles. Later on, she occasionally spoke of the times when she took a quick look at a good book just before her husband came home so that she could carry on a pleasant conversation at dinner.[26]

Agnes Sapper constantly doubts whether she is able to fulfill all the tasks which are expected of her, that is of a housewife among the ranks of the dignitaries of a small Swabian town. It is this attempt to live up to given standards and her sense of duty which later prevent her from pursuing her writing with a clear conscience.[27]

The fact that more and more middle-class women seek employment means that the career of a housewife is no longer viewed as the sole occupation for a woman. But those housewives who never had other employment are very much affected when they have to give up their own household. Agnes Sapper regards it as a form of deprivation to relinquish her household as long as she is healthy and active, and therefore refuses to move in with her widowed sister after the death of her husband.[28]

We see in these biographies and autobiographies of educated middle-class women how in the course of several generations a change of attitude takes place: marriage comes to be regarded not as the sole provision for a woman's existence; and working in a qualified profession to secure one's own existence gradually becomes accepted, especially when a profession is chosen which can be practiced at home. A way of life is then made possible which hardly differs from that of a single widow or a wealthy unmarried woman.

This small extract from the huge amount of autobiographical writings shows that autobiographies are not only useful in widening our knowledge on living conditions and ideologies—they also contain many and various clues to other types of sources.

NOTES

Translated by Dagmar Höher.

1. See Erika Adolphy's criticism of René Levy's three-stages model, in: Erika Adolphy, *Einige Gedanken zu der Frage: Was ist eigentlich eine normale Frauenbiographie?* (Some Thoughts on the Question: What is, in fact, a Normal Biography of a Woman?) Dokumentation der Tagung "Weibliche Biographien" (München 1982, Beiträge zur feministischen Theorie und Praxis 7), pp. 8–9.

2. In the autumn of 1982 a conference on "Female Biographies" took place in Bielefeld. The papers are published in a monograph: *Dokumentation der Tagung "Weibliche Biographien" in Bielefeld,* ed. by Sozialwissenschaftliche Forschung und Praxis für Frauen e.V. (München, 1982, Beiträge zur feministischen Theorie und Praxis 7).

3. Agnes Sapper, *Frau Pauline Brater. Lebensbild einer deutschen Frau* (Biographical Sketch of a German Woman) (München: Beck, n.d., 44th edition), preface p. iii.

4. Sapper, *Ein Gruß an die Freunde meiner Bücher* (Stuttgart: Gundert, 1922), pp. 58–59.

5. For example, Sapper, *Gruß,* p. 59.

6. Sapper, *Gruß,* p. 67.

7. Sapper, *Gruß,* p. 67; also Sapper, *Brater,* p. 89, from a letter to her husband: "The other day there was a large tea party at your mother's (cream cake!!!)."

8. Sapper, *Gruß,* p. 65.

9. Agnes Herding-Sapper: *Agnes Sapper. Ihr Weg und ihr Wirken* (Stuttgart: Gundert, 1936, 8.–10. Tsd.), p. 206.

10. Herding-Sapper, *Sapper,* p. 193.

11. Sapper, *Gruß,* p. 58.

12. Carroll Smith-Rosenberg, "Meine innig geliebte Freundin! Beziehungen zwischen Frauen im 19. Jahrhundert," *Listen der Ohnmacht. Zur Sozialgeschichte weiblicher Widerstandsformen,* ed. by Claudia Honegger and Bettina Heintz (Frankfurt: Europäische Verlagsanstalt, 1981), p. 357–92 (English edition: "The Female World of Love and Ritual: Relations between Women in Nineteenth-Century America," *Signs. Journal of Women in Culture and Society* 1, 1975, pp. 1–29).

13. For example, Herding-Sapper, *Sapper,* p. 99.

14. Sapper, *Brater,* for example pp. 101–2.

15. Herding-Sapper, *Sapper,* p. 131.

16. Herding-Sapper, *Sapper,* p. 140.

17. These seven children spring from three different marriages, for both parents were already married once before they met: Wilhelm Pfaff to the aristocrat von Patkul in Livonia when he was director of the observatory in Dorpat, and Luise, née Planck, to the Rev. Kraz. Both spouses died early in married life. Pauline was given the name Damajanti because at the time of her birth her father was translating the Indian "Nal and Damajanti" into German, together with his friend Prof. Friedrich Rückert, poet and orientalist; e.g. Sapper, *Brater,* pp. 4–5.

18. Sapper, *Brater,* p. 25.

19. From 1855 on, Karl Brater (1819–1869) was head of the editorial staff of Bluntschli's *Staatswörterbuch.* In 1858 he was elected to the Bavarian parliament as Nürnberg's constitutional and democratic party deputy. In 1859, he took over the editorship of the newly founded political daily *Süddeutsche Zeitung.*

20. Sapper, *Brater*, p. 122.

21. Herding-Sapper, *Sapper*, pp. 151–52.

22. Herding-Sapper, *Sapper*, p. 121; see also, for example, Sapper, *Brater*, p. 31.

23. Herding-Sapper, *Sapper*, p. 61.

24. She could not bear to observe a loss of heat. When she had scalded a pot full of milk, she was vexed by the thought that the heat of this milk (now eighty degrees Celsius) should go to waste. Therefore, this pot of milk was quickly placed into a bowl with cold water, and the moment was awaited when the temperature of the milk had reached that of the water, and the breakfast dishes were washed up in this water, warmed without any use of fuel.

25. Sapper, *Brater*, p. 283.

26. Herding-Sapper, *Sapper*, pp. 76–77; see also p. 49.

27. Sapper, *Gruß*, p. 19.

28. Sapper, *Gruß*, p. 70.

THE STRUGGLE FOR AN IDENTITY

WORKING-CLASS AUTOBIOGRAPHIES BY WOMEN IN NINETEENTH-CENTURY GERMANY

Juliane Jacobi-Dittrich

In this article I will present results from my research on the history of girlhood. The findings should be considered as first steps toward a more concise knowledge of the process through which women's identity was developed during the nineteenth century. Generally speaking, the century has been analyzed as the time when patriarchy, in tight connection with capitalism, shaped what Karin Hausen calls the "Polarisierung der Geschlechtscharaktere" (polarization of sexual characteristics).

In the following study I have analyzed three lower middle-class and working-class autobiographies. The class demarcation has been drawn in relation to a selection of upper middle-class autobiographies written by women that I previously analyzed under similar aspects.[1] After discussing the three individual texts according to the theoretical framework that will be outlined below, I will compare the result of this analysis to my findings from the upper middle-class autobiographies. This comparison will emphasize the question of class deferentiation within the general discussion of a specific female experience in building an identity. As an introduction, I will explain my selection and present briefly the analytical framework of identity and life cycle as developed in the work of Erik Erikson.[2]

My selections are not from the well-known short autobiographical sketches written by working-class authors that have been republished during recent years. With my interest in the history of education and childhood, I tend to focus more on the course of life than on the reconstruction of everyday life and work conditions as structural problems. Acknowledging Annette Kuhn's insightful remarks on the historical approach toward the category "gender" which generally is understood as a "natural" category,[3] I assume that what is considered "natural" undergoes constant change throughout history. To answer the question of how women developed an identity at a given time will thus add to the historical definition of "gender." The above-mentioned autobiographical sketches cannot be used for such an inquiry, since they do not deal with the authors' course of life, but with certain aspects of their lives in a more systematical way.

So as not to be misunderstood: I do not view female identity as an easily described psychological apparatus, molded in a process of socialization that can be generalized for every woman at any given time. I refer to the term "identity" and the process of how it is built up through the life-cycle as described by Erik Erikson, who states that identity is formed through the relationship of the child's ego to the historical prevailing images of his/her time. According to Erikson, identity is the result of the successive integration of all identifications throughout childhood and youth. The crystallizing of the ego-identity binds together early childhood, in which parents and the body have been dominant experiences for identification, with later stages that offer a diversity of social roles adaptable to the ego. Youth and adolescence have a special meaning for the modern process of building an identity, since they provide a psycho-social moratorium during which the young person can go through emotional extremes tentatively, to try out ideological alternatives, and to playfully master serious commitment. This concept of identity could be applied in this very broad sense to the male coming-of-age in the European middle classes during the second half of the nineteenth century. As to what extent it will be applicable to female youth and especially to those of working-class background will be shown in this paper.

Erikson's concept surely is based on the psychoanalytical observation of middle-class childhood and youth. The conditions for growing up provided by the working-class environment differed substantially from the middle-class background. For workers, there was no youthful moratorium, but simply a time of employment without the burden of raising a family. Their youth is a transitory stage dependent on the work place and the family, with less responsibility than an adult person in the working class. I am thus referring to a sex-determined, as well as a class-determined, concept of identity which, roughly spoken, views childhood and youth as a straightforward development toward a grown-up personality reflecting the various influences of family, society, and education. There are potential traps involved in this approach, but I prefer a male- and class-biased concept that takes biases into account to a speculative concept that emerged from "female discourse." Up to now, all attempts at a genuine female concept have tended to reformulate the idea of a "female nature." The reason why the concept of "identity" that I am employing is particularly useful lies in the fact that the genre I am dealing with, the nineteenth-century autobiography, is strongly male and middle class and thus reflects certain structural moments from the introduced concept of "identity."[4] This does not mean that I want to define the identity of women as a deviation from the male set norm. Rather, I intend to explain life courses as processes of developing an identity by using the autobiographical introspection of women.

I will deal with the breaks in their lives, not as breaking away from the male standards, but as events of finding their own way. Neither "the woman who acts like a man" is looked for, nor the woman who fulfills male demands in the image of the trinity of homemaker, mother, and wife. I am searching rather for developments in the process of building up an identity which give independence from these standards and show how women suffered and fought for conditions which would foster autonomy.

Thus I am posing the question: Has there been any consistent image (or images) that offered orientation to women while they grew up, and if so, how did it work? If not, why didn't it work? Their own concepts of their identity will be defined by their ideas of sex roles and sex relations, of political or ideological beliefs, of job achievements and family relations. Autobiographical introspection referring to these areas of experience as well as to how they relate them to the whole setting in which they grew up will be investigated.

It is clear that certain objective conditions such as economic controls on a family shaped the lives of these women, and will be reflected in their autobiographical texts. But the individual autobiography is shaped by the individual's encounter with these objective conditions and by a variety of factors that tend to vary from person to person. Thus the result of my investigation will not lead to a collective biography of working-class girlhood and youth, but rather to a presentation of single cases of women's lives that might indicate general tendencies in the process of building an identity as a woman at a given time in the given social environment.

All sources dealt with here tell exceptional stories. They also cannot simply be classified as "proletarian" stories. But since all these women either have a working-class background or have been employed as wage laborers during their childhood and youth or joined the working-class movement, I consider these three writings as quite different from middle-class autobiographical writings. It seems to be justifiable to arrange them under the heading of "working-class autobiographies." I have chosen Adelheid Popp's (1869–1939) "Die Jugendgeschichte einer Arbeiterin" (The Youth of a Female Worker) and "Erinnerungen aus meiner Kindheit und Jugend" (Memoirs from my Childhood and Youth), because these two writings present a real working-class auto-biography, in the sense that they come strikingly close to the bourgeois genre, while at the same time referring to a different class background.

Clara Mueller-Jahnke (1860–1905) tells the story of a girl who came from a middle-class family. Her father had only recently climbed the social ladder. Because of his early death, the author had to go out to work at the early age of fourteen. In her autobiographical text she considers herself as working class. The autobiography, first published before World War I, was published in a second edition in 1921 by the Dietz publishing company, and we can assume that it represents the literary and moral standards of an influential group within the organized social-democratic working class.

Marie Wegrainer's "Lebensgeschichte einer Arbeiterin, von ihr selbst erzählt" (The Life of a Working Woman, Told by Herself) tells the story of a girl from a declining craftman's family who has to earn a living as a domestic servant. This autobiography documents the fate of women from these declining families during the period of rapid industrialization. In contrast to Popp and Mueller-Jahnke, it tells of everyday aspects that the others would not even mention. Marie Wegrainer's life never took dramatic twists, but reflects the common fate of domestic servants who eventually got married to workers.

Both Mueller-Jahnke and Wegrainer employ the third person in the telling of their lives; Mueller-Jahnke even uses a new name. Among women's autobiographies this objectification can be found frequently (Hedwig Dohm, Lily Braun). It possibly expresses a desire to distance oneself and to maintain personal privacy. As for Wegrainer, I would assume that she wanted to give her story a more "professional" writer's look.

The selection of these autobiographical writings was made because of a need for a broad description of childhood and youth. The various aspects involved in the coming-of-age in this particular class background should be found in the narration. I did not want to confine the selection to autobiographies of activists in the working-class movement (like Popp and Mueller-Jahnke), and thus I included one by a woman who never considered herself able to fight for a better life. As I said before, I do not intend to write anything like a "collective biography"—others have recently done that, and on a much better empirical basis[5]—but I have been looking for individual life courses. That does not mean that no attempt to categorize these writings will be made, but my analysis centers around the individual introspection of the women.

Since the texts I am dealing with use the literary form of an autobiography, they have to be discussed within this genre. Wolfgang Emmerich categorizes the various forms of working-class autobiographical writing in terms of the following three main types: the story that is written to initiate a process of political learning, the story of the social climber, and the story of the social victim.[6] Popp definitely tries to evoke a political process of learning by describing her emerging class consciousness. Wegrainer thinks of herself as a social climber who failed. Male social climbers did not write and publish their autobiography unless they were successful. If they failed, they viewed themselves unambiguously as social victims, according to Emmerich's types of working-class autobiography.

Autobiography, a nineteenth-century male middle-class genre, has been employed by middle-class women as well as by working-class men and women. Differences within the genre caused by the different conditions of life in working-class autobiographies are the subject of Emmerich's introduction essay in his "Proletarische Lebensläufe" (Proletarian Life Courses). There he states that working-class autobiographies reflect the collective experience of the class more than do middle-class autobiographies and refer much less to individual experience. To verify his assertion, he quotes from Popp, who says in "Jugend einer Arbeiterin" (Youth of a Working Woman):

> I did not write my story because I considered it as an individually important story; to the contrary, I wrote it because I realized that my own fate was the fate of hundreds of thousands of women and girls from the proletariat. I wrote it because I recognized important phenomena of our society in the environment that caused my own predicaments.[7]

I think that Emmerich underestimates two aspects of working-class autobiography: first the use of the genre makes it almost inevitable for the writer to develop a deeper understanding of his/her individual life course. The perception by both middle-class and working-class writers of their identity was shaped by the conditions of rising bourgeois society in the nineteenth century, and those who wrote their autobiographies must have had a strong self-concept in that respect. And secondly, Emmerich disregards the sex-determined motif in autobiographical writing. Even if Popp claims to write because her life reflects a collective experience and even if she is doing it from the viewpoint of a class leader, her life course and the way she reflects it disclose a specific female view of class conditions, as I will demonstrate later. Thus Emmerich's main types of working class autobiographies reflect a strong male bias.

The case of Mueller-Jahnke's autobiography most clearly shows that the types developed by Emmerich do not apply very well to my selection of working-class autobiographies. More than Popp, she looks on herself not only as a class-conscious member of the working-class movement, but as a victim of sex discrimination as well. This awareness leads her to proletarian solidarity: a case not considered in Emmerich's scheme. It makes Mueller-Jahnke's autobiography a valuable key story for the interpretation of the remaining two. The meaning and the relevance of sex-defined identity are presented in her writing in such a precise way, that one wonders whether this might be the major subject of the other two texts as well. I will look for evidence of this hypothesis by interpreting the writings one by one. After a brief biographical sketch gleaned from the autobiographies, I will discuss various motifs within each text. The selection of these motifs is made out of the interest in identity processes they reflect. The first question to be asked concerns the motivation to write at all. The assumption that family relations tell of possible persons who offered chances for identification leads to the further subject of how the authors viewed their parents and their own position towards their families. What were the norms concerning sexual relations, partner selection, and marriage with which they were confronted? Education as a means of oppression or enforcement of autonomy appears in male as well as in female middle-class autobiographies as crucial for the process of building an identity. I will also look for possible motifs that are to be found exclusively in working-class female autobiographical writing. At the conclusion, I will attempt to consider how introspection concerning their own sexual role influenced each individual molding of autobiographical writing as a genre.

Clara Mueller-Jahnke[8]

Mueller-Jahnke was born as the daughter of a Pomeranian free-thinking minister, who himself came from a rural working-class background and received his parsonage as a result of the revolution of 1848. Because of the early death of her father, Clara, being the only surviving daughter, had to earn a living as a fourteen-year-old by private teaching. At sixteen, after only a brief school training, she went to Berlin to work as a clerical worker. Sexual harassment by her boss drove her back home to Pomerania, where she opened a boarding house at a seashore resort. A love affair with one of the guests, a Polish priest, led to pregnancy. She delivered the child incognito in Berlin, leaving home under the pretense of suffering from a serious disease that needed special treatment. The child died shortly after it was born. Clara went back home again and worked as a writer for the local newspaper. She broke completely with her mother, who had no understanding for the pregnancy and viewed Clara's suffering as a personal attack on her own standards of morality. The story stops at this point. It is told as a report to a beloved man (modelled after Hedwig Dohm's "Schicksale einer Seele" [Fate of a Soul]),[9] allowing the reader to know that later in her life Clara Mueller-Jahnke found a meaningful relationship with another man. From her biography, we know that she married a painter, very likely the "beloved" addressed in her book.

The motives of Mueller-Jahnke are obvious: "I confess" is a qualified title. She wants to uncover the sexual abuse of women, and a new morality based on the equality of the sexes is to be promoted through her text. The Protestant love of truth provided by her upbringing was joined to the material experience of a woman in wage-labor dependence to create this new morality. Sincerity as an ultimate Protestant concept is one of her ideals, and it certainly was her hard fate that the man whom she loved and who hurt her most was a Polish Catholic priest. The first part of her sad story contains the telling fact that the first man who affected her life through sexual assault was her boss, whom she describes as an immoral capitalist.[10] Thus Clara finds the male world utterly oppressive and opposed to her own ideas about love and personal relationship. Males not only commit sexual abuse, but also represent insincerity, wretchedness and dubious social values. The ideals of sincerity and pure love were central for her, and this is certainly the reason why the autobiography was republished with an introduction by Clara Bohm-Schuch, who points out the enlightening values of the book for women within the working-class movement.[11]

Among a large portion of the organized German working class these idealistic views were highly esteemed. The possible dangers of a liberated sexuality could thus be counteracted by new norms.

One might come to the conclusion that this autobiography is a product of plain ideology. When examined more closely, however, it reveals some traits that tell a different story. The therapeutic effect of a "confession" may give us the key. Mueller-Jahnke's life was so humiliating and painful that only the written confessions made under the conditions of a newly-found love and her new ideals helped her to cope with these experiences. The jobs available to an unmarried woman at the time (clerical work, running a boarding house) made her totally defenseless against male harassment, with no assistance offered by the conventional rules and mechanisms that apparently worked for other middle-class girls and young women—as the autobiographies of Lange, Baeumer, Tiburtius, and Weber (for example) point out. Under these particular conditions, the necessity to go out for work created a major danger for the physical and mental intactness of a woman. Without the protection of a father or close male relative, Clara Mueller-Jahnke was defenseless in her exposure to male harassment. But she presents this in a special, noteworthy way. By means of her Protestant "sincerity," she was able to reveal her own needs and desires in the relationship to the Catholic priest, portraying her own sexuality quite pitilessly despite an occasionally overdone sentimentality:

> My beloved, I shall try to describe my feelings during the trip. I was not a child in need of protection about to meet her fatal lot unsuspectingly. I knew exactly what I was in for. Nevertheless, stirred by a wild defiance and pushed by an invisible hand, I went on. . . . This was no longer me, Wilma, this pale obstinate woman. . . . I stood right next to me and watched every facet of her tense features, every convulsion of her feverish soul with a demonic cold desire for knowledge, and I maintained the desire. It remained within me when I walked at his side through the magnificent night in the light of the full moon, towards the little town in the middle of nowhere that we had chosen as the place for our encounter. [12]

We can tell from this quotation that sexuality and eroticism had a central meaning in this woman's life, and that she was aware of this. Oppression and solidarity with the suppressed were the result. Thus sex is seen as the most powerful force in her life. How did this develop during her childhood and how does she herself understand the shaping force of sexuality for her personal identity?

The idyllic life in the parsonage seems at first glance to have been far from influenced by dark carnal forces. But the author reveals that those forces existed and were closely related to the sex roles in the family:

> My mother cried a lot. Married at just eighteen to a man twenty years older, she had stayed a spoiled and pampered child in her narrow family circle despite her genuine intelligence. She raised five children, of which I was the youngest, under bitter sufferings, . . . and four children died very young.[13]

This quotation shows that the daughter had a deep understanding of the mother when she was an adult woman. She does not, however, talk about her relationship to the mother openly as long as she is dealing with her own childhood. In retrospect, it was her father who was influential in terms of educational ideas. He planned a professional career for her and wanted to send her to a Swiss university, quite an unusual idea at the time. She received the same instructions he gave to the boys boarding with the family who were being prepared for academic studies. Strangely enough, she writes less about what they studied than about her attraction to a handsome boy among them. The emphasis on this aspect of being educated among boys reveals that Clara as an author was very much aware that her sex and consequently her sexuality or eroticism shaped her relationship towards men and at a very early state formed her identity as a woman. This awareness is accompanied by a critical attitude toward conventional sex-roles. An early disdain for a "good match" is mentioned when she writes of her first passionte fondness for the young doctor of the family and describes the sad "good matches" of her schoolmates. Her mother was the one who firmly believed that Clara should herself look for a good marriage. The plan set up by her progressive father for her to become a doctor was destroyed by his early death; the mother refused to send her even to a one-year course in a normal school for women.

Briefly stated, this presentation of childhood and youth sharply depicts the contradictions in a woman's biography that arose so early because of the premature absence of a protecting father. The result was an extremely sensitive girl suffering from sexual defenselessness and very much inclined to get involved in romantic love affairs. She tries to cope with her bitter experience by writing these confessions denouncing the pretentious bourgeois morality her mother represents. The ultimate goal seems to be propaganda for the "new" old idea of a marriage among equals.[14]

As opposed to middle-class woman in the second half of the

nineteenth century, Mueller-Jahnke could not take ideological or emotional refuge in a job or a profession that would have been approved by the society as appropriate for a woman. She had to sell her work on the job market of the modern economic world and could not acquire training in a "feminine" profession accepted as approximating mothering as a genuine female occupation. That is what makes her story initially different from all middle-class biographies I have read and what justifies her inclusion in a selection of working-class autobiographies. She does not, however, present a straight working-class movement view of her life course. Her own coming-of-age is not interpreted through mere social-democratic idealism of clean and fair sex relations among men and women, but tells of deeper introspection of a process she views as molded through sex-related oppression. Her identity is not idealistically presented as shaped only by "sincerity" and diligent work, but also through the experience of erotic attraction as a constructive as well as a devastating force.

In this respect, Mueller-Jahnke's autobiography offers as a key for the understanding of working-class women's autobiography the importance of sex determination. It is blatant sexual abuse that constantly threatened the life of these women on the one hand, and, on the other, the insight that among women's rights there should be the right for an autonomous sexual life. Mueller-Jahnke explicitly declares that she found her path to the working-class movement through the experience of her sexual defenselessness. Her strong will to fight for a society of freedom emerged from these sufferings. This is a case of autobiographical writing in which class determination can only be understood through sex determination.

Adelheid Popp[15]

Popp's "Jugendgeschichte einer Arbeiterin" (Youth of a Working Woman) is one of the best-known autobiographies written by a woman from the second half of the nineteenth century. Although it is the explicit goal of these memoirs to show the development from oppression to a class-conscious proletariat, implicitly there are other issues included in this autobiography, therapeutic ones as in Mueller-Jahnke's.

Popp's childhood was marked by poverty, loneliness, and severe illness. Her youth was endangered by unemployment and sexual abuse at her place of work. Her life story gives us the impression that she finally emerged from the dark days of her childhood into the bright light of a social-democratic organizer who then knew all about how to fight poverty, illness, and ignorance. Popp points out that she had very little schooling. As a ten-year-old she considered herself no longer a child and thus avoided registration as a child and bypassed compulsory school attendance. She began work as a wage laborer. Despite her deficient education, she had always read a lot and apparently had a special gift to describe what she had read to others. Her later achievements as a party organizer originated from this ability.

Popp tells about her early life as a working child in considerable detail. Exploitation of children, especially of female children, by so-called *Zwischenmeister* (intermediate supervisors) is a major theme. Working in a factory for bronze articles and in a glass factory caused a serious nervous attack. Although she was only fourteen, she was placed in a psychiatric ward and, having been totally abandoned by her mother, finally ended up in a workhouse. A reader oriented toward middle-class ideas of the family might be surprised that Popp does not blame her mother for leaving her alone, but rather blames the condition of psychiatric wards at the time. As for the psychic disease that put her in these institutions, she does not describe it clearly but calls it a "nervous attack." She says only that this type of nervous attack had been a constant threat in her youth because she feared ending up in an institution like a workhouse or a hospital for good.

"Die Jugendgeschichte einer Arbeiterin" does not deal with the problem of sex relations as Popp did very didactically in her "Erinnerungen" (Memoirs). In this first autobiographical text, she gives instead an account of the sexual harassment that marked her childhood. There was a boarder in the family's house who, according to her judgement, had not been sufficiently called to account for what he did to her. Her mother as well as her brother treated the man with indulgence and pointed out to her quite clearly that their interest wasn't as much in Adelheid's intactness as a person as in the establishment and retaining of a hypocritical morality. Popp had to experience these socially accepted standards yet again when the travel agent of the factory where she worked tried to seduce her. She immediately quit, since she felt endangered and humiliated. Brother and mother had no understanding of her predicament and forced her to go back to work.

The relationship to her mother seems to have been very strong. Popp claims that although her mother in her old age had become an almost unbearable burden, she could never abandon her. She admires her mother because she had been someone "who never wanted to depend on anyone." Quite contrary to Clara Mueller-Jahnke, Popp sees herself deeply influenced by her mother's image. The personal strength of the mother enabled her to develop her own strength as a working-class organizer.

The choice of a partner is talked about at length in the more didactically oriented "Erinnerungen." Popp points out that she always had high aspirations, but in her youth never met anybody who would have really met her expectations. Her self-described prudishness as a young person seems to prevent her from describing how she met her future husband. She tells about dreams of the desirable man, but these dreams turn out to be not very sensual: "Whenever I thought about marriage, I dreamed of a man who would share my ideals. I expected not only happiness from him, but also support for my own personal development." Here again, we find the ideal male-female relationship that seemed to prevail among socialist women at the time. It symbolizes the change in her personal life as a result of political insight, but at the same time shows that she has always been very aware of the suppressive effects of the dominant conventional sex-roles. Even when Popp sees working conditions as constituting the main influence on her personal development, she has a clear sense of the importance of sex-related oppression.

She gives a touching account of the significance of beauty in her life: outfits and jewelry embellished the youth of this proletarian fighter, and on occasion she reports at great length on how to dress despite her poverty.[16] In comparison to most of the middle-class autobiographies I have examined, this subject is more important to working-class women. When Popp began work, she commented: "Now I had nice dresses according to my taste at the time; I was allowed to buy fancy shoes and other things a young girl enjoys."[17] A remarkable tale of feudal mercy and fancy outfit is included that underlines this aspect. As a young child, she was often given a certain amount of money and new clothes by a dutchess, which, of course, brought about no long-term improvement in the living conditions of the family. Her relating of the story, however, makes it hard to believe that it is written by a social democratic leader, since she does not pay much attention at all to the class struggle aspects of the anecdote—it seems more like a miraculous fairy tale.

On her first visit to the castle bedecked in her new clothes, she suddenly sees herself in a mirror door and wonders who this person might be with a mysterious resemblance to herself in terms of color of hair and clothing. After coming home, she talks it over with her mother, but the two of them can find no explanation because they do not know that doors covered with mirrors exist. The real event surely has symbolic significance, even if the author herself does not allude to it and might not even have interpreted it in that way. The very fact that she recalls the event and considers it worth telling in her autobiography gives us a hint that this woman, even as a child, was quite aware of the problem of self-consciousness. The reflection in the mirror enclosed a mystery about herself that she tried to uncover. At the same time, this tale reveals her self-perception as a nicely dressed girl.

It is insufficient to characterize Popp's autobiography as a working-class autobiography "in which the decisive step [is taken] to view a proletarian life no longer from the perspective of the more or less helpless victim in history, but to see a strong relationship between individual development of class and society."[18] The author adds very special personal aspects originating from her fate as a female member of her class. No male writer of her political background has paid that much attention to problems of sexuality, beauty, and psychological explanations of parent(mother)-child relationship. It is a specific characteristic of Popp that even when she explains family conditions through class struggle, she still deals with the "personal affairs" that contrast so noticeably with male working-class autobiography.[19]

Popp's coming-of-age is viewed as particularly influenced by the fact that to grow up as a woman means to become potentially or actually a victim of male power. As opposed to Mueller-Jahnke, she does not have the experience of ambivalence toward her own desires for love, although I tend to interpret her attitude toward female beauty as her way to experience the positive aspects of her gender. Thus Popp adds a motif to her autobiography which otherwise adopts significant aspects from the male-shaped idea of a working-class autobiography. Her story reflects her sexually-defined role not merely as being a victim, but also as providing beauty in her life.

Marie Wegrainer

Marie Wegrainer's *Lebensgeschichte einer Arbeiterin* (Life Story of a Working Woman)[20] tells the story of a child born in a workhouse near Rothenburg ob der Tauber in 1852 as the illegitimate daughter of a servant who had been left by the father of her child. She grew up with foster parents and was sent to Munich to work as a domestic servant in a shopowner's household when she turned thirteen. At the age of sixteen, she was asked by her birth-mother, who had in the meantime married a wealthy shopowner, to return home. Two years later, Marie left home again after her stepfather had tried to rape her. She went back to Munich and worked as a chambermaid. After a disappointing affair with an artist, she met a young craftsman. A long period of betrothal followed because her fiancé had to serve in the army. During this time she gave birth to a child who died briefly thereafter. Finally she married the craftsman, had four children, and lived in poverty most of her life, since her husband, an independant cabinetmaker, was unable to adapt to changes caused by rapid industrialization in the late nineteenth century. Although she suffered considerable hardship, she claims that the motivation to record her autobiography derives from a satisfying life course. Clearly the success of her children (mainly that of the youngest son, the writer Leonhard Frank) was the joy of her life. She says of her son Leonhard: "He had inherited a sense of delicacy from his mother. Only she had a deep understanding for him and was obsessed by the wish that he would one day achieve what had been denied to her by a hard fate. He should rise up and not be submerged in the misery of life that had threatened and almost overtaken her life."[21] He was able to fulfill the goals she had only dreamed of. The end of the story reveals more about the author's motivation: she had looked on herself as somebody appointed for a higher destination and in retrospect she tries to justify her lack of success. We know from other studies in social history that the prevailing self-perception of domestic servants throughout the nineteenth century was that of being people between the classes.

It is no accident that Wegrainer dreams of being an artist, a status between the classes. She was neither a socially descending person nor a class-conscious climber (like Popp). Calling herself a working-class woman, she can be viewed as a woman from those social classes that have been forced into the status of proletarian workers by industrializa-tion. Women of this class background very often had to lower their sights and become domestic servants. Wegrainer adjusted to poverty and assumed it to be her personal fate since she had married a good-for-nothing.

As a child, she had the maximum amount of schooling for her class background, although she says that she would have liked to have gone on beyond her confirmation in order to learn sewing and other skills. Her unwed mother could not afford a lengthier education. Unlike Popp, Wegrainer never suffered from unemployment during her youth and had instead a wide range of social experience among the upper class. The extremely bad relationship to her mother was improved when her mother gained modest wealth through her marriage.

It seems as if everything improved in Marie Wegrainer's life, which she defines as a moderate story with moderate expectations. This modesty, accompanied by narrow-mindedness, can be very clearly shown in the depiction of sexual experience, deliberately chosen or shaped by her actual encounters with men. She is pregnant while still unwed and loses the child, but the relationship with her fiancé stays stable. The rape attempted by her father is named as such, but does not cause a radical change in her family relations; new grass grows, and after two or three years everybody has forgotten the assault. It is a general tendency in Wegrainer's story to describe the most dramatic events undramatically. The course of a normal life is the line she wants to follow. Aspects of pain, despair, suffering, or pleasure are named, but put in no relation to the "normal" life. There is a heavy pressure on her to harmonize the whole description of her life. The destiny of life is well planned from the outset: a "good marriage," well-arranged circumstances of life, modest wealth, a nice home, and successful children who achieve what Wegrainer as a mother thinks they should achieve, are the central values in her life.

Since her own mother initially had to give her children away in order to make a living, the foster mother had a much closer relationship to Marie during her childhood, but the author nevertheless does not mention her after leaving her house. The birth-mother is portrayed in a very ambivalent way: on the one hand, she was hard-hearted enough not to allow her another year of school, yet on the other hand, Marie returns home to her without any question. The father, who never cared for her at all, is seen in the general mild light of her report: "Only once and only for a short quarter of an hour was Marie allowed to see her father."[22] Returning from America, he visited the inn next door and asked to see his child before he had to travel on. He was friendly to her, was a "real handsome young man," asked her questions "with tears in his eyes." She describes the end of the meeting: "And even if the father had done so much wrong to her and her mother, for her he remained a beautiful recollection, since he had kissed and caressed her."[23] It is common in women's autobiographies that the father appears in a radiant light despite his total retreat from responsibility.

Her lack of a possible better education is never blamed on social conditions, but rather on the hard-heartedness of her mother or bad luck, as when the possible financial support from an old man in Munich who believes in her talents is withdrawn. "Luck had only touched her slightly"[24] is her fatalistic comment on the death of that possible sponsor. The author never thinks of herself as someone capable of struggling against oppressive conditions, but she strives mightily to gain a better education for her children. One of them becomes an artist, thus fulfilling her own hopes which are revealed only at the very end of her report. In her dreams, she apparently envisioned herself as an artist. Although her first love was a painter, she avoided any mention of her own dreams of becoming an artist in her account of that affair. It is only very indirectly that we find further hints in her autobiography of a possible interest in this kind of work.

Wegrainer talks a lot about her beauty. She depicts herself as a beautiful girl and adds lengthy descriptions of clothes. Female beauty is important for her; even in her depiction of men, she often refers to their good looks. Her later husband, a social disaster, was very good looking, always dressed well, and thus she falls in love with him. She gives this picture of him without questioning her own judgement. It seems as if Wegrainer wrote down her life because she thought of herself as a person with an outstanding sense for beauty, but it is only in the last few passages of her narration that she links this sense of beauty with possible professional achievement, and here she is projecting her wishes onto her son's career. At the same time, her son represents her superego. She finishes her book with the following dedication: "After my death to my son Gerhard. And if he finds his mother guilty, he should not condemn her but keep in mind that she has paid early for her guilt."[25] The only possible guilt she might be referring to is the illegitimate child and its early death or the near-rape by her stepfather. The repentance she could have in mind is the life with the good-for-nothing husband. The outline of the book would not evoke this interpretation, since guilt is at no point a topic in the narration. But the concluding passages indicate that Wegrainer viewed her life's course as structured initially by a fateful sexual relationship.

This interpretation of Wegrainer's autobiography gives support to the following conclusion: her own view of how her identity has been established puts an emphasis on her crucial relationship to men. In that respect, her autobiography is not that different from Mueller-Jahnke's and Popp's: she did not find a way out of this predicament through joining the working-class movement, but projected her dreams of professional achievements onto a narration of lost love and onto her support for her beloved son.

As I pointed out before, she perceives herself as a potential social climber who failed. Her solution to project her aspirations onto her son's life is a woman's solution. A man possibly would have interpreted a similar life course as his fate as an unrecognized genius, an idea Wegrainer did not have in mind. The question is thus raised: does she see herself as a victim? And does my initial thesis apply at all: that all three women struggled through their lives by breaking away from conventional rules and fighting for autonomy? Wegrainer sees herself as a victim. She did not only suffer, however, and positively views her own life before marriage in her work as a chambermaid; she also purposefully strives for a better future for her own children, and tries to avoid what her mother had done to her. Another break from the prescribed life course remains only weakly expressed, but appears in dreams. The assumed collective experience within working-class autobiographies, however, does not apply to her story.

The question as to why these women wrote their biographies can be easily answered: Mueller-Jahnke and Popp shared the same motive of wanting to present their lives in the public sphere, of describing their individual fate as that of a woman and a class in such a way that other women could learn from it. In both cases therapeutic motives entered in as well. Through writing, they liberated themselves from the pain they had suffered. Therapeutic motivation is also evident in Wegrainer's autobiography, although she has no class-related political goal for the publication of her life's story. Writing in a way very close to the middle-class autobiographical style of the time, Mueller-Jahnke, Popp, and Wegrainer made an attempt to present their childhood and youth as moving along an upward path.[26] It turned out, however, that in the lives of none of these women does such an "upward path" become apparent. The reason quite clearly lies in their gender. In various ways the definition of what they were supposed to become as adult women and the threat of male abuse caused deviations and twists in their lives which were brought on by their sex-role. This, at least, is the ultimate motivation for telling their stories publicly.

In conclusion I will focus my comments on certain key motifs in the above works: family relations, educational chances, job possibilities and aspirations and the subjective perception of sex-roles, and male sexuality and eroticism. In a second step, I will compare my findings with the results from the interpretation of female middle-class autobiographies, an interpretation that has been guided by similar questions: How did these women become who they were? What have been the most influential personal relations, images, and structures in their lives that molded their identity as they became adult? Finally, I will sum up what kind of identity these working-class women developed in reference to Erikson's concept of identity.

Family relationship is dealt with in all three autobiographies in reference only to the mother and father. The relationship to the mother is reported as being problematic in all cases, although each woman attempts to analyze and find legitimate explanations of why her mother treated her as she did. None of the mothers seemed to the authors to have helped them in their development and instead constrained the

lives of their daughters by hard-heartedness and narrowly-defined social norms. Of the fathers, none shared their lives consistently in childhood and youth, but both Wegrainer and Mueller-Jahnke describe
their fathers with much indulgence and only Popp presents hers in a
negative way. The well-known belief that it is the task of mothers to
impose society's demands on their children can be found even in
nineteenth-century working-class autobiography.[27] Manuals of educational advice repeatedly demanded this role of women throughout the
century, and the great pedagogical ideas of the time as proposed by
Rousseau and Pestalozzi underlined the importance of this task. Even
the daughters of the lower classes reflected these demands on
mothers, as illustrated by Popp:

> My feelings for childhood recollections are different. No light, no sun-
> beam, no cosy home, where motherly love and care led me through
> childhood, come to mind. Nevertheless, I had a good and devoted
> mother who didn't allow herself a minute's rest; she was always driven
> by necessity and the strong will to raise her children properly and to
> protect them against hunger."[28]

Despite a desperate situation, the mother fulfilled her task.

I think that the high esteem of the father finds its explanation in the
fact that in Wegrainer's as in Mueller-Jahnke's life he was far less
influential in their real lives than the mother and thus could be
idealized. On the other hand, all three women refused the demand to
live the kind of life their mothers had, and this was the severest break
in their life course. In Mueller-Jahnke's story, this aspect comes up
frequently; Popp several times relates incidents that point out quite
clearly that she does not share her mother's view of how to shape her
relationship to men. Wegrainer puts strong emphasis on her own family life; she sees herself as a much more concerned mother than her
own mother and blames her mother for missed chances in life.

The education of all these women was poor. Mueller-Jahnke and
Wegrainer at least attended school for eight years; Popp spent only
three years in school, but emerged an enthusiastic reader. Wegrainer
apparently enjoyed the time she spent in school and would have liked
to have stayed longer. She regrets her brief education again and again.

None of these women worked in the fields that became accessible
through the middle-class women's movement, namely education and
social work, in which feminine qualities in the sense of "motherly"
qualities were demanded. Mueller-Jahnke tells the story of a midwife
who had worked as a clerical worker and who helped her at her
delivery. She describes the work of this woman apparently in order to

show that militant action for access to meaningful jobs is important. She herself did not strive for a goal in the field of these "mothering professions" but confined herself to clerical work.[29] Popp was never in a position to be able to develop "career plans" at all, since she was bound to become a worker anyway. Wegrainer's role as a domestic servant represents just another case of female proletarian fate that cannot be concealed by her description of the fancy life among the upper class. The "right to work" did not have to be fought for in the lives of these women. The simple necessity to survive did not allow much reflection on what type of work they were doing. One of the most significant characteristics in these women's process of finding an identity was that they did not become aware of their condition through *Bildung,* but through direct suffering from exploitation at the work place and through the ever-present danger of sexual abuse.

Sexuality, sensuality, a sense of aesthetics, and eroticism are themes that belong together in the stories they tell about their lives. Mueller-Jahnke talks romantically about beauty and erotic attraction when she tells of her childhood. Popp deals at length with problems of how to dress as a young working woman, which surprises the reader, because otherwise she takes such a firmly moralistic class-conscious stand. Wegrainer's major motive in writing her story lies in her sensuality, which she connects directly to eroticism and sexuality.

Male sexuality is a basic threat in the lives of the three women. There are other more positive aspects of how they encounter male relationships in their stories, but the emphasis is undoubtedly placed on danger. Popp describes the relationship to her "ideal" man as absolutely chaste and thus locates the danger outside the bounds of marriage. Even if she does not point out in the narration of her own life's course the aspect of danger that much, she speaks of the defense through her "iron morality" as a growing girl. Wegrainer and Mueller-Jahnke look at themselves as victims of male abuse and this leads them to autobiographical writing. Men (or one man) have been important figures in the lives of these three women and have given direction to their life course more than anything else. Their identity as women has been shaped throughout their childhood and youth under the overall assumption that they were to become the submissive objects of male desires. I tend to explain the male orientation of Mueller-Jahnke and Wegrainer through the general predicament of women of their time to find a way out of prescribed submission. They have been influenced by the prevailing ideology of mutual complementary relations between the sexes, and consequently, they all express an ambivalent attitude toward men. Men are not only potential and real oppressors, but offer images as autonomous persons and thus bring about dreams of ideal partners who would accept their autonomous lives. Wegrainer did not have sufficient positive experience for such dreams, but must confine herself to seeing her successful son as the "ideal man."

In my final section, I will compare the writings of these women, who in a very basic way were connected to the working class, with the writings of contemporaneous middle-class women. My previous research dealt with the autobiographical writings of the following: Fanny Lewald (writer), Hedwig Dohm (writer), Mathilde Franziska Anneke (writer, politician, principal of a girl's school), Franziska Tiburtius (doctor), Helene Lange (teacher and women's movement activist), Marianne Weber (academic), Lily Braun (writer and politician), Ellen Hauss-Knapp (politician and teacher), and Gertrud Bäumer (teacher and activist of the women's movement).[30] Although the classification "proletarian" versus "middle-class" is not entirely satisfactory, I am tentatively sticking to it for the purpose of discriminating the various work experiences of those women.

Almost all the writers of either group were very critical toward their mothers. The mother-daughter relationship is not only a current topic of interest (Hammer, Friday[31]), but was already a problem among women in the nineteenth century. The fathers generally are treated with much more indulgence by both groups. Many middle-class autobiographies even claim that had there not been these fathers, the women would not have become what they were. Mueller-Jahnke corresponds most precisely to this pattern (Braun, Lewald, Baeumer). Only Popp, as I said before, unforgivingly portrays her father as a tyrant under whom the whole family had to suffer. The father clearly represented a positively identified figure for these women who, however, was in a position with which they never could really identify. This kept him above criticism as an unreachable image. But while the middle-class autobiographies portray the father as the image for the possibility to live a life outside the narrow house, two of the working-class autobiographies give a much more idealized and colorless picture of the fathers, while Popp confines his role to that of an oppressor.

The accent on educational opportunities and training represents a large part of almost all autobiographies, since by definition a nineteenth-century personality gains self consciousness through school and *Bildung* in childhood and youth. There is a significant difference between the two groups, however. Middle-class women deal with education as a means of finding meaning in life, and thus the striving for a good education was the motivation for personal and political action. Even those among them who did not have to fight for an education and might have taken up other interests for their professional career ended up as teachers for young girls (Heuss-Knapp). Popp, Wegrainer, and Mueller-Jahnke had to work for a living and did not need to oppose family or society for the right to work outside the house. There was no opportunity for them to live a life as a *hoehere Tochter,* as a wife, or as an unmarried aunt, who in all three cases could stay at home. I do not want to belittle this choice for a middle-class woman, but it made a difference for the course of a life. Since working-class women did not have these choices, they did not work in those areas which had been fought for and established by the middle-class women's movement and which had produced the idea of a *geistige Mütterlichkeit* (spiritual motherhood). Working-class women did not reflect on job profiles, but took any available wage-labor jobs in the industrial, commercial, or domestic labor market.

Another basic difference can be found in the differing attention paid to eroticism and sexuality. The activists from the women's movement (Tiburtius, Lange, Baeumer, Weber, and Heuss-Knapp) do not talk about this topic in a way comparable to the treatment it finds in the working-class autobiographies. Indeed, Tiburtius, Lange, and Baeumer give the impression that there was no such thing in their lives. Weber theorizes on sex relations and eroticism and tells at length about the sexual fate of her domestic servants. Heuss-Knapp confines herself to some very soft hints. Only the married radicals (i.e., Lewald, Dohm, and Braun) talk about their sexual and erotic relations with men. The potential danger of male violence caused by sexual desires is stressed only by Dohm and Braun.

The relationship to a particular man was of major importance for a number of women from the middle-class group. Very often it led to the specific direction their life took and produced characteristic twists in the process of personal development. For the working-class writers, the relationship to men was marked by danger. Despite their ideas about the "ideal man," it wasn't he who shaped their experiences with men when they were young. Although some of the middle-class women no doubt had quite similar experiences with men, they do not talk about it. Did rules of convention really protect those women, as Tiburtius claims, or did rules of convention only keep them from publicly denouncing those humiliating experiences? There are certain indications that the latter assumption is correct. Dohm tells briefly of sexual harassment by male teachers and other men of her bourgeois environment. In Marianne Weber's biography of her husband Max Weber, she portrays at length the rape of her beloved aunt, the mother of her later husband, which took place in the best of Heidelberg academic circles. She also describes her mother-in-law's miserable life as a married woman oppressed sexually by her husband, a highly esteemed member of the Reichstag. What was Marianne Weber's motive in writing this bizarre introduction to the life of her famous sociologist husband?[32] Education and rules of convention for middle-class women made it possible for them to repress this whole field of experience and to build an environment as adults which kept this threat under control.

In comparison to their sisters from the middle-class women's movement, Wegrainer, Mueller-Jahnke, and Popp did not strive for education *(Bildung)* as a means for a self-defined identity in itself. Too often they had been threatened by male abuse and economic disaster. Strategies for economic and personal independence were less important for them, but the threat of violence called for basic protection of women through better working conditions, for abolishment of male-dominated morality, and for the acknowledgement of the equality of sexes. They expressed this call either through political action or through the hope for a better future for their children.

Autobiography as a nineteenth-century literary genre has been viewed as the description of the acquirement of a certain education. The molding of an identity in Germany through *Bildung* led to a certain social position in the public arena. Consequently, the middle class autobiographies I have dealt with have been significantly influenced by this view, even if most of them tell the story of the struggle against restrictions set by a male-dominated society. The working-class women of my sample who adopted the genre do not reflect that struggle for an education. They emphasize much more the bleak oppression of working conditions and economic exploitation. In that respect, they resemble male working-class autobiographies as defined by Emmerich. They differ significantly from Emmerich's scheme, however, in their focus on the sex-related forms of oppression and in their descriptions of the "private" experience of aesthetic values.

These women depicted their lives within the accepted genre. In addition to the therapeutic motivation, they considered themselves capable of relating a consistent individualized life course. Yet the consistency was not provided by the prerequisites of an acknowledged idea of what they were to become, but rather by their fight against the restrictive life of a working woman and—in the case of Mueller-Jahnke and Popp—for an autonomous life. This specific adoption of the genre leads to the question: to what extent could their view of coming-of-age be interpreted in the framework that Erikson offered for the process of building an identity.

My discussion of their writings indicates that there was no consistent concept of identity offering orientation to these women. The prevailing stereotypes of male and female personalities and relationships and their consequences for the female life course cannot be addressed as a concept for identity as long as one shares Erikson's notion of an identity that includes the active acquisition of personality traits and qualities. The dominant ideas of the female personality were not acceptable for two of the authors (Popp, Mueller-Jahnke); Wegrainer manages in her depiction to harmonize her ideal goals with her female fate, but the underlying contradictions are easily disclosed. Popp's self-acknowledged prudishness, Mueller-Jahnke's disdain for "good matches," and even Wegrainer's escapist dreams of a beauty admired by upper classes indicate counter-concepts they developed themselves in their childhood and youth. They all wanted to take an active part in shaping their lives. They refused to accept a role as a victim of a male-dominated love life, and they developed personal and/or political goals for themselves. The process of building up an identity did not involve a close relationship with parents for unquestioned identification or a moratorium during their youth. No successive integration of all identifications through childhood and youth, as Erikson puts it, shaped their identity, but rather severe breaks, most dramatically indicated by the decision to break away from the kind of life their mothers lived and the negative experience brought on by their gender.

NOTES

1. Juliane Jacobi-Dittrich, " 'Hausfrau, Gattin und Mutter,' Lebensläufe und Bildungsgänge von Frauen im 19. Jahrhundert" (Homemaker, Wife and Mother, Life Course and Education of Women in the Nineteenth Century), *Frauen in der Geschichte IV* (Düsseldorf: Schwann, 1983), pp. 262–81.

2. Erik Erikson, *Identität und Lebenszyklus* (Frankfurt: Suhrkamp, 1969).

3. Annette Kuhn, "Das Geschlecht—eine historische Kategorie?" (Gender—a Historical Category?), *Frauen in der Geschichtiv,* pp. 29–50.

4. Bernd Neumann, *Identität und Rollenzwang, Zur Theorie der Autobiographie* (Frankfurt: Athenäum, 1970).

5. Sabine Richebächer, *Uns fehlt nur eine Kleinigkeit,* Deutsche Proletarische Frauenbewegung 1890–1914 (We only lack a small last bit, German proletarian women's movement 1890–1914) (Frankfurt: Fischer, 1982).

6. Wolfgang Emmerich, *Proletarische Lebensläufe,* Bd.1 (Proletarian Life Courses) (Hamburg: Rowolt, 1974) pp. 22–26.

7. Emmerich, p. 21.

8. Clara Mueller-Jahnke, *Ich bekenne* (I Confess) (Berlin: Dietz, 1922); Klaus Osterroth, *Biographisches Lexikon des Sozialismus,* Bd.1 (Biographical Encyclopedia of Socialism) (Hannover: Dietz, 1960) p. 227.

9. Hedwig Dohm, *Schicksale einer Seele* (Fates of a Soul) (Berlin: S. Fischer, 1899).

10. I must omit discussion of another interesting twist illustrated by this work, that is the strange German mixture of nationalism, populism, and Protestant religious beliefs of the late nineteenth century among certain social democrats.

11. Clara Bohm-Schuch was Clara Zetkin's successor as editor of *Die Gleichheit* (Equality), the women's periodical of the Socialist party after the party's split in 1917.

12. Mueller-Jahnke, pp. 140–41.

13. Mueller-Jahnke, pp. 9–10.

14. It would be interesting to go through social democratic autobiographical writings under this aspect.

15. Adelheid Popp, *Jugend einer Arbeiterin* (Youth of a Working Woman) ed. H. J. Schuetz (Berlin-Bonn: Dietz, 1977) contains the two autobiographical writings: "Jugendgeschichte einer Arbeiterin" (Youth of a Working Woman) and "Erinnerungen aus meiner Kindheit und Jugend" (Memoirs from My Childhood and Youth).

16. Popp, p. 61; 132.

17. Popp, p. 40.

18. Emmerich, p. 22.

19. Compare the family life record given by Moritz Bromme, *Lebensgeschichte eines modernen Fabrikarbeiters* (The Life of a Modern Factory Worker) ed. Paul Göhre (Jena: Diederich, 1905).

20. Marie Wegrainer, *Die Lebensgeschichte einer Arbeiterin von ihr selbst erzählt,* (The Life Story of a Working Woman, Told by Herself) (München: Delphin, 1914).

21. Wegrainer, p. 182.

22. Wegrainer, p. 9.

23. Wegrainer, p. 9.

24. Wegrainer, p. 32.

25. Wegrainer, p. 186.

26. Cf. Eckhard Dittrich and Juliane Dittrich-Jacobi, "Autobiographien als Quelle zur Sozialgeschichte der Erziehung" (autobiographies as source material for a social history in education) in *Aus Geschichten lernen,* ed. Dieter Baacke and Theodor Schulze (München: Juventa, 1979).

27. Uta Enders-Dragässer, *Die Mütterdressur* (The Mother's Taming) (Basel: Mondbuch, 1981).

28. Popp, p. 25.

29. Cf. Ute Frevert, "Vom Klavier zur Schreibmaschine. Weiblicher Arbeitsmarkt und Rollenzuweisungen am Beispiel weiblicher Angestellter in der Weimarer Republik" (From Piano to Typewriter, Female-Labor-market and Role Assignment as Exemplified by Female Employees during the Weimar Republic) *Frauen in der Geschichte,* Bd.II. (Düsseldorf: Schwann, 1979) pp. 82–112.

30. Fanny Lewald, *Meine Lebensgeschichte,* (My Life's Story) ed. Gisela Brinker-Gabler (Frankfurt: Fischer, 1980). Hedwig Dohm, *Schicksale einer Seele* (Fates of a Soul) (Berlin: S. Fischer, 1899). Mathilde Franziska Anneke, "Autobiographisches Fragment," *Mathilde Franziska Anneke in Selbstzeugnissen und Dokumenten,* ed. Maria Wagner (Frankfurt: Fischer, 1980). Franziska Tiburtius, *Erinnerungen einer Achtzigjährigen.* (Memoirs of an Eighty-year-old) (Berlin: Schwetschke, 1925). Helene Lange, *Lebenserinnerungen* (Memoirs) (Berlin: Herbig, 1927). Marianne Weber,

Lebenserinnerungen (Memoirs) (Bremen: Strohm, 1948). Lily Braun, *Memoiren einer Sozialistin* (Memoirs of a Socialist) 2 vols., (München: Langen, 1909). Elly Heuss-Knapp, *Ausblick vom Münsterturm* (View from the Cathedral's Tower) (Tübingen: Wunderlich, 1952). Gertrud Baeumer, *Lebensweg durch eine Zeitwende,* (A Life Course in Changing Times) (Tübingen: Wunderlich, 1933).

31. Signe Hammer, *Mütter und Töchter* (Mothers and Daughters) (Frankfurt: Fischer, 1977). Nancy Friday, *My Mother/Myself* (New York: Delacorte Press, 1977).

32. Marianne Weber, *Max Weber. Ein Lebensbild* (Max Weber, A Portrait) (Tübingen: Mohr, 1926).

CONTRIBUTORS

HANS ADLER received his Ph.D. from the Ruhr University, Bochum, in 1978 and teaches there now. His research interests focus on German literature of the eighteenth to twentieth centuries, the theory of literature, semiotics of literature, narratology, and the social history of literature. His publications include *Soziale Romane im Vormärz* (1980), *Literarische Geheimberichte 1840–1848* (2 vols., 1977/81), an edition of C. A. Schloenbach's *Die Hasenschlinge und andere Erzählungen* (1984), as well as articles on linguistic issues, the German social novel of the eighteenth and nineteenth centuries, and Georg Büchner.

JAMES C. ALBISETTI received his doctoral degree in History from Yale University in 1976. He is currently teaching at the University of Kentucky. He has written several articles on secondary and higher education in Germany, and is also interested in the entry of women into the professions in Germany. He has published a book, *Secondary School Reform in Imperial Germany* (Princeton, 1983).

RUTH P. DAWSON received her Ph.D. from the University of Michigan and is now Assistant Professor of Women's Studies and Director of the Liberal Studies Program at the University of Hawaii at Manoa. She is interested in all aspects of the literary life of women in late eighteenth-century Germany.

RICHARD J. EVANS received his doctorate in 1972 from Oxford University. He is currently professor of European History at the University of East Anglia, Norwich. He has been visiting Associate Professor of European History at Columbia University. He is the author of numerous articles and reviews on German history and women's history, and of *The Feminist Movement in Germany 1894–1933* (1976) and *The Feminists* (1977), and editor, with W. R. Lee, of *The German Family* (1981).

JOHN C. FOUT received his Ph.D. in History from the University of Minnesota in 1969 and teaches at Bard College. His research interests include the social history of women in Europe and the German Christian Socialist movement. He has written several articles and edited collections of documents and essays, including *European*

Women: A Documentary History, 1789–1945 (New York, 1980) and his forthcoming *German Women in the Nineteenth Century: A Social History* (New York, 1984).

KAY GOODMAN received her Ph.D. from the University of Wisconsin, Madison in 1977 and teaches at Brown University. She is interested in women in German literature and has written several articles on that topic. She is currently working on a book-length study of women's autobiography in Germany.

PATRICIA HERMINGHOUSE is Professor of German and Chair of the Department of Foreign Languages, Literature and Linguistics at the University of Rochester. She received her Ph.D. from Washington University in St. Louis, where she was one of the founders of the Women's Studies Program. Beyond her interest in women as writers, she has published widely and edited two volumes on East German literature (1976, 1983) and a major series on the writings of German political emigrés in the United States.

DEBORAH HERTZ received her Ph.D. in History from the University of Minnesota in 1979. She currently teaches at the State University of New York at Binghamton. She has written several articles on Rahel Varnhagen and on the Jewish community of Berlin in the eighteenth century. She has also edited a collection of Rahel's letters, *Rahel Varnhagens Zensierte Briefe* (Cologne, 1984).

JULIANE JACOBI-DITTRICH received her Ph.D. from the University of Bielefeld, where she now teaches educational history. Besides her studies in the field of the history of childhood, especially girlhood, she is working on a project dealing with German immigrants and the education of their children in the United States in the nineteenth century.

RUTH-ELLEN BOETCHER JOERES, coeditor of this volume, received her Ph.D. in German literature in 1971 at the Johns Hopkins University and is now Professor of German and Director of the Center for Advanced Feminist Studies at the University of Minnesota. Her particular areas of interest are the social history of German literature in the eighteenth through twentieth centuries and German women writers. She has translated and commented Karl Gutzkow's *Wally the Skeptic* (Lang, 1974), has edited a catalogue for the German holdings in the Gerritsen Collection of Women's History, is the author of *Die Anfänge der deutschen Frauenbewegung: Louise Otto-Peters* (Fischer, 1983) and, with Annette Kuhn, is editing volume VI of the *Frauen in der Geschichte* series.

MARY JO MAYNES, coeditor of this volume, received her Ph.D. in History from the University of Michigan in 1977. She currently teaches at the University of Minnesota. Her research interests include European social history, history of the family and history of education, as well as women's history. She has written several articles on these topics and has two books in press: *Schooling for the People: Comparative Local Studies of Schooling History in France and Germany, 1750–1850* (New York, 1984) and *Schooling in Western Europe: A Social History* (Albany, 1985).

RENATE MÖHRMANN is Professor of Theatre, Film, and Television Studies at the University of Cologne. She studied German, French, philosophy, and the media in Hamburg, Lyon, and New York, and completed her doctorate at the City University of New York in 1972. She is the author of *Der vereinsamte Mensch: Studien zum Wandel des Einsamkeitsmotivs im Roman von Raabe bis Musil* (Bouvier, 1974), *Die andere Frau. Emanzipationsansätze deutscher Schriftstellerinnen im Vorfeld der Achtundvierziger-Revolution* (Metzler, 1977), *Frauenemanzipation im Vormärz. Texte und Dokumente* (Reclam, 1978), *Die Frau mit der Kamera. Filmemacherinnen in der Bundesrepublik Deutschland* (Hanser, 1980). She is also editor of the series Studium zum Theater, Film und Fernsehen (Lang, 1981).

ROSEMARY ORTHMANN is a Ph.D. candidate in history at Indiana University. She is currently writing a dissertation on the economic role of women within the working-class family economy in Berlin during the period of high industrialization. She is the recent recipient of research fellowships from the Social Science Research Council, the Fulbright Commission, and the International Research and Exchanges Board.

CATHERINE M. PRELINGER received her Ph.D. in German history from Yale University. She is Associate Editor at the Papers of Benjamin Franklin, Yale University. Her contribution to this collection was completed while she served as Research Associate and Visiting Lecturer in Women's Studies at Harvard Divinity School. She has published widely in the field of mid-nineteenth century German feminism; she has completed a book-length manuscript documenting the religious context of the early German women's movement and is currently engaged in a comparative study of the restored female diaconate in Germany, England, and the United States.

JEAN H. QUATAERT is Associate Professor of European History at the University of Houston, Clear Lake. She received her Ph.D. from the University of California, Los Angeles. She is the author of *Re-luctant Feminists in German Social Democracy 1885–1917* (Prince-ton, 1979) and coauthor, with Marilyn Boxer, of *Socialist Women: Studies in European Socialist Feminism in the Nineteenth and Early Twentieth Centuries* (New York, 1978). Currently, she is working on a book about nineteenth-century work and family life of weavers in a textile district in historic Saxony and seamstresses in Berlin.

REGULA VENSKE studied law, German, and English at the Univer-sities of Heidelberg and Hamburg and completed a master's thesis on the later writings of Fanny Lewald. At present she is a lecturer at both the Literaturwissenschaftliches Seminar at the University of Hamburg and at the John F. Kennedy Institut für Amerikastudien at the Free University of Berlin. She has published several articles on contemporary women's literature, on Fanny Lewald, and on femi-nist rhetoric theory and is at work on a dissertation concerning the depiction of men in women's fiction.

GUDRUN WEDEL has studied at the University of Frankfurt and the Free University of Berlin, where she is working on a doctoral project on nineteenth-century German women's autobiographies. She has published several papers on this topic.

WULF WÜLFING received his Ph.D. in German literature from Bonn University and is currently Akademischer Oberrat at the Ruhr University in Bochum. His publications include works on slogans, rhetoric, travel literature, the mythicizing of women (Rahel Varnha-gen, Bettina von Arnim, Charlotte Stieglitz, Queen Luise of Prussia), on Napoleon, Goethe, and Heine, as well as books on *Junges Deutschland.*

INDEX

Abensour, Léon, 250
abortion, 249
actress, 70, 72, 162, 163, 178
Adele, 176
Adler, Hans, 216
age, and occupation, 49. *See also* life cycle
alcoholism, 238, 239
alienation, 179, 187
America, 298–99
anarchism, 199
Anneke, Mathilde Franziska, 62, 340
anonymous authorship, 84, 86, 280
Anthony, Katharine, 111, 124
apprenticeship, 33, 49, 51, 68
Arbeiterinnen-Zeitung, 232
Arendt, Hannah, 272, 273
aristocratic women, 307
Arm und Reich, 205–207
art, occupations in, 64, 65, 68, 70, 112, 162
Association for Women's Education and University Studies, 103
Association of Catholic Women Teachers, 102, 103
Aston, Louise, 62, 65, 66, 193–214
atheism, 199
Augspurg, Anita, 95, 103, 248
Aus dem Leben einer Frau, 200
autobiographical material, 42, 44, 217
autobiographies, 230–46, 289, 305–20, 321–45
Awakening, 216, 217

Baader, Ottilie, 232, 235–36, 241
Bacheracht, Therese von, 62, 65, 91
Baldinger, Friderika, 153
Barth, Carola, 105
Bartky, Sandra Lee, 164
Bauer, Bruno, 198, 199
Bauer, Edgar, 198, 204
Bäumer, Gertrud, 68, 102, 117, 118, 119, 120, 248, 249, 340
Bautzen archives for the Oberlausitz, 12
Bavaria, 100
Beck, Dr. Oskar, 310, 311, 312
Becker, August *(pseud.). See* Varnhagen von Ense, Karl August
belles lettres, 61–77, 78–93

Berdrow, Otto, 84, 283
Berger, John, 151–52
Berlepsch, Emilie, 160, 164, 167, 169, 172
Berlin, 42, 87, 90, 95, 96, 97, 99, 180, 204, 232, 290, 327; Aston's expulsion from, 197, 198–99; female factory workers in, 24–41; social and intellectual life, 278–88
Berlin, University of, 101
Bernstein, Eduard, 116
Bertheau, Caroline. *See* Fliedner, Caroline
Beutelmayer, Marie, 238, 241
biographies, 175, 305–20
Bliebtreu, Adelheid, 224
Bloch, Ernst, 203
Bluhm, Agnes, 96, 97
Bohm-Schuch, Clara, 327
Bonn, University of, 101
Boschek, Anna, 233
bourgeoisie, 83, 216, 232, 299
Bovenschen, Silvia, 61, 150, 152, 157, 283
Brater, Karl, 314
Brater, Pauline, 308–18
Braun, Dr. G., 237
Braun, Lily, 121–23, 124, 340
Brausewetter, Ernst, 79
Bré, Ruth, 111
Bremer, Friedericke, 218
Brinker-Gabler, Gisela, 69, 89, 180
Brinkmann, Gustav von, 277
Brümmer, Franz, 79
Brussels lace, 295
Buhl, Franz, 199
Bülow, Helene von, 224
Bundesrat, 17
Burgsdorff, Wilhelm von, 277

Calm, Marie, 97
capitalism, 321
Catholic Women's League, 255
Catholicism, 97, 98, 99, 102, 103, 200, 203, 216, 295, 327, 328
Cauer, Minna, 103
censorship, 150, 152, 182; interior, 175, 182
charities, 56, 126, 215–29
children and child care, 17, 25, 28, 51, 55, 56, 57, 58, 68, 112, 121, 124, 160, 169, 335

children's books, 310
Christ, Lena, 233, 236, 238, 243
Cixous, Hélène, 110
Claassen, Ria, 123
classes and class distinctions, 6, 224, 230–46, 293
Clementine, 185
clothing, 332
coeducation, 103, 105
Continental System, Napoleonic, 10
cottage industries, 6–23, 49, 55, 64, 82
cottagers, 9, 14
cotton manufacturing, 10–11
Crepaz, Adele, 125–26

demographic revolution, 217
Diers, Marie, 116
deaconessate, Kaiserswerth, 215–29
discipline, 175–92, 198, 283
Disselhof, Julius, 224
Dittmer, Louise, 62, 63
division of labor, 4, 18, 80, 112, 167, 168, 255. *See also* domestic sphere
divorce, 162, 184, 186, 277
Dohm, Hedwig, 111, 112, 113, 116, 138, 327, 340, 341
domestic industry, 6–23, 49, 55, 64
domestic service and servants, 32, 43, 57, 64, 65, 69, 237, 239, 242, 243, 324, 333, 334; in fiction, 66, 67, 68
domestic sphere, 4, 85–86, 112, 122, 124, 171, 189, 199–200, 205
Droste-Hülshoff, Annette von, 87
Duensing, Frieda, 96
Dulden, 233, 237, 238, 243

Eberle, Sophie, 218
education, 88, 94, 141, 143, 147, 152, 158, 161, 164–65, 171, 172, 217, 315; advanced, 89, 99–101, 102, 181; early childhood, 223; financial support, 101, 102; middle-class women, 64, 85; and occupation, 307, 316–17; opportunities for, 112, 116, 220–25; for self-reliance, 300; weaving schools, 12; working-class women, 326, 334, 338, 340, 342. *See also* apprenticeship; universities
Edwards, Lee, 150
ehemännliche Wirtschaft, 13
eheweibliche Wirtschaft, 13
eheweibliches Einbringen, 13
Ehrmann, Marianne, 160–61, 163, 164, 167, 168, 169–70, 172
Eigenliebe, 143, 148–49, 152
Ellis, Havelock, 114, 115, 117
emancipation, 153, 175, 179, 185, 188, 197,

199, 300; movement, 193–94, 207
Emmerich, Wolfgang, 325, 326, 342
employment opportunity, 62, 94, 112, 115, 166
Engelsing, Rolf, 281
England, trade with, 10
entrepreneurs, female, 49
equal rights, 250, 255, 289
Erikson, Erik, 321, 322, 337, 343
ethical movements, 42–43
Ethische Gesellschaft, 42
Ethische Kultur, 42
expenditure patterns, 24–41
exploitation, 47, 50, 115

factory owners, 43, 47, 51
factory work, 18, 49, 64, 113, 118, 120
factory workers, 24–41, 232, 233–34, 239–40, 331
family, 63, 147, 249, 297; bonds, 276; cult of, 80–81; as a model, 119, 215–29; norms, 73; obligations, 50; relationships, 29, 237; supportive, 104; work patterns, 6–23
family history, 24–25
family life, 43, 56, 316
father-daughter relationship, 185–86, 235–36, 237–38, 329, 335, 338, 340
feminists and feminism, 110–11, 114, 119, 167, 230; consciousness, 157–74, 225; controversy, 193–214; literary, 272; in literature, 137–56; middle-class, 5, 43; "reluctant feminists," 241; theory and concept, 47–58, 110
fertility, 114, 121
Fichte, Johann, 277
fiction, 61–77, 137–56. *See also* novel
Fliedner, Caroline, 220, 225
Fliedner, Theodor, 215–16, 218–24, 225
food, 26, 36, 51, 52, 53, 56, 57
franchise, 113, 248, 254
Frank, Leonhard, 334
Frauen-Zeitung, 194, 197, 203, 208, 223, 224
Frauenroman, 139–56
Frederick II, the Great, 275
Freiburg, University of, 97
French Revolution, 160
Freytag, Thekla, 100, 104, 105
Friedan, Betty, 110
Friedländer, Moses, 277
Friedländer, Rebecca, 271–88
Friedrich Wilhelm III, 216
Friedrich Wilhelm IV, 200, 221
Friedrichs, Elisabeth, 79
Fröbel, Friedrich, 223, 298
Frohberg, Regina. *See* Friedländer, Rebecca

Gedenkbuch, 232
Geib, Margarethe, 225
gender roles, 3–23, 143, 144, 168
General Association of German Writers, 82
General German League of Charitable Institutions for Academically and Technically Trained Women Teachers, 102
German Evangelical Women's League, 251
German Pension Institute for Women Teachers and Educators, 102
German Women Teachers' Association, 102
German Women's Association, 94, 95, 101, 102
Geschichte des Fräuleins von Sternheim, 137–56
Geschlechtscharaktere, 143
Gleim, Betty, 183
Goethe, Johann Wolfgang von, 297
Goodman, Kay, 279
Göttingen, 99
Gottschall, Rudolf, 88
governess, 64, 70, 85, 181, 239
Gross, Heinrich, 79, 85
guilds, 8, 11–12, 19, 63
Gundert, D., 310
Gutzkow, Karl, 180, 298

Hacker, Agnes, 97
Hahn-Hahn, Ida, Countess, 62, 66–67, 68, 299–300
Hamburg, 223
Hansemann, Ottilie von, 101
Hausen, Karin, 143, 321
Hauss-Knapp, Ellen, 340
hawking of goods, 14–15, 17
health, 49, 53, 56, 57, 330
Heimburg, W., 82, 84
Heim-Voegtlin, Marie, 101
Heine, Heinrich, 183, 272, 297, 299, 300
Heller, Agnes, 179
Heller, Otto, 88
Herber, Pauline, 102
Herding, Fritz, 316
Herding-Sapper, Agnes, 309–18
heroines, in women's literature, 61, 74, 137
Herz, Henriette, 275
Herz, Markus, 275
Heyse, Paul, 279
Hippel, Theodor Gottlieb von, 115, 117, 158–59, 160, 162, 165, 167, 168, 169, 172
Hobsbawm, E. J., 247
Hohendahl, Peter, 145
Holtzendorff, Franz von, 95
Holy Alliance, 200
home industry, 6–23, 49, 55, 64

home weavers, 232
homeweaving, 3–23
hospitals, 216
housekeeping, 17, 25, 28, 51, 53, 55, 57, 58, 62, 80, 157, 166, 168, 314, 316, 317–18; tasks shared, 5
housewife, 110, 120, 300
housing, 26, 29, 30–31, 34–38, 53
Huch, Ricarda, 104
Huguenots, 10, 290
Humboldt, Alexander von, 277
Humboldt, Wilhelm von, 277

illegitimacy, 217
Im Kampf ums Dasein, 233, 237, 238, 239, 243
imagination, 183, 187, 315
independence, economic, 115, 179
industrial capitalism, 5, 12
industrial revolution, 4, 5, 80, 205, 250
industry and industrialization, 295, 324, 334; workers and working conditions, 24–41, 42–60
inequality, social, 81
inheritance, wife's, 13–14
Inner Mission, 221
intellect and intellectual competence, 114, 117, 121, 143, 144, 145, 152, 170, 276, 297, 313, 316
international economy, 10, 11, 19
Irigaray, Luce, 110

Jagiellonian Library, Krakow, 273
Janssen-Jurreit, Marieluise, 138
Jesuits, 200, 203, 296
Jewish women, 85, 271–88
Jewish Women's League, 255
Joeres, Ruth-Ellen B., 197
Jones, Agnes, 224
journalism, 80, 160, 204
journals, 80, 82, 102, 153, 281

Kaiserswerth, deaconessate, 215–29
Kant, Immanuel, 81, 85, 139, 185
Kaplan, Marion, 255
Kempin, Emilie, 95
Kettler, Hedwig, 95
Keudell, Elise von, 105
Key, Ellen, 111–12, 114, 115, 116, 117, 118, 120, 121, 122, 123, 124
Kinkel, Johanna, 291
Kollontai, Alexandra, 252
Kolodny, Annette, 139, 143
Königsberg, 85, 185
Krankenkasse, 51, 52, 53, 54, 57
Kristeva, Julia, 110

Kuhn, Annette, 322
Kuhnow, Anna, 96

labor force, female, 6–23, 24–41
lady's maid, 65; in fiction, 66, 67
landownership, 9
Lange, Helene, 97, 100, 102, 103, 104, 116, 117, 118, 119, 340
Langer, Angela, 233, 236, 239, 242
La Roche, Sophie von, 137–56, 161
Eine Lebensfrage, 186
legal profession, 95–96
Lehmus, Emilie, 96, 97
Lepel, Franziska von, 224
Lette Association, 94, 95
letter-writing, 281–82, 312–13, 315
Levin, Rahel. *See* Varnhagen, Rahel
Lewald, August, 86
Lewald, Fanny, 62, 63, 65, 66, 68–69, 71, 72, 74, 83–84, 85–87, 88, 115, 175–92, 340; quoted, 90
Lewis, Jill, 110
Leyen, Else von der, 104
libraries, lending, 51, 80
life cycle, 24–41, 54
Linden, Countess Marie von, 101, 104
linen manufacture and trade, 8
literacy, 55, 57, 80, 90, 142, 181
literary critics, 73, 89
literary enterprise, 61–77, 78–93, 99
literary marketplace, 80, 90
literature, 61–77, 79, 80, 137–56, 232
Loeper-Housselle, Marie, 102
Lombroso, Cesare, 114, 117
love, as an ideal, 71, 143, 144, 327, 329
Luther, Martin, 201, 226

male-female relationship, 332
Marholm, Laura, 116, 117, 120
market economy, 19
Marlitt, E., 82, 84
marriage, 52, 64, 146, 153, 160, 164, 166, 168, 172, 225, 306, 326, 327, 335; and age, 29; arranged, 115; economic contribution, 13; of equals, 329; in fiction, 68, 201; immoral, 199; intermarriage, 200, 274, 276; Lewald's view of, 184
married women: occupations, 48, 50, 54–57; physicians, 103–104; teachers, 103; writers, 87
Märten, Lu, 180
medicine, 95, 96–97, 158
Medick, Hans, 17
Memoiren einer Idealistin, 290
Meysenbug, Malwida, 289–304
middle-class women, 64, 68, 94, 181, 306, 316, 340–42

migrant workers, 56
migration, 32
Mill, John Stuart, 111, 254
misogyny, 81, 161, 164, 165, 171, 241
"Missbrauchte Frauenkraft," 111, 112, 113, 123
Möbius, Paul Julius, 114
Möhrmann, Renate, 185, 186, 199
Monod, Gabriel, 291
morality, 196–97
Mosegaard, Anna, 232, 239
mother-daughter relationship, 186–87, 237, 276, 313, 329, 331–32, 334, 335, 337–38, 340
motherhood, 249; and work, 110–27
Mueller-Jahnke, Clara, 324, 326, 327–30, 336, 340
Mühlbach, Luise, 62, 66, 67–68, 69, 71, 72, 73, 74, 91
Munich, 97
Münster, Friedericke, 215, 218, 219, 220
Münster, 99
Mutterschutz, 111

networks, 237–38
New York Society for Ethical Culture, 42
newspapers, 55, 80, 234, 242, 281, 309, 312, 316, 327
Nietzsche, Friedrich, 81, 290–91
Nigg, Marianne, 78
Nightingale, Florence, 218, 224
noblewomen, 68, 105
novel, 75, 80, 88, 188, 201, 278, 280; commercialization of, 80; epistolary, 140, 142; *Frauenroman,* 139–56; romantic, 64; and self-definition, 236–37; tendentious, 63
nursing, 216, 221, 224, 306, 313, 316, 317

Oberlausitz, 5–23
O'Brien, Mary, 110
occupations, 47, 50–57, 162, 249, 339; by age, 31–33; and education, 316–17; literary, 62, 78–93, 99, 162–63, 181; professions, 94–109, 158, 306–307, 329; range and variety, 47–48; suitable for women, 64, 112–13, 117, 121, 122, 181, 189
Olberg, Oda, 121
O'Neill, William L., 254
Otto, Louise. *See* Otto-Peters, Louise
Otto-Peters, Louise, 62, 63, 65, 66, 84, 115, 138, 193–214, 223, 224

Pankhurst, Emmeline, 111
Pataky, Sophie, 78, 79
paternal authority, 184–86
patriarchy, 7, 215, 219, 321
patriotism, 249

Perthen, Anna, 241
Pfaff, Else, 311
Pfaff, Luise, 314, 316
physicians, 103–4, 181; organizations, 101
piecework wages, 45, 52, 55
poetry and poets, 194–96, 236
politics, 198, 234, 242, 316
Pomona, 153
Popp, Adelheid, 232, 234, 238, 240, 242, 324, 325, 326, 330–33, 336, 340
poverty, 19, 56, 243, 330, 332, 334
preindustrial society, 4, 17, 19
private sphere, 157, 199–200. *See also* domestic sphere
professions, and women, 94–109, 158–59, 306–307, 329
progress, 299–300
proletariat, 63, 64, 252, 253. *See also* working-class women
propaganda, 230
Protestant women, 103, 162, 215–29, 327, 328
protoindustrial society, 4, 17, 19
Prussia, 99, 100, 101, 162, 175, 275
Prutz, Robert, 188
pseudonymns. *See* anonymous authorship
public speaking, 233–36
public sphere, 4, 122, 149, 157
publishing, 79, 80, 90, 139, 181, 275, 281–82, 283, 306

Quataert, Jean, 241

Radcliffe Richards, Janet, 252, 253
railroads, 291–94
Rantzau, Marie von, 224
rape, 333, 335
reading, 167, 331
The Redemptrice, 177–78
Reformation, 222
Eine Reise nach Ostende, 291–99
religion, 112, 197–209, 216, 296, 313
reproductive sphere, 110. *See also* domestic sphere
respectability, 170–71
Revolution of 1848, 291
Richardson, Samuel, 139, 142, 143
Richter, Amalie, 219
Riehl, Wilhelm Heinrich, 81–82
Rittershaus-Bjarnason, Adeline, 101
Robert, Ludwig, 278
role sharing, 16
roles: determined by sex, 4, 143, 144, 168, 323, 329; work, 3–23, 80
Roth, Aurelia, 238
Rousseau, Jean Jacques, 139, 145, 151, 164, 165–66, 338

Runge, Max, 114
rural manufacturing, 6–23
rural women, 307

salary, 18, 30, 45, 46, 47, 50, 51, 58, 100, 182
Salomon, Rebecca. *See* Friedländer, Rebecca
salons, 271, 275, 276, 278, 282, 284
Sapper, Agnes, 308–18
Saumoneau, Louise, 252
Saxony, 100, 200; homeweaving, 3–23
Schapire, Anna, 123
Scharnhorst, Agnes von, 224
Scherr, Johannes, 84
Schiller, Friedrich, 208
Schlegel, Friedrich, 277
Schleiermacher, Friedrich, 277
Schloß und Fabrik, 205
Schmerz der Liebe, 280
Schreiner, Olive, 117
Schumann, Sabine, 153
Schurmann, Anna Maria, 170
Schwarz, Sybilla, 170
Scott, Joan, 47
seduction, 68
Seidl, Amalie, 233
self-reliance, 157–74, 300
Sengle, Friedrich, 200
serfdom, 8
sex discrimination, 326
sexual abuse, 335
sexual equality, 159
sexual harassment, 57, 239–40, 327, 330, 331
sexuality, 119, 120, 194, 196, 238, 240, 279, 328, 339, 341
Silesian weavers, 206
Simon, Heinrich, 187
single women, 216–17; factory workers, 24–41; occupations, 50–54, 94; writers, 87
Smith-Rosenberg, Carroll, 312
social climbing, 71
social differentiation, 8
social work, 96
socialism, 116, 203–204, 249, 295–96, 297, 301
socialist women, 43, 53, 232–33, 238–42
Socialists-of-the-Chair, 5
solidarity, 101–103, 194, 326
Sowerwine, Charles, 253
Spiero, Heinrich, 88
Sponer, Marie, 233
Springer, Jenny, 97
Sprengel, Auguste, 99
Stahr, Adolf, 83, 181, 183, 184
standard of living, 45

state regulation, 12, 15, 19–20
Steinhauer, Marieluise, 83
Stier, Sieglinde, 97
Stirner, Max, 199
Stites, Richard, 252, 254
Straus, Rahel, 101, 103, 104
Strauss, Ida, 123, 124
Stritt, Marie, 248
suffrage movement, 111, 118, 119, 248, 254
supervision of workers, 47, 50, 51, 57
Szepe, Helena, 88

teaching, 64, 70, 95, 102, 158, 181, 306,
    307, 315, 317, 327, 341; Kaiserswerth
    deaconessate, 221–24; Lewald's teachers,
    175, 183; rise of the profession, 97–99
teamwork, and Saxon families, 3–23
technology, 16, 19, 206
textile manufacturing, 7–23
textile workers, 33
theater, 51, 53, 73
theft, 206
Thirty Years' War, 8
Tiburtius, Franziska, 96, 97, 104
Tieck, Ludwig, 277
Tilly, Louise, 47
trade and trading regulations, 63, 64, 206,
    250
travel and travel literature, 289–304, 315,
    316
Travel Companions, 177

unions, 43–44, 51, 52, 53, 54, 56, 57
universities, 95, 96, 97, 100, 102, 118, 181,
    329
upper classes, 63, 138
urban life, 30
Utopian socialists, 250

Varnhagen, Rahel, 90, 272–88
Varnhagen von Ense, Karl August, 273, 280
Varnhagen Collection, 273
Verein für Sozialpolitik, 5
Vienna, 232, 233–34; working conditions,
    42–60
Viennese Enquête (1896), 42–60
Vilar, Esther, 65

violence, 238, 239, 341
Vormärz, 62, 75
Vorwerk, Anna, 99, 102, 104

wages, 18, 30, 45, 46, 47, 50, 51, 52, 55, 58,
    100, 182
Wagner, Sister Sophie, 218
Wartensleben, Countess Gabriele von, 105
Watt, Ian, 142, 143
weaving, 8–23
Weber, Marianne, 340, 341–42
Weber, Mathilde, 96, 101
Weber, Max, 341
Wedel, Christine von, 105
Wegrainer, Marie, 324, 325, 333–37
Wichern, Johann Hinrich, 221
Wienbarg, Ludolf, 297
Winckel, Franz, 101
Winterhalter, Elizabeth, 96
Wollstonecraft, Mary, 157, 160, 165, 167,
    250
Women Teachers' Association, 103
Women, Work and Family, 47
Women's Advanced School, Hamburg, 290,
    299
women's movement, 123, 223, 225, 230–
    46, 248, 306
Women's Reform Association, 95
Woolf, Virginia, 75, 76, 180–81, 184
work and women, 42–60, 166, 170, 172,
    178; in literature, 61–77; and mother-
    hood, 110–27; roles, 3–23
working-class women, 42–60, 66, 89, 115,
    124, 230–46, 307, 321–45
working conditions, 3–23, 42–60, 78–93,
    115, 215–29, 327–28, 333
writers and writing, 61–77, 78–93, 162–63,
    175–92, 271–88, 305–20, 324–45

Yeazell, Ruth, 137

Zetkin, Klara, 115, 120–21, 124, 248, 252,
    253
Ziegler, Hildegard, 101, 105
Zurich: First International Congress, *Ethische
    Gesellschaft*, 42
Zurich, University of, 95, 96, 101